Stream Processing with Apache Spark

Mastering Structured Streaming and
Spark Streaming

Gerard Maas and François Garillot

Beijing · Boston · Farnham · Sebastopol · Tokyo

Stream Processing with Apache Spark

by Gerard Maas and François Garillot

Copyright © 2019 François Garillot and Gerard Maas Images. All rights reserved.

Published by O'Reilly Media, Inc., 1005 Gravenstein Highway North, Sebastopol, CA 95472.

O'Reilly books may be purchased for educational, business, or sales promotional use. Online editions are also available for most titles (*http://oreilly.com*). For more information, contact our corporate/institutional sales department: 800-998-9938 or *corporate@oreilly.com*.

Acquisitions Editor: Rachel Roumeliotis
Developmental Editor: Jeff Bleiel
Production Editor: Nan Barber
Copyeditor: Octal Publishing Services, LLC
Proofreader: Kim Cofer

Indexer: Judith McConville
Interior Designer: David Futato
Cover Designer: Karen Montgomery
Illustrator: Rebecca Demarest

June 2019:   First Edition

Revision History for the First Edition
2019-06-12:   First Release

See *http://oreilly.com/catalog/errata.csp?isbn=9781491944240* for release details.

978-1-491-94424-0

[LSI]

Table of Contents

Part I. Fundamentals of Stream Processing with Apache Spark

Part II.   Structured Streaming

Part III. Spark Streaming

Foreword

Welcome to *Stream Processing with Apache Spark*!

It's very exciting to see how much both the Apache Spark project, as well as stream processing with Apache Spark have come along since it was first started by Matei Zaharia at University of California Berkeley in 2009. Apache Spark started off as the first unified engine for big data processing and has grown into the de-facto standard for all things big data.

Stream Processing with Apache Spark is an excellent introduction to the concepts, tools, and capabilities of Apache Spark as a stream processing engine. This book will first introduce you to the core Spark concepts necessary to understand modern distributed processing. Then it will explore different stream processing architectures and the fundamental architectural trade-offs between then. Finally, it will illustrate how Structured Streaming in Apache Spark makes it easy to implement distributed streaming applications. In addition, it will also cover the older Spark Streaming (aka, DStream) APIs for building streaming applications with legacy connectors.

In all, this book covers everything you'll need to know to master building and operating streaming applications using Apache Spark! We look forward to hearing about what you'll build!

— Tathagata Das
Cocreator of Spark Streaming and
Structured Streaming

— Michael Armbrust
Cocreator of Spark SQL and Structured Streaming

— Bill Chambers
Coauthor of Spark: The Definitive Guide
May 2019

Preface

Who Should Read This Book?

We created this book for software professionals who have an affinity for data and who want to improve their knowledge and skills in the area of stream processing, and who are already familiar with or want to use Apache Spark for their streaming applications.

We have included a comprehensive introduction to the concepts behind stream processing. These concepts form the foundations to understand the two streaming APIs offered by Apache Spark: Structured Streaming and Spark Streaming.

We offer an in-depth exploration of these APIs and provide insights into their features, application, and practical advice derived from our experience.

Beyond the coverage of the APIs and their practical applications, we also discuss several advanced techniques that belong in the toolbox of every stream-processing practitioner.

Readers of all levels will benefit from the introductory parts of the book, whereas more experienced professionals will draw new insights from the advanced techniques covered and will receive guidance on how to learn more.

We have made no assumptions about your required knowledge of Spark, but readers who are not familiar with Spark's data-processing capabilities should be aware that in this book, we focus on its streaming capabilities and APIs. For a more general view of the Spark capabilities and ecosystem, we recommend *Spark: The Definitive Guide* by Bill Chambers and Matei Zaharia (O'Reilly).

The programming language used across the book is Scala. Although Spark provides bindings in Scala, Java, Python, and R, we think that Scala is the language of choice for streaming applications. Even though many of the code samples could be translated into other languages, some areas, such as complex stateful computations, are best approached using the Scala programming language.

Installing Spark

Spark is an Apache open source project hosted officially by the Apache Foundation, but which mostly uses GitHub (*http://bit.ly/2J5cWCL*) for its development. You can also download it as a binary, pre-compiled package at the following address: *https://spark.apache.org/downloads.html*.

From there, you can begin running Spark on one or more machines, which we will explain later. Packages exist for all of the major Linux distributions, which should help installation.

For the purposes of this book, we use examples and code compatible with Spark 2.4.0, and except for minor output and formatting details, those examples should stay compatible with future Spark versions.

Note, however, that Spark is a program that runs on the Java Virtual Machine (JVM), which you should install and make accessible on every machine on which any Spark component will run.

To install a Java Development Kit (JDK), we recommend OpenJDK (*http://bit.ly/2GK7ym0*), which is packaged on many systems and architectures, as well.

You can also install the Oracle JDK (*http://bit.ly/2ZMMkwe*).

Spark, as any Scala program, runs on any system on which a JDK version 6 or later is present. The recommended Java runtime for Spark depends on the version:

- For Spark versions below 2.0, Java 7 is the recommended version.
- For Spark versions 2.0 and above, Java 8 is the recommended version.

Learning Scala

The examples in this book are in Scala. This is the implementation language of core Spark, but it is by far not the only language in which it can be used; as of this writing, Spark offers APIs in Python, Java, and R.

Scala is one of the most feature-complete programming languages today, in that it offers both functional and object-oriented aspects. Yet, its concision and type inference makes the basic elements of its syntax easy to understand.

> Scala as a beginner language has many advantages from a pedagogical viewpoint, its regular syntax and semantics being one of the most important.
>
> —Björn Regnell, *Lund University*

Hence, we hope the examples will stay clear enough for any reader to pick up their meanings. However, for the readers who might want a primer on the language and who are more comfortable learning using a book, we advise *Atomic Scala* [Eckel2013]. For users looking for a reference book to touch up on their knowledge, we recommend *Programming in Scala* [Odersky2016].

The Way Ahead

This book is organized in five parts:

- Part I expands on and deepens the concepts that we've been discussing in this preface. We cover the fundamental concepts of stream processing, the general blueprints of the architectures that implement streaming, and study Spark in detail.

- In Part II, we learn Structured Streaming, its programming model, and how to implement streaming applications, from relatively simple stateless transformations to advanced stateful operations. We also discuss its integration with monitoring tools supporting 24/7 operations and discover the experimental areas currently under development.

- In Part III, we study Spark Streaming. In a similar organization to Structured Streaming, we learn how to create streaming applications, operate Spark Streaming jobs, and integrate it with other APIs in Spark. We close this part with a brief guide to performance tuning.

- Part IV introduces advanced streaming techniques. We discuss the use of probabilistic data structures and approximation techniques to address stream-processing challenges and examine the limited space of online machine learning with Spark Streaming.

- To close, Part V brings us to streaming beyond Apache Spark. We survey other available stream processors and provide a glimpse into further steps to keep learning about Spark and stream processing.

We recommend that you to go through Part I to gain an understanding of the concepts supporting stream processing. This will facilitate the use of a common language and concepts across the rest of the book.

Part II, Structured Streaming, and Part III, Spark Streaming, follow a consistent structure. You can choose to cover one or the other first, to match your interest and most immediate priorities:

- Maybe you are starting a new project and want to know Structured Streaming? Check! Start in Part II.

- Or you might be jumping into an existing code base that uses Spark Streaming and you want to understand it better? Start in Part III.

Part IV initially goes deep into some mathematical background required to understand the probabilistic structures discussed. We like to think of it as "the road ahead is steep but the scenery is beautiful."

Part V will put stream processing using Spark in perspective with other available frameworks and libraries out there. It might help you decide to try one or more alternatives before settling on a particular technology.

The online resources of the book complement your learning experience with notebooks and code that you can use and experiment with on your own. Or, you can even take a piece of code to bootstrap your own project. The online resources are located at *https://github.com/stream-processing-with-spark*.

We truly hope that you enjoy reading this book as much as we enjoyed compiling all of the information and bundling the experience it contains.

Bibliography

- [Eckel2013] Eckel, Bruce and Dianne Marsh, *Atomic Scala* (Mindview LLC, 2013).
- [Odersky2016] Odersky, Martin, Lex Spoon, and Bill Venners, *Programming in Scala*, 3rd ed. (Artima Press, 2016).

Conventions Used in This Book

The following typographical conventions are used in this book:

Italic
> Indicates new terms, URLs, email addresses, filenames, and file extensions.

`Constant width`
> Used for program listings, as well as within paragraphs to refer to program elements such as variable or function names, databases, data types, environment variables, statements, and keywords.

`Constant width bold`
> Shows commands or other text that should be typed literally by the user.

`Constant width italic`
> Shows text that should be replaced with user-supplied values or by values determined by context.

This element signifies a tip or suggestion.

 This element signifies a general note.

 This element indicates a warning or caution.

Using Code Examples

The online repository for this book contains supplemental material to enhance the learning experience with interactive notebooks, working code samples, and a few projects that let you experiment and gain practical insights on the subjects and techniques covered. It can be found at *https://github.com/stream-processing-with-spark*.

The notebooks included run on the Spark Notebook, an open source, web-based, interactive coding environment developed with a specific focus on working with Apache Spark using Scala. Its live widgets are ideal to work with streaming applications as we can visualize the data as it happens to pass through the system.

The Spark Notebook can be found at *https://github.com/spark-notebook/spark-notebook*, and pre-built versions can be downloaded directly from their distribution site at *http://spark-notebook.io*.

This book is here to help you get your job done. In general, if example code is offered with this book, you may use it in your programs and documentation. You do not need to contact us for permission unless you're reproducing a significant portion of the code. For example, writing a program that uses several chunks of code from this book does not require permission. Selling or distributing a CD-ROM of examples from O'Reilly books does require permission. Answering a question by citing this book and quoting example code does not require permission. Incorporating a significant amount of example code from this book into your product's documentation does require permission.

We appreciate, but do not require, attribution. An attribution usually includes the title, author, publisher, and ISBN. For example: *"Stream Processing with Apache Spark* by Gerard Maas and François Garillot (O'Reilly). Copyright 2019 François Garillot and Gerard Maas Images, 978-1-491-94424-0."

If you feel your use of code examples falls outside fair use or the permission given above, feel free to contact us at *permissions@oreilly.com*.

O'Reilly Online Learning

 For almost 40 years, *O'Reilly Media* has provided technology and business training, knowledge, and insight to help companies succeed.

Our unique network of experts and innovators share their knowledge and expertise through books, articles, conferences, and our online learning platform. O'Reilly's online learning platform gives you on-demand access to live training courses, in-depth learning paths, interactive coding environments, and a vast collection of text and video from O'Reilly and 200+ other publishers. For more information, please visit *http://oreilly.com*.

How to Contact Us

Please address comments and questions concerning this book to the publisher:

O'Reilly Media, Inc.
1005 Gravenstein Highway North
Sebastopol, CA 95472
800-998-9938 (in the United States or Canada)
707-829-0515 (international or local)
707-829-0104 (fax)

We have a web page for this book, where we list errata, examples, and any additional information. You can access this page at *http://bit.ly/stream-proc-apache-spark*.

To comment or ask technical questions about this book, send email to *bookquestions@oreilly.com*.

For more information about our books, courses, conferences, and news, see our website at *http://www.oreilly.com*.

Find us on Facebook: *http://facebook.com/oreilly*

Follow us on Twitter: *http://twitter.com/oreillymedia*

Watch us on YouTube: *http://www.youtube.com/oreillymedia*

Acknowledgments

This book drastically evolved from its original inception as a learning manual for Spark Streaming to become a comprehensive resource on the streaming capabilities of Apache Spark. We would like to thank our reviewers for their invaluable feedback that helped steer this book into its current form. We are especially grateful to Russell Spitzer from Datastax, Serhat Yilmaz from Facebook, and Giselle Van Dongen from Klarrio.

We would like to extend our gratitude to Holden Karau for her help and advice in the early stages of the draft and to Bill Chambers for his continued support as we added coverage of Structured Streaming.

Our editor at O'Reilly, Jeff Bleiel, has been a stronghold of patience, feedback, and advice as we progressed from early ideas and versions of the draft until the completion of the content you have on your hands. We also would like to thank Shannon Cutt, our first editor at O'Reilly for all of her help in getting this project started. Other people at O'Reilly were there to assist us at many stages and help us move forward.

We thank Tathagata Das for the many interactions, in particular during the early days of Spark Streaming, when we were pushing the limits of what the framework could deliver.

From Gerard

I would like to thank my colleagues at Lightbend for their support and understanding while I juggled between book writing and work responsibilities. A very special thank you to Ray Roestenburg for his pep talks in difficult moments; to Dean Wampler for always being supportive of my efforts in this book; and to Ruth Stento for her excellent advice on writing style.

A special mention to Kurt Jonckheer, Patrick Goemaere, and Lieven Gesquière who created the opportunity and gave me the space to deepen my knowledge of Spark; and to Andy Petrella for creating the Spark Notebook, but more importantly, for his contagious passion and enthusiasm that influenced me to keep exploring the intersection of programming and data.

Most of all, I would like to express my infinite gratitude to my wife, Ingrid, my daughters Layla and Juliana, and my mother, Carmen. Without their love, care, and understanding, I wouldn't have been able to get through this project.

From François

I'm very grateful to my colleagues at Swisscom and Facebook for their support during the writing of this book; to Chris Fregly, Paco Nathan, and Ben Lorica for their advice and support; and to my wife AJung for absolutely everything.

Fundamentals of Stream Processing with Apache Spark

The first part of this book is dedicated to building solid foundations on the concepts that underpin stream processing and a theoretical understanding of Apache Spark as a streaming engine.

We begin with a discussion on what motivating drivers are behind the adoption of stream-processing techniques and systems in the enterprise today (Chapter 1). We then establish vocabulary and concepts common to stream processing (Chapter 2). Next, we take a quick look at how we got to the current state of the art as we discuss different streaming architectures (Chapter 3) and outline a theoretical understanding of Apache Spark as a streaming engine (Chapter 4).

At this point, the readers have the opportunity to directly jump to the more practical-oriented discussion of Structured Streaming in Part II or Spark Streaming in Part III.

For those who prefer to gain a deeper understanding before adventuring into APIs and runtimes, we suggest that you continue reading about Spark's Distributed Processing model in Chapter 5, in which we lay the core concepts that will later help you to better understand the different implementations, options, and features offered by Spark Streaming and Structured Streaming.

In Chapter 6, we deepen our understanding of the resilience model implemented by Spark and how it takes away the pain from the developer to implement robust streaming applications that can run enterprise-critical workloads 24/7.

With this new knowledge, we are ready to venture into the two streaming APIs of Spark, which we do in the subsequent parts of this book.

CHAPTER 1
Introducing Stream Processing

In 2011, Marc Andreessen famously said that "software is eating the world," referring to the booming digital economy, at a time when many enterprises were facing the challenges of a digital transformation. Successful online businesses, using "online" and "mobile" operation modes, were taking over their traditional "brick-and-mortar" counterparts.

For example, imagine the traditional experience of buying a new camera in a photography shop: we would visit the shop, browse around, maybe ask a few questions of the clerk, make up our mind, and finally buy a model that fulfilled our desires and expectations. After finishing our purchase, the shop would have registered a credit card transaction—or only a cash balance change in case of a cash payment—and the shop manager would that know they have one less inventory item of that particular camera model.

Now, let's take that experience online: first, we begin searching the web. We visit a couple of online stores, leaving digital traces as we pass from one to another. Advertisements on websites suddenly begin showing us promotions for the camera we were looking at as well as for competing alternatives. We finally find an online shop offering us the best deal and purchase the camera. We create an account. Our personal data is registered and linked to the purchase. While we complete our purchase, we are offered additional options that are allegedly popular with other people who bought the same camera. Each of our digital interactions, like searching for keywords on the web, clicking some link, or spending time reading a particular page generates a series of events that are collected and transformed into business value, like personalized advertisement or upsale recommendations.

Commenting on Andreessen's quote, in 2015, Dries Buytaert said "no, actually, *data* is eating the world." What he meant is that the disruptive companies of today are no longer disruptive because of their software, but because of the unique data they collect and their ability to transform that data into value.

The adoption of stream-processing technologies is driven by the increasing need of businesses to improve the time required to react and adapt to changes in their operational environment. This way of processing data as it comes in provides a technical and strategical advantage. Examples of this ongoing adoption include sectors such as internet commerce, continuously running data pipelines created by businesses that interact with customers on a 24/7 basis, or credit card companies, analyzing transactions as they happen in order to detect and stop fraudulent activities as they happen.

Another driver of stream processing is that our ability to generate data far surpasses our ability to make sense of it. We are constantly increasing the number of computing-capable devices in our personal and professional environments<m-dash>televisions, connected cars, smartphones, bike computers, smart watches, surveillance cameras, thermostats, and so on. We are surrounding ourselves with devices meant to produce event logs: streams of messages representing the actions and incidents that form part of the history of the device in its context. As we interconnect those devices more and more, we create an ability for us to access and therefore analyze those event logs. This phenomenon opens the door to an incredible burst of creativity and innovation in the domain of near real-time data analytics, on the condition that we find a way to make this analysis tractable. In this world of aggregated event logs, stream processing offers the most resource-friendly way to facilitate the analysis of streams of data.

It is not a surprise that not only is data eating the world, but so is *streaming data*.

In this chapter, we start our journey in stream processing using Apache Spark. To prepare us to discuss the capabilities of Spark in the stream-processing area, we need to establish a common understanding of what stream processing is, its applications, and its challenges. After we build that common language, we introduce Apache Spark as a generic data-processing framework able to handle the requirements of batch and streaming workloads using a unified model. Finally, we zoom in on the streaming capabilities of Spark, where we present the two available APIs: Spark Streaming and Structured Streaming. We briefly discuss their salient characteristics to provide a sneak peek into what you will discover in the rest of this book.

What Is Stream Processing?

Stream processing is the discipline and related set of techniques used to extract information from *unbounded data*.

In his book *Streaming Systems*, Tyler Akidau defines unbounded data as follows:

A type of dataset that is infinite in size (at least theoretically).

Given that our information systems are built on hardware with finite resources such as memory and storage capacity, they cannot possibly hold unbounded datasets. Instead, we observe the data as it is received at the processing system in the form of a flow of events over time. We call this a *stream* of data.

In contrast, we consider *bounded data* as a dataset of known size. We can count the number of elements in a bounded dataset.

Batch Versus Stream Processing

How do we process both types of datasets? With *batch processing*, we refer to the computational analysis of bounded datasets. In practical terms, this means that those datasets are available and retrievable as a whole from some form of storage. We know the size of the dataset at the start of the computational process, and the duration of that process is limited in time.

In contrast, with *stream processing* we are concerned with the processing of data as it arrives to the system. Given the unbounded nature of data streams, the stream processors need to run constantly for as long as the stream is delivering new data. That, as we learned, might be—theoretically—forever.

Stream-processing systems apply programming and operational techniques to make possible the processing of potentially infinite data streams with a limited amount of computing resources.

The Notion of Time in Stream Processing

Data can be encountered in two forms:

- At rest, in the form of a file, the contents of a database, or some other kind of record
- In motion, as continuously generated sequences of signals, like the measurement of a sensor or GPS signals from moving vehicles

We discussed already that a stream-processing program is a program that assumes its input is potentially infinite in size. More specifically, a stream-processing program assumes that its input is a sequence of signals of indefinite length, *observed over time*.

From the point of view of a timeline, *data at rest* is data from the past: arguably, all bounded datasets, whether stored in files or contained in databases, were initially a stream of data collected over time into some storage. The user's database, all the orders from the last quarter, the GPS coordinates of taxi trips in a city, and so on all started as individual events collected in a repository.

Trying to reason about *data in motion* is more challenging. There is a time difference between the moment data is originally generated and when it becomes available for processing. That time delta might be very short, like web log events generated and processed within the same datacenter, or much longer, like GPS data of a car traveling through a tunnel that is dispatched only when the vehicle reestablishes its wireless connectivity after it leaves the tunnel.

We can observe that there's a timeline when the events were produced and another for when the events are handled by the stream-processing system. These timelines are so significant that we give them specific names:

Event time
> The time when the event was created. The time information is provided by the local clock of the device generating the event.

Processing time
> The time when the event is handled by the stream-processing system. This is the clock of the server running the processing logic. It's usually relevant for technical reasons like computing the processing lag or as criteria to determine duplicated output.

The differentiation among these timelines becomes very important when we need to correlate, order, or aggregate the events with respect to one another.

The Factor of Uncertainty

In a timeline, data at rest relates to the past, and data in motion can be seen as the present. But what about the future? One of the most subtle aspects of this discussion is that it makes no assumptions on the throughput at which the system receives events.

In general, streaming systems do not require the input to be produced at regular intervals, all at once, or following a certain rhythm. This means that, because computation usually has a cost, it's a challenge to predict peak load: matching the sudden arrival of input elements with the computing resources necessary to process them.

If we have the computing capacity needed to match a sudden influx of input elements, our system will produce results as expected, but if we have not planned for such a burst of input data, some streaming systems might face delays, resource constriction, of failure.

Dealing with uncertainty is an important aspect of stream processing.

In summary, stream processing lets us extract information from infinite data streams observed as events delivered over time. Nevertheless, as we receive and process data, we need to deal with the additional complexity of event-time and the uncertainty introduced by an unbounded input.

Why would we want to deal with the additional trouble? In the next section, we glance over a number of use cases that illustrate the value added by stream processing and how it delivers on the promise of providing faster, actionable insights, and hence business value, on data streams.

Some Examples of Stream Processing

The use of stream processing goes as wild as our capacity to imagine new real-time, innovative applications of data. The following use cases, in which the authors have been involved in one way or another, are only a small sample that we use to illustrate the wide spectrum of application of stream processing:

Device monitoring

A small startup rolled out a cloud-based Internet of Things (IoT) device monitor able to collect, process, and store data from up to 10 million devices. Multiple stream processors were deployed to power different parts of the application, from real-time dashboard updates using in-memory stores, to continuous data aggregates, like unique counts and minimum/maximum measurements.

Fault detection

A large hardware manufacturer applies a complex stream-processing pipeline to receive device metrics. Using time-series analysis, potential failures are detected and corrective measures are automatically sent back to the device.

Billing modernization

A well-established insurance company moved its billing system to a streaming pipeline. Batch exports from its existing mainframe infrastructure are streamed through this system to meet the existing billing processes while allowing new real-time flows from insurance agents to be served by the same logic.

Fleet management

A fleet management company installed devices able to report real-time data from the managed vehicles, such as location, motor parameters, and fuel levels, allowing it to enforce rules like geographical limits and analyze driver behavior regarding speed limits.

Media recommendations

A national media company deployed a streaming pipeline to ingest new videos, such as news reports, into its recommendation system, making the videos available to its users' personalized suggestions almost as soon as they are ingested into the company's media repository. The company's previous system would take hours to do the same.

Faster loans

A bank active in loan services was able to reduce loan approval from hours to seconds by combining several data streams into a streaming application.

A common thread among those use cases is the need of the business to process the data and create actionable insights in a short period of time from when the data was received. This time is relative to the use case: although *minutes* is a very fast turnaround for a loan approval, a milliseconds response is probably necessary to detect a device failure and issue a corrective action within a given service-level threshold.

In all cases, we can argue that *data* is better when consumed as fresh as possible.

Now that we have an understanding of what stream processing is and some examples of how it is being used today, it's time to delve into the concepts that underpin its implementation.

Scaling Up Data Processing

Before we discuss the implications of distributed computation in stream processing, let's take a quick tour through *MapReduce*, a computing model that laid the foundations for scalable and reliable data processing.

MapReduce

The history of programming for distributed systems experienced a notable event in February 2003. Jeff Dean and Sanjay Gemawhat, after going through a couple of iterations of rewriting Google's crawling and indexing systems, began noticing some operations that they could expose through a common interface. This led them to develop *MapReduce*, a system for distributed processing on large clusters at Google.

> Part of the reason we didn't develop MapReduce earlier was probably because when we were operating at a smaller scale, then our computations were using fewer machines, and therefore robustness wasn't quite such a big deal: it was fine to periodically checkpoint some computations and just restart the whole computation from a checkpoint if a machine died. Once you reach a certain scale, though, that becomes fairly untenable since you'd always be restarting things and never make any forward progress.
>
> —Jeff Dean, *email to Bradford F. Lyon, August 2013*

MapReduce is a programming API first, and a set of components second, that make programming for a distributed system a relatively easier task than all of its predecessors.

Its core tenets are two functions:

Map

The map operation takes as an argument a function to be applied to every element of the collection. The collection's elements are read in a distributed manner, through the distributed filesystem, one chunk per executor machine. Then, all of the elements of the collection that reside in the local chunk see the function applied to them, and the executor emits the result of that application, if any.

Reduce

The reduce operation takes two arguments: one is a neutral element, which is what the *reduce* operation would return if passed an empty collection. The other is an aggregation operation, that takes the current value of an aggregate, a new element of the collection, and lumps them into a new aggregate.

Combinations of these two higher-order functions are powerful enough to express every operation that we would want to do on a dataset.

The Lesson Learned: Scalability and Fault Tolerance

From the programmer's perspective, here are the main advantages of MapReduce:

- It has a simple API.
- It offers very high expressivity.
- It significantly offloads the difficulty of distributing a program from the shoulders of the programmer to those of the library designer. In particular, resilience is built into the model.

Although these characteristics make the model attractive, the main success of MapReduce is its ability to sustain growth. As data volumes increase and growing business requirements lead to more information-extraction jobs, the MapReduce model demonstrates two crucial properties:

Scalability

As datasets grow, it is possible to add more resources to the cluster of machines in order to preserve a stable processing performance.

Fault tolerance

The system can sustain and recover from partial failures. All data is replicated. If a data-carrying executor crashes, it is enough to relaunch the task that was running on the crashed executor. Because the master keeps track of that task, that does not pose any particular problem other than rescheduling.

These two characteristics combined result in a system able to constantly sustain workloads in an environment fundamentally unreliable, *properties that we also require for stream processing.*

Distributed Stream Processing

One fundamental difference of stream processing with the MapReduce model, and with batch processing in general, is that although batch processing has access to the complete dataset, with streams, we see only a small portion of the dataset at any time.

This situation becomes aggravated in a distributed system; that is, in an effort to distribute the processing load among a series of executors, we further split up the input stream into partitions. Each executor gets to see only a partial view of the complete stream.

The challenge for a distributed stream-processing framework is to provide an abstraction that hides this complexity from the user and lets us reason about the stream as a whole.

Stateful Stream Processing in a Distributed System

Let's imagine that we are counting the votes during a presidential election. The classic batch approach would be to wait until all votes have been cast and then proceed to count them. Even though this approach produces a correct end result, it would make for very boring news over the day because no (intermediate) results are known until the end of the electoral process.

A more exciting scenario is when we can count the votes per candidate as each vote is cast. At any moment, we have a partial count by participant that lets us see the current standing as well as the voting trend. We can probably anticipate a result.

To accomplish this scenario, the stream processor needs to keep an internal register of the votes seen so far. To ensure a consistent count, this register must recover from any partial failure. Indeed, we can't ask the citizens to issue their vote again due to a technical failure.

Also, any eventual failure recovery cannot affect the final result. We can't risk declaring the wrong winning candidate as a side effect of an ill-recovered system.

This scenario illustrates the challenges of stateful stream processing running in a distributed environment. Stateful processing poses additional burdens on the system:

- We need to ensure that the state is preserved over time.
- We require data consistency guarantees, even in the event of partial system failures.

As you will see throughout the course of this book, addressing these concerns is an important aspect of stream processing.

Now that we have a better sense of the drivers behind the popularity of stream processing and the challenging aspects of this discipline, we can introduce Apache Spark. As a unified data analytics engine, Spark offers data-processing capabilities for both batch and streaming, making it an excellent choice to satisfy the demands of the data-intensive applications, as we see next.

Introducing Apache Spark

Apache Spark is a fast, reliable, and fault-tolerant distributed computing framework for large-scale data processing.

The First Wave: Functional APIs

In its early days, Spark's breakthrough was driven by its novel use of memory and expressive functional API. The Spark memory model uses RAM to cache data as it is being processed, resulting in up to 100 times faster processing than Hadoop MapReduce, the open source implementation of Google's MapReduce for batch workloads.

Its core abstraction, the *Resilient Distributed Dataset* (RDD), brought a rich functional programming model that abstracted out the complexities of distributed computing on a cluster. It introduced the concepts of *transformations* and *actions* that offered a more expressive programming model than the map and reduce stages that we discussed in the MapReduce overview. In that model, many available *transformations* like `map`, `flatmap`, `join`, and `filter` express the lazy conversion of the data from one internal representation to another, whereas eager operations called *actions* materialize the computation on the distributed system to produce a result.

The Second Wave: SQL

The second game-changer in the history of the Spark project was the introduction of Spark SQL and *DataFrames* (and later, *Dataset*, a strongly typed DataFrame). From a high-level perspective, Spark SQL adds SQL support to any dataset that has a schema. It makes it possible to query a comma-separated values (CSV), Parquet, or JSON dataset in the same way that we used to query a SQL database.

This evolution also lowered the threshold of adoption for users. Advanced distributed data analytics were no longer the exclusive realm of software engineers; it was now accessible to data scientists, business analysts, and other professionals familiar with SQL. From a performance point of view, SparkSQL brought a query optimizer and a physical execution engine to Spark, making it even faster while using fewer resources.

A Unified Engine

Nowadays, Spark is a unified analytics engine offering batch and streaming capabilities that is compatible with a polyglot approach to data analytics, offering APIs in Scala, Java, Python, and the R language.

While in the context of this book we are going to focus our interest on the streaming capabilities of Apache Spark, its batch functionality is equally advanced and is highly complementary to streaming applications. Spark's unified programming model means that developers need to learn only one new paradigm to address both batch and streaming workloads.

 In the course of the book, we use *Apache Spark* and *Spark* interchangeably. We use *Apache Spark* when we want to make emphasis on the project or open source aspect of it, whereas we use *Spark* to refer to the technology in general.

Spark Components

Figure 1-1 illustrates how Spark consists of a core engine, a set of abstractions built on top of it (represented as horizontal layers), and libraries that use those abstractions to address a particular area (vertical boxes). We have highlighted the areas that are within the scope of this book and grayed out those that are not covered. To learn more about these other areas of Apache Spark, we recommend *Spark, The Definitive Guide* by Bill Chambers and Matei Zaharia (O'Reilly), and *High Performance Spark* by Holden Karau and Rachel Warren (O'Reilly).

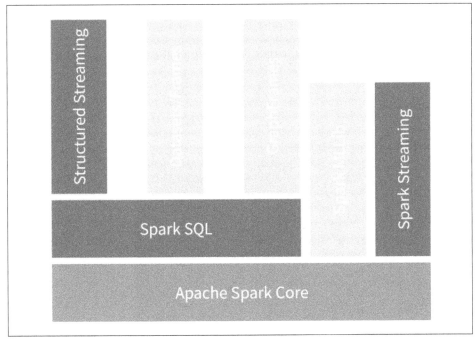

Figure 1-1. Abstraction layers (horizontal) and libraries (vertical) offered by Spark

As abstraction layers in Spark, we have the following:

Spark Core

Contains the Spark core execution engine and a set of low-level functional APIs used to distribute computations to a cluster of computing resources, called *executors* in Spark lingo. Its cluster abstraction allows it to submit workloads to YARN, Mesos, and Kubernetes, as well as use its own standalone cluster mode, in which Spark runs as a dedicated service in a cluster of machines. Its datasource abstraction enables the integration of many different data providers, such as files, block stores, databases, and event brokers.

Spark SQL

Implements the higher-level `Dataset` and `DataFrame` APIs of Spark and adds SQL support on top of arbitrary data sources. It also introduces a series of performance improvements through the Catalyst query engine, and code generation and memory management from project Tungsten.

The libraries built on top of these abstractions address different areas of large-scale data analytics: *MLLib* for machine learning, *GraphFrames* for graph analysis, and the two APIs for stream processing that are the focus of this book: Spark Streaming and Structured Streaming.

Spark Streaming

Spark Streaming was the first stream-processing framework built on top of the distributed processing capabilities of the core Spark engine. It was introduced in the Spark 0.7.0 release in February of 2013 as an alpha release that evolved over time to become today a mature API that's widely adopted in the industry to process large-scale data streams.

Spark Streaming is conceptually built on a simple yet powerful premise: apply Spark's distributed computing capabilities to stream processing by transforming continuous streams of data into discrete data collections on which Spark could operate. This approach to stream processing is called the *microbatch* model; this is in contrast with the *element-at-time* model that dominates in most other stream-processing implementations.

Spark Streaming uses the same functional programming paradigm as the Spark core, but it introduces a new abstraction, the *Discretized Stream* or *DStream*, which exposes a programming model to operate on the underlying data in the stream.

Structured Streaming

Structured Streaming is a stream processor built on top of the Spark SQL abstraction. It extends the `Dataset` and `DataFrame` APIs with streaming capabilities. As such, it adopts the schema-oriented transformation model, which confers the *structured* part of its name, and inherits all the optimizations implemented in Spark SQL.

Structured Streaming was introduced as an experimental API with Spark 2.0 in July of 2016. A year later, it reached *general availability* with the Spark 2.2 release becoming eligible for production deployments. As a relatively new development, Structured Streaming is still evolving fast with each new version of Spark.

Structured Streaming uses a declarative model to acquire data from a stream or set of streams. To use the API to its full extent, it requires the specification of a schema for the data in the stream. In addition to supporting the general transformation model provided by the `Dataset` and `DataFrame` APIs, it introduces stream-specific features such as support for event-time, streaming joins, and separation from the underlying runtime. That last feature opens the door for the implementation of runtimes with different execution models. The default implementation uses the classical microbatch approach, whereas a more recent *continuous processing* backend brings experimental support for near-real-time continuous execution mode.

Structured Streaming delivers a unified model that brings stream processing to the same level of batch-oriented applications, removing a lot of the cognitive burden of reasoning about stream processing.

Where Next?

If you are feeling the urge to learn either of these two APIs right away, you could directly jump to Structured Streaming in Part II or Spark Streaming in Part III.

If you are not familiar with stream processing, we recommend that you continue through this initial part of the book because we build the vocabulary and common concepts that we use in the discussion of the specific frameworks.

## CHAPTER 2

Stream-Processing Model

In this chapter, we bridge the notion of a data stream—a source of data "on the move" —with the programming language primitives and constructs that allow us to express stream processing.

We want to describe simple, fundamental concepts first before moving on to how Apache Spark represents them. Specifically, we want to cover the following as components of stream processing:

- Data sources
- Stream-processing pipelines
- Data sinks

We then show how those concepts map to the specific stream-processing model implemented by Apache Spark.

Next, we characterize stateful stream processing, a type of stream processing that requires bookkeeping of past computations in the form of some intermediate state needed to process new data. Finally, we consider streams of timestamped events and basic notions involved in addressing concerns such as "what do I do if the order and timeliness of the arrival of those events do not match expectations?"

Sources and Sinks

As we mentioned earlier, Apache Spark, in each of its two streaming systems—Structured Streaming and Spark Streaming—is a programming framework with APIs in the Scala, Java, Python, and R programming languages. It can only operate on data that enters the runtime of programs using this framework, and it ceases to operate on the data as soon as it is being sent to another system.

This is a concept that you are probably already familiar with in the context of data at rest: to operate on data stored as a file of records, we need to read that file into memory where we can manipulate it, and as soon as we have produced an output by computing on this data, we have the ability to write that result to another file. The same principle applies to databases—another example of data at rest.

Similarly, data streams can be made accessible as such, in the streaming framework of Apache Spark using the concept of streaming *data sources*. In the context of stream processing, accessing data from a stream is often referred to as *consuming the stream*. This abstraction is presented as an interface that allows the implementation of instances aimed to connect to specific systems: Apache Kafka, Flume, Twitter, a TCP socket, and so on.

Likewise, we call the abstraction used to write a data stream outside of Apache Spark's control a *streaming sink*. Many connectors to various specific systems are provided by the Spark project itself as well as by a rich ecosystem of open source and commercial third-party integrations.

In Figure 2-1, we illustrate this concept of sources and sinks in a stream-processing system. Data is consumed from a source by a processing component and the eventual results are produced to a sink.

Figure 2-1. Simplified streaming model

The notion of sources and sinks represents the system's boundary. This labeling of system boundaries makes sense given that a distributed framework can have a highly complex footprint among our computing resources. For example, it is possible to connect an Apache Spark cluster to another Apache Spark cluster, or to another distributed system, of which Apache Kafka is a frequent example. In that context, one framework's sink is the downstream framework's source. This chaining is commonly known as a *pipeline*. The name of sources and sinks is useful to both describe data passing from one system to the next and which point of view we are adopting when speaking about each system independently.

Immutable Streams Defined from One Another

Between sources and sinks lie the programmable constructs of a stream-processing framework. We do not want to get into the details of this subject yet—you will see them appear later in Part II and Part III for Structured Streaming and Spark Streaming, respectively. But we can introduce a few notions that will be useful to understand how we express stream processing.

Both stream APIs in Apache Spark take the approach of functional programming: they declare the transformations and aggregations they operate on data streams, assuming that those streams are immutable. As such, for one given stream, it is impossible to mutate one or several of its elements. Instead, we use transformations to express how to process the contents of one stream to obtain a derived data stream. This makes sure that at any given point in a program, any data stream can be traced to its inputs by a sequence of transformations and operations that are explicitly declared in the program. As a consequence, any particular process in a Spark cluster can reconstitute the content of the data stream using only the program and the input data, making computation unambiguous and reproducible.

Transformations and Aggregations

Spark makes extensive use of *transformations* and *aggregations*. Transformations are computations that express themselves in the same way for every element in the stream. For example, creating a derived stream that doubles every element of its input stream corresponds to a transformation. Aggregations, on the other hand, produce results that depend on many elements and potentially every element of the stream observed until now. For example, collecting the top five largest numbers of an input stream corresponds to an aggregation. Computing the average value of some reading every 10 minutes is also an example of an aggregation.

Another way to designate those notions is to say that transformations have *narrow dependencies* (to produce one element of the output, you need only one of the elements of the input), whereas aggregations have *wide dependencies* (to produce one element of the output you would need to observe many elements of the input stream encountered so far). This distinction is useful. It lets us envision a way to express basic functions that produces results using higher-order functions.

Although Spark Streaming and Structured Streaming have distinct ways of representing a data stream, the APIs they operate on are similar in nature. They both present themselves under the form of a series of transformations applied to immutable input streams and produce an output stream, either as a bona fide data stream or as an output operation (data sink).

Window Aggregations

Stream-processing systems often feed themselves on actions that occur in real time: social media messages, clicks on web pages, ecommerce transactions, financial events, or sensor readings are also frequently encountered examples of such events. Our streaming application often has a centralized view of the logs of several places, whether those are retail locations or simply web servers for a common application. Even though seeing every transaction individually might not be useful or even practical, we might be interested in seeing the properties of events seen over a recent period of time; for example, the last 15 minutes or the last hour, or maybe even both.

Moreover, the very idea of stream processing is that the system is supposed to be long-running, dealing with a continuous stream of data. As these events keep coming in, the older ones usually become less and less relevant to whichever processing you are trying to accomplish.

We find many applications of regular and recurrent time-based aggregations that we call *windows*.

Tumbling Windows

The most natural notion of a window aggregation is that of "a grouping function each x period of time." For instance, "the maximum and minimum ambient temperature each hour" or "the total energy consumption (kW) each 15 minutes" are examples of window aggregations. Notice how the time periods are inherently consecutive and nonoverlapping. We call this grouping of a fixed time period, in which each group follows the previous and does not overlap, *tumbling windows*.

Tumbling windows are the norm when we need to produce aggregates of our data over regular periods of time, with each period independent from previous periods. Figure 2-2 shows a tumbling window of 10 seconds over a stream of elements. This illustration demonstrates the tumbling nature of tumbling windows.

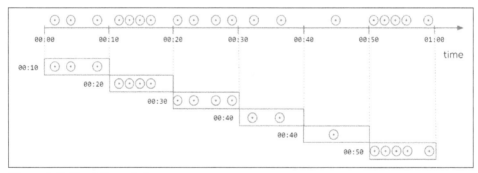

Figure 2-2. Tumbling windows

Sliding Windows

Sliding windows are aggregates over a period of time that are reported at a higher frequency than the aggregation period itself. As such, sliding windows refer to an aggregation with two time specifications: the window length and the reporting frequency. It usually reads like "a grouping function over a time interval x reported each y frequency." For example, "the average share price over the last day reported hourly." As you might have noticed already, this combination of a sliding window with the average function is the most widely known form of a sliding window, commonly known as a *moving average*.

Figure 2-3 shows a sliding window with a window size of 30 seconds and a reporting frequency of 10 seconds. In the illustration, we can observe an important characteristic of *sliding windows*: they are not defined for periods of time smaller than the size of the window. We can see that there are no windows reported for time `00:10` and `00:20`.

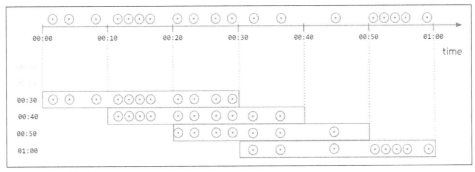

Figure 2-3. Sliding windows

Although you cannot see it in the final illustration, the process of drawing the chart reveals an interesting feature: we can construct and maintain a sliding window by adding the most recent data and removing the expired elements, while keeping all other elements in place.

It's worth noting that tumbling windows are a particular case of sliding windows in which the frequency of reporting is equal to the window size.

Stateless and Stateful Processing

Now that we have a better notion of the programming model of the streaming systems in Apache Spark, we can look at the nature of the computations that we want to apply on data streams. In our context, data streams are fundamentally long collections of elements, observed over time. In fact, Structured Streaming pushes this logic by considering a data stream as a virtual table of records in which each row corresponds to an element.

Stateful Streams

Whether streams are viewed as a continuously extended collection or as a table, this approach gives us some insight into the kind of computation that we might find interesting. In some cases, the emphasis is put on the continuous and independent processing of elements or groups of elements: those are the cases for which we want to operate on some elements based on a well-known heuristic, such as alert messages coming from a log of events.

This focus is perfectly valid but hardly requires an advanced analytics system such as Apache Spark. More often, we are interested in a real-time reaction to new elements based on an analysis that depends on the whole stream, such as detecting outliers in a collection or computing recent aggregate statistics from event data. For example, it might be interesting to find higher than usual vibration patterns in a stream of airplane engine readings, which requires understanding the regular vibration measurements for the kind of engine we are interested in.

This approach, in which we are simultaneously trying to understand new data in the context of data already seen, often leads us to *stateful stream processing*. Stateful stream processing is the discipline by which we compute something out of the new elements of data observed in our input data stream and refresh internal data that helps us perform this computation.

For example, if we are trying to do anomaly detection, the internal state that we want to update with every new stream element would be a machine learning model, whereas the computation we want to perform is to say whether an input element should be classified as an anomaly or not.

This pattern of computation is supported by a distributed streaming system such as Apache Spark because it can take advantage of a large amount of computing power and is an exciting new way of reacting to real-time data. For example, we could compute the running mean and standard deviation of the elements seen as input numbers and output a message if a new element is further away than five standard deviations from this mean. This is a simple, but useful, way of marking particular extreme outliers of the distribution of our input elements.[1] In this case, the internal state of the stream processor only stores the running mean and standard deviation of our stream —that is, a couple of numbers.

---

[1] Thanks to the Chebycheff inequality, we know that alerts on this data stream should occur with less than 5% probability.

Bounding the Size of the State

One of the common pitfalls of practitioners new to the field of stream processing is the temptation to store an amount of internal data that is proportional to the size of the input data stream. For example, if you would like to remove duplicate records of a stream, a naive way of approaching that problem would be to store every message already seen and compare new messages to them. That not only increases computing time with each incoming record, but also has an unbounded memory requirement that will eventually outgrow any cluster.

This is a common mistake because the premise of stream processing is that there is no limit to the number of input events and, while your available memory in a distributed Spark cluster might be large, it is always limited. As such, intermediary state representations can be very useful to express computation that operates on elements relative to the global stream of data on which they are observed, but it is a somewhat unsafe approach. If you choose to have intermediate data, you need to make absolutely sure that the amount of data you might be storing at any given time is strictly bounded to a certain upper limit that is less than your available memory, independent of the amount of data that you might encounter as input.

An Example: Local Stateful Computation in Scala

To gain intuition into the concept of statefulness without having to go into the complexity of distributed stream processing, we begin with a simple nondistributed stream example in Scala.

The Fibonacci Sequence is classically defined as a stateful stream: it's the sequence starting with 0 and 1, and thereafter composed of the sum of its two previous elements, as shown in Example 2-1.

Example 2-1. A stateful computation of the Fibonacci elements

```
scala> val ints = Stream.from(0)
ints: scala.collection.immutable.Stream[Int] = Stream(0, ?)

scala> val fibs = (ints.scanLeft((0, 1)){ case ((previous, current), index) =>
        (current, (previous + current))})

fibs: scala.collection.immutable.Stream[(Int, Int)] = Stream((0,1), ?)

scala> fibs.take(8).print
(0,1), (1,1), (1,2), (2,3), (3,5), (5,8), (8,13), (13,21), empty
```

```
Scala> fibs.map{ case (x, y) => x}.take(8).print
0, 1, 1, 2, 3, 5, 8, 13, empty
```

Stateful stream processing refers to any stream processing that looks to past information to obtain its result. It's necessary to maintain some *state* information in the process of computing the next element of the stream.

Here, this is held in the recursive argument of the scanLeft function, in which we can see fibs having a tuple of two elements for each element: the sought result, and the next value. We can apply a simple transformation to the list of tuples fibs to retain only the leftmost element and thus obtain the classical Fibonacci Sequence.

The important point to highlight is that to get the value at the *nth* place, we must process all *n-1* elements, keeping the intermediate (i-1, i) elements as we move along the stream.

Would it be possible to define it without referring to its prior values, though, purely statelessly?

A Stateless Definition of the Fibonacci Sequence as a Stream Transformation

To express this computation as a stream, taking as input the integers and outputting the Fibonacci Sequence, we express this as a stream transformation that uses a stateless map function to transform each number to its Fibonacci value. We can see the implementation of this approach in Example 2-2.

Example 2-2. A stateless computation of the Fibonacci elements

```
scala> import scala.math.{pow, sqrt}
import scala.math.{pow, sqrt}

scala> val phi = (sqrt(5)+1) / 2
phi: Double = 1.618033988749895

scala> def fibonacciNumber(x: Int): Int =
  ((pow(phi,x) - pow(-phi,-x))/sqrt(5)).toInt
fibonacciNumber: (x: Int)Int

scala> val integers = Stream.from(0)
integers: scala.collection.immutable.Stream[Int] = Stream(0, ?)
scala> integers.take(10).print
0, 1, 2, 3, 4, 5, 6, 7, 8, 9, empty

scala> val fibonacciSequence = integers.map(fibonacciNumber)
fibonacciSequence: scala.collection.immutable.Stream[Int] = Stream(0, ?)
```

```
scala>fibonacciSequence.take(8).print
0, 1, 1, 2, 3, 5, 8, 13, empty
```

This rather counterintuitive definition uses a stream of integers, starting from the single integer (0), to then define the Fibonacci Sequence as a computation that takes as input an integer *n* received over the stream and returns the *n-th* element of the Fibonacci Sequence as a result. This uses a floating-point number formula known as the *Binet formula* to compute the *n-th* element of the sequence directly, without requiring the previous elements; that is, without requiring knowledge of the state of the stream.

Notice how we take a limited number of elements of this sequence and print them in Scala, as an explicit operation. This is because the computation of elements in our stream is executed lazily, which calls the evaluation of our stream only when required, considering the elements needed to produce them from the last materialization point to the original source.

Stateless or Stateful Streaming

We illustrated the difference between stateful and stateless stream processing with a rather simple case that has a solution using the two approaches. Although the stateful version closely resembles the definition, it requires more computing resources to produce a result: it needs to traverse a stream and keep intermediate values at each step.

The stateless version, although contrived, uses a simpler approach: we use a stateless function to obtain a result. It doesn't matter whether we need the Fibonacci number for 9 or 999999, in both cases the computational cost is roughly of the same order.

We can generalize this idea to stream processing. Stateful processing is more costly in terms of the resources it uses and also introduces concerns in face of failure: what happens if our computation fails halfway through the stream? Although a safe rule of thumb is to choose for the stateless option, if available, many of the interesting questions we can ask over a stream of data are often stateful in nature. For example: how long was the user session on our site? What was the path the taxi used across the city? What is the moving average of the pressure sensor on an industrial machine?

Throughout the book, we will see that stateful computations are more general but they carry their own constraints. It's an important aspect of the stream-processing framework to provide facilities to deal with these constraints and free the user to create the solutions that the business needs dictate.

The Effect of Time

So far, we have considered how there is an advantage in keeping track of intermediary data as we produce results on each element of the data stream because it allows us to analyze each of those elements relative to the data stream that they are part of as long as we keep this intermediary data of a bounded and reasonable size. Now, we want to consider another issue unique to stream processing, which is the operation on time-stamped messages.

Computing on Timestamped Events

Elements in a data stream always have a *processing time*. That is, by definition, the time at which the stream-processing system observes a new event from a data source. That time is entirely determined by the processing runtime and completely independent of the content of the stream's element.

However, for most data streams, we also speak of a notion of *event time*, which is the time when the event actually happened. When the capabilities of the system sensing the event allow for it, this time is usually added as part of the message payload in the stream.

Timestamping is an operation that consists of adding a register of time at the moment of the generation of the message, which will become a part of the data stream. It is a ubiquitous practice that is present in both the most humble embedded devices (provided they have a clock) as well as the most complex logs in financial transaction systems.

Timestamps as the Provider of the Notion of Time

The importance of time stamping is that it allows users to reason on their data considering the moment at which it was generated.

For example, if I register my morning jog using a wearable device and I synchronize the device to my phone when I get back home, I would like to see the details of my heart rate and speed as I ran through the forest moments ago, and not see the data as a timeless sequence of values as they are being uploaded to some cloud server. As we can see, timestamps provide the context of time to data.

So, because event logs form a large proportion of the data streams being analyzed today, those timestamps help make sense of what happened to a particular system at a given time. This complete picture is something that is often made more elusive by the fact that transporting the data from the various systems or devices that have created it to the cluster that processes it is an operation prone to different forms of failure in which some events could be delayed, reordered, or lost.

Often, users of a framework such as Apache Spark want to compensate for those hazards without having to compromise on the reactivity of their system. Out of this desire was born a discipline for producing the following:

- Clearly marked correct and reordered results
- Intermediary prospective results

With that classification reflecting the best knowledge that a stream-processing system has of the timestamped events delivered by the data stream and under the proviso that this view could be completed by the late arrival of delayed stream elements. This process constitutes the basis for *event-time processing*.

In Spark, this feature is offered natively only by Structured Streaming. Even though Spark Streaming lacks built-in support for event-time processing, it is a question of development effort and some data consolidation processes to manually implement the same sort of primitives, as you will see in Chapter 22.

Event Time Versus Processing Time

We recognize that there is a timeline in which the events are created and a different one when they are processed:

- *Event time* refers to the timeline when the events were originally generated. Typically, a clock available at the generating device places a timestamp in the event itself, meaning that all events from the same source could be chronologically ordered even in the case of transmission delays.

- *Processing time* is the time when the event is handled by the stream-processing system. This time is relevant only at the technical or implementation level. For example, it could be used to add a processing timestamp to the results and in that way, differentiate duplicates, as being the same output values with different processing times.

Imagine that we have a series of events produced and processed over time, as illustrated in Figure 2-4.

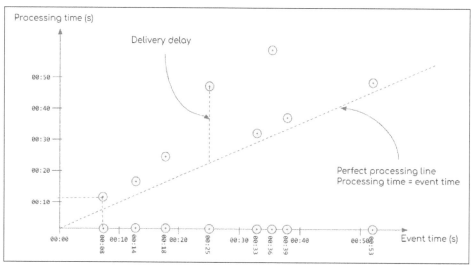

Figure 2-4. Event versus processing time

Let's look at this more closely:

- The x-axis represents the event timeline and the dots on that axis denote the time at which each event was generated.

- The y-axis is the processing time. Each dot on the chart area corresponds to when the corresponding event in the x-axis is processed. For example, the event created at 00:08 (first on the x-axis) is processed at approximately 00:12, the time that corresponds to its mark on the y-axis.

- The diagonal line represents the perfect processing time. In an ideal world, using a network with zero delay, events are processed immediately as they are created. Note that there can be no processing events below that line, because it would mean that events are processed before they are created.

- The vertical distance between the diagonal and the processing time is the *delivery delay*: the time elapsed between the production of the event and its eventual consumption.

With this framework in mind, let's now consider a 10-second window aggregation, as demonstrated in Figure 2-5.

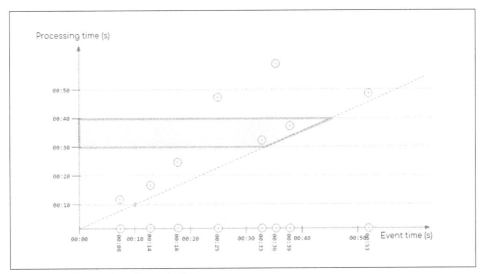

Figure 2-5. Processing-time windows

We start by considering windows defined on processing time:

- The stream processor uses its internal clock to measure 10-second intervals.
- All events that fall in that time interval belong to the window.
- In Figure 2-5, the horizontal lines define the 10-second windows.

We have also highlighted the window corresponding to the time interval `00:30-00:40`. It contains two events with event time `00:33` and `00:39`.

In this window, we can appreciate two important characteristics:

- The window boundaries are well defined, as we can see in the highlighted area. This means that the window has a defined start and end. We know what's in and what's out by the time the window closes.
- Its contents are arbitrary. They are unrelated to when the events were generated. For example, although we would assume that a `00:30-00:40` window would contain the event `00:36`, we can see that it has fallen out of the resulting set because it was late.

Let's now consider the same 10-second window defined on event time. For this case, we use the *event creation time* as the window aggregation criteria. Figure 2-6 illustrates how these windows look radically different from the processing-time windows we saw earlier. In this case, the window `00:30-00:40` contains all the events that were *created* in that period of time. We can also see that this window has no natural upper boundary that defines when the window ends. The event created at `00:36` was late for more than 20 seconds. As a consequence, to report the results of the window `00:30-00:40`, we need to wait at least until `01:00`. What if an event is dropped by the network and never arrives? How long do we wait? To resolve this problem, we introduce an arbitrary deadline called a *watermark* to deal with the consequences of this open boundary, like lateness, ordering, and deduplication.

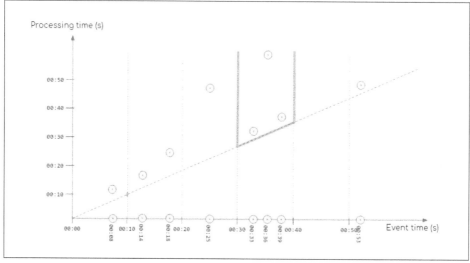

Figure 2-6. Event-time windows

Computing with a Watermark

As we have noticed, stream processing produces periodic results out of the analysis of the events observed in its input. When equipped with the ability to use the timestamp contained in the event messages, the stream processor is able to bucket those messages into two categories based on a notion of a watermark.

The watermark is, at any given moment, *the oldest timestamp that we will accept on the data stream*. Any events that are older than this expectation are not taken into the results of the stream processing. The streaming engine can choose to process them in an alternative way, like report them in a *late arrivals* channel, for example.

However, to account for possibly delayed events, this watermark is usually much larger than the average delay we expect in the delivery of the events. Note also that this watermark is a fluid value that monotonically increases over time,[2] sliding a window of delay-tolerance as the time observed in the data-stream progresses.

---

2 Watermarks are nondecreasing by nature.

When we apply this concept of watermark to our event-time diagram, as illustrated in Figure 2-7, we can appreciate that the watermark closes the open boundary left by the definition of event-time window, providing criteria to decide what events belong to the window, and what events are too late to be considered for processing.

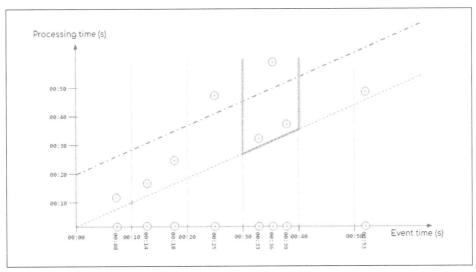

Figure 2-7. Watermark in event time

After this notion of watermark is defined for a stream, the stream processor can operate in one of two modes with relation to that specific stream: either it is producing output relative to events that are all older than the watermark, in which case the output is final because all of those elements have been observed so far, and no further event older than that will ever be considered, or it is producing an output relative to the data that is before the watermark and a new, delayed element newer than the watermark could arrive on the stream at any moment and can change the outcome. In this latter case, we can consider the output as provisional because newer data can still change the final outcome, whereas in the former case, the result is final and no new data will be able to change it.

We examine in detail how to concretely express and operate this sort of computation in Chapter 12.

Note finally that with provisionary results, we are storing intermediate values and in one way or another, we require a method to revise their computation upon the arrival of delayed events. This process requires some amount of memory space. As such, event-time processing is another form of stateful computation and is subject to the same limitation: to handle watermarks, the stream processor needs to store a lot of intermediate data and, as such, consume a significant amount of memory that roughly corresponds to *the length of the watermark × the rate of arrival × message size.*

Also, since we need to wait for the watermark to expire to be sure that we have all elements that comprise an interval, stream processes that use a watermark and want to have a unique, final result for each interval, must delay their output for at least the length of the watermark.

 We want to outline event-time processing because it is an exception to the general rule we have given in Chapter 1 of making no assumptions on the throughput of events observed in its input stream.

With event-time processing, we make the assumption that setting our watermark to a certain value is appropriate. That is, we can expect the results of a streaming computation based on event-time processing to be meaningful only if the watermark allows for the delays that messages of our stream will actually encounter between their creation time and their order of arrival on the input data stream.

A too small watermark will lead to dropping too many events and produce severely incomplete results. A too large watermark will delay the output of results deemed complete for too long and increase the resource needs of the stream processing system to pre-serve all intermediate events.

It is left to the users to ensure they choose a watermark suitable for the event-time processing they require and appropriate for the computing resources they have available, as well.

Summary

In this chapter, we explored the main notions unique to the stream-processing programming model:

- Data sources and sinks
- Stateful processing
- Event-time processing

We explore the implementation of these concepts in the streaming APIs of Apache Spark as we progress through the book.

## CHAPTER 3

Streaming Architectures

The implementation of a distributed data analytics system has to deal with the management of a pool of computational resources, as in-house clusters of machines or reserved cloud-based capacity, to satisfy the computational needs of a division or even an entire company. Since teams and projects rarely have the same needs over time, clusters of computers are best amortized if they are a shared resource among a few teams, which requires dealing with the problem of multitenancy.

When the needs of two teams differ, it becomes important to give each a fair and secure access to the resources for the cluster, while making sure the computing resources are best utilized over time.

This need has forced people using large clusters to address this heterogeneity with modularity, making several functional blocks emerge as interchangeable pieces of a data platform. For example, when we refer to database storage as the functional block, the most common component that delivers that functionality is a relational database such as PostgreSQL or MySQL, but when the streaming application needs to write data at a very high throughput, a scalable column-oriented database like Apache Cassandra would be a much better choice.

In this chapter, we briefly explore the different parts that comprise the architecture of a streaming data platform and see the position of a processing engine relative to the other components needed for a complete solution. After we have a good view of the different elements in a streaming architecture, we explore two architectural styles used to approach streaming applications: the Lambda and the Kappa architectures.

Components of a Data Platform

We can see a data platform as a composition of standard components that are expected to be useful to most stakeholders and specialized systems that serve a purpose specific to the challenges that the business wants to address.

Figure 3-1 illustrates the pieces of this puzzle.

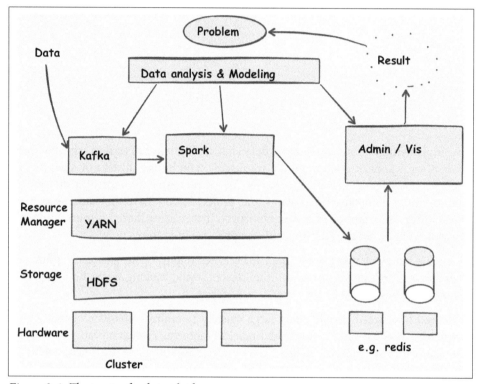

Figure 3-1. The parts of a data platform

Going from the bare-metal level at the bottom of the schema to the actual data processing demanded by a business requirement, you could find the following:

The hardware level

On-premises hardware installations, datacenters, or potentially virtualized in homogeneous cloud solutions (such as the T-shirt size offerings of Amazon, Google, or Microsoft), with a base operating system installed.

The persistence level

On top of that baseline infrastructure, it is often expected that machines offer a shared interface to a persistence solution to store the results of their computation as well as perhaps its input. At this level, you would find distributed storage solutions like the Hadoop Distributed File System (HDFS)—among many other distributed storage systems. On the cloud, this persistence layer is provided by a dedicated service such as Amazon Simple Storage Service (Amazon S3) or Google Cloud Storage.

The resource manager

After persistence, most cluster architectures offer a single point of negotiation to submit jobs to be executed on the cluster. This is the task of the resource manager, like YARN and Mesos, and the more evolved *schedulers* of the *cloud-native* era, like Kubernetes.

The execution engine

At an even higher level, there is the execution engine, which is tasked with executing the actual computation. Its defining characteristic is that it holds the interface with the programmer's input and describes the data manipulation. Apache Spark, Apache Flink, or MapReduce would be examples of this.

A data ingestion component

Besides the execution engine, you could find a data ingestion server that could be plugged directly into that engine. Indeed, the old practice of reading data from a distributed filesystem is often supplemented or even replaced by another data source that can be queried in real time. The realm of messaging systems or log processing engines such as Apache Kafka is set at this level.

A processed data sink

On the output side of an execution engine, you will frequently find a high-level data sink, which might be either another analytics system (in the case of an execution engine tasked with an *Extract, Transform and Load* [ETL] job), a NoSQL database, or some other service.

A visualization layer

We should note that because the results of data-processing are useful only if they are integrated in a larger framework, those results are often plugged into a visualization. Nowadays, since the data being analyzed evolves quickly, that visualization has moved away from the old static report toward more real-time visual interfaces, often using some web-based technology.

In this architecture, Spark, as a computing engine, focuses on providing data processing capabilities and relies on having functional interfaces with the other blocks of the picture. In particular, it implements a cluster abstraction layer that lets it interface with YARN, Mesos, and Kubernetes as resource managers, provides connectors to many data sources while new ones are easily added through an easy-to-extend API, and integrates with output data sinks to present results to upstream systems.

Architectural Models

Now we turn our attention to the link between stream processing and batch processing in a concrete architecture. In particular, we're going to ask ourselves the question of whether batch processing is still relevant if we have a system that can do stream processing, and if so, why?

In this chapter, we contrast two conceptions of streaming application architecture: the *Lambda architecture*, which suggests duplicating a streaming application with a batch counterpart running in parallel to obtain complementary results, and the *Kappa architecture*, which purports that if two versions of an application need to be compared, those should both be streaming applications. We are going to see in detail what those architectures intend to achieve, and we examine that although the Kappa architecture is easier and lighter to implement in general, there might be cases for which a Lambda architecture is still needed, and why.

The Use of a Batch-Processing Component in a Streaming Application

Often, if we develop a batch application that runs on a periodic interval into a streaming application, we are provided with batch datasets already—and a batch program representing this periodic analysis, as well. In this evolution use case, as described in the prior chapters, we want to evolve to a streaming application to reap the benefits of a lighter, simpler application that gives faster results.

In a greenfield application, we might also be interested in creating a reference batch dataset: most data engineers don't work on merely solving a problem once, but revisit their solution, and continuously improve it, especially if value or revenue is tied to the performance of their solution. For this purpose, a batch dataset has the advantage of setting a benchmark: after it's collected, it does not change anymore and can be used as a "test set." We can indeed replay a batch dataset to a streaming system to compare its performance to prior iterations or to a known benchmark.

In this context, we identify three levels of interaction between the batch and the stream-processing components, from the least to the most mixed with batch processing:

Code reuse

Often born out of a reference batch implementation, seeks to reemploy as much of it as possible, so as not to duplicate efforts. This is an area in which Spark shines, since it is particularly easy to call functions that transform Resilient Distributed Databases (RDDs) and DataFrames—they share most of the same APIs, and only the setup of the data input and output is distinct.

Data reuse

> Wherein a streaming application feeds itself from a feature or data source prepared, at regular intervals, from a batch processing job. This is a frequent pattern: for example, some international applications must handle time conversions, and a frequent pitfall is that daylight saving rules change on a more frequent basis than expected. In this case, it is good to be thinking of this data as a new dependent source that our streaming application feeds itself off.

Mixed processing

> Wherein the application itself is understood to have both a batch and a streaming component during its lifetime. This pattern does happen relatively frequently, out of a will to manage both the precision of insights provided by an application, and as a way to deal with the versioning and the evolution of the application itself.

The first two uses are uses of convenience, but the last one introduces a new notion: using a batch dataset as a benchmark. In the next subsections, we see how this affects the architecture of a streaming application.

Referential Streaming Architectures

In the world of replay-ability and performance analysis over time, there are two historical but conflicting recommendations. Our main concern is about how to measure and test the performance of a streaming application. When we do so, there are two things that can change in our setup: the nature of our model (as a result of our attempt at improving it) and the data that the model operates on (as a result of organic change). For instance, if we are processing data from weather sensors, we can expect a seasonal pattern of change in the data.

To ensure we compare apples to apples, we have already established that replaying a *batch dataset* to two versions of our streaming application is useful: it lets us make sure that we are not seeing a change in performance that is really reflecting a change in the data. Ideally, in this case, we would test our improvements in yearly data, making sure we're not overoptimizing for the current season at the detriment of performance six months after.

However, we want to contend that a comparison with a *batch analysis* is necessary, as well, beyond the use of a benchmark dataset—and this is where the architecture comparison helps.

The Lambda Architecture

The Lambda architecture (Figure 3-2) suggests taking a batch analysis performed on a periodic basis—say, nightly—and to supplement the model thus created with streaming refinements as data comes, until we are able to produce a new version of the batch analysis based on the entire day's data.

It was introduced as such by Nathan Marz in a blog post, "How to beat the CAP Theorem" (*http://bit.ly/1ATyjbD*).[1] It proceeds from the idea that we want to emphasize two novel points beyond the precision of the data analysis:

- The historical replay-ability of data analysis is important
- The availability of results proceeding from fresh data is also a very important point

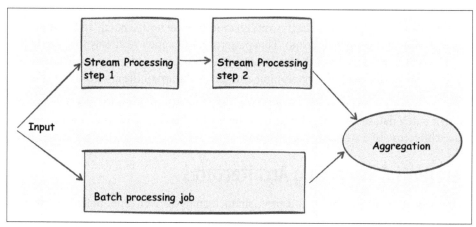

Figure 3-2. The Lambda architecture

This is a useful architecture, but its drawbacks seem obvious, as well: such a setup is complex and requires maintaining two versions of the same code, for the same purpose. Even if Spark helps in letting us reuse most of our code between the batch and streaming versions of our application, the two versions of the application are distinct in life cycles, which might seem complicated.

An alternative view on this problem suggests that it would be enough to keep the ability to feed the same dataset to two versions of a streaming application (the new, improved experiment, and the older, stable workhorse), helping with the maintainability of our solution.

The Kappa Architecture

This architecture, as outlined in Figure 3-3, compares two streaming applications and does away with any batching, noting that if reading a batch file is needed, a simple

---

1 We invite you to consult the original article if you want to know more about the link with the CAP theorem (also called Brewer's theorem). The idea was that it concentrated some limitations fundamental to distributed computing described by the theorem to a limited part of the data-processing system. In our case, we're focusing on the practical implications of that constraint.

component can replay the contents of this file, record by record, as a streaming data source. This simplicity is still a great benefit, since even the code that consists in feeding data to the two versions of this application can be reused. In this paradigm, called the *Kappa architecture* ([Kreps2014]), there is no deduplication and the mental model is simpler.

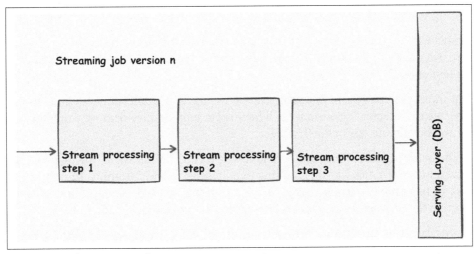

Figure 3-3. The Kappa architecture

This begs the question: is batch computation still relevant? Should we convert our applications to be all streaming, all the time?

We think some concepts stemming from the Lambda architecture are still relevant; in fact, they're vitally useful in some cases, although those are not always easy to figure out.

There are some use cases for which it is still useful to go through the effort of implementing a batch version of our analysis and then compare it to our streaming solution.

Streaming Versus Batch Algorithms

There are two important considerations that we need to take into account when selecting a general architectural model for our streaming application:

- Streaming algorithms are sometimes completely different in nature
- Streaming algorithms can't be guaranteed to measure well against batch algorithms

Let's explore these thoughts in the next two sections using motivating examples.

Streaming Algorithms Are Sometimes Completely Different in Nature

Sometimes, it is difficult to deduce batch from streaming, or the reverse, and those two classes of algorithms have different characteristics. This means that at first glance we might not be able to reuse code between both approaches, but also, and more important, that relating the performance characteristics of those two modes of processing should be done with high care.

To make things more precise, let's look at an example: the buy or rent problem. In this case, we decide to go skiing. We can buy skis for $500 or rent them for $50. Should we rent or buy?

Our intuitive strategy is to first rent, to see if we like skiing. But suppose we do: in this case, we will eventually realize we will have spent more money than we would have if we had bought the skis in the first place.

In the batch version of this computation, we proceed "in hindsight," being given the total number of times we will go skiing in a lifetime. In the streaming, or online version of this problem, we are asked to make a decision (produce an output) on each discrete skiing event, as it happens. The strategy is fundamentally different.

In this case, we can consider the competitive ratio of a streaming algorithm. We run the algorithm on the worst possible input, and then compare its "cost" to the decision that a batch algorithm would have taken, "in hindsight."

In our buy-or-rent problem, let's consider the following streaming strategy: we rent until renting makes our total spending as much as buying, in which case we buy.

If we go skiing nine times or fewer, we are optimal, because we spend as much as what we would have in hindsight. The competitive ratio is one. If we go skiing 10 times or more, we pay $450 + $500 = $950. The worst input is to receive 10 "ski trip" decision events, in which case the batch algorithm, in hindsight, would have paid $500. The competitive ratio of this strategy is (2 − 1/10).

If we were to choose another algorithm, say "always buy on the first occasion," then the worst possible input is to go skiing only once, which means that the competitive ratio is $500 / $50 = 10.

 The performance ratio or competitive ratio is a measure of how far from the optimal the values returned by an algorithm are, given a measure of optimality. An algorithm is formally ρ-competitive if its objective value is no more than ρ times the optimal offline value for all instances.

A better competitive ratio is smaller, whereas a competitive ratio above one shows that the streaming algorithm performs measurably worse on some inputs. It is easy to see that with the worst input condition, the batch algorithm, which proceeds in hindsight with strictly more information, is always expected to perform better (the competitive ratio of any streaming algorithm is greater than one).

Streaming Algorithms Can't Be Guaranteed to Measure Well Against Batch Algorithms

Another example of those unruly cases is the bin-packing problem. In the bin-packing problem, an input of a set of objects of different sizes or different weights must be fitted into a number of bins or containers, each of them having a set volume or set capacity in terms of weight or size. The challenge is to find an assignment of objects into bins that minimizes the number of containers used.

In computational complexity theory, the offline ration of that algorithm is known to be *NP-hard*. The simple variant of the problem is the *decision* question: knowing whether that set of objects will fit into a specified number of bins. It is itself NP-complete, meaning (for our purposes here) computationally very difficult in and of itself.

In practice, this algorithm is used very frequently, from the shipment of actual goods in containers, to the way operating systems match memory allocation requests, to blocks of free memory of various sizes.

There are many variations of these problems, but we want to focus on the distinction between online versions—for which the algorithm has as input a stream of objects—and offline versions—for which the algorithm can examine the entire set of input objects before it even starts the computing process.

The online algorithm processes the items in arbitrary order and then places each item in the first bin that can accommodate it, and if no such bin exists, it opens a new bin and puts the item within that new bin. This greedy approximation algorithm always allows placing the input objects into a set number of bins that is, at worst, suboptimal; meaning we might use more bins than necessary.

A better algorithm, which is still relatively intuitive to understand, is the *first fit decreasing strategy*, which operates by first sorting the items to be inserted in decreasing order of their sizes, and then inserting each item into the first bin in the list with sufficient remaining space. That algorithm was proven in 2007 to be much closer to the optimal algorithm producing the absolute minimum number of bins ([Dosa2007]).

The first fit decreasing strategy, however, relies on the idea that we can first sort the items in decreasing order of sizes before we begin processing them and packing them into bins.

Now, attempting to apply such a method in the case of the online bin-packing problem, the situation is completely different in that we are dealing with a stream of elements for which sorting is not possible. Intuitively, it is thus easy to understand that the online bin-packing problem—which by its nature lacks foresight when it operates—is much more difficult than the offline bin-packing problem.

 That intuition is in fact supported by proof if we consider the competitive ratio of streaming algorithms. This is the ratio of resources consumed by the online algorithm to those used by an online optimal algorithm delivering the minimal number of bins by which the input set of objects encountered so far can be packed. This competitive ratio for the knapsack (or bin-packing) problem is in fact arbitrarily bad (that is, large; see [Sharp2007]), meaning that it is always possible to encounter a "bad" sequence in which the performance of the online algorithm will be arbitrarily far from that of the optimal algorithm.

The larger issue presented in this section is that there is no guarantee that a streaming algorithm will perform better than a batch algorithm, because those algorithms must function without foresight. In particular, some online algorithms, including the knapsack problem, have been proven to have an arbitrarily large performance ratio when compared to their offline algorithms.

What this means, to use an analogy, is that we have one worker that receives the data as batch, as if it were all in a *storage room* from the beginning, and the other worker receiving the data in a streaming fashion, as if it were on a *conveyor belt*, then *no matter how clever our streaming worker is, there is always a way to place items on the conveyor belt in such a pathological way that he will finish his task with an arbitrarily worse result than the batch worker.*

The takeaway message from this discussion is twofold:

- Streaming systems are indeed "lighter": their semantics can express a lot of low-latency analytics in expressive terms.
- Streaming APIs invite us to implement analytics using streaming or online algorithms in which heuristics are sadly limited, as we've seen earlier.

Summary

In conclusion, the news of batch processing's demise is overrated: batch processing is still relevant, at least to provide a baseline of performance for a streaming problem. Any responsible engineer should have a good idea of the performance of a batch algorithm operating "in hindsight" on the same input as their streaming application:

- If there is a known competitive ratio for the streaming algorithm at hand, and the resulting performance is acceptable, running just the stream processing might be enough.
- If there is no known competitive ratio between the implemented stream processing and a batch version, running a batch computation on a regular basis is a valuable benchmark to which to hold one's application.

## CHAPTER 4

Apache Spark as a Stream-Processing Engine

In Chapter 3, we pictured a general architectural diagram of a streaming data platform and identified where Spark, as a distributed processing engine, fits in a big data system.

This architecture informed us about what to expect in terms of interfaces and links to the rest of the ecosystem, especially as we focus on stream data processing with Apache Spark. Stream processing, whether in its Spark Streaming or Structured Streaming incarnation, is another *execution mode* for Apache Spark.

In this chapter, we take a tour of the main features that make Spark stand out as a stream-processing engine.

The Tale of Two APIs

As we mentioned in "Introducing Apache Spark" on page 11, Spark offers two different stream-processing APIs, Spark Streaming and Structured Streaming:

Spark Streaming
> This is an API and a set of connectors, in which a Spark program is being served small batches of data collected from a stream in the form of microbatches spaced at fixed time intervals, performs a given computation, and eventually returns a result at every interval.

Structured Streaming
> This is an API and a set of connectors, built on the substrate of a SQL query optimizer, Catalyst. It offers an API based on `DataFrames` and the notion of continu-

ous queries over an unbounded table that is constantly updated with fresh records from the stream.

The interface that Spark offers on these fronts is particularly rich, to the point where this book devotes large parts explaining those two ways of processing streaming datasets. One important point to realize is that both APIs rely on the core capabilities of Spark and share many of the low-level features in terms of distributed computation, in-memory caching, and cluster interactions.

As a leap forward from its MapReduce predecessor, Spark offers a rich set of operators that allows the programmer to express complex processing, including machine learning or event-time manipulations. We examine more specifically the basic properties that allow Spark to perform this feat in a moment.

We would just like to outline that these interfaces are by design as simple as their batch counterparts—operating on a `DStream` feels like operating on an `RDD`, and operating on a streaming `Dataframe` looks eerily like operating on a batch one.

Apache Spark presents itself as a unified engine, offering developers a consistent environment whenever they want to develop a batch or a streaming application. In both cases, developers have all the power and speed of a distributed framework at hand.

This versatility empowers development agility. Before deploying a full-fledged stream-processing application, programmers and analysts first try to discover insights in interactive environments with a fast feedback loop. Spark offers a built-in shell, based on the Scala *REPL* (short for Read-Eval-Print-Loop) that can be used as prototyping grounds. There are several notebook implementations available, like Zeppelin, Jupyter, or the Spark Notebook, that take this interactive experience to a user-friendly web interface. This prototyping phase is essential in the early phases of development, and so is its velocity.

If you refer back to the diagram in Figure 3-1, you will notice that what we called *results* in the chart are actionable insights—which often means revenue or cost-savings—are generated every time a loop (starting and ending at the business or scientific problem) is traveled fully. In sum, this loop is a crude representation of the experimental method, going through observation, hypothesis, experiment, measure, interpretation, and conclusion.

Apache Spark, in its streaming modules, has always made the choice to carefully manage the cognitive load of switching to a streaming application. It also has other major design choices that have a bearing on its stream-processing capabilities, starting with its in-memory storage.

Spark's Memory Usage

Spark offers in-memory storage of slices of a dataset, which must be initially loaded from a data source. The data source can be a distributed filesystem or another storage medium. Spark's form of in-memory storage is analogous to the operation of caching data.

Hence, a *value* in Spark's in-memory storage has a *base*, which is its initial data source, and layers of successive operations applied to it.

Failure Recovery

What happens in case of a failure? Because Spark knows exactly which data source was used to ingest the data in the first place, and because it also knows all the operations that were performed on it thus far, it can reconstitute the segment of lost data that was on a crashed executor, from scratch. Obviously, this goes faster if that reconstitution (*recovery*, in Spark's parlance), does not need to be totally *from scratch*. So, Spark offers a replication mechanism, quite in a similar way to distributed filesystems.

However, because memory is such a valuable yet limited commodity, Spark makes (by default) the cache short lived.

Lazy Evaluation

As you will see in greater detail in later chapters, a good part of the operations that can be defined on values in Spark's storage have a lazy execution, and it is the execution of a final, eager output operation that will trigger the actual execution of computation in a Spark cluster. It's worth noting that if a program consists of a series of linear operations, with the previous one feeding into the next, the intermediate results *disappear* right after said next step has consumed its input.

Cache Hints

On the other hand, what happens if we have several operations to do on a single intermediate result? Should we have to compute it several times? Thankfully, Spark lets users specify that an intermediate value is important and how its contents should be safeguarded for later.

Figure 4-1 presents the data flow of such an operation.

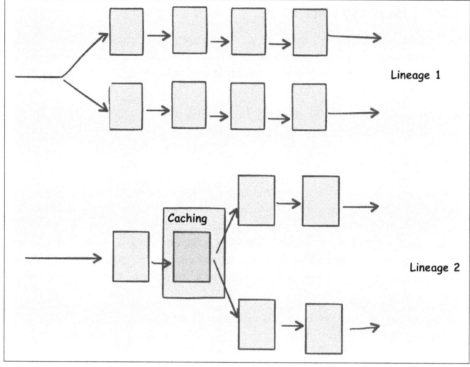

Figure 4-1. Operations on cached values

Finally, Spark offers the opportunity to spill the cache to secondary storage in case it runs out of memory on the cluster, extending the in-memory operation to secondary —and significantly slower—storage to preserve the functional aspects of a data process when faced with temporary peak loads.

Now that we have an idea of the main characteristics of Apache Spark, let's spend some time focusing on one design choice internal to Spark, namely, the latency versus throughput trade-off.

Understanding Latency

Spark Streaming, as we mentioned, makes the choice of microbatching. It generates a chunk of elements on a fixed interval, and when that interval "tick" elapses, it begins processing the data collected over the last interval. Structured Streaming takes a slightly different approach in that it will make the interval in question as small as possible (the processing time of the last microbatch)—and proposing, in some cases, a continuous processing mode, as well. Yet, nowadays, microbatching is still the dominating internal execution mode of stream processing in Apache Spark.

A consequence of microbatching is that any microbatch delays the processing of any particular element of a batch by at least the time of the batch interval.

Firstly, microbatches create a baseline latency. The jury is still out on how small it is possible to make this latency, though approximately one second is a relatively common number for the lower bound. For many applications, a latency in the space of a few minutes is sufficient; for example:

- Having a dashboard that refreshes you on key performance indicators of your website over the last few minutes
- Extracting the most recent trending topics in a social network
- Computing the energy consumption trends of a group of households
- Introducing new media in a recommendation system

Whereas Spark is an equal-opportunity processor and delays all data elements for (at most) one batch before acting on them, some other streaming engines exist that can fast-track some elements that have priority, ensuring a faster responsivity for them. If your response time is essential for these specific elements, alternative stream processors like Apache Flink or Apache Storm might be a better fit. But if you're just interested in fast processing *on average*, such as when monitoring a system, Spark makes an interesting proposition.

Throughput-Oriented Processing

All in all, where Spark truly excels at stream processing is with throughput-oriented data analytics.

We can compare the microbatch approach to a train: it arrives at the station, waits for passengers for a given period of time and then transports all passengers that boarded to their destination. Although taking a car or a taxi for the same trajectory might allow one passenger to travel faster door to door, the batch of passengers in the train ensures that far more travelers arrive at their destination. The train offers higher throughput for the same trajectory, at the expense that some passengers must wait until the train departs.

The Spark core engine is optimized for distributed batch processing. Its application in a streaming context ensures that large amounts of data can be processed per unit of time. Spark amortizes the overhead of distributed task scheduling by having many elements to process at once and, as we saw earlier in this chapter, it utilizes in-memory techniques, query optimizations, caching, and even code generation to speed up the transformational process of a dataset.

When using Spark in an end-to-end application, an important constraint is that downstream systems receiving the processed data must also be able to accept the full output provided by the streaming process. Otherwise, we risk creating application bottlenecks that might cause cascading failures when faced with sudden load peaks.

Spark's Polyglot API

We have now outlined the main design foundations of Apache Spark as they affect stream processing, namely a rich API and an in-memory processing model, defined within the model of an execution engine. We have explored the specific streaming modes of Apache Spark, and still at a high level, we have determined that the predominance of microbatching makes us think of Spark as more adapted to throughput-oriented tasks, for which more data yields more quality. We now want to bring our attention to one additional aspect where Spark shines: its programming ecosystem.

Spark was first coded as a Scala-only project. As its interest and adoption widened, so did the need to support different user profiles, with different backgrounds and programming language skills. In the world of scientific data analysis, Python and R are arguably the predominant languages of choice, whereas in the enterprise environment, Java has a dominant position.

Spark, far from being just a library for distributing computation, has become a polyglot framework that the user can interface with using Scala, Java, Python, or the R language. The development language is still Scala, and this is where the main innovations come in.

The coverage of the Java API has for a long time been fairly synchronized with Scala, owing to the excellent Java compatibility offered by the Scala language. And although in Spark 1.3 and earlier versions Python was lagging behind in terms of functionalities, it is now mostly caught up. The newest addition is R, for which feature-completeness is an enthusiastic work in progress.

This versatile interface has let programmers of various levels and backgrounds flock to Spark for implementing their own data analytics needs. The amazing and growing richness of the contributions to the Spark open source project are a testimony to the strength of Spark as a federating framework.

Nevertheless, Spark's approach to best catering to its users' computing goes beyond letting them use their favorite programming language.

Fast Implementation of Data Analysis

Spark's advantages in developing a streaming data analytics pipeline go beyond offering a concise, high-level API in Scala and compatible APIs in Java and Python. It also offers the simple model of Spark as a practical shortcut throughout the development process.

Component reuse with Spark is a valuable asset, as is access to the Java ecosystem of libraries for machine learning and many other fields. As an example, Spark lets users benefit from, for instance, the Stanford CoreNLP (*http://bit.ly/2UMALSk*) library with ease, letting you avoid the painful task of writing a tokenizer. All in all, this lets you quickly prototype your streaming data pipeline solution, getting first results quickly enough to choose the right components at every step of the pipeline development.

Finally, stream processing with Spark lets you benefit from its model of fault tolerance, leaving you with the confidence that faulty machines are not going to bring the streaming application to its knees. If you have enjoyed the automatic restart of failed Spark jobs, you will doubly appreciate that resiliency when running a 24/7 streaming operation.

In conclusion, Spark is a framework that, while making trade-offs in latency, optimizes for building a data analytics pipeline with agility: fast prototyping in a rich environment and stable runtime performance under adverse conditions are problems it recognizes and tackles head-on, offering users significant advantages.

To Learn More About Spark

This book is focused on streaming. As such, we move quickly through the Spark-centric concepts, in particular about batch processing. The most detailed references are [Karau2015] and [Chambers2018].

On a more low-level approach, the official documentation in the Spark Programming guide (*http://bit.ly/1Bns1XZ*) is another accessible must-read.

Summary

In this chapter, you learned about Spark and where it came from.

- You saw how Spark extends that model with key performance improvements, notably in-memory computing, as well as how it expands on the API with new higher-order functions.

- We also considered how Spark integrates into the modern ecosystem of big data solutions, including the smaller footprint it focuses on, when compared to its older brother, Hadoop.

- We focused on the streaming APIs and, in particular, on the meaning of their microbatching approach, what uses they are appropriate for, as well as the applications they would not serve well.

- Finally, we considered stream processing in the context of Spark, and how building a pipeline with agility, along with a reliable, fault-tolerant deployment is its best use case.

## CHAPTER 5

Spark's Distributed Processing Model

As a distributed processing system, Spark relies on the availability and addressability of computing resources to execute any arbitrary workload.

Although it's possible to deploy Spark as a standalone distributed system to solve a punctual problem, organizations evolving in their data maturity level are often required to deploy a complete data architecture, as we discussed in Chapter 3.

In this chapter, we want to discuss the interaction of Spark with its computational environment and how, in turn, it needs to adapt to the features and constraints of the environment of choice.

First, we survey the current choices for a cluster manager: YARN, Mesos, and Kubernetes. The scope of a cluster manager goes beyond running data analytics, and therefore, there are plenty of resources available to get in-depth knowledge on any of them. For our purposes, we are going to provide additional details on the cluster manager provider by Spark as a reference.

After you have an understanding of the role of the cluster manager and the way Spark interacts with it, we look into the aspects of fault tolerance in a distributed environment and how the execution model of Spark functions in that context.

With this background, you will be prepared to understand the data reliability guarantees that Spark offers and how they apply to the streaming execution model.

Running Apache Spark with a Cluster Manager

We are first going to look at the discipline of distributing stream processing on a set of machines that collectively form a *cluster*. This set of machines has a general purpose and needs to receive the streaming application's runtime binaries and launching scripts—something known as *provisioning*. Indeed, modern clusters are managed automatically and include a large number of machines in a situation of *multitenancy*, which means that many stakeholders want to access and use the same cluster at various times in the day of a business. The clusters are therefore managed by *cluster managers*.

Cluster managers are pieces of software that receive utilization requests from a number of users, match them to some resources, reserve the resources on behalf of the users for a given duration, and place user applications onto a number of resources for them to use. The challenges of the cluster manager's role include nontrivial tasks such as figuring out the best placements of user requests among a pool of available machines or securely isolating the user applications if several share the same physical infrastructure. Some considerations where these managers can shine or break include fragmentation of tasks, optimal placement, availability, preemption, and prioritization. Cluster management is, therefore, a discipline in and of itself, beyond the scope of Apache Spark. Instead, Apache Spark takes advantage of existing cluster managers to distribute its workload over a cluster.

Examples of Cluster Managers

Some examples of popular cluster managers include the following:

- Apache YARN, which is a relatively mature cluster manager born out of the Apache Hadoop project
- Apache Mesos, which is a cluster manager based on Linux's container technology, and which was originally the reason for the existence of Apache Spark
- Kubernetes, which is a modern cluster manager born out of service-oriented deployment APIs, originated in practice at Google and developed in its modern form under the flag of the Cloud Native Computing Foundation

Where Spark can sometimes confuse people is that Apache Spark, as a distribution, includes a cluster manager of its own, meaning Apache Spark has the ability to serve as its own particular deployment orchestrator.

In the rest of this chapter we look at the following:

- Spark's own cluster managers and how their *special purpose* means that they take on less responsibility in the domain of fault tolerance or multitenancy than production cluster managers like Mesos, YARN, or Kubernetes.
- How there is a standard level of *delivery guarantees* expected out of a distributed streaming application, how they differ from one another, and how Spark meets those guarantees.

- How microbatching, a distinctive factor of Spark's approach to stream processing, comes from the decade-old model of *bulk-synchronous processing* (BSP), and paves the evolution path from Spark Streaming to Structured Streaming.

Spark's Own Cluster Manager

Spark has two internal cluster managers:

The local cluster manager
> This emulates the function of a cluster manager (or resource manager) for testing purposes. It reproduces the presence of a cluster of distributed machines using a threading model that relies on your local machine having only a few available cores. This mode is usually not very confusing because it executes only on the user's laptop.

The standalone cluster manager
> A relatively simple, Spark-only cluster manager that is rather limited in its availability to slice and dice resource allocation. The standalone cluster manager holds and makes available the entire worker node on which a Spark executor is deployed and started. It also expects the executor to have been predeployed there, and the actual shipping of that *.jar* to a new machine is not within its scope. It has the ability to take over a specific number of executors, which are part of its deployment of worker nodes, and execute a task on it. This cluster manager is extremely useful for the Spark developers to provide a bare-bones resource management solution that allows you to focus on improving Spark in an environment without any bells and whistles. The standalone cluster manager is not recommended for production deployments.

As a summary, Apache Spark is a *task scheduler* in that what it schedules are *tasks*, units of distribution of computation that have been extracted from the user program. Spark also communicates and is deployed through cluster managers including Apache Mesos, YARN, and Kubernetes, or allowing for some cases its own standalone cluster manager. The purpose of that communication is to reserve a number of *executors*, which are the units to which Spark understands equal-sized amounts of computation resources, a virtual "node" of sorts. The reserved resources in question could be provided by the cluster manager as the following:

- Limited processes (e.g., in some basic use cases of YARN), in which processes have their resource consumption metered but are not prevented from accessing each other's resource by default.

- *Containers* (e.g., in the case of Mesos or Kubernetes), in which containers are a relatively lightweight resource reservation technology that is born out of the cgroups and namespaces of the Linux kernel and have known their most popular iteration with the Docker project.

- They also could be one of the above deployed on *virtual machines* (VMs), themselves coming with specific cores and memory reservation.

Cluster Operations

Detailing the different levels of isolations entailed by these three techniques is beyond the scope of this book but well worth exploring for production setups.

Note that in an enterprise-level production cluster management domain, we also encounter notions such as job queues, priorities, multitenancy options, and preemptions that are properly the domain of that cluster manager and therefore not something that is very frequently talked about in material that is focused on Spark.

However, it will be essential for you to have a firm grasp of the specifics of your cluster manager setup to understand how to be a "good citizen" on a cluster of machines, which are often shared by several teams. There are many good practices on how to run a proper cluster manager while many teams compete for its resources. And for those recommendations, you should consult both the references listed at the end of this chapter and your local DevOps team.

Understanding Resilience and Fault Tolerance in a Distributed System

Resilience and fault tolerance are absolutely essential for a distributed application: they are the condition by which we will be able to perform the user's computation to completion. Nowadays, clusters are made of commodity machines that are ideally operated near peak capacity over their lifetime.

To put it mildly, hardware breaks quite often. A *resilient* application can make progress with its process despite latencies and noncritical faults in its distributed environment. A *fault-tolerant* application is able to succeed and complete its process despite the unplanned termination of one or several of its nodes.

This sort of resiliency is especially relevant in stream processing given that the applications we're scheduling are supposed to live for an undetermined amount of time. That undetermined amount of time is often correlated with the life cycle of the data source. For example, if we are running a retail website and we are analyzing transactions and website interactions as they come into the system against the actions and clicks and navigation of users visiting the site, we potentially have a data source that will be available for the entire duration of the lifetime of our business, which we hope to be very long, if our business is going to be successful.

As a consequence, a system that will process our data in a streaming fashion should run uninterrupted for long periods of time.

This "show must go on" approach of streaming computation makes the resiliency and fault-tolerance characteristics of our applications more important. For a batch job, we could launch it, hope it would succeed, and relaunch if we needed to change it or in case of failure. For an online streaming Spark pipeline, this is not a reasonable assumption.

Fault Recovery

In the context of fault tolerance, we are also interested in understanding how long it takes to recover from failure of one particular node. Indeed, stream processing has a particular aspect: data continues being generated by the data source in real time. To deal with a batch computing failure, we always have the opportunity to restart from scratch and accept that obtaining the results of computation will take longer. Thus, a very primitive form of fault tolerance is detecting the failure of a particular node of our deployment, stopping the computation, and restarting from scratch. That process can take more than twice the original duration that we had budgeted for that computation, but if we are not in a hurry, this still acceptable.

For stream processing, *we need to keep receiving data* and thus potentially storing it, if the recovering cluster is not ready to assume any processing yet. This can pose a problem at a high throughput: if we try restarting from scratch, we will need not only to reprocess all of the data that we have observed since the beginning of the application—which in and of itself can be a challenge—but during that reprocessing of historical data, we will need it to continue receiving and thus potentially storing new data that was generated while we were trying to catch up. This pattern of restarting from scratch is something so intractable for streaming that we will pay special attention to Spark's ability to restart only *minimal* amounts of computation in the case that a node becomes unavailable or nonfunctional.

Cluster Manager Support for Fault Tolerance

We want to highlight why it is still important to understand Spark's fault tolerance guarantees, even if there are similar features present in the cluster managers of YARN, Mesos, or Kubernetes. To understand this, we can consider that cluster managers help with fault tolerance when they work hand in hand with a framework that is able to report failures and request new resources to cope with those exceptions. Spark possesses such capabilities.

For example, *production* cluster managers such as YARN, Mesos, or Kubernetes have the ability to detect a node's failure by inspecting endpoints on the node and asking the node to report on its own readiness and liveness state. If these cluster managers detect a failure and they have spare capacity, they will replace that node with another, made available to Spark. That particular action implies that the Spark executor code will start anew in another node, and then attempt to join the existing Spark cluster.

The cluster manager, by definition, does not have introspection capabilities into the applications being run on the nodes that it reserves. Its responsibility is limited to the container that runs the user's code.

That responsibility boundary is where the Spark resilience features start. To recover from a failed node, Spark needs to do the following:

- Determine whether that node contains some state that should be reproduced in the form of checkpointed files
- Understand at which stage of the job a node should rejoin the computation

The goal here is for us to explore that if a node is being replaced by the cluster manager, Spark has capabilities that allow it to take advantage of this new node and to distribute computation onto it.

Within this context, our focus is on Spark's responsibilities as an application and underline the capabilities of a cluster manager only when necessary: for instance, a node could be replaced because of a hardware failure or because its work was simply preempted by a higher-priority job. Apache Spark is blissfully unaware of the *why*, and focuses on the *how*.

Data Delivery Semantics

As you have seen in the streaming model, the fact that streaming jobs act on the basis of data that is generated in real time means that intermediate results need to be provided to the *consumer* of that streaming pipeline on a regular basis.

Those results are being produced by some part of our cluster. Ideally, we would like those observable results to be coherent, in line, and in real time with respect to the arrival of data. This means that we want results that are exact, and we want them as soon as possible. However, distributed computation has its own challenges in that it sometimes includes not only individual nodes failing, as we have mentioned, but it also encounters situations like *network partitions*, in which some parts of our cluster are not able to communicate with other parts of that cluster, as illustrated in Figure 5-1.

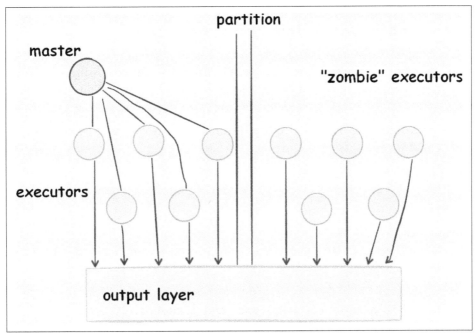

Figure 5-1. A network partition

Spark has been designed using a *driver/executor* architecture. A specific machine, the *driver*, is tasked with keeping track of the *job progression* along with the job submissions of a user, and the computation of that program occurs as the data arrives. However, if the network partitions separate some part of the cluster, the *driver* might be able to keep track of only the part of the executors that form the initial cluster. In the other section of our partition, we will find nodes that are entirely able to function, but will simply be unable to account for the proceedings of their computation to the *driver*.

This creates an interesting case in which those "zombie" nodes do not receive new tasks, but might well be in the process of completing some fragment of computation that they were previously given. Being unaware of the partition, they will report their results as any executor would. And because this reporting of results sometimes does not go through the *driver* (for fear of making the *driver* a bottleneck), the reporting of these zombie results could succeed.

Because the *driver*, a single point of bookkeeping, does not know that those zombie executors are still functioning and reporting results, it will reschedule the same tasks that the lost executors had to accomplish on new nodes. This creates a *double-answering* problem in which the zombie machines lost through partitioning and the machines bearing the rescheduled tasks both report the same results. This bears real consequences: one example of stream computation that we previously mentioned is routing tasks for financial transactions. A double withdrawal, in that context, or double stock purchase orders, could have tremendous consequences.

It is not only the aforementioned problem that causes different processing semantics. Another important reason is that when output from a stream-processing application and state checkpointing cannot be completed in one atomic operation, it will cause data corruption if failure happens between checkpointing and outputting.

These challenges have therefore led to a distinction between *at least once* processing and *at most once* processing:

At least once
> This processing ensures that every element of a stream has been processed once or more.

At most once
> This processing ensures that every element of the stream is processed once or less.

Exactly once
> This is the combination of "at least once" and "at most once."

At-least-once processing is the notion that we want to make sure that every chunk of initial data has been dealt with—it deals with the node failure we were talking about earlier. As we've mentioned, when a streaming process suffers a partial failure in which some nodes need to be replaced or some data needs to be recomputed, we need to reprocess the lost units of computation while keeping the ingestion of data going. That requirement means that if you do not respect at-least-once processing, there is a chance for you, under certain conditions, to lose data.

The antisymmetric notion is called at-most-once processing. At-most-once processing systems guarantee that the zombie nodes repeating the same results as a rescheduled node are treated in a coherent manner, in which we keep track of only one set of results. By keeping track of *what data* their results *were about*, we're able to make sure we can discard repeated results, yielding at-most-once processing guarantees. The way in which we achieve this relies on the notion of *idempotence* applied to the "last mile" of result reception. Idempotence qualifies a function such that if we apply it twice (or more) to any data, we will get the same result as the first time. This can be achieved by keeping track of the data that we are reporting a result for, and having a bookkeeping system at the output of our streaming process.

Microbatching and One-Element-at-a-Time

In this section, we want to address two important approaches to stream processing: *bulk-synchronous processing*, and *one-at-a-time record processing*.

The objective of this is to connect those two ideas to the two APIs that Spark possesses for stream processing: Spark Streaming and Structured Streaming.

Microbatching: An Application of Bulk-Synchronous Processing

Spark Streaming, the more mature model of stream processing in Spark, is roughly approximated by what's called a *Bulk Synchronous Parallelism* (BSP) system.

The gist of BSP is that it includes two things:

- A split distribution of asynchronous work
- A synchronous barrier, coming in at fixed intervals

The split is the idea that each of the successive steps of work to be done in streaming is separated in a number of parallel chunks that are roughly proportional to the number of executors available to perform this task. Each executor receives its own chunk (or chunks) of work and works separately until the second element comes in. A particular resource is tasked with keeping track of the progress of computation. With Spark Streaming, this is a synchronization point at the "driver" that allows the work to progress to the next step. Between those scheduled steps, all of the executors on the cluster are doing the same thing.

Note that what is being passed around in this scheduling process are the functions that describe the processing that the user wants to execute on the data. The data is already on the various executors, most often being delivered directly to these resources over the lifetime of the cluster.

This was coined "function-passing style" by Heather Miller in 2016 (and formalized in [Miller2016]): asynchronously pass safe functions to distributed, stationary, immutable data in a stateless container, and use lazy combinators to eliminate intermediate data structures.

The frequency at which further rounds of data processing are scheduled is dictated by a time interval. This time interval is an arbitrary duration that is measured in batch processing time; that is, what you would expect to see as a "wall clock" time observation in your cluster.

For stream processing, we choose to implement barriers at small, fixed intervals that better approximate the real-time notion of data processing.

Bulk-Synchronous Parallelism

BSP is a very generic model for thinking about parallel processing, introduced by Leslie Valiant in the 1990s. Intended as an abstract (mental) model above all else, it was meant to provide a pendant to the Von Neumann model of computation for parallel processing.

It introduces three key concepts:

- A number of components, each performing processing and/or memory functions
- A router that delivers messages point to point between components
- Facilities for synchronizing all or a subset of the component at a regular time interval L, where L is the periodicity parameter

The purpose of the bulk-synchronous model is to give clear definitions that allow thinking of the moments when a computation can be performed by agents each acting separately, while pooling their knowledge together on a regular basis to obtain one single, aggregate result. Valiant introduces the notion:

> A computation consists of a sequence of supersteps. In each superstep, each component is allocated a task consisting of some combination of local computation steps, message transmissions and (implicitly) message arrivals from other components. After each period of L time units, a global check is made to determine whether the superstep has been completed by all the components. If it has, the machine proceeds to the next superstep. Otherwise, the next period of L units is allocated to the unfinished superstep.

This model also proceeds to give guarantees about the scalability and cost of this mode of computation. (To learn more about this, consult [Valiant1990].) It was influential in the design of modern graph processing systems such as Google's Pregel. Here, we use it as a way to speak of the timing of synchronization of parallel computation in Spark's `DStreams`.

One-Record-at-a-Time Processing

By contrast, one-record-at-a-time processing functions by *pipelining*: it analyzes the whole computation as described by user-specified functions and deploys it as pipelines using the resources of the cluster. Then, the only remaining matter is to flow data through the various resources, following the prescribed pipeline. Note that in this latter case, each step of the computation is materialized at some place in the cluster at any given point.

Systems that function mostly according to this paradigm include Apache Flink, Naiad, Storm, and IBM Streams. (You can read more on these in Chapter 29.) This does not necessarily mean that those systems are incapable of microbatching, but rather characterizes their major or most native mode of operation and makes a statement on their dependency on the process of pipelining, often at the heart of their processing.

The minimum latency, or time needed for the system to react to the arrival of one particular event, is very different between those two: minimum latency of the microbatching system is therefore the time needed to complete the reception of the current microbatch (the batch interval) plus the time needed to start a task at the executor where this data falls (also called scheduling time). On the other hand, a system processing records one by one can react as soon as it meets the event of interest.

Microbatching Versus One-at-a-Time: The Trade-Offs

Despite their higher latency, microbatching systems offer significant advantages:

- They are able to *adapt* at the synchronization barrier boundaries. That adaptation might represent the task of recovering from failure, if a number of executors have been shown to become deficient or lose data. The periodic synchronization can also give us an opportunity to add or remove executor nodes, giving us the possibility to grow or shrink our resources depending on what we're seeing as the cluster load, observed through the throughput on the data source.

- Our BSP systems can sometimes have an easier time providing *strong consistency* because their batch determinations—that indicate the beginning and the end of a particular batch of data—are deterministic and recorded. Thus, any kind of computation can be redone and produce the same results the second time.

- Having data available *as a set* that we can probe or inspect at the beginning of the microbatch allows us to perform efficient optimizations that can provide ideas on the way to compute on the data. Exploiting that on *each* microbatch, we can consider the specific case rather than the general processing, which is used for all possible input. For example, we could take a sample or compute a statistical measure before deciding to process or drop each microbatch.

More importantly, the simple presence of the microbatch as a well-identified element also allows an efficient way of specifying programming for both batch processing (where the data is at rest and has been saved somewhere) and streaming (where the data is in flight). The microbatch, even for mere instants, *looks* like data at rest.

Bringing Microbatch and One-Record-at-a-Time Closer Together

The marriage between microbatching and one-record-at-a-time processing as is implemented in systems like Apache Flink or Naiad is still a subject of research.[1].]

Although it does not solve every issue, Structured Streaming, which is backed by a main implementation that relies on microbatching, does not expose that choice at the API level, allowing for an evolution that is independent of a fixed-batch interval. In fact, the default internal execution model of Structured Streaming is that of microbatching with a dynamic batch interval. Structured Streaming is also implementing continuous processing for some operators, which is something we touch upon in Chapter 15.

Dynamic Batch Interval

What is this notion of *dynamic batch interval*? The dynamic batch interval is the notion that the recomputation of data in a streaming `DataFrame` or `Dataset` consists of an update of existing data with the new elements seen over the wire. This update is occurring based on a trigger and the usual basis of this would be time duration. That time duration is still determined based on a fixed world clock signal that we expect to be synchronized within our entire cluster and that represents a single synchronous source of time that is shared among every executor.

However, this trigger can also be the statement of "as often as possible." That statement is simply the idea that a new batch should be started as soon as the previous one has been processed, given a reasonable initial duration for the first batch. This means that the system will launch batches as often as possible. In this situation, the latency that can be observed is closer to that of one-element-at-a-time processing. The idea here is that the microbatches produced by this system will converge to the smallest manageable size, making our stream flow faster through the executor computations that are necessary to produce a result. As soon as that result is produced, a new query will be started and scheduled by the Spark driver.

---

1 One interesting Spark-related project that recently came out of the University of Berkeley is called Drizzle and uses "group scheduling" to form a sort of longer-lived pipeline that persists across several batches, for the purpose of creating near-continuous queries. See [Venkataraman2016

Structured Streaming Processing Model

The main steps in Structured Streaming processing are as follows:

1. When the Spark driver triggers a new batch, processing starts with updating the account of data read from a data source, in particular, getting data offsets for the beginning and the end of the latest batch.

2. This is followed by logical planning, the construction of successive steps to be executed on data, followed by query planning (intrastep optimization).

3. And then the launch and scheduling of the actual computation by adding a new batch of data to update the continuous query that we're trying to refresh.

Hence, from the point of view of the computation model, we will see that the API is significantly different from Spark Streaming.

The Disappearance of the Batch Interval

We now briefly explain what Structured Streaming batches mean and their impact with respect to operations.

In Structured Streaming, the batch interval that we are using is no longer a computation budget. With Spark Streaming, the idea was that if we produce data every two minutes and flow data into Spark's memory every two minutes, we should produce the results of computation on that batch of data in at least two minutes, to clear the memory from our cluster for the next microbatch. Ideally, as much data flows out as flows in, and the usage of the collective memory of our cluster remains stable.

With Structured Streaming, without this fixed time synchronization, our ability to see performance issues in our cluster is more complex: a cluster that is unstable—that is, unable to "clear out" data by finishing to compute on it as fast as new data flows in— will see ever-growing batch processing times, with an accelerating growth. We can expect that keeping a hand on this batch processing time will be pivotal.

However, if we have a cluster that is correctly sized with respect to the throughput of our data, there are a lot of advantages to have an as-often-as-possible update. In particular, we should expect to see very frequent results from our Structured Streaming cluster with a higher granularity than we used to in the time of a conservative batch interval.

## CHAPTER 6

Spark's Resilience Model

In most cases, a streaming job is a long-running job. By definition, streams of data observed and processed over time lead to jobs that run continuously. As they process data, they might accumulate intermediary results that are difficult to reproduce after the data has left the processing system. Therefore, the cost of failure is considerable and, in some cases, complete recovery is intractable.

In distributed systems, especially those relying on commodity hardware, failure is a function of size: the larger the system, the higher the probability that some component fails at any time. Distributed stream processors need to factor this chance of failure in their operational model.

In this chapter, we look at the resilience that the Apache Spark platform provides us: how it's able to recover partial failure and what kinds of guarantees we are given for the data passing through the system when a failure occurs. We begin by getting an overview of the different internal components of Spark and their relation to the core data structure. With this knowledge, you can proceed to understand the impact of failure at the different levels and the measures that Spark offers to recover from such failure.

Resilient Distributed Datasets in Spark

Spark builds its data representations on *Resilient Distributed Datasets* (RDDs). Introduced in 2011 by the paper "Resilient Distributed Datasets: A Fault-Tolerant Abstraction for In-Memory Cluster Computing" [Zaharia2011], RDDs are the foundational data structure in Spark. It is at this ground level that the strong fault tolerance guarantees of Spark start.

RDDs are composed of partitions, which are segments of data stored on individual nodes and tracked by the Spark driver that is presented as a location-transparent data structure to the user.

We illustrate these components in Figure 6-1 in which the classic *word count* application is broken down into the different elements that comprise an RDD.

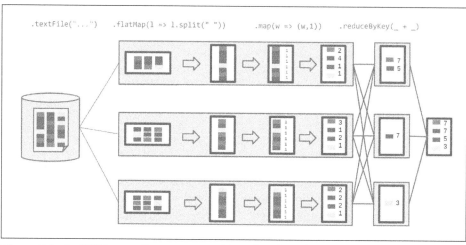

Figure 6-1. An RDD operation represented in a distributed system

The colored blocks are data elements, originally stored in a distributed filesystem, represented on the far left of the figure. The data is stored as partitions, illustrated as columns of colored blocks inside the file. Each partition is read into an executor, which we see as the horizontal blocks. The actual data processing happens within the executor. There, the data is transformed following the transformations described at the RDD level:

- `.flatMap(l => l.split(" "))` separates sentences into words separated by space.

- `.map(w => (w,1))` transforms each word into a tuple of the form (`<word>`, 1) in this way preparing the words for counting.

- `.reduceByKey(_ + _)` computes the count, using the `<word>` as a key and applying a sum operation to the attached number.

- The final result is attained by bringing the partial results together using the same `reduce` operation.

RDDs constitute the programmatic core of Spark. All other abstractions, batch and streaming alike, including `DataFrames`, `DataSets`, and `DStreams` are built using the facilities created by RDDs, and, more important, they inherit the same fault tolerance capabilities. We provide a brief introduction of the RDDs programming model in "RDDs as the Underlying Abstraction for DStreams" on page 213.

Another important characteristic of RDDs is that Spark will try to keep their data preferably in-memory for as long as it is required and provided enough capacity in the system. This behavior is configurable through storage levels and can be explicitly controlled by calling caching operations.

We mention those structures here to present the idea that Spark tracks the progress of the user's computation through modifications of the data. Indeed, knowing how far along we are in what the user wants to do through inspecting the control flow of his program (including loops and potential recursive calls) can be a daunting and error-prone task. It is much more reliable to define types of distributed data collections, and let the user create one from another, or from other data sources.

In Figure 6-2, we show the same *word count* program, now in the form of the user-provided code (left) and the resulting internal RDD chain of operations. This dependency chain forms a particular kind of graph, a Directed Acyclic Graph (DAG). The DAG informs the scheduler, appropriately called DAGScheduler, on how to distribute the computation and is also the foundation of the failure-recovery functionality, because it represents the internal data and their dependencies.

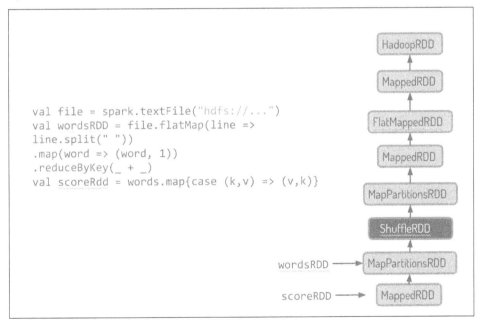

Figure 6-2. RDD lineage

As the system tracks the ordered creation of these distributed data collections, it tracks the work done, and what's left to accomplish.

Spark Components

To understand at what level fault tolerance operates in Spark, it's useful to go through an overview of the nomenclature of some core concepts. We begin by assuming that the user provides a program that ends up being divided into chunks and executed on various machines, as we saw in the previous section, and as depicted in Figure 6-3.

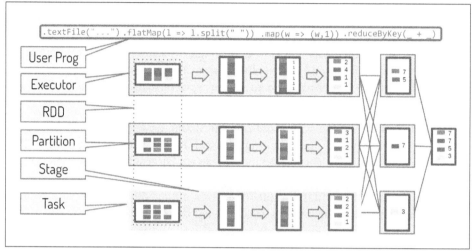

Figure 6-3. Spark nomenclature

Let's run down those steps, illustrated in Figure 6-3, which define the vocabulary of the Spark runtime:

User Program
> The user application in Spark Streaming is composed of user-specified *function calls* operating on a resilient data structure (RDD, DStream, streaming DataSet, and so on), categorized as *actions* and *transformations*.

Transformed User Program
> The user program may undergo adjustments that modify some of the specified calls to make them simpler, the most approachable and understandable of which is map-fusion.[1] Query plan is a similar but more advanced concept in Spark SQL.

RDD
> A logical representation of a distributed, resilient, dataset. In the illustration, we see that the initial RDD comprises three parts, called partitions.

---

1 The process by which l.map(foo).map(bar) is changed into l.map((x) => bar(foo(x)))

Partition

A partition is a physical segment of a dataset that can be loaded independently.

Stages

The user's operations are then grouped into *stages*, whose boundary separates user operations into steps that must be executed separately. For example, operations that require a shuffle of data across multiple nodes, such as a join between the results of two distinct upstream operations, mark a distinct stage. Stages in Apache Spark are the unit of sequencing: they are executed one after the other. At most one of any interdependent stages can be running at any given time.

Jobs

After these *stages* are defined, what internal actions Spark should take is clear. Indeed, at this stage, a set of interdependent *jobs* is defined. And jobs, precisely, are the vocabulary for a unit of scheduling. They describe the work at hand from the point of view of an entire Spark cluster, whether it's waiting in a queue or currently being run across many machines. (Although it's not represented explicitly, in Figure 6-3, the job is the complete set of transformations.)

Tasks

Depending on where their source data is on the cluster, jobs can then be cut into *tasks*, crossing the conceptual boundary between distributed and single-machine computing: a task is a unit of local computation, the name for the local, executor-bound part of a job.

Spark aims to make sure that all of these steps are safe from harm and to recover quickly in the case of any incident occurring in any stage of this process. This concern is reflected in fault-tolerance facilities that are structured by the aforementioned notions: restart and checkpointing operations that occur at the task, job, stage, or program level.

Spark's Fault-Tolerance Guarantees

Now that we have seen the "pieces" that constitute the internal machinery in Spark, we are ready to understand that failure can happen at many different levels. In this section, we see Spark fault-tolerance guarantees organized by "increasing blast radius," from the more modest to the larger failure. We are going to investigate the following:

- How Spark mitigates Task failure through restarts
- How Spark mitigates Stage failure through the shuffle service
- How Spark mitigates the disappearance of the *orchestrator* of the user program, through driver restarts

When you've completed this section, you will have a clear mental picture of the guarantees Spark affords us at runtime, letting you understand the failure scenarios that a well-configured Spark job can deal with.

Task Failure Recovery

Tasks can fail when the infrastructure on which they are running has a failure or logical conditions in the program lead to an sporadic job, like OutOfMemory, network, storage errors, or problems bound to the quality of the data being processed (e.g., a parsing error, a NumberFormatException, or a NullPointerException to name a few common exceptions).

If the input data of the task was stored, through a call to cache() or persist() and if the chosen storage level implies a replication of data (look for a storage level whose setting ends in _2 , such as MEMORY_ONLY_SER_2), the task does not need to have its input recomputed, because a copy of it exists in complete form on another machine of the cluster. We can then use this input to restart the task. Table 6-1 summarizes the different storage levels configurable in Spark and their chacteristics in terms of memory usage and replication factor.

Table 6-1. Spark storage levels

Level	Uses disk	Uses memory	Uses off-heap storage	Object (deserialized)	# of replicated copies
NONE					1
DISK_ONLY	X				1
DISK_ONLY_2	X				2
MEMORY_ONLY		X		X	1
MEMORY_ONLY_2		X		X	2
MEMORY_ONLY_SER		X			1
MEMORY_ONLY_SER_2		X			2
MEMORY_AND_DISK	X	X		X	1
MEMORY_AND_DISK_2	X	X		X	2
MEMORY_AND_DISK_SER	X	X			1
MEMORY_AND_DISK_SER_2	X	X			2
OFF_HEAP			X		1

If, however, there was no persistence or if the storage level does not guarantee the existence of a copy of the task's input data, the Spark driver will need to consult the DAG that stores the user-specified computation to determine which segments of the job need to be recomputed.

Consequently, without enough precautions to save either on the caching or on the storage level, the failure of a task can trigger the recomputation of several others, up to a stage boundary.

Stage boundaries imply a shuffle, and a shuffle implies that intermediate data will somehow be materialized: as we discussed, the shuffle transforms executors into data servers that can provide the data to any other executor serving as a destination.

As a consequence, these executors have a copy of the map operations that led up to the shuffle. Hence, executors that participated in a shuffle have a copy of the map operations that led up to it. But that's a lifesaver if you have a dying downstream executor, able to rely on the upstream servers of the shuffle (which serve the output of the map-like operation). What if it's the contrary: you need to face the crash of one of the upstream executors?

Stage Failure Recovery

We've seen that task failure (possibly due to executor crash) was the most frequent incident happening on a cluster and hence the most important event to mitigate. Recurrent task failures will lead to the failure of the stage that contains that task. This brings us to the second facility that allows Spark to resist arbitrary stage failures: the *shuffle service*.

When this failure occurs, it always means some rollback of the data, but a shuffle operation, by definition, depends on all of the prior executors involved in the step that precedes it.

As a consequence, since Spark 1.3 we have the shuffle service, which lets you work on map data that is saved and distributed through the cluster with a good locality, but, more important, through a server that is not a Spark task. It's an external file exchange service written in Java that has no dependency on Spark and is made to be a much longer-running service than a Spark executor. This additional service attaches as a separate process in all cluster modes of Spark and simply offers a data file exchange for executors to transmit data reliably, right before a shuffle. It is highly optimized through the use of a netty backend, to allow a very low overhead in transmitting data. This way, an executor can shut down after the execution of its map task, as soon as the shuffle service has a copy of its data. And because data transfers are faster, this transfer time is also highly reduced, reducing the vulnerable time in which any executor could face an issue.

Driver Failure Recovery

Having seen how Spark recovers from the failure of a particular task and stage, we can now look at the facilities Spark offers to recover from the failure of the driver program. The driver in Spark has an essential role: it is the depository of the block manager, which knows where each block of data resides in the cluster. It is also the place where the DAG lives.

Finally, it is where the scheduling state of the job, its metadata, and logs resides. Hence, if the driver is lost, a Spark cluster as a whole might well have lost which stage it has reached in computation, what the computation actually consists of, and where the data that serves it can be found, in one fell swoop.

Cluster-mode deployment

Spark has implemented what's called the *cluster deployment mode*, which allows the driver program to be hosted on the cluster, as opposed to the user's computer.

The deployment mode is one of two options: in client mode, the driver is launched in the same process as the client that submits the application. In cluster mode, however, the driver is launched from one of the worker processes inside the cluster, and the client process exits as soon as it fulfills its responsibility of submitting the application without waiting for the application to finish.

This, in sum, allows Spark to operate an automatic driver restart, so that the user can start a job in a "fire and forget fashion," starting the job and then closing their laptop to catch the next train. Every cluster mode of Spark offers a web UI that will let the user access the log of their application. Another advantage is that driver failure does not mark the end of the job, because the driver process will be relaunched by the cluster manager. But this only allows recovery from scratch, given that the temporary state of the computation—previously stored in the driver machine—might have been lost.

Checkpointing

To avoid losing intermediate state in case of a driver crash, Spark offers the option of checkpointing; that is, recording periodically a snapshot of the application's state to disk. The setting of the `sparkContext.setCheckpointDirectory()` option should point to reliable storage (e.g., Hadoop Distributed File System [HDFS]) because having the driver try to reconstruct the state of intermediate RDDs from its local filesystem makes no sense: those intermediate RDDs are being created on the executors of the cluster and should as such not require any interaction with the driver for backing them up.

We come back to the subject of checkpointing in detail much later, in Chapter 24. In the meantime, there is still one component of any Spark cluster whose potential failure we have not yet addressed: the master node.

Summary

This tour of Spark-core's fault tolerance and high-availability modes should have given you an idea of the main primitives and facilities offered by Spark and of their defaults. Note that none of this is so far specific to Spark Streaming or Structured Streaming, but that all these lessons apply to the streaming APIs in that they are required to deliver long-running, fault-tolerant and yet performant applications.

Note also that these facilities reflect different concerns in the frequency of faults for a particular cluster. These facilities reflect different concerns for the frequency of faults in a particular cluster:

- Features such as setting up a failover master node kept up-to-date through Zookeeper are really about avoiding a single point of failure in the design of a Spark application.
- The Spark Shuffle Service is here to avoid any problems with a shuffle step at the end of a long list of computation steps making the whole fragile through a faulty executor.

The later is a much more frequent occurrence. The first is about dealing with every possible condition, the second is more about ensuring smooth performance and efficient recovery.

APPENDIX A

References for Part I

- [Armbrust2018] Armbrust, M., T. Das, J. Torres, B. Yavuz, S. Zhu, R. Xin, A. Ghodsi, I. Stoica, and M. Zaharia. "Structured Streaming: A Declarative API for Real-Time Applications in Apache Spark," May 27, 2018. *https://stanford.io/2Jia3iY*.

- [Bhartia2016] Bhartia, R. "Optimize Spark-Streaming to Efficiently Process Amazon Kinesis Streams," AWS Big Data blog, February 26, 2016. *https://amzn.to/2E7I69h*.

- [Chambers2018] Chambers, B., and Zaharia, M., *Spark: The Definitive Guide*. O'Reilly, 2018.

- [Chintapalli2015] Chintapalli, S., D. Dagit, B. Evans, R. Farivar, T. Graves, M. Holderbaugh, Z. Liu, K. Musbaum, K. Patil, B. Peng, and P. Poulosky. "Benchmarking Streaming Computation Engines at Yahoo!" Yahoo! Engineering, December 18, 2015. *http://bit.ly/2bhgMJd*.

- [Das2013] Das, Tathagata. "Deep Dive With Spark Streaming," Spark meetup, June 17, 2013. *http://bit.ly/2Q8Xzem*.

- [Das2014] Das, Tathagata, and Yuan Zhong. "Adaptive Stream Processing Using Dynamic Batch Sizing," 2014 ACM Symposium on Cloud Computing. *http://bit.ly/2WTOuby*.

- [Das2015] Das, Tathagata. "Improved Fault Tolerance and Zero Data Loss in Spark Streaming," Databricks Engineering blog. January 15, 2015. *http://bit.ly/2HqH614*.

- [Dean2004] Dean, Jeff, and Sanjay Ghemawat. "MapReduce: Simplified Data Processing on Large Clusters," OSDI San Francisco, December, 2004. *http://bit.ly/15LeQej*.

- [Doley1987] Doley, D., C. Dwork, and L. Stockmeyer. "On the Minimal Synchronism Needed for Distributed Consensus," *Journal of the ACM* 34(1) (1987): 77-97. *http://bit.ly/2LHRy9K*.

- [Dosa2007] Dósa, Gÿorgy. "The Tight Bound of First fit Decreasing Bin-Packing Algorithm Is FFD(I)≤(11/9)OPT(I)+6/9." In *Combinatorics, Algorithms, Probabilistic and Experimental Methodologies*. Springer-Verlag, 2007.

- [Dunner2016] Dünner, C., T. Parnell, K. Atasu, M. Sifalakis, and H. Pozidis. "High-Performance Distributed Machine Learning Using Apache Spark," December 2016. *http://bit.ly/2JoSgH4*.

- [Fischer1985] Fischer, M. J., N. A. Lynch, and M. S. Paterson. "Impossibility of distributed consensus with one faulty process," *Journal of the ACM* 32(2) (1985): 374–382. *http://bit.ly/2Ee9tPb*.

- [Gibbons2004] Gibbons, J. "An unbounded spigot algorithm for the digits of π," *American Mathematical Monthly* 113(4) (2006): 318-328. *http://bit.ly/2VwwvH2*.

- [Greenberg2015] Greenberg, David. *Building Applications on Mesos*. O'Reilly, 2015.

- [Halevy2009] Halevy, Alon, Peter Norvig, and Fernando Pereira. "The Unreasonable Effectiveness of Data," *IEEE Intelligent Systems* (March/April 2009). *http://bit.ly/2VCveD3*.

- [Karau2015] Karau, Holden, Andy Konwinski, Patrick Wendell, and Matei Zaharia. *Learning Spark*. O'Reilly, 2015.

- [Kestelyn2015] Kestelyn, J. "Exactly-once Spark Streaming from Apache Kafka," Cloudera Engineering blog, March 16, 2015. *http://bit.ly/2EniQfJ*.

- [Kleppmann2015] Kleppmann, Martin. "A Critique of the CAP Theorem," arXiv.org:1509.05393, September 2015. *http://bit.ly/30jxsG4*.

- [Koeninger2015] Koeninger, Cody, Davies Liu, and Tathagata Das. "Improvements to Kafka Integration of Spark Streaming," Databricks Engineering blog, March 30, 2015. *http://bit.ly/2Hn7dat*.

- [Kreps2014] Kreps, Jay. "Questioning the Lambda Architecture," O'Reilly Radar, July 2, 2014. *https://oreil.ly/2LSEdqz*.

- [Lamport1998] Lamport, Leslie. "The Part-Time Parliament," *ACM Transactions on Computer Systems* 16(2): 133–169. *http://bit.ly/2W3zr1R*.

- [Lin2010] Lin, Jimmy, and Chris Dyer. *Data-Intensive Text Processing with MapReduce*. Morgan & ClayPool, 2010. *http://bit.ly/2YD9wMr*.

- [Lyon2013] Lyon, Brad F. "Musings on the Motivations for Map Reduce," Nowhere Near Ithaca blog, June, 2013, *http://bit.ly/2Q3OHXe*.

- [Maas2014] Maas, Gérard. "Tuning Spark Streaming for Throughput," Virdata Engineering blog, December 22, 2014. *http://www.virdata.com/tuning-spark/*.

- [Marz2011] Marz, Nathan. "How to beat the CAP theorem," Thoughts from the Red Planet blog, October 13, 2011. *http://bit.ly/2KpKDQq*.

- [Marz2015] Marz, Nathan, and James Warren. *Big Data: Principles and Best Practices of Scalable Realtime Data Systems.* Manning, 2015.

- [Miller2016] Miller, H., P. Haller, N. Müller, and J. Boullier "Function Passing: A Model for Typed, Distributed Functional Programming," *ACM SIGPLAN Conference on Systems, Programming, Languages and Applications: Software for Humanity, Onward!* November 2016: (82-97). *http://bit.ly/2EQASaf*.

- [Nasir2016] Nasir, M.A.U. "Fault Tolerance for Stream Processing Engines," arXiv.org:1605.00928, May 2016. *http://bit.ly/2Mpz66f*.

- [Shapira2014] Shapira, Gwen. "Building The Lambda Architecture with Spark Streaming," Cloudera Engineering blog, August 29, 2014. *http://bit.ly/2XoyHBS*.

- [Sharp2007] Sharp, Alexa Megan. "Incremental algorithms: solving problems in a changing world," PhD diss., Cornell University, 2007. *http://bit.ly/2Ie8MGX*.

- [Valiant1990] Valiant, L.G. "Bulk-synchronous parallel computers," *Communications of the ACM* 33:8 (August 1990). *http://bit.ly/2IgX3ar*.

- [Vavilapalli2013] Vavilapalli, et al. "Apache Hadoop YARN: Yet Another Resource Negotiator," ACM Symposium on Cloud Computing, 2013. *http://bit.ly/2Xn3tuZ*.

- [Venkat2015] Venkat, B., P. Padmanabhan, A. Arokiasamy, and R. Uppalapati. "Can Spark Streaming survive Chaos Monkey?" The Netflix Tech Blog, March 11, 2015. *http://bit.ly/2WkDJmr*.

- [Venkataraman2016] Venkataraman, S., P. Aurojit, K. Ousterhout, A. Ghodsi, M. J. Franklin, B. Recht, and I. Stoica. "Drizzle: Fast and Adaptable Stream Processing at Scale," Tech Report, UC Berkeley, 2016. *http://bit.ly/2HW08Ot*.

- [White2010] White, Tom. *Hadoop: The Definitive Guide*, 4th ed. O'Reilly, 2015.

- [Zaharia2011] Zaharia, Matei, Mosharaf Chowdhury, et al. "Resilient Distributed Datasets: A Fault-Tolerant Abstraction for In-Memory Cluster Computing," UCB/EECS-2011-82. *http://bit.ly/2IfZE4q*.

- [Zaharia2012] Zaharia, Matei, Tathagata Das, et al. "Discretized Streams: A Fault-Tolerant Model for Scalable Stream Processing," UCB/EECS-2012-259. *http://bit.ly/2MpuY6c*.

## PART II

Structured Streaming

In this part, we examine Structured Streaming.

We begin our journey by exploring a practical example that should help you build your intuition for the model. From there, we examine the API and get into the details of the following aspects of stream processing:

- Consuming data using sources
- Building data-processing logic using the rich Streaming Dataframe/Dataset API
- Understanding and working with event time
- Dealing with state in streaming applications
- Learning about arbitrary stateful transformations
- Writing the results to other systems using sinks

Before closing, we provide an overview of the operational aspects of Structured Streaming.

Finally, we explore the current developments in this exciting new streaming API and provide insights into experimental areas like machine learning applications and near-real-time data processing with continuous streaming.

CHAPTER 7

Introducing Structured Streaming

In data-intensive enterprises, we find many large datasets: log files from internet-facing servers, tables of shopping behavior, and NoSQL databases with sensor data, just to name a few examples. All of these datasets share the same fundamental life cycle: They started out empty at some point in time and were progressively filled by arriving data points that were directed to some form of secondary storage. This process of data arrival is nothing more than a *data stream* being materialized onto secondary storage. We can then apply our favorite analytics tools on those datasets *at rest*, using techniques known as *batch processing* because they take large chunks of data at once and usually take considerable amounts of time to complete, ranging from minutes to days.

The `Dataset` abstraction in *Spark SQL* is one such way of analyzing data at rest. It is particularly useful for data that is *structured* in nature; that is, it follows a defined schema. The `Dataset` API in Spark combines the expressivity of a SQL-like API with type-safe collection operations that are reminiscent of the Scala collections and the `Resilient Distributed Dataset` (RDD) programming model. At the same time, the `Dataframe` API, which is in nature similar to Python Pandas and R Dataframes, widens the audience of Spark users beyond the initial core of data engineers who are used to developing in a functional paradigm. This higher level of abstraction is intended to support modern data engineering and data science practices by enabling a wider range of professionals to jump onto the big data analytics train using a familiar API.

What if, instead of having to wait for the data to *"settle down,"* we could apply the same `Dataset` concepts to the data while it is in its original stream form?

The Structured Streaming model is an extension of the `Dataset` SQL-oriented model to handle data on the move:

- The data arrives from a *source* stream and is assumed to have a defined schema.

- The stream of events can be seen as rows that are appended to an unbounded table.

- To obtain results from the stream, we express our computation as queries over that table.

- By continuously applying the same query to the updating table, we create an output stream of processed events.

- The resulting events are offered to an output *sink*.

- The *sink* could be a storage system, another streaming backend, or an application ready to consume the processed data.

In this model, our theoretically *unbounded* table must be implemented in a physical system with defined resource constraints. Therefore, the implementation of the model requires certain considerations and restrictions to deal with a potentially infinite data inflow.

To address these challenges, Structured Streaming introduces new concepts to the `Dataset` and `DataFrame` APIs, such as support for event time, *watermarking*, and different output modes that determine for how long past data is actually stored.

Conceptually, the Structured Streaming model blurs the line between batch and streaming processing, removing a lot of the burden of reasoning about analytics on fast-moving data.

First Steps with Structured Streaming

In the previous section, we learned about the high-level concepts that constitute Structured Streaming, such as sources, sinks, and queries. We are now going to explore Structured Streaming from a practical perspective, using a simplified web log analytics use case as an example.

Before we begin delving into our first streaming application, we are going to see how classical batch analysis in Apache Spark can be applied to the same use case.

This exercise has two main goals:

- First, most, if not all, streaming data analytics start by studying a static data sample. It is far easier to start a study with a file of data, gain intuition on how the data looks, what kind of patterns it shows, and define the process that we require to extract the intended knowledge from that data. Typically, it's only after we have defined and tested our data analytics job, that we proceed to transform it into a streaming process that can apply our analytic logic to data on the move.

- Second, from a practical perspective, we can appreciate how Apache Spark simplifies many aspects of transitioning from a batch exploration to a streaming application through the use of uniform APIs for both batch and streaming analytics.

This exploration will allow us to compare and contrast the batch and streaming APIs in Spark and show us the necessary steps to move from one to the other.

Online Resources

For this example, we use Apache Web Server logs from the public 1995 NASA Apache web logs, originally from *http://ita.ee.lbl.gov/html/contrib/NASA-HTTP.html*.

For the purpose of this exercise, the original log file has been split into daily files and each log line has been formatted as JSON. The compressed `NASA-weblogs` file can be downloaded from *https://github.com/stream-processing-with-spark*.

Download this dataset and place it in a folder on your computer.

Batch Analytics

Given that we are working with archive log files, we have access to all of the data at once. Before we begin building our streaming application, let's take a brief *intermezzo* to have a look at what a classical batch analytics job would look like.

Online Resources

For this example, we will use the `batch_weblogs` notebook in the online resources for the book, located at *https://github.com/stream-processing-with-spark*][*https://github.com/stream-processing-with-spark*].

First, we load the log files, encoded as JSON, from the directory where we unpacked them:

```
// This is the location of the unpackaged files. Update accordingly
val logsDirectory = ???
val rawLogs = sparkSession.read.json(logsDirectory)
```

Next, we declare the schema of the data as a `case class` to use the typed `Dataset` API. Following the formal description of the dataset (at NASA-HTTP (*http://bit.ly/2YwMAhG*)), the log is structured as follows:

The logs are an ASCII file with one line per request, with the following columns:

- Host making the request. A hostname when possible, otherwise the Internet address if the name could not be looked up.

- Timestamp in the format "DAY MON DD HH:MM:SS YYYY," where DAY is the day of the week, MON is the name of the month, DD is the day of the month, HH:MM:SS is the time of day using a 24-hour clock, and YYYY is the year. The timezone is −0400.

- Request given in quotes.

- HTTP reply code.

- Bytes in the reply.

Translating that schema to Scala, we have the following `case class` definition:

```
import java.sql.Timestamp
case class WebLog(host: String,
                  timestamp: Timestamp,
                  request: String,
                  http_reply: Int,
                  bytes: Long
                  )
```

We use `java.sql.Timestamp` as the type for the timestamp because it's internally supported by Spark and does not require any additional `cast` that other options might require.

We convert the original JSON to a typed data structure using the previous schema definition:

```
import org.apache.spark.sql.functions._
import org.apache.spark.sql.types.IntegerType
// we need to narrow the `Interger` type because
// the JSON representation is interpreted as `BigInteger`
val preparedLogs = rawLogs.withColumn("http_reply",
                                      $"http_reply".cast(IntegerType))
val weblogs = preparedLogs.as[WebLog]
```

Now that we have the data in a structured format, we can begin asking the questions that interest us. As a first step, we would like to know how many records are contained in our dataset:

```
val recordCount = weblogs.count
>recordCount: Long = 1871988
```

A common question would be: "what was the most popular URL per day?" To answer that, we first reduce the timestamp to the day of the month. We then group by this new `dayOfMonth` column and the request URL and we count over this aggregate. We finally order using descending order to get the top URLs first:

```
val topDailyURLs = weblogs.withColumn("dayOfMonth", dayofmonth($"timestamp"))
                          .select($"request", $"dayOfMonth")
                          .groupBy($"dayOfMonth", $"request")
                          .agg(count($"request").alias("count"))
                          .orderBy(desc("count"))

topDailyURLs.show()
+----------+------------------------------------------+-----+
|dayOfMonth|                                   request|count|
+----------+------------------------------------------+-----+
|        13|GET /images/NASA-logosmall.gif HTTP/1.0   |12476|
|        13|GET /htbin/cdt_main.pl HTTP/1.0           | 7471|
|        12|GET /images/NASA-logosmall.gif HTTP/1.0   | 7143|
|        13|GET /htbin/cdt_clock.pl HTTP/1.0          | 6237|
|         6|GET /images/NASA-logosmall.gif HTTP/1.0   | 6112|
|         5|GET /images/NASA-logosmall.gif HTTP/1.0   | 5865|
         ...
```

Top hits are all images. What now? It's not unusual to see that the top URLs are images commonly used across a site. Our true interest lies in the content pages generating the most traffic. To find those, we first filter on html content and then proceed to apply the top aggregation we just learned.

As we can see, the request field is a quoted sequence of [HTTP_VERB] URL [HTTP_VER SION]. We will extract the URL and preserve only those ending in *.html*, *.htm*, or no extension (directories). This is a simplification for the purpose of this example:

```
val urlExtractor = """^GET (.+) HTTP/\d.\d""".r
val allowedExtensions = Set(".html",".htm", "")
val contentPageLogs = weblogs.filter {log =>
  log.request match {
    case urlExtractor(url) =>
      val ext = url.takeRight(5).dropWhile(c => c != '.')
      allowedExtensions.contains(ext)
    case _ => false
  }
}
```

With this new dataset that contains only *.html*, *.htm*, and directories, we proceed to apply the same *top-k* function as earlier:

```
val topContentPages = contentPageLogs
  .withColumn("dayOfMonth", dayofmonth($"timestamp"))
  .select($"request", $"dayOfMonth")
  .groupBy($"dayOfMonth", $"request")
  .agg(count($"request").alias("count"))
  .orderBy(desc("count"))

topContentPages.show()
+----------+------------------------------------------+-----+
|dayOfMonth|                                   request|count|
+----------+------------------------------------------+-----+
```

```
|   13| GET /shuttle/countdown/liftoff.html HTTP/1.0"  |  4992|
|    5| GET /shuttle/countdown/ HTTP/1.0"               |  3412|
|    6| GET /shuttle/countdown/ HTTP/1.0"               |  3393|
|    3| GET /shuttle/countdown/ HTTP/1.0"               |  3378|
|   13| GET /shuttle/countdown/ HTTP/1.0"               |  3086|
|    7| GET /shuttle/countdown/ HTTP/1.0"               |  2935|
|    4| GET /shuttle/countdown/ HTTP/1.0"               |  2832|
|    2| GET /shuttle/countdown/ HTTP/1.0"               |  2330|
    . . .
```

We can see that the most popular page that month was *liftoff.html*, corresponding to
the coverage of the launch of the Discovery shuttle, as documented on the NASA
archives (*https://go.nasa.gov/2Q9HBQX*). It's closely followed by countdown/, the days
prior to the launch.

Streaming Analytics

In the previous section, we explored historical NASA web log records. We found
trending events in those records, but much later than when the actual events happened.

One key driver for streaming analytics comes from the increasing demand of organizations to have timely information that can help them make decisions at many different levels.

We can use the lessons that we have learned while exploring the archived records
using a batch-oriented approach and create a streaming job that will provide us with
trending information as it happens.

The first difference that we observe with the batch analytics is the source of the data.
For our streaming exercise, we will use a TCP server to simulate a web system that
delivers its logs in real time. The simulator will use the same dataset but will feed it
through a TCP socket connection that will embody the stream that we will be analyzing.

Online Resources

For this example, we will use the notebooks weblog_TCP_server
and streaming_weblogs found in the online resources for the
book, located at *https://github.com/stream-processing-with-spark*.

Connecting to a Stream

If you recall from the introduction of this chapter, Structured Streaming defines the
concepts of sources and sinks as the key abstractions to consume a stream and produce a result. We are going to use the TextSocketSource implementation to connect
to the server through a TCP socket. Socket connections are defined by the host of the

server and the port where it is listening for connections. These two configuration elements are required to create the socket source:

```
val stream = sparkSession.readStream
  .format("socket")
  .option("host", host)
  .option("port", port)
  .load()
```

Note how the creation of a stream is quite similar to the declaration of a static data-source in the batch case. Instead of using the read builder, we use the readStream construct and we pass to it the parameters required by the streaming source. As you will see during the course of this exercise and later on as we go into the details of Structured Streaming, the API is basically the same DataFrame and Dataset API for static data but with some modifications and limitations that you will learn in detail.

Preparing the Data in the Stream

The socket source produces a streaming DataFrame with one column, value, which contains the data received from the stream. See "The Socket Source" on page 130 for additional details.

In the batch analytics case, we could load the data directly as JSON records. In the case of the Socket source, that data is plain text. To transform our raw data to WebLog records, we first require a schema. The schema provides the necessary information to parse the text to a JSON object. It's the *structure* when we talk about *structured* streaming.

After defining a schema for our data, we proceed to create a Dataset, following these steps:

```
import java.sql.Timestamp
case class WebLog(host:String,
                  timestamp: Timestamp,
                  request: String,
                  http_reply:Int,
                  bytes: Long
                  )
val webLogSchema = Encoders.product[WebLog].schema      ❶
val jsonStream = stream.select(from_json($"value", webLogSchema) as "record")   ❷
val webLogStream: Dataset[WebLog] = jsonStream.select("record.*").as[WebLog]    ❸
```

❶ Obtain a schema from the case class definition

❷ Transform the text value to JSON using the JSON support built into Spark SQL

❸ Use the Dataset API to transform the JSON records to WebLog objects

As a result of this process, we obtain a Streaming Dataset of WebLog records.

Operations on Streaming Dataset

The `webLogStream` we just obtained is of type `Dataset[WebLog]` like we had in the batch analytics job. The difference between this instance and the batch version is that `webLogStream` is a streaming `Dataset`.

We can observe this by querying the object:

```
webLogStream.isStreaming
> res: Boolean = true
```

At this point in the batch job, we were creating the first query on our data: How many records are contained in our dataset? This is a question that we can easily answer when we have access to all of the data. However, how do we count records that are constantly arriving? The answer is that some operations that we consider usual on a static `Dataset`, like counting all records, do not have a defined meaning on a `Streaming Dataset`.

As we can observe, attempting to execute the `count` query in the following code snippet will result in an `AnalysisException`:

```
val count = webLogStream.count()
> org.apache.spark.sql.AnalysisException: Queries with streaming sources must
be executed with writeStream.start();;
```

This means that the direct queries we used on a static `Dataset` or `DataFrame` now need two levels of interaction. First, we need to declare the transformations of our stream, and then we need to start the stream process.

Creating a Query

What are popular URLs? In what time frame? Now that we have immediate analytic access to the stream of web logs, we don't need to wait for a day or a month (or more than 20 years in the case of these NASA web logs) to have a rank of the popular URLs. We can have that information as trends unfold in much shorter windows of time.

First, to define the period of time of our interest, we create a window over some timestamp. An interesting feature of Structured Streaming is that we can define that time interval on the timestamp when the data was produced, also known as *event time*, as opposed to the time when the data is being processed.

Our window definition will be of five minutes of event data. Given that our timeline is simulated, the five minutes might happen much faster or slower than the clock time. In this way, we can clearly appreciate how Structured Streaming uses the timestamp information in the events to keep track of the event timeline.

As we learned from the batch analytics, we should extract the URLs and select only content pages, like *.html*, *.htm*, or directories. Let's apply that acquired knowledge first before proceeding to define our windowed query:

```scala
// A regex expression to extract the accessed URL from weblog.request
val urlExtractor = """^GET (.+) HTTP/\d.\d""".r
val allowedExtensions = Set(".html", ".htm", "")

val contentPageLogs: String => Boolean = url => {
  val ext = url.takeRight(5).dropWhile(c => c != '.')
  allowedExtensions.contains(ext)
}

val urlWebLogStream = webLogStream.flatMap { weblog =>
  weblog.request match {
    case urlExtractor(url) if (contentPageLogs(url)) =>
      Some(weblog.copy(request = url))
    case _ => None
  }
}
```

We have converted the request to contain only the visited URL and filtered out all noncontent pages. Now, we define the windowed query to compute the top trending URLs:

```scala
val rankingURLStream = urlWebLogStream
    .groupBy($"request", window($"timestamp", "5 minutes", "1 minute"))
    .count()
```

Start the Stream Processing

All of the steps that we have followed so far have been to define the process that the stream will undergo. But no data has been processed yet.

To start a Structured Streaming job, we need to specify a `sink` and an `output mode`. These are two new concepts introduced by Structured Streaming:

- A `sink` defines where we want to materialize the resulting data; for example, to a file in a filesystem, to an in-memory table, or to another streaming system such as Kafka.

- The `output mode` defines how we want the results to be delivered: do we want to see all data every time, only updates, or just the new records?

These options are given to a `writeStream` operation. It creates the streaming query that starts the stream consumption, materializes the computations declared on the query, and produces the result to the output `sink`.

We visit all these concepts in detail later on. For now, let's use them empirically and observe the results.

For our query, shown in Example 7-1, we use the `memory` `sink` and output mode `com` `plete` to have a fully updated table each time new records are added to the result of keeping track of the URL ranking.

Example 7-1. Writing a stream to a sink

```
val query = rankingURLStream.writeStream
  .queryName("urlranks")
  .outputMode("complete")
  .format("memory")
  .start()
```

The memory sink outputs the data to a temporary table of the same name given in the `queryName` option. We can observe this by querying the tables registered on `Spark` `SQL`:

```
scala> spark.sql("show tables").show()
+--------+---------+-----------+
|database|tableName|isTemporary|
+--------+---------+-----------+
|        | urlranks|       true|
+--------+---------+-----------+
```

In the expression in Example 7-1, `query` is of type `StreamingQuery` and it's a handler to control the query life cycle.

Exploring the Data

Given that we are accelerating the log timeline on the producer side, after a few seconds, we can execute the next command to see the result of the first windows, as illustrated in Figure 7-1.

Note how the processing time (a few seconds) is decoupled from the event time (hundreds of minutes of logs):

```
urlRanks.select($"request", $"window", $"count").orderBy(desc("count"))
```

request	window	count
"/shuttle/missions/sts-70/mission-sts-70.html"	{"start":"2018-02-02T18:18:00.000+01:00","end":"2018-02-02T18:23:00.000+01:00"}	8
"/shuttle/countdown/"	{"start":"2018-02-02T18:17:00.000+01:00","end":"2018-02-02T18:22:00.000+01:00"}	8
"/shuttle/countdown/"	{"start":"2018-02-02T18:18:00.000+01:00","end":"2018-02-02T18:23:00.000+01:00"}	8
"/shuttle/countdown/"	{"start":"2018-02-02T18:20:00.000+01:00","end":"2018-02-02T18:25:00.000+01:00"}	7
"/shuttle/countdown/"	{"start":"2018-02-02T18:21:00.000+01:00","end":"2018-02-02T18:26:00.000+01:00"}	7
"/shuttle/countdown/liftoff.html"	{"start":"2018-02-02T18:22:00.000+01:00","end":"2018-02-02T18:27:00.000+01:00"}	7
"/shuttle/missions/sts-70/mission-sts-70.html"	{"start":"2018-02-02T18:17:00.000+01:00","end":"2018-02-02T18:22:00.000+01:00"}	7
"/shuttle/countdown/liftoff.html"	{"start":"2018-02-02T18:20:00.000+01:00","end":"2018-02-02T18:25:00.000+01:00"}	6
"/shuttle/countdown/"	{"start":"2018-02-02T18:16:00.000+01:00","end":"2018-02-02T18:21:00.000+01:00"}	6
"/ksc.html"	{"start":"2018-02-02T18:17:00.000+01:00","end":"2018-02-02T18:22:00.000+01:00"}	6

Figure 7-1. URL ranking: query results by window

We explore event time in detail in Chapter 12.

Summary

In these first steps into Structured Streaming, you have seen the process behind the development of a streaming application. By starting with a batch version of the process, you gained intuition about the data, and using those insights, we created a streaming version of the job. In the process, you could appreciate how close the *structured* batch and the streaming APIs are, albeit we also observed that some usual batch operations do now apply in a streaming context.

With this exercise, we hope to have increased your curiosity about Structured Streaming. You're now ready for the learning path through this section.

## CHAPTER 8

The Structured Streaming
Programming Model

Structured Streaming builds on the foundations laid on top of the Spark SQL `Data Frames` and `Datasets` APIs of Spark SQL. By extending these APIs to support streaming workloads, Structured Streaming inherits the traits of the high-level language introduced by Spark SQL as well as the underlying optimizations, including the use of the Catalyst query optimizer and the low overhead memory management and code generation delivered by Project Tungsten. At the same time, Structured Streaming becomes available in all the supported language bindings for Spark SQL. These are: Scala, Java, Python, and R, although some of the advanced state management features are currently available only in Scala. Thanks to the intermediate query representation used in Spark SQL, the performance of the programs is identical regardless of the *language binding* used.

Structured Streaming introduces support for event time across all windowing and aggregation operations, making it easy to program logic that uses the time when events were generated, as opposed to the time when they enter the processing engine, also known as *processing time*. You learned these concepts in "The Effect of Time" on page 25.

With the availability of Structured Streaming in the Spark ecosystem, Spark manages to unify the development experience between *classic* batch and stream-based data processing.

In this chapter, we examine the programming model of Structured Streaming by following the sequence of steps that are usually required to create a streaming job with Structured Streaming:

- Initializing Spark
- Sources: acquiring streaming data
- Declaring the operations we want to apply to the streaming data
- Sinks: output the resulting data

Initializing Spark

Part of the visible unification of APIs in Spark is that `SparkSession` becomes the single entry point for *batch* and *streaming* applications that use Structured Streaming.

Therefore, our entry point to create a Spark job is the same as when using the Spark batch API: we instantiate a `SparkSession` as demonstrated in Example 8-1.

Example 8-1. Creating a local Spark Session

```
import org.apache.spark.sql.SparkSession

val spark = SparkSession
  .builder()
  .appName("StreamProcessing")
  .master("local[*]")
  .getOrCreate()
```

Using the Spark Shell

When using the Spark shell to explore Structured Streaming, the `SparkSession` is already provided as `spark`. We don't need to create any additional context to use Structured Streaming.

Sources: Acquiring Streaming Data

In Structured Streaming, a *source* is an abstraction that lets us consume data from a streaming data producer. Sources are not directly created. Instead, the `sparkSession` provides a builder method, `readStream`, that exposes the API to specify a streaming source, called a *format*, and provide its configuration.

For example, the code in Example 8-2 creates a `File` streaming source. We specify the type of source using the `format` method. The method `schema` lets us provide a schema for the data stream, which is mandatory for certain source types, such as this `File` source.

Example 8-2. File streaming source

```
val fileStream = spark.readStream
  .format("json")
  .schema(schema)
  .option("mode","DROPMALFORMED")
  .load("/tmp/datasrc")

>fileStream:
org.apache.spark.sql.DataFrame = [id: string, timestamp: timestamp ... ]
```

Each source implementation has different options, and some have tunable parameters. In Example 8-2, we are setting the option `mode` to `DROPMALFORMED`. This option instructs the JSON stream processor to drop any line that neither complies with the JSON format nor matches the provided schema.

Behind the scenes, the call to `spark.readStream` creates a `DataStreamBuilder` instance. This instance is in charge of managing the different options provided through the builder method calls. Calling `load(...)` on this `DataStreamBuilder` instance validates the options provided to the builder and, if everything checks, it returns a streaming `DataFrame`.

We can appreciate the symmetry in the Spark API: while `read Stream` provides the options to declare the source of the stream, `writeStream` lets us specify the output sink and the output mode required by our process. They are the counterparts of `read` and `write` in the `DataFrame` APIs. As such, they provide an easy way to remember the execution mode used in a Spark program:

- `read`/`write`: Batch operation
- `readStream`/`writeStream`: Streaming operation

In our example, this streaming `DataFrame` represents the stream of data that will result from monitoring the provided *path* and processing each new file in that path as JSON-encoded data, parsed using the schema provided. All malformed code will be dropped from this data stream.

Loading a streaming source is lazy. What we get is a representation of the stream, embodied in the streaming `DataFrame` instance, that we can use to express the series of transformations that we want to apply to it in order to implement our specific business logic. Creating a streaming `DataFrame` does not result in any data actually being consumed or processed until the stream is materialized. This requires a *query*, as you will see further on.

Available Sources

As of Spark v2.4.0, the following streaming sources are supported:

json, orc, parquet, csv, text, textFile
> These are all file-based streaming sources. The base functionality is to monitor a path (folder) in a filesystem and consume files atomically placed in it. The files found will then be parsed by the formatter specified. For example, if json is provided, the Spark json reader will be used to process the files, using the schema information provided.

socket
> Establishes a client connection to a TCP server that is assumed to provide text data through a socket connection.

kafka
> Creates Kafka consumer able to retrieve data from Kafka.

rate
> Generates a stream of rows at the rate given by the rowsPerSecond option. It's mainly intended as a testing source.

We look at sources in detail in Chapter 10.

Transforming Streaming Data

As we saw in the previous section, the result of calling load is a streaming DataFrame. After we have created our streaming DataFrame using a source, we can use the Data set or DataFrame API to express the logic that we want to apply to the data in the stream in order to implement our specific use case.

> Remember that DataFrame is an alias for Dataset[Row]. Although this might seem like a small technical distinction, when used from a typed language such as Scala, the Dataset API presents a typed interface, whereas the DataFrame usage is untyped. When the structured API is used from a dynamic language such as Python, the DataFrame API is the only available API.
>
> There's also a performance impact when using operations on a typed Dataset. Although the SQL expressions used by the Data Frame API can be understood and further optimized by the query planner, closures provided in Dataset operations are opaque to the query planner and therefore might run slower than the exact same DataFrame counterpart.

Assuming that we are using data from a sensor network, in Example 8-3 we are selecting the fields `deviceId`, `timestamp`, `sensorType`, and `value` from a `sensor Stream` and filtering to only those records where the sensor is of type `temperature` and its `value` is higher than the given `threshold`.

Example 8-3. Filter and projection

```
val highTempSensors = sensorStream
  .select($"deviceId", $"timestamp", $"sensorType", $"value")
  .where($"sensorType" === "temperature" && $"value" > threshold)
```

Likewise, we can aggregate our data and apply operations to the groups over time. Example 8-4 shows that we can use `timestamp` information from the event itself to define a time window of five minutes that will slide every minute. We cover event time in detail in Chapter 12.

What is important to grasp here is that the Structured Streaming API is practically the same as the `Dataset` API for batch analytics, with some additional provisions specific to stream processing.

Example 8-4. Average by sensor type over time

```
val avgBySensorTypeOverTime = sensorStream
  .select($"timestamp", $"sensorType", $"value")
  .groupBy(window($"timestamp", "5 minutes", "1 minute"), $"sensorType")
  .agg(avg($"value"))
```

If you are not familiar with the structured APIs of Spark, we suggest that you familiarize yourself with it. Covering this API in detail is beyond the scope of this book. We recommend *Spark: The Definitive Guide* (O'Reilly, 2018) by Bill Chambers and Matei Zaharia as a comprehensive reference.

Streaming API Restrictions on the DataFrame API

As we hinted in the previous chapter, some operations that are offered by the standard `DataFrame` and `Dataset` API do not make sense on a streaming context.

We gave the example of `stream.count`, which does not make sense to use on a stream. In general, operations that require immediate materialization of the underlying dataset are not allowed.

These are the API operations not directly supported on streams:

- `count`
- `show`

- describe
- limit
- take(n)
- distinct
- foreach
- sort
- multiple stacked aggregations

Next to these operations, stream-stream and static-stream `joins` are partially supported.

Understanding the limitations

Although some operations, like `count` or `limit`, do not make sense on a stream, some other stream operations are computationally difficult. For example, `distinct` is one of them. To filter duplicates in an arbitrary stream, it would require that you remember all of the data seen so far and compare each new record with all records already seen. The first condition would require infinite memory and the second has a computational complexity of $O(n^2)$, which becomes prohibitive as the number of elements (n) increases.

Operations on aggregated streams

Some of the unsupported operations become defined after we apply an aggregation function to the stream. Although we can't `count` the stream, we could `count` messages received per minute or `count` the number of devices of a certain type.

In Example 8-5, we define a `count` of events per `sensorType` per minute.

Example 8-5. Count of sensor types over time

```
val avgBySensorTypeOverTime = sensorStream
  .select($"timestamp", $"sensorType")
  .groupBy(window($"timestamp", "1 minutes", "1 minute"), $"sensorType")
  .count()
```

Likewise, it's also possible to define a `sort` on aggregated data, although it's further restricted to queries with output mode `complete`. We examine about output modes in greater detail in "outputMode" on page 103.

Stream deduplication

We discussed that `distinct` on an arbitrary stream is computationally difficult to implement. But if we can define a key that informs us when an element in the stream has already been seen, we can use it to remove duplicates:

```
stream.dropDuplicates("<key-column>") ...
```

Workarounds

Although some operations are not supported in the exact same way as in the *batch* model, there are alternative ways to achieve the same functionality:

`foreach`
> Although `foreach` cannot be directly used on a stream, there's a *foreach sink* that provides the same functionality.
>
> Sinks are specified in the output definition of a stream.

`show`
> Although `show` requires an immediate materialization of the query, and hence it's not possible on a streaming `Dataset`, we can use the `console` sink to output data to the screen.

Sinks: Output the Resulting Data

All operations that we have done so far—such as creating a stream and applying transformations on it—have been declarative. They define from where to consume the data and what operations we want to apply to it. But up to this point, there is still no data flowing through the system.

Before we can initiate our stream, we need to first define *where* and *how* we want the output data to go:

- *Where* relates to the streaming sink: the receiving side of our streaming data.
- *How* refers to the output mode: how to treat the resulting records in our stream.

From the API perspective, we materialize a stream by calling `writeStream` on a streaming `DataFrame` or `Dataset`, as shown in Example 8-6.

Calling `writeStream` on a streaming `Dataset` creates a `DataStreamWriter`. This is a builder instance that provides methods to configure the output behavior of our streaming process.

Example 8-6. File streaming sink

```
val query = stream.writeStream
  .format("json")
  .queryName("json-writer")
  .outputMode("append")
  .option("path", "/target/dir")
  .option("checkpointLocation", "/checkpoint/dir")
  .trigger(ProcessingTime("5 seconds"))
  .start()

>query: org.apache.spark.sql.streaming.StreamingQuery = ...
```

We cover sinks in detail in Chapter 11.

format

The `format` method lets us specify the output sink by providing the name of a built-in sink or the fully qualified name of a custom sink.

As of Spark v2.4.0, the following streaming sinks are available:

`console` *sink*

> A sink that prints to the standard output. It shows a number of rows configurable with the option `numRows`.

file sink

> File-based and format-specific sink that writes the results to a filesystem. The format is specified by providing the format name: `csv`, `hive`, `json`, `orc`, `parquet`, `avro`, or `text`.

`kafka` *sink*

> A Kafka-specific producer sink that is able to write to one or more Kafka topics.

`memory` *sink*

> Creates an in-memory table using the provided query name as table name. This table receives continuous updates with the results of the stream.

`foreach` *sink*

> Provides a programmatic interface to access the stream contents, one element at the time.

`foreachBatch` *sink*

> `foreachBatch` is a programmatic sink interface that provides access to the complete `DataFrame` that corresponds to each underlying microbatch of the Structured Streaming execution.

outputMode

The `outputMode` specifies the semantics of how records are added to the output of the streaming query. The supported modes are `append`, `update`, and `complete`:

append

> (default mode) Adds only *final* records to the output stream. A record is considered *final* when no new records of the incoming stream can modify its value. This is always the case with linear transformations like those resulting from applying projection, filtering, and mapping. This mode guarantees that each resulting record will be output only once.

update

> Adds new and updated records since the last trigger to the output stream. `update` is meaningful only in the context of an aggregation, where aggregated values change as new records arrive. If more than one incoming record changes a single result, all changes between trigger intervals are collated into one output record.

complete

> `complete` mode outputs the complete internal representation of the stream. This mode also relates to aggregations, because for nonaggregated streams, we would need to remember all records seen so far, which is unrealistic. From a practical perspective, `complete` mode is recommended only when you are aggregating values over low-cardinality criteria, like *count of visitors by country*, for which we know that the number of countries is bounded.

Understanding the append semantic

When the streaming query contains aggregations, the definition of final becomes nontrivial. In an aggregated computation, new incoming records might change an existing aggregated value when they comply with the aggregation criteria used. Following our definition, we cannot output a record using `append` until we know that its value is final. Therefore, the use of the `append` output mode in combination with aggregate queries is restricted to queries for which the aggregation is expressed using event-time and it defines a `watermark`. In that case, `append` will output an event as soon as the `watermark` has expired and hence it's considered that no new records can alter the aggregated value. As a consequence, output events in `append` mode will be delayed by the aggregation time window plus the watermark offset.

queryName

With `queryName`, we can provide a name for the query that is used by some sinks and also presented in the job description in the Spark Console, as depicted in Figure 8-1.

Figure 8-1. Completed Jobs in the Spark UI showing the query name in the job description

option

With the `option` method, we can provide specific key–value pairs of configuration to the stream, akin to the configuration of the source. Each sink can have specific configuration we can customize using this method.

We can add as many `.option(...)` calls as necessary to configure the sink.

options

`options` is an alternative to `option` that takes a `Map[String, String]` containing all the key–value configuration parameters that we want to set. This alternative is more friendly to an externalized configuration model, where we don't know *a priori* the settings to be passed to the sink's configuration.

trigger

The optional `trigger` option lets us specify the frequency at which we want the results to be produced. By default, Structured Streaming will process the input and produce a result as soon as possible. When a trigger is specified, output will be produced at each trigger interval.

`org.apache.spark.sql.streaming.Trigger` provides the following supported triggers:

`ProcessingTime(<interval>)`
    Lets us specify a time interval that will dictate the frequency of the query results.

`Once()`
    A particular `Trigger` that lets us execute a streaming job once. It is useful for testing and also to apply a defined streaming job as a single-shot batch operation.

`Continuous(<checkpoint-interval>)`
    This trigger switches the execution engine to the experimental `continuous` engine for low-latency processing. The `checkpoint-interval` parameter indi-

cates the frequency of the asynchronous checkpointing for data resilience. It should not be confused with the `batch interval` of the `ProcessingTime` trigger. We explore this new execution option in Chapter 15.

start()

To materialize the streaming computation, we need to start the streaming process. Finally, `start()` materializes the complete job description into a streaming computation and initiates the internal scheduling process that results in data being consumed from the source, processed, and produced to the sink. `start()` returns a `Streaming Query` object, which is a handle to manage the individual life cycle of each query. This means that we can simultaneously start and stop multiple queries independently of one other within the same `sparkSession`.

Summary

After reading this chapter, you should have a good understanding of the Structured Streaming programming model and API. In this chapter, you learned the following:

- Each streaming program starts by defining a source and what sources are currently available.
- We can reuse most of the familiar `Dataset` and `DataFrame` APIs for transforming the streaming data.
- Some common operations from the `batch` API do not make sense in streaming mode.
- Sinks are the configurable definition of the stream output.
- The relation between output modes and aggregation operations in the stream.
- All transformations are lazy and we need to `start` our stream to get data flowing through the system.

In the next chapter, you apply your newly acquired knowledge to create a comprehensive stream-processing program. After that, we will zoom into specific areas of the Structured Streaming API, such as event-time handing, window definitions, the concept of watermarks, and arbitrary state handling.

## CHAPTER 9

Structured Streaming in Action

Now that we have a better understanding of the Structured Streaming API and programming model, in this chapter, we create a small but complete Internet of Things (IoT)-inspired streaming program.

Online Resources

For this example, we will use the `Structured-Streaming-in-action` notebook in the online resources for the book, located on *https://github.com/stream-processing-with-spark*.

Our use case will be to consume a stream of sensor readings from Apache Kafka as the streaming source.

We are going to correlate incoming IoT sensor data with a static reference file that contains all known sensors with their configuration. That way, we enrich each incoming record with specific sensor parameters that we require to process the reported data. We then save all correctly processed records to a file in Parquet format.

Apache Kafka

Apache Kafka is one of the most popular choices for a scalable messaging broker that is used to decouple producers from consumers in an event-driven system. It is is a highly scalable distributed streaming platform based on the abstraction of a distributed commit log. It provides functionality similar to message queues or enterprise messaging systems but differentiates from its predecessors in three important areas:

- Runs are distributed on a commodity cluster, making it highly scalable.

- Fault-tolerant data storage guarantees consistency of data reception and delivery.

- Pull-based consumers allow consumption of the data at a different time and pace, from real time, to microbatch, to batch, creating the possibility of feeding data to a wide range of applications.

You can find Kafka at *http://kafka.apache.org*.

Consuming a Streaming Source

The first part of our program deals with the creation of the streaming `Dataset`:

```
val rawData = sparkSession.readStream
    .format("kafka")
    .option("kafka.bootstrap.servers", kafkaBootstrapServer)
    .option("subscribe", topic)
    .option("startingOffsets", "earliest")
    .load()

> rawData: org.apache.spark.sql.DataFrame
```

The entry point of Structured Streaming is an existing Spark Session (`sparkSession`). As you can appreciate on the first line, the creation of a streaming `Dataset` is almost identical to the creation of a static `Dataset` that would use a `read` operation instead. `sparkSession.readStream` returns a `DataStreamReader`, a class that implements the builder pattern to collect the information needed to construct the streaming source using a *fluid* API. In that API, we find the `format` option that lets us specify our source provider, which, in our case, is `kafka`. The options that follow it are specific to the source:

`kafka.bootstrap.servers`
  Indicates the set of bootstrap servers to contact as a comma-separated list of `host:port` addresses

---

```
subscribe
```
Specifies the topic or topics to subscribe to

```
startingOffsets
```
The offset reset policy to apply when this application starts out fresh

We cover the details of the Kafka streaming provider later in Chapter 10.

The `load()` method evaluates the `DataStreamReader` builder and creates a `DataFrame` as a result, as we can see in the returned value:

```
> rawData: org.apache.spark.sql.DataFrame
```

A `DataFrame` is an alias for `Dataset[Row]` with a known schema. After creation, you can use streaming `Datasets` just like regular `Datasets`. This makes it possible to use the full-fledged `Dataset` API with Structured Streaming, albeit some exceptions apply because not all operations, such as `show()` or `count()`, make sense in a streaming context.

To programmatically differentiate a streaming `Dataset` from a static one, we can ask a `Dataset` whether it is of the streaming kind:

```
rawData.isStreaming
res7: Boolean = true
```

And we can also explore the schema attached to it, using the existing `Dataset` API, as demonstrated in Example 9-1.

Example 9-1. The Kafka schema

```
rawData.printSchema()

root
 |-- key: binary (nullable = true)
 |-- value: binary (nullable = true)
 |-- topic: string (nullable = true)
 |-- partition: integer (nullable = true)
 |-- offset: long (nullable = true)
 |-- timestamp: timestamp (nullable = true)
 |-- timestampType: integer (nullable = true)
```

In general, Structured Streaming requires the explicit declaration of a schema for the consumed stream. In the specific case of `kafka`, the schema for the resulting `Dataset` is fixed and is independent of the contents of the stream. It consists of a set of fields specific to the Kakfa source: `key`, `value`, `topic`, `partition`, `offset`, `timestamp`, and `timestampType`, as we can see in Example 9-1. In most cases, applications will be mostly interested in the contents of the `value` field where the actual payload of the stream resides.

Application Logic

Recall that the intention of our job is to correlate the incoming IoT sensor data with a reference file that contains all known sensors with their configuration. That way, we would enrich each incoming record with specific sensor parameters that would allow us to interpret the reported data. We would then save all correctly processed records to a Parquet file. The data coming from unknown sensors would be saved to a separate file for later analysis.

Using Structured Streaming, our job can be implemented in terms of `Dataset` operations:

```
val iotData = rawData.select($"value").as[String].flatMap{record =>
  val fields = record.split(",")
  Try {
    SensorData(fields(0).toInt, fields(1).toLong, fields(2).toDouble)
  }.toOption
}

val sensorRef = sparkSession.read.parquet(s"$workDir/$referenceFile")
sensorRef.cache()

val sensorWithInfo = sensorRef.join(iotData, Seq("sensorId"), "inner")

val knownSensors = sensorWithInfo
  .withColumn("dnvalue", $"value"*($"maxRange"-$"minRange")+$"minRange")
  .drop("value", "maxRange", "minRange")
```

In the first step, we transform our CSV-formatted records back into `SensorData` entries. We apply Scala functional operations on the typed `Dataset[String]` that we obtained from extracting the `value` field as a `String`.

Then, we use a streaming `Dataset` to static `Dataset` `inner join` to correlate the sensor data with the corresponding reference using the `sensorId` as key.

To complete our application, we compute the real values of the sensor reading using the minimum-maximum ranges in the reference data.

Writing to a Streaming Sink

The final step of our streaming application is to write the enriched IoT data to a Parquet-formatted file. In Structured Streaming, the `write` operation is crucial: it marks the completion of the declared transformations on the stream, defines a *write mode*, and upon calling start(), the processing of the continuous query will begin.

In Structured Streaming, all operations are lazy declarations of what we want to do with the streaming data. Only when we call `start()` will the actual consumption of the stream begin and the query operations on the data materialize into actual results:

```
val knownSensorsQuery = knownSensors.writeStream
  .outputMode("append")
  .format("parquet")
  .option("path", targetPath)
  .option("checkpointLocation", "/tmp/checkpoint")
  .start()
```

Let's break this operation down:

- `writeStream` creates a builder object where we can configure the options for the desired write operation, using a *fluent* interface.

- With `format`, we specify the sink that will materialize the result downstream. In our case, we use the built-in `FileStreamSink` with Parquet format.

- `mode` is a new concept in Structured Streaming: given that we, theoretically, have access to all the data seen in the stream so far, we also have the option to produce different views of that data.

- The `append` mode, used here, implies that the new records affected by our streaming computation are produced to the output.

The result of the `start` call is a `StreamingQuery` instance. This object provides methods to control the execution of the query and request information about the status of our running streaming query, as shown in Example 9-2.

Example 9-2. Query progress

```
knownSensorsQuery.recentProgress

res37: Array[org.apache.spark.sql.streaming.StreamingQueryProgress] =
Array({
  "id" : "6b9fe3eb-7749-4294-b3e7-2561f1e840b6",
  "runId" : "0d8d5605-bf78-4169-8cfe-98311fc8365c",
  "name" : null,
  "timestamp" : "2017-08-10T16:20:00.065Z",
  "numInputRows" : 4348,
  "inputRowsPerSecond" : 395272.7272727273,
  "processedRowsPerSecond" : 28986.666666666668,
  "durationMs" : {
    "addBatch" : 127,
    "getBatch" : 3,
    "getOffset" : 1,
    "queryPlanning" : 7,
    "triggerExecution" : 150,
    "walCommit" : 11
  },
  "stateOperators" : [ ],
  "sources" : [ {
    "description" : "KafkaSource[Subscribe[iot-data]]",
    "startOffset" : {
```

```
    "iot-data" : {
      "0" : 19048348
    }
  },
  "endOffset" : {
    "iot-data" : {
      "0" : 19052696
    }
  },
  "numInputRow...
```

In Example 9-2, we can see the `StreamingQueryProgress` as a result of calling known `SensorsQuery.recentProgress`. If we see nonzero values for the `numInputRows`, we can be certain that our job is consuming data. We now have a Structured Streaming job running properly.

Summary

Hopefully, this hands-on chapter has shown you how to create your first nontrivial application using Structured Streaming.

After reading this chapter, you should have a better understanding of the structure of a Structured Streaming program and how to approach a streaming application, from consuming the data, to processing it using the `Dataset` and `DataFrames` APIs, to producing the data to an external output. At this point, you should be just about ready to take on the adventure of creating your own streaming processing jobs.

In the next chapters, you learn in depth the different aspects of Structured Streaming.

## CHAPTER 10

Structured Streaming Sources

The previous chapters provided a good overview of the Structured Streaming programming model and how you can apply it in a practical way. You also saw how sources are the starting point of each Structured Streaming program. In this chapter, we study the general characteristics of a source and review the available sources in greater detail, including their different configuration options and modes of operation.

Understanding Sources

In Structured Streaming, a source is an abstraction that represents streaming data providers. The concept behind the source interface is that streaming data is a continuous flow of events over time that can be seen as a sequence, indexed with a monotonously incrementing counter.

Figure 10-1 illustrates how each event in the stream is considered to have an ever-increasing offset.

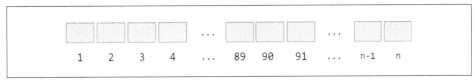

Figure 10-1. A stream seen as an indexed sequence of events

Offsets, as shown in Figure 10-2, are used to request data from the external source and to indicate what data has already been consumed. Structured Streaming knows when there is data to process by asking the current offset from the external system and comparing it to the last processed offset. The data to be processed is requested by getting a *batch* between two offsets start and end. The source is informed that data has been processed by committing a given offset. The source contract guarantees that all data with an offset less than or equal to the committed offset has been processed and that subsequent requests will stipulate only offsets greater than that committed offset. Given these guarantees, sources might opt to discard the processed data to free up system resources.

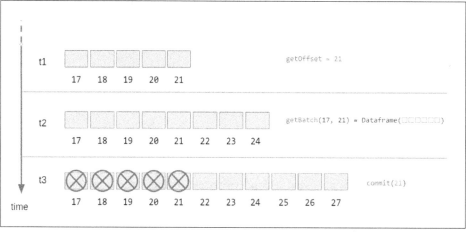

Figure 10-2. Offset process sequence

Let's take a closer look at the dynamics of the offset-based processing shown in Figure 10-2:

1. At *t1*, the system calls `getOffset` and obtains the current offset for the *source*.

2. At *t2*, the system obtains the batch up to the last known offset by calling `get Batch(start, end)`. Note that new data might have arrived in the meantime.

3. At *t3*, the system `commits` the offset and the source drops the corresponding records.

This process repeats constantly, ensuring the acquisition of streaming data. To recover from eventual failure, offsets are often *checkpointed* to external storage.

Besides the offset-based interaction, sources must fulfill two requirements: to be reliable, sources must be replayable in the same order; and sources must provide a schema.

Reliable Sources Must Be Replayable

In Structured Streaming, *replayability* is the capacity to request a part of the stream that had been already requested but not committed yet. Just like we can rewind that Netflix series we are watching to see a piece we just missed because of a distraction, sources must offer the capability to replay a piece of the stream that was already requested but not committed. This is done by calling `getBatch` with the offset range that we want to receive again.

A source is considered to be reliable when it can produce an uncommitted offset range even after a total failure of the Structured Streaming process. In this failure recovery process, offsets are restored from their last known checkpoint and are requested again from the source. This requires the actual streaming system that is backing the source implementation to store data safely outside the `streaming` process. By requiring replayability from the source, Structured Streaming delegates recovery responsibility to the source. This implies that only reliable sources work with Structured Streaming to create strong end-to-end delivery guarantees.

Sources Must Provide a Schema

A defining characteristic of the structured APIs of Spark is that they rely on schema information to handle the data at different levels. As opposed to processing opaque Strings or Byte Array blobs, schema information provides insights on how the data is shaped in terms of fields and types. We can use schema information to drive optimizations at different levels in the stack, from query planning to the internal binary representation of data, storage, and access to it.

Sources must provide schema information that describes the data they produce. Some source implementations allow this schema to be configured and use this configuration information to automatically parse incoming data and transform it into valid records. In fact, many file-based streaming sources such as JSON or comma-separated values (CSV) files follow this model, in which the user must provide the schema used by the file format to ensure proper parsing. Some other sources use a fixed internal schema that expresses the metadata information of every record and leaves the parsing of the payload to the application.

From an architectural perspective, creating schema-driven streaming applications is desirable because it facilitates the global understanding of how data flows through the system and drives the formalization of the different stages of a multiprocess streaming pipeline.

Defining schemas

In Structured Streaming, we reuse the Spark SQL API for creating schema definitions. There are several different methods that we can use to define the schema that defines the content of the stream—programmatically, inferred from a `case class` definition, or loaded from an existing dataset:

Programmatically

We use the `StructType` and `StructField` classes to build up a representation of the schema. For example, to represent a tracked vehicle with *id*, *type*, and *location coordinates*, we can construct the corresponding schema structure as follows:

```
import org.apache.spark.sql.{StructType, StructField}_
import org.apache.spark.sql.types._

val schema = StructType(
  List(
    StructField("id", StringType, true),
    StructField("type", StringType, true),
    StructField("location", StructType(List(
        StructField("latitude", DoubleType, false),
        StructField("longitude", DoubleType, false)
        )), false)
    )
  )
```

`StructField` can contain nested `StructTypes`, making it possible to create schemas of arbitrary depth and complexity.

By inference

In Scala, the schema also can be represented using arbitrary combinations of `case classes`. Given a single `case class` or a `case class` hierarchy, the schema representation can be computed by creating an `Encoder` for the `case class` and obtaining the schema from that `encoder` instance.

Using this method, the same schema definition used in the preceding example can be obtained like so:

```
import org.apache.spark.sql.Encoders

// Define the case class hierarchy
case class Coordinates(latitude: Double, longitude: Double)
case class Vehicle(id: String, `type`: String, location: Coordinates )
// Obtain the Encoder, and the schema from the Encoder
val schema = Encoders.product[Vehicle].schema
```

Extract from a dataset

A practical method of obtaining a schema definition is by maintaining a sample data file in a schema-aware format, such as Parquet. To obtain our schema definition, we load the sample dataset and get the schema definition from the loaded `DataFrame`:

```
val sample = spark.read.parquet(<path-to-sample>)
val schema = sample.schema
```

The programmatic way of defining schemas is powerful but requires effort and is complex to maintain, often leading to errors. Loading a dataset might be practical at the prototyping stage, but it requires keeping the sample dataset up-to-date, which in some cases can lead to accidental complexity.

Although the best method to choose might be different from one use case to the other, in general, when working with Scala, we prefer to use the inference method, when possible.

Available Sources

The following are the sources currently available in the Spark distribution of Structured Streaming:

File
> Allows the ingestion of data stored as files. In most cases, the data is transformed in records that are further processed in streaming mode. This supports these formats: JSON, CSV, Parquet, ORC, and plain text.

Kafka
> Allows the consumption of streaming data from Apache Kafka.

Socket
> A TCP socket client able to connect to a TCP server and consume a text-based data stream. The stream must be encoded in the UTF-8 character set.

Rate
> Produces an internally generated stream of (`timestamp, value`) records with a configurable production rate. This is normally used for learning and testing purposes.

As we discussed in "Understanding Sources" on page 113, sources are considered reliable when they provide replay capabilities from an offset, even when the structured streaming process fails. Using this criterion, we can classify the available sources as follows:

Reliable
> File source, Kafka source

Unreliable
> Socket source, Rate source

The unreliable sources may be used in a production system only when the loss of data can be tolerated.

The streaming source API is currently undergoing evolution. As of this writing, there is no stable public API to develop custom sources. This is expected to change in the near future.

In the next part of this chapter, we explore in detail the sources currently available. As production-ready sources, the File and the Kafka sources have many options that we discuss in detail. The Socket and the Rate source are limited in features, which will be evident by their concise coverage.

The File Source

The File source is a simple streaming data source that reads files from a monitored directory in a filesystem. A file-based handover is a commonly used method to bridge a batch-based process with a streaming system. The batch process produces its output in a file format and drops it in a common directory where a suitable implementation of the File source can pick these files up and transform their contents into a stream of records for further processing in streaming mode.

Specifying a File Format

The files are read using a specified format, which is provided with the `.format(<for mat_name>)` method in the `readStream` builder, or by using the dedicated methods in the `DataStreamReader` that indicate the format to use; for example, `readStream.par quet('/path/to/dir/')`. When using the dedicated methods corresponding to each supported format, the method call should be done as the last call of the builder.

For example, the three forms in Example 10-1 are equivalent.

Example 10-1. Building a FileStream

```
// Use format and load path
val fileStream = spark.readStream
  .format("parquet")
  .schema(schema)
  .load("hdfs://data/exchange")

// Use format and path options
val fileStream = spark.readStream
  .format("parquet")
  .option("path", "hdfs://data/exchange")
  .schema(schema)
  .load()

// Use dedicated method
val fileStream = spark.readStream
```

```
.schema(schema)
.parquet("hdfs://data/exchange")
```

As of Spark v2.3.0, the following file-based formats are supported by Structured Streaming. These are the same file formats supported by the static `DataFrame`, `Data set`, and SQL APIs:

- CSV
- JSON
- Parquet
- ORC
- text
- textFile

Common Options

Regardless of the specific format, the general functionality of the File source is to monitor a directory in a shared filesystem identified by its specific URL. All file formats support a common set of options that control the file inflow and define the aging criteria of the files.

 As Apache Spark is a fast-evolving project, APIs and their options might change in future versions. Also, in this section, we cover only the most relevant options that apply to streaming workloads. For the most up-to-date information, always check the API documentation corresponding to your Spark version (*http:// spark.apache.org/*).

These options can be set for all file-based sources:

`maxFilesPerTrigger` *(Default: unset)*
Indicates how many files will be consumed at each query trigger. This setting limits the number of files processed at each trigger, and in doing so, it helps to control the data inflow in the system.

`latestFirst` *(Default:* `false`*)*
When this flag is set to `true`, newer files are elected for processing first. Use this option when the most recent data has higher priority over older data.

`maxFileAge` *(Default:* `7 days`*)*
Defines an age threshold for the files in the directory. Files older than the threshold will not be eligible for processing and will be effectively ignored. This thres-

hold is relative to the most recent file in the directory and not to the system clock. For example, if `maxFileAge` is 2 days and the most recent file is from yesterday, the threshold to consider a file too old will be *older than three days ago*. This dynamic is similar to watermarks on event time.

`fileNameOnly` *(Default:* `false`*)*

When set to `true`, two files will be considered the same if they have the same name; otherwise, the full path will be considered.

 When `latestFirst` is set to `true` and the `maxFilesPerTrigger` option is configured, `maxFileAge` is ignored because there might be a condition in which files that are valid for processing become older than the threshold because the system gives priority to the most recent files found. In such cases, no aging policy can be set.

Common Text Parsing Options (CSV, JSON)

Some file formats, such as CSV and JSON, use a configurable parser to transform the text data in each file into structured records. It's possible for upstream processes to create records that do not fulfill the expected format. These records are considered corrupted.

Streaming systems are characterized by their continuous running. A streaming process should not fail when bad data is received. Depending on the business requirements, we can either drop the invalid records or route the data considered corrupted to a separate error-handling flow.

Handing parsing errors

The following options allow for the configuration of the parser behavior to handle those records that are considered corrupted:

`mode` *(default* `PERMISSIVE`*)*

Controls the way that corrupted records are handled during parsing. Allowed values are `PERMISSIVE`, `DROPMALFORMED`, and `FAILFAST`.

- `PERMISSIVE`: The value of the corrupted record is inserted in a special field configured by the option `columnNameOfCorruptRecord` that must exist in the schema. All other fields are set to `null`. If the field does not exist, the record is dropped (same behavior as `DROPMALFORMED`).

- `DROPMALFORMED`: Corrupted records are dropped.

- `FAILFAST`: An exception is thrown when a corrupted record is found. This method is not recommended in a streaming process, because the propagation of the exception will potentially make the streaming process fail and stop.

`columnNameOfCorruptRecord` *(default: "_corrupt_record")*

Permits the configuration of the special field that contains the string value of malformed records. This field can also be configured by setting `spark.sql.colum nNameOfCorruptRecord` in the Spark configuration. If both `spark.sql.columnNa meOfCorruptRecord` and this option are set, this option takes precedence.

Schema inference

`inferSchema` *(default:* `false`*)*

Schema inference is not supported. Setting this option is ignored. Providing a *schema* is mandatory.

Date and time formats

`dateFormat` *(default:* `"yyyy-MM-dd"`*)*

Configures the pattern used to parse `date` fields. Custom patterns follow the formats defined at java.text.SimpleDateFormat (*https://docs.oracle.com/javase/8/ docs/api/java/text/SimpleDateFormat.html*).

`timestampFormat` *(default:* `"yyyy-MM-dd'T'HH:mm:ss.SSSXXX"`*)*

Configures the pattern used to parse `timestamp` fields. Custom patterns follow the formats defined at java.text.SimpleDateFormat (*https://docs.oracle.com/ javase/8/docs/api/java/text/SimpleDateFormat.html*).

JSON File Source Format

The JSON format support for the File source lets us consume text files encoded as JSON, in which each line in the file is expected to be a valid JSON object. The JSON records are parsed using the provided schema. Records that do not follow the schema are considered invalid, and there are several options available to control the handling of invalid records.

JSON parsing options

By default, the JSON File source expects the file contents to follow the JSON Lines specification (*http://jsonlines.org/*). That is, each independent line in the file corresponds to a valid JSON document that complies with the specified schema. Each line should be separated by a newline (`\n`) character. A CRLF character (`\r\n`) is also supported because trailing white spaces are ignored.

We can tweak the tolerance of the JSON parser to process data that does not fully comply with the standard. It's also possible to change the behavior to handle those records that are considered corrupted. The following options allow for the configuration of the parser behavior:

allowComments *(default: `false`)*

When enabled, comments in Java/C++ style are allowed in the file and the corresponding line will be ignored; for example:

```
// Timestamps are in ISO 8601 compliant format
{"id":"x097abba", "timestamp": "2018-04-01T16:32:56+00:00"}
{"id":"x053ba0bab", "timestamp": "2018-04-01T16:35:02+00:00"}
```

Otherwise, comments in the JSON file are considered corrupted records and handled following the mode setting.

allowNumericLeadingZeros *(default: `false`)*

When enabled, leading zeros in numbers are allowed (e.g., 00314). Otherwise, the leading zeros are considered invalid numeric values, the corresponding record is deemed corrupted, and it is handled following the mode setting.

allowSingleQuotes *(default: `true`)*

Allows the use of single quotes to demark fields. When enabled, both single quotes and double quotes are allowed. Regardless of this setting, quote characters cannot be nested and must be properly escaped when used within a value; for example:

```
// valid record
{"firstname":"Alice", 'lastname': 'Wonderland'}
// invalid nesting
{"firstname":'Elvis "The King"', 'lastname': 'Presley'}
// correct escaping
{"firstname":'Elvis \"The King\"', 'lastname': 'Presley'}
```

allowUnquotedFieldNames *(default: `false`)*

Allows unquoted JSON field names (e.g., {firstname:"Alice"}). Note that it's not possible to have spaces in field names when using this option (e.g., {first name:"Alice"} is considered corrupted even when the field name matches the schema). Use with caution.

multiLine *(default: `false`)*

When enabled, instead of parsing JSON Lines, the parser will consider the contents of each file as a single valid JSON document and will attempt to parse its contents as records following the defined schema.

Use this option when the producer of the file can output only complete JSON documents as files. In such cases, use a top-level array to group the records, as shown in Example 10-2.

Example 10-2. Using a top-level array to group records

```
[
  {"firstname":"Alice", "last name":"Wonderland", "age": 7},
  {"firstname":"Coraline", "last name":"Spin"    , "age":15}
]
```

primitivesAsString *(default* false*)*

> When enabled, primitive value types are considered strings. This allows you to read documents having fields of mixed types, but all values are read as a String.
>
> In Example 10-3 the resulting age field is of type String, containing values age="15" for *"Coraline"* and age="unknown" for *"Diana"*.

Example 10-3. primitivesAsString usage

```
{"firstname":"Coraline", "last name":"Spin", "age": 15}
{"firstname":"Diana", "last name":"Prince", "age": "unknown"}
```

CSV File Source Format

CSV is a popular tabular data storage and exchange format that is widely supported by enterprise applications. The File Source CSV format support allows us to ingest and process the output of such applications in a Structured Streaming application. Although the name "CSV" originally indicated that values are separated by commas, often the separation character can be freely configured. There are many configuration options available to control the way data is transformed from plain text to structured records.

In the rest of this section, we cover the most common options and, in particular, those that are relevant for the streaming process. For formatting-related options, refer to the latest documentation (*https://spark.apache.org/docs/latest/api/scala/index.html#org.apache.spark.sql.DataFrameReader#csv*). These are the most commonly used CSV parsing options:

CSV parsing options

comment *(default: "" [disabled])*

> Configures a character that marks lines considered as comments; for example, when using option("comment","#"), we can parse the following CSV with a comment in it:

```
#Timestamps are in ISO 8601 compliant format
x097abba, 2018-04-01T16:32:56+00:00, 55
x053ba0bab, 2018-04-01T16:35:02+00:00, 32
```

header *(default:* `false`*)*
> Given that a schema must be provided, the header line is ignored and has no effect.

`multiline` *(default:* `false`*)*
> Consider each file as one record spanning all of the lines in the file.

quote *(default:* `"` *[double quote])*
> Configures the character used to enclose values that contain a column separator.

sep *(default:* `,` *[comma])*
> Configures the character that separates the fields in each line.

Parquet File Source Format

Apache Parquet is a column-oriented, file-based data storage format. The internal representation splits original rows into chunks of columns that are stored using compression techniques. As a consequence, queries that require specific columns do not need to read the complete file. Instead, the relevant pieces can be independently addressed and retrieved. Parquet supports complex nested data structures and preserves the schema structure of the data. Due to its enhanced query capabilities, efficient use of storage space and the preservation of schema information, Parquet is a popular format for storing large, complex datasets.

Schema definition

To create a streaming source from Parquet files, it is sufficient to provide the schema of the data and the directory location. The schema provided during the streaming declaration is fixed for the duration of the streaming source definition.

Example 10-4 shows the creation of a Parquet-based File source from a folder in `hdfs://data/folder` using the provided schema.

Example 10-4. Building a Parquet source example

```
// Use format and load path
val fileStream = spark.readStream
  .schema(schema)
  .parquet("hdfs://data/folder")
```

Text File Source Format

The text format for the File source supports the ingestion of plain-text files. Using configuration options, it's possible to ingest the text either line by line or the entire file as a single text blob. The schema of the data produced by this source is naturally `StringType` and does not need to be specified. This is a generic format that we can use to ingest arbitrary text for further programmatic processing, from the famous word count to custom parsing of proprietary text formats.

Text ingestion options

Next to the common options for the File source that we saw in "Common Options" on page 119, the text file format supports reading text files as a whole using the `whole text` option:

`wholetext` (*default* `false`)
>   If true, read the complete file as a single text blob. Otherwise, split the text into lines using the standard line separators (`\n`, `\r\n`, `\r`) and consider each line a record.

text and textFile

The text format supports two API alternatives:

`text`
>   Returns a dynamically typed `DataFrame` with a single `value` field of type `String Type`

`textFile`
>   Returns a statically typed `Dataset[String]`

We can use the `text` format specification as a terminating method call or as a `format` option. To obtain a statically typed `Dataset`, we must use `textFile` as the last call of the stream builder call. The examples in Example 10-5 illustrate the specific API usage.

Example 10-5. Text format API usage

```
// Text specified as format
>val fileStream = spark.readStream.format("text").load("hdfs://data/folder")
fileStream: org.apache.spark.sql.DataFrame = [value: string]

// Text specified through dedicated method
>val fileStream = spark.readStream.text("hdfs://data/folder")
fileStream: org.apache.spark.sql.DataFrame = [value: string]

// TextFile specified through dedicated method
val fileStream = spark.readStream.textFile("/tmp/data/stream")
fileStream: org.apache.spark.sql.Dataset[String] = [value: string]
```

The Kafka Source

Apache Kafka is a Publish/Subscribe (pub/sub) system based on the concept of a distributed log. Kafka is highly scalable and offers high-throughput, low-latency handling of the data at the consumer and producer sides. In Kafka, the unit of organization is a topic. Publishers send data to a topic and subscribers receive data from the topic to which they subscribed. This data delivery happens in a reliable way. Apache Kafka has become a popular choice of messaging infrastructure for a wide range of streaming use cases.

The Structured Streaming source for Kafka implements the subscriber role and can consume data published to one or several topics. This is a reliable source. Recall from our discussion in "Understanding Sources" on page 113, this means that data delivery semantics are guaranteed even in case of partial or total failure and restart of the streaming process.

Setting Up a Kafka Source

To create a Kafka source, we use the `format("kafka")` method with the `create Stream` builder on the Spark Session. We need two mandatory parameters to connect to Kafka: the addresses of the Kafka brokers, and the topic(s) to which we want to connect.

The address of the Kafka brokers to connect to is provided through the option `kafka.bootstrap.servers` as a `String` containing a comma-separated list of `host:port` pairs.

Example 10-6 presents a simple Kafka source definition. It subscribes to a single topic, `topic1`, by connecting to the brokers located at `host1:port1`, `host2:port2`, and `host3:port3`.

Example 10-6. Creating a Kafka source

```
>val kafkaStream = spark.readStream
  .format("kafka")
  .option("kafka.bootstrap.servers", "host1:port1,host2:port2,host3:port3")
  .option("subscribe", "topic1")
  .option("checkpointLocation", "hdfs://spark/streaming/checkpoint")
  .load()

kafkaStream: org.apache.spark.sql.DataFrame =
  [key: binary, value: binary ... 5 more fields]

>kafkaStream.printSchema

root
 |-- key: binary (nullable = true)
```

```
|-- value: binary (nullable = true)
|-- topic: string (nullable = true)
|-- partition: integer (nullable = true)
|-- offset: long (nullable = true)
|-- timestamp: timestamp (nullable = true)
|-- timestampType: integer (nullable = true)

>val dataStream = kafkaStream.selectExpr("CAST(key AS STRING)",
                                         "CAST(value AS STRING)")
                             .as[(String, String)]

dataStream: org.apache.spark.sql.Dataset[(String, String)] =
  [key: string, value: string]
```

The result of that call is a `DataFrame` with five fields: `key`, `value`, `topic`, `partition`, `offset`, `timestamp`, `timestampType`. Having a schema consisting of these five fields is fixed the Kafka source. It provides the raw `key` and `values` from Kafka and the metadata of each consumed record.

Usually, we are interested in only the `key` and `value` of the message. Both the `key` and the `value` contain a binary payload, represented internally as a `Byte Array`. When the data is written to Kafka using a `String` serializer, we can read that data back by casting the values to `String` as we have done in the last expression in the example. Although text-based encoding is a common practice, it's not the most space-efficient way of exchanging data. Other encodings, such as the schema-aware AVRO format, might offer a better space efficiency with the added benefit of embedding the schema information.

The additional metadata in the message, such as `topic`, `partition`, or `offset` can be used in more complex scenarios. For example, the topic field will contain the *topic* that produced the record and could be used as a label or discriminator, in case we subscribe to several topics at the same time.

Selecting a Topic Subscription Method

There are three different ways to specify the topic or topics that we want to consume:

- `subscribe`
- `subscribePattern`
- `assign`

The Kafka source setup must contain one and only one of these subscription options. They provide different levels of flexibility to select the topic(s) and even the partitions to subscribe to:

subscribe

> Takes a single topic or a list of comma-separated topics: `topic1`, `topic2`, `...`, `topicn`. This method subscribes to each topic and creates a single, unified stream with the data of the union of all the topics; for example, `.option("subscribe", "topic1,topic3")`.

subscribePattern

> This is similar to `subscribe` in behavior, but the topics are specified with a regular expression pattern. For example, if we have topics `'factory1Sensors'`, `'factory2Sensors'`, `'street1Sensors'`, `'street2Sensors'`, we can subscribe to all "factory" sensors with the expression `.option("subscribePattern", "factory[\\d]+Sensors")`.

assign

> Allows the fine-grained specification of specific partitions per topic to consume. This is known as `TopicPartitions` in the Kafka API. The partitions per topic are indicated using a JSON object, in which each key is a topic and its value is an array of partitions. For example, the option definition `.option("assign", """{"sensors":[0,1,3]}""")` would subscribe to the partitions 0, 1, and 3 of topic *sensors*. To use this method we need information about the topic partitioning. We can obtain the partition information programmatically by using the Kafka API or through configuration.

Configuring Kafka Source Options

There are two categories of configuration options for the Structured Streaming source for Kafka: dedicated source configuration, and pass-through options that are given directly to the underlying Kafka consumer.

Kafka source-specific options

The following options configure the behavior of the Kafka source. They relate in particular to how offsets are consumed:

startingOffsets *(default:* `latest`*)*

> Accepted values are `earliest`, `latest`, or a JSON object representing an association between topics, their partitions, and a given offset. Actual offset values are always positive numbers. There are two special offset values: `-2` denotes `earliest` and `-1` means `latest`; for example, `""" {"topic1": { "0": -1, "1": -2, "2":1024 }} """`
>
> `startingOffsets` are only used the first time a query is started. All subsequent restarts will use the *checkpoint* information stored. To restart a streaming job from a specific offset, we need to remove the contents of the *checkpoint*.

`failOnDataLoss` *(default:* `true`*)*

> This flag indicates whether to fail the restart of a streaming query in case data might be lost. This is usually when offsets are out of range, topics are deleted, or topics are rebalanced. We recommend setting this option to `false` during the develop/test cycle because stop/restart of the query side with a continuous producer will often trigger a failure. Set this back to `true` for production deployment.

`kafkaConsumer.pollTimeoutMs` *(default:* `512`*)*

> The poll timeout (in milliseconds) to wait for data from Kafka in the distributed consumers running on the Spark executors.

`fetchOffset.numRetries` *(default:* `3`*)*

> The number of retries before failing the fetch of Kafka offsets.

`fetchOffset.retryIntervalMs` *(default:* `10`*)*

> The delay between offset fetch retries in milliseconds.

`maxOffsetsPerTrigger` *(default: not set)*

> This option allows us to set a rate limit to the number of total records to be consumed at each query trigger. The limit configured will be equally distributed among the set of partitions of the subscribed topics.

Kafka Consumer Options

It's possible to pass configuration options through to the underlying Kafka consumer of this source. We do this by adding a `'kafka.'` prefix to the configuration key that we want to set.

For example, to configure Transport Layer Security (TLS) options for the Kafka source, we can set the Kafka consumer configuration option `security.protocol` by setting `kafka.security.protocol` in the source configuration.

Example 10-7 demonstrates how to configure TLS for the Kafka source using this method.

Example 10-7. Kafka source TLS configuration example

```
val tlsKafkaSource = spark.readStream.format("kafka")
  .option("kafka.bootstrap.servers", "host1:port1, host2:port2")
  .option("subscribe", "topsecret")
  .option("kafka.security.protocol", "SSL")
  .option("kafka.ssl.truststore.location", "/path/to/truststore.jks")
  .option("kafka.ssl.truststore.password", "truststore-password")
  .option("kafka.ssl.keystore.location", "/path/to/keystore.jks")
  .option("kafka.ssl.keystore.password", "keystore-password")
```

```
.option("kafka.ssl.key.password", "password")
.load()
```

 For an exhaustive listing of the Kafka consumer configuration options, refer to the official Kafka documentation (*http://bit.ly/ 2HnFl63*).

Banned configuration options

Not all options from the standard consumer configuration can be used because they conflict with the internal process of the source, which is controlled with the settings we saw in "Kafka source-specific options" on page 128.

These options are prohibited, as shown in Table 10-1. This means that attempting to use any of them will result in an `IllegalArgumentException`.

Table 10-1. Banned Kafka options

option	Reason	Alternative
auto.offset.reset	Offsets are managed within Structured Streaming	use startingOffsets instead
enable.auto.commit	Offsets are managed within Structured Streaming	
group.id	A unique group ID is managed internally per query	
key.deserializer	Payload is always represented as a Byte Array	Deserialization into specific formats is done programmatically
value.deserializer	Payload is always represented as a Byte Array	Deserialization into specific formats is done programmatically
interceptor.classes	A consumer interceptor might break the internal data representation	

The Socket Source

The Transmission Control Protocol (or TCP) is a connection-oriented protocol that enables bidirectional communication between a client and a server. This protocol underpins many of the higher-level communication protocols over the internet, such as FTP, HTTP, MQTT, and many others. Although application layer protocols like HTTP add additional semantics on top of a TCP connection, there are many applications that offer a vanilla, text-based TCP connection over a UNIX socket to deliver data.

The Socket source is a TCP socket client able to connect to a TCP server that offers a UTF-8 encoded text-based data stream. It connects to a TCP server using a host and port provided as mandatory options.

Configuration

To connect to a TCP server, we need the address of the host and a port number. It's also possible to configure the Socket source to add the timestamp at which each line of data is received.

These are the configuration options:

host *(mandatory)*
> The DNS hostname or IP address of the TCP server to which to connect.

port *(mandatory)*
> The port number of the TCP server to which to connect.

includeTimestamp *(default:* false*)*
> When enabled, the Socket source adds the timestamp of arrival to each line of data. It also changes the schema produced by this *source*, adding the timestamp as an additional field.

In Example 10-8, we observe the two modes of operation that this source offers. With the host, port configuration, the resulting streaming DataFrame has a single field named value of type String. When we add the flag includeTimestamp set to true, the schema of the resulting streaming DataFrame contains the fields value and time stamp, where value is of type String as before, and timestamp is of type Timestamp. Also, observe the log warning this source prints at creation.

Example 10-8. Socket source examples

```
// Only using host and port

>val stream = spark.readStream
  .format("socket")
  .option("host", "localhost")
  .option("port", 9876)
  .load()

18/04/14 17:02:34 WARN TextSocketSourceProvider:
The socket source should not be used for production applications!
It does not support recovery.

stream: org.apache.spark.sql.DataFrame = [value: string]

// With added timestamp information

val stream = spark.readStream
  .format("socket")
  .option("host", "localhost")
  .option("port", 9876)
  .option("includeTimestamp", true)
```

```
  .load()
```

```
18/04/14 17:06:47 WARN TextSocketSourceProvider:
The socket source should not be used for production applications!
It does not support recovery.
```

```
stream: org.apache.spark.sql.DataFrame = [value: string, timestamp: timestamp]
```

Operations

The Socket source creates a TCP client that connects to a TCP server specified in the configuration. This client runs on the Spark driver. It keeps the incoming data in memory until it is consumed by the query and the corresponding offset is committed. The data from committed offsets is evicted, keeping the memory usage stable under normal circumstances.

Recall from the discussion in "Understanding Sources" on page 113, a source is considered reliable if it can replay an uncommitted offset even in the event of failure and restart of the streaming process. This source is not considered to be reliable, because a failure of the Spark driver will result in losing all uncommitted data in memory.

This source should be used only for cases in which data loss is acceptable for the use case.

> A common architectural alternative to directly connecting to a TCP server using the Socket source is to use Kafka as a reliable intermediate storage. A robust microservice can be used to bridge the TCP server and Kafka. This microservice collects the data from the TCP server and delivers it atomically to Kafka. Then, we can use the reliable Kafka source to consume the data and further process it in Structured Streaming.

The Rate Source

The Rate source is an internal stream generator that produces a sequence of records at a configurable frequency, given in records/second. The output is a stream of records (timestamp, value) where timestamp corresponds to the moment of generation of the record, and value is an ever-increasing counter:

```
> val stream = spark.readStream.format("rate").load()

stream: org.apache.spark.sql.DataFrame = [timestamp: timestamp, value: bigint]
```

This is intended for benchmarks and for exploring Structured Streaming, given that it does not rely on external systems to work. As we can appreciate in the previous example, it is very easy to create and completely self-contained.

The code in Example 10-9 creates a rate stream of 100 rows per second with a ramp-up time of 60 seconds. The schema of the resulting `DataFrame` contains two fields: `timestamp` of type `Timestamp`, and `value`, which is a `BigInt` at schema level, and a `Long` in the internal representation.

Example 10-9. Rate source example

```
> val stream = spark.readStream.format("rate")
  .option("rowsPerSecond", 100)
  .option("rampUpTime",60)
  .load()
stream: org.apache.spark.sql.DataFrame = [timestamp: timestamp, value: bigint]
```

Options

The Rate source supports a few options that control the throughput and level of parallelism:

`rowsPerSecond` *(default: 1)*
    The number of rows to generate each second.

`rampUpTime` *(default: 0)*
    At the start of the stream, the generation of records will increase progressively until this time has been reached. The increase is linear.

`numPartitions` *(default: default spark parallelism level)*
    The number of partitions to generate. More partitions increase the parallelism level of the record generation and downstream query processing.

## CHAPTER 11

Structured Streaming Sinks

In the previous chapter, you learned about sources, the abstraction that allows Structured Streaming to acquire data for processing. After that data has been processed, we would want to do something with it. We might want to write it to a database for later querying, to a file for further (batch) processing, or to another streaming backend to keep the data in motion.

In Structured Streaming, *sinks* are the abstraction that represents how to produce data to an external system. Structured Streaming comes with several built-in sources and defines an API that lets us create custom sinks to other systems that are not natively supported.

In this chapter, we look at how a sink works, review the details of the sinks provided by Structured Streaming, and explore how to create custom sinks to write data to systems not supported by the default implementations.

Understanding Sinks

Sinks serve as output adaptors between the internal data representation in Structured Streaming and external systems. They provide a write path for the data resulting from the stream processing. Additionally, they must also close the loop of reliable data delivery.

To participate in the end-to-end reliable data delivery, sinks must provide an *idempotent* write operation. Idempotent means that the result of executing the operation two or more times is equal to executing the operation once. When recovering from a failure, Spark might reprocess some data that was partially processed at the time the failure occurred. At the side of the source, this is done by using the replay functionality. Recall from "Understanding Sources" on page 113, reliable sources must provide a means of replaying uncommitted data, based on a given offset. Likewise, sinks must provide the means of removing duplicated records before those are written to the external source.

The combination of a replayable source and an idempotent sink is what grants Structured Streaming its *effectively exactly once* data delivery semantics. Sinks that are not able to implement the idempotent requirement will result in end-to-end delivery guarantees of at most "at least once" semantics. Sinks that are not able to recover from the failure of the streaming process are deemed "unreliable" because they might lose data.

In the next section, we go over the available sinks in Structured Streaming in detail.

 Third-party vendors might provide custom Structured Streaming sinks for their products. When integrating one of these external sinks in your project, consult their documentation to determine the data delivery warranties they support.

Available Sinks

Structured Streaming comes with several sinks that match the supported sources as well as sinks that let us output data to temporary storage or to the console. In rough terms, we can divide the provided sinks into reliable and learning/experimentation support. In addition, it also offers a programmable interface that allows us to work with arbitrary external systems.

Reliable Sinks

The sinks considered reliable or production ready provide well-defined data delivery semantics and are resilient to total failure of the streaming process.

The following are the provided reliable sinks:

The File sink
   This writes data to files in a directory in the filesystem. It supports the same file formats as the File source: JSON, Parquet, comma-separated values (CSV), and Text.

The Kafka sink
   This writes data to Kafka, effectively keeping the data "on the move." This is an interesting option to integrate the results of our process with other streaming frameworks that rely on Kafka as the data backbone.

Sinks for Experimentation

The following sinks are provided to support interaction and experimentation with Structured Streaming. They do not provide failure recovery and therefore their use in production is discouraged because it can result in data loss.

The following are nonreliable sinks:

The Memory sink
> This creates a temporary table with the results of the streaming query. The resulting table can be queried within the same Java virtual machine (JVM) process, which allows in-cluster queries to access the results of the streaming process.

The Console sink
> This prints the results of the query to the console. This is useful at development time to visually inspect the results of the stream process.

The Sink API

Next to the built-in sinks, we also have the option to create a sink programmatically. This is achieved with the `foreach` operation that, as its name implies, offers access to each individual resulting record of the output stream. Finally, it is possible to develop our own custom sinks using the `sink` API directly.

Exploring Sinks in Detail

In the rest of this chapter, we explore the configuration and options available for each sink. We present in-depth coverage of the reliable sinks that should provide a thorough view of their applicability and can serve as a reference when you begin developing your own applications.

The experimental sinks are limited in scope, and that is also reflected in the level of coverage that follows.

Toward the end of this chapter, we look at the custom `sink` API options and review the considerations we need to take when developing our own sinks.

 If you are in your initial exploration phase of Structured Streaming, you might want to skip this section and come back to it later, when you are busy developing your own Structured Streaming jobs.

The File Sink

Files are a common intersystem boundary. When used as a sink for a streaming process, they allow the data to become *at rest* after the stream-oriented processing. Those files can become part of a *data lake* or can be consumed by other (batch) processes as part of a larger processing pipeline that combines streaming and batch modes.

Scalable, reliable, and distributed filesystems—such as HDFS or object stores like Amazon Simple Storage Service (Amazon S3)—make it possible to store large datasets as files in arbitrary formats. When running in local mode, at exploration or development time, it's possible to use the local filesystem for this sink.

The File sink supports the same formats as the File source:

- CSV
- JSON
- Parquet
- ORC
- Text

 Structured Streaming shares the same File *Data Source* implementation used in batch mode. The write options offered by the Data FrameWriter for each File format are also available in streaming mode. In this section, we highlight the most commonly used options. For the most up-to-date list, always consult the online documentation for your specific Spark version.

Before going into the details of each format, let's explore a general File sink example that's presented in Example 11-1.

Example 11-1. File sink example

```
// assume an existing streaming dataframe df
val query = stream.writeStream
  .format("csv")
  .option("sep", "\t")
  .outputMode("append")
  .trigger(Trigger.ProcessingTime("30 seconds"))
  .option("path","<dest/path>")
  .option("checkpointLocation", "<checkpoint/path>")
  .start()
```

In this example, we are using the `csv` format to write the stream results to the `<dest/ path>` destination directory using `TAB` as the custom separator. We also specify a `checkpointLocation`, where the checkpoint metadata is stored at regular intervals.

The File sink supports only `append` as `outputMode`, and it can be safely omitted in the `writeStream` declaration. Attempting to use another mode will result in the following exception when the query starts: `org.apache.spark.sql.AnalysisException: Data source ${format} does not support ${output_mode} output mode;`.

Using Triggers with the File Sink

One additional parameter that we see in Example 11-1 is the use of a `trigger`. When no trigger is specified, Structured Streaming starts the processing of a new batch as soon as the previous one is finished. In the case of the File sink, and depending on the throughput of the input stream, this might result in the generation of many small files. This might be detrimental for the filesystem storage capacity and performance.

Consider Example 11-2.

Example 11-2. Rate source with File sink

```
val stream = spark.readStream.format("rate").load()
val query = stream.writeStream
  .format("json")
  .option("path","/tmp/data/rate")
  .option("checkpointLocation", "/tmp/data/rate/checkpoint")
  .start()
```

If we let this query run for a little while and then we check the target directory, we should observe a large number of small files:

```
$ ls -1
part-00000-03a1ed33-3203-4c54-b3b5-dc52646311b2-c000.json
part-00000-03be34a1-f69a-4789-ad65-da351c9b2d49-c000.json
part-00000-03d296dd-c5f2-4945-98a8-993e3c67c1ad-c000.json
part-00000-0645a678-b2e5-4514-a782-b8364fb150a6-c000.json
...

# Count the files in the directory
$ ls -1 | wc -l
562

# A moment later
$ ls -1 | wc -l
608

# What's the content of a file?
$ cat part-00007-e74a5f4c-5e04-47e2-86f7-c9194c5e85fa-c000.json
{"timestamp":"2018-05-13T19:34:45.170+02:00","value":104}
```

As we learned in Chapter 10, the Rate source generates one record per second by default. When we see the data contained in one file, we can indeed see that single record. The query is, in fact, generating one file each time new data is available. Although the contents of that file is not large, filesystems incur some overhead in keeping track of the number of files in the filesystem. Even more, in the Hadoop Distributed File System (HDFS) each file occupies a block and replicates n times regardless of the contents. Given that the typical HDFS block is 128 MB, we can see how our naive query that uses a File sink can quickly deplete our storage.

The `trigger` configuration is there to help us avoid this situation. By providing time triggers for the production of files, we can ensure that we have a reasonably sufficient amount of data in each file.

We can observe the effect of a time `trigger` by modifying our previous example as follows:

```
import org.apache.spark.sql.streaming.Trigger

val stream = spark.readStream.format("rate").load()
val query = stream.writeStream
  .format("json")
  .trigger(Trigger.ProcessingTime("1 minute")) // <-- Add Trigger configuration
  .option("path","/tmp/data/rate")
  .option("checkpointLocation", "/tmp/data/rate/checkpoint")
  .start()
```

Let's issue the query and wait for a couple of minutes. When we inspect the target directory, we should see considerably fewer files than before, and each file should contain more records. The number of records per file depends on the `DataFrame` partitioning:

```
$ ls -1
part-00000-2ffc26f9-bd43-42f3-93a7-29db2ffb93f3-c000.json
part-00000-3cc02262-801b-42ed-b47e-1bb48c78185e-c000.json
part-00000-a7e8b037-6f21-4645-9338-fc8cf1580eff-c000.json
part-00000-ca984a73-5387-49fe-a864-bd85e502fd0d-c000.json
...

# Count the files in the directory
$ ls -1 | wc -l
34

# Some seconds later
$ ls -1 | wc -l
42

# What's the content of a file?

$ cat part-00000-ca984a73-5387-49fe-a864-bd85e502fd0d-c000.json
{"timestamp":"2018-05-13T22:02:59.275+02:00","value":94}
```

```
{"timestamp":"2018-05-13T22:03:00.275+02:00","value":95}
{"timestamp":"2018-05-13T22:03:01.275+02:00","value":96}
{"timestamp":"2018-05-13T22:03:02.275+02:00","value":97}
{"timestamp":"2018-05-13T22:03:03.275+02:00","value":98}
{"timestamp":"2018-05-13T22:03:04.275+02:00","value":99}
{"timestamp":"2018-05-13T22:03:05.275+02:00","value":100}
```

If you are trying this example on a personal computer, the number of partitions defaults to the number of cores present. In our case, we have eight cores, and we observe seven or eight records per partition. That's still very few records, but it shows the principle that can be extrapolated to real scenarios.

Even though a `trigger` based on the number of records or the size of the data would arguably be more interesting in this scenario, currently, only time-based triggers are supported. This might change in the future, as Structured Streaming evolves.

Common Configuration Options Across All Supported File Formats

We have already seen in previous examples the use of the method `option` that takes a key and a value to set configuration options in a sink.

All supported file formats share the following configuration options:

path
> A directory in a target filesystem where the streaming query writes the data files.

checkpointLocation
> A directory in a resilient filesystem where the checkpointing metadata is stored. New checkpoint information is written with each query execution interval.

compression *(default: None)*
> All supported file formats share the capability to compress the data, although the available compression `codecs` might differ from format to format. The specific compression algorithms are shown for each format in their corresponding section.

 When configuring options of the File sink, it's often useful to remember that any file written by the File sink can be read back using the corresponding File source. For example, when we discussed "JSON File Source Format" on page 121, we saw that it normally expects each line of the file to be a valid JSON document. Likewise, the JSON sink format will produce files containing one record per line.

Common Time and Date Formatting (CSV, JSON)

Text-based files formats such as CSV and JSON accept custom formatting for date and timestamp data types:

dateFormat *(default:* yyyy-MM-dd*)*
> Configures the pattern used to format date fields. Custom patterns follow the formats defined at java.text.SimpleDateFormat (*http://bit.ly/2VwrLku*).

timestampFormat *(default "yyyy-MM-dd'T'HH:mm:ss.SSSXXX")*
> Configures the pattern used to format timestamp fields. Custom patterns follow the formats defined at java.text.SimpleDateFormat (*http://bit.ly/2VwrLku*).

timeZone *(default: local timezone)*
> Configures the time zone to use to format timestamps.

The CSV Format of the File Sink

Using the CSV File format, we can write our data in a ubiquitous tabular format that can be read by many programs, from spreadsheet applications to a wide range of enterprise software.

Options

The CSV support in Spark supports many options to control the field separator, quoting behavior, and the inclusion of a header. In addition to that, the common File sink options and the date formatting options apply to the CSV sink.

> In this section, we list the most commonly used options. For a comprehensive list, check the online documentation (*http://bit.ly/2EdjVqe*).

Following are the commonly used options for the CSV sink:

header *(default:* false*)*
> A flag to indicate whether we should include a header to the resulting file. The header consists of the name of the fields in this streaming DataFrame.

quote *(default: " [double quote])*
> Sets the character used to quote records. Quoting is necessary when records might contain the separator character, which, without quoting, would result in corrupt records.

quoteAll *(default: `false`)*
> A flag used to indicate whether all values should be quoted or only those that contain a separator character. Some external systems require all values to be quoted. When using the CSV format to import the resulting files in an external system, check that system's import requirements to correctly configure this option.

sep *(default: `,` [comma])*
> Configures the separator character used between fields. The separator must be a single character. Otherwise, the query will throw an `IllegalArgumentException` at runtime when it starts.

The JSON File Sink Format

The JSON File sink lets us write output data to files using the JSON Lines format. This format transforms each record in the output dataset into a valid JSON document written in a line of text. The JSON File sink is symmetrical to the JSON source. As we would expect, files written with this format can be read again using the JSON source.

> When using third-party JSON libraries to read the resulting files, we should take care of first reading the file(s) as lines of text and then parse each line as a JSON document representing one record.

Options

Next to the common file and text format options, the JSON sink supports these specific configurations:

encoding *(default: `UTF-8`)*
> Configures the charset encoding used to write the JSON files.

lineSep *(default: `\n`)*
> Sets the line separator to be used between JSON records.

Supported `compression` options (default: `none`): `none`, `bzip2`, `deflate`, `gzip`, `lz4`, and `snappy`.

The Parquet File Sink Format

The Parquet File sink supports the common File sink configuration and does not have format-specific options.

Supported `compression` options (default: `snappy`): `none`, `gzip`, `lzo`, and `snappy`.

The Text File Sink Format

The text file sink writes plain-text files. Although the other file formats would perform a conversion from the streaming `DataFrame` or `Dataset` schema to the particular file format structure, the text sink expects either a flattened streaming `Dataset[String]` or a streaming `DataFrame` with a schema containing a single `value` field of `StringType`.

The typical use of the text file format is to write custom text-based formats not natively supported in Structured Streaming. To achieve this goal, we first transform programmatically the data into the desired text representation. After that, we use the text format to write the data to files. Attempting to write any complex schema to a text sink will result in an error.

Options

Beside the common options for sinks and text-based formats, the text sink supports the following configuration option:

`lineSep` (*default:* \n)
  Configures the line separator used for terminating each text line.

The Kafka Sink

As we discussed in "The Kafka Source" on page 126, Kafka is a Publish/Subscribe (pub/sub) system. Although the Kafka source functions as a subscriber, the Kafka sink is the publisher counterpart. The Kafka sink allows us to write data (back) to Kafka, which then can be consumed by other subscribers to continue a chain of streaming processors.

Downstream consumers might be other streaming processors, implemented using Structured Streaming or any of the other streaming frameworks available, or (micro) services that consume the streaming data to fuel applications in the enterprise ecosystem.

Understanding the Kafka Publish Model

In Kafka, data is represented as key–value records exchanged over a topic. Topics are composed of distributed partitions. Each partition maintains the messages in the order in which they were received. This ordering is indexed by an offset, which, in turn, is used by the consumer to indicate the record(s) to read. When a record is published to a topic, it's placed in a partition of a topic. The choice of the partition depends on the key. The ruling principle is that a record with the same key will land in the same partition. As a result, the ordering in Kafka is partial. The sequence of

---

records from a single partition will be ordered sequentially by arrival time but there are no ordering guarantees among partitions.

This model is highly scalable and Kafka implementation ensures low-latency reads and writes, making it an excellent carrier for streaming data.

Using the Kafka Sink

Now that you've learned about the Kafka publishing model, we can look at the practical side of producing data to Kafka. We just saw that the Kafka records are structured as key–value pairs. We need to structure our data in the same shape.

In a minimal implementation, we must ensure that our streaming `DataFrame` or `Data set` has a `value` field of `BinaryType` or `StringType`. The implication of this requirement is that we usually need to encode our data into a transport representation before sending it to Kafka.

When the key is not specified, Structured Streaming will replace the `key` with `null`. This makes the Kafka sink use a round-robin assignment of the partition for the corresponding topic.

If we want to preserve control over the key assignment, we must have a `key` field, also of `BinaryType` or `StringType`. This `key` is used for the partition assignment, resulting in a guaranteed ordering between records with equal keys.

Optionally, we can control the destination topic at the record level by adding a `topic` field. If present, the `topic` value must correspond to a Kafka topic. Setting the `topic` on the `writeStream` option overrides the value in the `topic` field.

The related record will be published to that topic. This option is useful when implementing a fan-out pattern in which incoming records are sorted in different dedicated topics for further processing. Think for example about classifying incoming support tickets into dedicated sales, technical, and troubleshooting topics that are consumed downstream by their corresponding (micro) service.

After we have the data in the right shape, we also need the address of the target bootstrap servers in order to connect to the brokers.

In practical terms, this generally involves two steps:

1. Transform each record as a single field called `value` and optionally assign a key and a topic to each record.

2. Declare our stream sink using the `writeStream` builder.

Example 11-3 shows these steps in use.

Example 11-3. Kafka sink example

```
// Assume an existing streaming dataframe 'sensorData'
// with schema: id: String, timestamp: Long, sensorType: String, value: Double

// Create a key and a value from each record:

val kafkaFormattedStream = sensorData.select(
  $"id" as "key",
  to_json(
    struct($"id", $"timestamp", $"sensorType", $"value")
  ) as "value"
)

// In step two, we declare our streaming query:

val kafkaWriterQuery = kafkaFormat.writeStream
  .queryName("kafkaWriter")
  .outputMode("append")
  .format("kafka") // determines that the kafka sink is used
  .option("kafka.bootstrap.servers", kafkaBootstrapServer)
  .option("topic", targetTopic)
  .option("checkpointLocation", "/path/checkpoint")
  .option("failOnDataLoss", "false") // use this option when testing
  .start()
```

When we add `topic` information at the record level, we must omit the `topic` configuration option.

In Example 11-4, we modify the previous code to write each record to a dedicated topic matching the `sensorType`. That is, all `humidity` records go to the humidity topic, all `radiation` records go to the radiation topic, and so on.

Example 11-4. Kafka sink to different topics

```
// assume an existing streaming dataframe 'sensorData'
// with schema: id: String, timestamp: Long, sensorType: String, value: Double

// Create a key, value and topic from each record:

val kafkaFormattedStream = sensorData.select(
  $"id" as "key",
  $"sensorType" as "topic",
  to_json(struct($"id", $"timestamp", $"value")) as "value"
)

// In step two, we declare our streaming query:

val kafkaWriterQuery = kafkaFormat.writeStream
  .queryName("kafkaWriter")
  .outputMode("append")
```

```
.format("kafka") // determines that the kafka sink is used
.option("kafka.bootstrap.servers", kafkaBootstrapServer)
.option("checkpointLocation", "/path/checkpoint")
.option("failOnDataLoss", "false") // use this option when testing
.start()
```

Note that we have removed the setting `option("topic", targetTopic)` and added a `topic` field to each record. This results in each record being routed to the topic corresponding to its `sensorType`. If we leave the setting `option("topic", targetTopic)` in place, the value of the `topic` field would have no effect. The `option("topic", targetTopic)` setting takes precedence.

Choosing an encoding

When we look closely at the code in Example 11-3, we see that we create a single `value` field by converting the existing data into its JSON representation. In Kafka, each record consists of a key and a value. The `value` field contains the payload of the record. To send or receive a record of arbitrary complexity to and from Kafka, we need to convert said record into a single-field representation that we can fit into this `value` field. In Structured Streaming, the conversion to and from this transport value representation to the actual record must be done through user code. Ideally, the encoding we choose can be easily transformed into a structured record to take advantage of the Spark capabilities to manipulate data.

A common encoding format is JSON. JSON has native support in the structured APIs of Spark, and that extends to Structured Streaming. As we saw in Example 11-4, we write JSON by using the SQL function `to_json`: `to_json(struct($"id", $"timestamp", $"value")) as "value")`.

Binary representations such as AVRO and ProtoBuffers are also possible. In such cases, we treat the `value` field as a `BinaryType` and use third-party libraries to do the encoding/decoding.

As of this writing, there is no built-in support for binary encodings, but AVRO support has been announced for an upcoming version.

An important factor to consider when choosing an encoding format is schema support. In a multiservice model that uses Kafka as the communications backbone, it's typical to find services producing data that use a different programming model, language, and/or framework than a streaming processor or other service that consumes it.

To ensure interoperability, schema-oriented encodings are the preferred choice. Having a schema definition allows for the creation of artifacts in different languages and ensures that produced data can be consumed later on.

The Memory Sink

The Memory sink is a nonreliable sink that saves the results of the stream processing in an in-memory temporary table. It is considered nonreliable because all data will be lost in the case the streaming process ends, but it's certainly useful in scenarios for which low-latency access to the streaming results are is required.

The temporary table created by this sink is named after the query name. This table is backed up by the streaming query and will be updated at each trigger following the semantics of the chosen outputMode.

The resulting table contains an up-to-date view of the query results and can be queried using classical Spark SQL operations. The query must be executed in the same process (JVM) where the Structured Streaming query is started.

The table maintained by the Memory Sink can be accessed interactively. That property makes it an ideal interface with interactive data exploration tools like the Spark REPL or a notebook.

Another common use is to provide a query service on top of the streaming data. This is done by combining a server module, like an HTTP server, with the Spark driver. Calls to specific HTTP endpoints can then be served with data from this in-memory table.

Example 11-5 assumes a sensorData streaming dataset. The result of the stream processing is materialized in this in-memory table, which is available in the SQL context as sample_memory_query.

Example 11-5. Memory sink example

```
val sampleMemoryQuery = sensorData.writeStream
  .queryName("sample_memory_query")    // this query name will be the SQL table name
  .outputMode("append")
  .format("memory")
  .start()
```

```
// After the query starts we can access the data in the temp table
val memData = session.sql("select * from sample_memory_query")
memData.count() // show how many elements we have in our table
```

Output Modes

The Memory sink supports all output modes: Append, Update, and Complete. Hence, we can use it with all queries, including aggregations. The combination of the Memory sink with the Complete mode is particularly interesting because it provides a fast, in-memory queryable store for the up-to-date computed complete state. Note that for a query to support Complete state, it must aggregate over a bounded-cardinality key. This is to ensure that the memory requirements to handle the state are likewise bounded within the system resources.

The Console Sink

For all of us who love to print "Hello, world!" to the screen output, we have the Console sink. Indeed, the Console sink lets us print a small sample of the results of the query to the standard output.

Its use is limited to debugging and data exploration in an interactive shell-based environment, such as the spark-shell. As we would expect, this sink is not reliable given that it does not commit any data to another system.

You should avoid using the Console sink in production environments, much like printlns are frowned upon from an operational code base.

Options

Here are the configurable options for the Console sink:

numRows *(default:* 20*)*
: The maximum number of rows to show at each query trigger.

truncate *(default:* true*)*
: A flag that indicates whether the output of each cell in a row should be truncated.

Output Modes

As of Spark 2.3, the Console sink supports all output modes: Append, Update, and Complete.

The Foreach Sink

There are times when we need to integrate our stream-processing applications with legacy systems in the enterprise. Also, as a young project, the range of available sinks in Structured Streaming is rather limited.

The foreach sink consists of an API and sink definition that provides access to the results of the query execution. It extends the writing capabilities of Structured Streaming to any external system that provides a Java virtual machine (JVM) client library.

The ForeachWriter Interface

To use the Foreach sink we must provide an implementation of the ForeachWriter interface. The ForeachWriter controls the life cycle of the writer operation. Its execution takes place distributed on the executors, and the methods are called for each partition of the streaming DataFrame or Dataset, as demonstrated in Example 11-6.

Example 11-6. The API definition of the ForeachWriter

```
abstract class ForeachWriter[T] extends Serializable {

  def open(partitionId: Long, version: Long): Boolean

  def process(value: T): Unit

  def close(errorOrNull: Throwable): Unit

}
```

As we can see in Example 11-6, the ForeachWriter is bound to a type [T] that corresponds to the type of the streaming Dataset or to spark.sql.Row in case of a streaming DataFrame. Its API consists of three methods: open, process, and close:

open

> This is called at every trigger interval with the partitionId and a unique version number. Using these two parameters, the ForeachWriter must decide whether to process the partition being offered. Returning true will lead to the processing of each element using the logic in the process method. If the method returns false, the partition will be skipped for processing.

process

> This provides access to the data, one element at a time. The function applied to the data must produce a side effect, such as inserting the record in a database,

calling a REST API, or using a networking library to communicate the data to another system.

close

> This is called to notify the end of writing a partition. The error object will be null when the output operation terminated successfully for this partition or will contain a Throwable otherwise. close is called at the end of every partition writing operation, even when open returned false (to indicate that the partition should not be processed).

This contract is part of the data delivery semantics because it allows us to remove duplicated partitions that might already have been sent to the sink but are reprocessed by Structured Streaming as part of a recovery scenario. For that mechanism to properly work, the sink must implement some persistent way to remember the parti tion/version combinations that it has already seen.

After we have our ForeachWriter implementation, we use the customary write Stream method of declaring a sink and we call the dedicated foreach method with the ForeachWriter instance.

The ForeachWriter implementation must be Serializable. This is mandatory because the ForeachWriter is executed distributedly on each node of the cluster that contains a partition of the streaming Dataset or DataFrame being processed. At runtime, a new deserialized copy of the provided ForeachWriter instance will be created for each partition of the Dataset or DataFrame. As a consequence, we might not pass any state in the initial constructor of the ForeachWriter.

Let's put this all together in a small example that shows how the Foreach sink works and illustrates the subtle intricacies of dealing with the state handling and serialization requirements.

TCP Writer Sink: A Practical ForeachWriter Example

For this example, we are going to develop a text-based TCP sink that transmits the results of the query to an external TCP socket receiving server. In this example, we will be using the spark-shell utility that comes with the Spark installation.

In Example 11-7, we create a simple TCP client that can connect and write text to a server socket, provided its host and port. Note that this class is not Serializable. Sockets are inherently nonserializable because they are dependent on the underlying system I/O ports.

Example 11-7. TCP socket client

```scala
class TCPWriter(host:String, port: Int) {
  import java.io.PrintWriter
  import java.net.Socket
  val socket = new Socket(host, port)
  val printer = new PrintWriter(socket.getOutputStream, true)
  def println(str: String) = printer.println(str)
  def close() = {
    printer.flush()
    printer.close()
    socket.close()
  }
}
```

Next, in Example 11-8, we use this TCPWriter in a ForeachWriter implementation.

Example 11-8. TCPForeachWriter implementation

```scala
import org.apache.spark.sql.ForeachWriter
class TCPForeachWriter(host: String, port: Int)
    extends ForeachWriter[RateTick] {

  @transient var writer: TCPWriter = _
  var localPartition: Long = 0
  var localVersion: Long = 0

  override def open(
      partitionId: Long,
      version: Long
    ): Boolean = {
    writer = new TCPWriter(host, port)
    localPartition = partitionId
    localVersion = version
    println(
      s"Writing partition [$partitionId] and version[$version]"
    )
    true // we always accept to write
  }

  override def process(value: RateTick): Unit = {
    val tickString = s"${v.timestamp}, ${v.value}"
    writer.println(
      s"$localPartition, $localVersion, $tickString"
    )
  }

  override def close(errorOrNull: Throwable): Unit = {
    if (errorOrNull == null) {
      println(
        s"Closing partition [$localPartition] and version[$localVersion]"
```

```
      )
      writer.close()
    } else {
      print("Query failed with: " + errorOrNull)
    }
  }
}
```

Pay close attention to how we have declared the TCPWriter variable: @transient var
writer:TCPWriter = _. @transient means that this reference should not be serialized. The initial value is null (using the empty variable initialization syntax _). It's
only in the call to open that we create an instance of TCPWriter and assign it to our
variable for later use.

Also, note how the process method takes an object of type RateTick. Implementing
a ForeachWriter is easier when we have a typed Dataset to start with as we deal with
a specific object structure instead of spark.sql.Rows, which are the generic data container for *streaming DataFrames*. In this case, we transformed the initial streaming
DataFrame to a typed Dataset[RateTick] before proceeding to the sink phase.

Now, to complete our example, we create a simple Rate source and write the produced stream directly to our newly developed TCPForeachWriter:

```
case class RateTick(timestamp: Long, value: Long)

val stream = spark.readStream.format("rate")
                  .option("rowsPerSecond", 100)
                  .load()
                  .as[RateTick]

val writerInstance = new TCPForeachWriter("localhost", 9876)

val query = stream
      .writeStream
      .foreach(writerInstance)
      .outputMode("append")
```

Before starting our query, we run a simple TCP server to observe the results. For this
purpose, we use an nc, a useful *nix command to create TCP/UDP clients and servers
in the command line. In this case, we use a TCP server listening to port 9876:

```
# Tip: the syntax of netcat is system-specific.
# The following command should work on *nix and on OSX nc managed by homebrew.
# Check your system documentation for the proper syntax.
nc -lk 9876
```

Finally, we start our query:

```
val queryExecution = query.start()
```

In the shell running the nc command, we should see output like the following:

```
5, 1, 1528043018, 72
5, 1, 1528043018, 73
5, 1, 1528043018, 74
0, 1, 1528043018, 0
0, 1, 1528043018, 1
0, 1, 1528043018, 2
0, 1, 1528043018, 3
0, 1, 1528043018, 4
0, 1, 1528043018, 5
0, 1, 1528043018, 6
0, 1, 1528043018, 7
0, 1, 1528043018, 8
0, 1, 1528043018, 9
0, 1, 1528043018, 10
0, 1, 1528043018, 11
7, 1, 1528043019, 87
7, 1, 1528043019, 88
7, 1, 1528043019, 89
7, 1, 1528043019, 90
7, 1, 1528043019, 91
7, 1, 1528043019, 92
```

In the output, the first column is the `partition`, and the second is the `version`, followed by the data produced by the `Rate` source. It's interesting to note that the data is ordered within a partition, like `partition 0` in our example, but there are no ordering guarantees among different partitions. Partitions are processed in parallel in different machines of the cluster. There's no guarantee which one comes first.

Finally, to end the query execution, we call the `stop` method:

```
queryExecution.stop()
```

The Moral of this Example

In this example, you have seen how to correctly use a minimalistic `socket` client to output the data of a streaming query with the Foreach sink. Socket communication is the underlying interaction mechanism of most database drivers and many other application clients in the wild. The method that we have illustrated here is a common pattern that you can effectively apply to write to a variety of external systems that offer a JVM-based client library. In a nutshell, we can summarize this pattern as follows:

1. Create a `@transient` mutable reference to our driver class in the body of the `Fore`
   `achWriter`.

2. In the `open` method, initialize a connection to the external system. Assign this connection to the mutable reference. It's guaranteed that this reference will be used by a single thread.

3. In `process`, publish the provided data element to the external system.

4. Finally, in `close`, we terminate all connections and clean up any state.

Troubleshooting ForeachWriter Serialization Issues

In Example 11-8, we saw how we needed an uninitialized mutable reference to the TCPWriter: `@transient var writer:TCPWriter = _`. This seemingly elaborate construct is required to ensure that we instantiate the nonserializable class only when the `ForeachWriter` is already deserialized and running remotely, in an executor.

If we want to explore what happens when we attempt to include a nonserializable reference in a `ForeachWriter` implementation, we could declare our `TCPWriter` instance like this, instead:

```
import org.apache.spark.sql.ForeachWriter
class TCPForeachWriter(host: String, port: Int) extends ForeachWriter[RateTick] {

  val nonSerializableWriter:TCPWriter = new TCPWriter(host,port)
  // ... same code as before ...
}
```

Although this looks simpler and more familiar, when we attempt to run our query with this `ForeachWriter` implementation, we get a `org.apache.spark.SparkExcep tion: Task not serializable`. This produces a very long *stack trace* that contains a best-effort attempt at pointing out the offending class. We must follow the stack trace until we find the `Caused by` statement, such as that shown in the following trace:

```
Caused by: java.io.NotSerializableException: $line17.$read$$iw$$iw$TCPWriter
Serialization stack:
  - object not serializable (class: $line17.$read$$iw$$iw$TCPWriter,
      value: $line17.$read$$iw$$iw$TCPWriter@4f44d3e0)
  - field (class: $line20.$read$$iw$$iw$TCPForeachWriter,
      name: nonSerializableWriter, type: class $line17.$read$$iw$$iw$TCPWriter)
  - object (class $line20.$read$$iw$$iw$TCPForeachWriter,
      $line20.$read$$iw$$iw$TCPForeachWriter@54832ad9)
  - field (class: org.apache.spark.sql.execution.streaming.ForeachSink, name:
      org$apache$spark$sql$execution$streaming$ForeachSink$$writer,
      type: class org.apache.spark.sql.ForeachWriter)
```

As this example was running in the `spark-shell`, we find some weird $$-notation, but when we remove that noise, we can see that the nonserializable object is `object not serializable (class: TCPWriter)`, and the reference to it is the field `field name: nonSerializableWriter, type: class TCPWriter`.

Serialization issues are common in `ForeachWriter` implementations. Hopefully, with the tips in this section, you will be able to avoid any trouble in your own implementation. But for cases when this happens, Spark makes a best-effort attempt at determining the source of the problem. This information, provided in the stack trace, is very valuable to debug and solve these serialization issues.

## CHAPTER 12

Event Time–Based Stream Processing

In "The Effect of Time" on page 25, we discussed the effect of time in stream processing from a general perspective.

As we recall, *event-time processing* refers to looking at the stream of events from the timeline at which they were produced and applying the processing logic from that perspective. When we are interested in analyzing the patterns of the event data over time, it is necessary to process the events as if we were observing them at the time they were produced. To do this, we require the device or system that produces the event to "stamp" the events with the time of creation. Hence, the usual name "timestamp" to refer to a specific event-bound time. We use that time as our frame of reference for how time evolves.

To illustrate this concept, let's explore a familiar example. Consider a network of weather stations used to monitor local weather conditions. Some remote stations are connected through the mobile network, whereas others, hosted at volunteering homes, have access to internet connections of varying quality. The weather monitoring system cannot rely on the arrival order of the events because that order is mostly dependent on the speed and reliability of the network they are connected to. Instead, the weather application relies on each weather station to timestamp the events delivered. Our stream processing then uses these timestamps to compute the time-based aggregations that feed the weather forecasting system.

The capability of a stream-processing engine to use event time is important because we are usually interested in the relative order in which events were produced, not the sequence in which the events are processed. In this chapter, we learn how Structured Streaming provides seamless support for event-time processing.

Understanding Event Time in Structured Streaming

At the server side, the notion of time is ruled by the internal clock of the computers running any given application. In the case of distributed applications running on a cluster of machines, it is a mandatory practice to use a clock synchronization technique and protocol such as *Network Time Protocol* (NTP) to align all clocks to the same time. The purpose is that the different parts of a distributed application running on a cluster of computers can make consistent decisions about the timeline and relative ordering of events.

However, when data is coming from external devices, such as sensor networks, other datacenters, mobile phones, or connected cars, to name few examples, we have no guarantees that their clocks are aligned with our cluster of machines. We need to interpret the timeline of the incoming events from the perspective of the producing system and not in reference to the internal clock of the processing system. Figure 12-1 depicts this scenario.

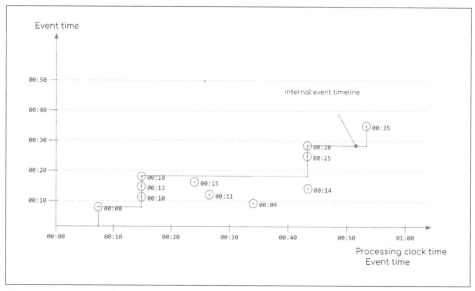

Figure 12-1. Internal event timeline

In Figure 12-1, we visualize how the time is handled in Structured Streaming:

- In the x-axis, we have the processing time, the clock time of the processing system.
- The y-axis represents the internal representation of the event time timeline.
- Events are represented with a circle with their corresponding event time label next to them.

- The event arrival time corresponds to the time on the x-axis.

As events arrive in the system, our internal notion of time progresses:

1. The first event, `00:08`, arrives into the system at `00:07`, "early" from the point of view of the machine clock. We can appreciate that the internal clock time does not affect our perception of the event timeline.

2. The event timeline advances to `00:08`.

3. The next batch of events, `00:10`, `00:12`, `00:18` arrive for processing. The event timeline moves up to `00:18` because it's the maximum observed time so far.

4. `00:15` enters the system. The event timeline remains in its current value of `00:18` as `00:15` is earlier than the current internal time.

5. Likewise, `00:11` and `00:09` are received. Should we process these events or are they too late?

6. When the next set of events are processed, `00:14`, `00:25`, `00:28`, the streaming clock increases up to their maximum of `00:28`.

In general, Structured Streaming infers the timeline of the events processed with event time by keeping a monotonically increasing upper bound of the field declared as timestamp in the events. This nonlinear timeline is the ruling clock used for the time-based processing features in this chapter. The ability of Structured Streaming to understand the time flow of the event source decouples the event generation from the event processing time. In particular, we can replay a sequence of past events and have Structured Streaming produce the correct results for all event-time aggregations. We could, for example, replay a week's worth of events in a few minutes and have our system produce results consistent with a week period. This would be impossible if time were governed by the computer clock.

Using Event Time

In Structured Streaming, we can take advantage of the built-in support for event time in two areas: time-based aggregation and state management.

In both cases, the first step is to have a field in our data in the right format for Structured Streaming to understand it as a timestamp.

Spark SQL supports `java.sql.Timestamp` as a `Timestamp` type. For other base types, we need to first convert the value to a `Timestamp` before we can use it for event-time processing. In Table 12-1, the initial `ts` field contains the timestamp of a given type, and we summarize how to obtain the corresponding `Timestamp` type.

Table 12-1. Obtaining a Timestamp field

ts base type	SQL function
Long	`$"ts".cast(TimestampType))`
String with default format *yyyy-MM-dd HH:mm:ss*	`$"ts".cast(TimestampType)`
String with default format *yyyy-MM-dd HH:mm:ss* (alternative)	`to_timestamp($"ts")`
String with a custom format. eg.*dd-MM-yyyy HH:mm:ss*	`to_timestamp($"ts", "dd-MM-yyyy HH:mm:ss")`

Processing Time

As we discussed in the introduction of this section, we make a distinction between event-time and processing-time processing. Event time relates to the timeline at which events were produced and is independent of the time of processing. In contrast, processing time is the timeline when events are ingested by the engine, and it is based on the clock of the computers processing the event stream. It's is the "now" when the events enter the processing engine.

There are cases in which the event data does not contain time information, but we still want to take advantage of the native time-based functions offered by Structured Streaming. In those cases, we can add a *processing-time* timestamp to the event data and use that timestamp as the event time.

Continuing with the same example, we can add processing-time information using the `current_timestamp` SQL function:

```
// Lets assume an existing streaming dataframe of weather station readings
// (id: String, pressure: Double, temperature: Double)

// we add a processing-time timestamp
val timeStampEvents = raw.withColumn("timestamp", current_timestamp())
```

Watermarks

At the beginning of the chapter, we learned that external factors can affect the delivery of event messages and, hence, when using event time for processing, we didn't have a guarantee of order or delivery. Events might be late or never arrive at all. How late is too late? For how long do we hold partial aggregations before considering them complete? To answer these questions, the concept of watermarks was introduced in Structured Streaming. A watermark is a time threshold that dictates how long we wait for events before declaring that they are too late. Events that are considered late beyond the watermark are discarded.

Watermarks are computed as a threshold based on the internal time representation. As we can appreciate in Figure 12-2, the watermark line is a shifted line from the event-time timeline inferred from the event's time information. In this chart, we can observe that all events falling in the "gray area" below the *watermark* line are considered "too late" and will not be taken into consideration in the computations consuming this event stream.

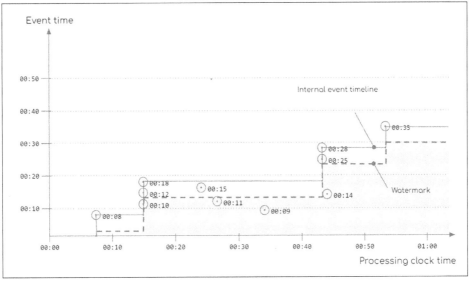

Figure 12-2. Watermark with the internal event timeline

We declare a watermark by linking our `timestamp` field with the time threshold corresponding to the watermark. Continuing with the Table 12-1, we declare a watermark like this:

```
// Lets assume an existing streaming dataframe of weather station readings
// (id: String, ts:Long, pressure: Double, temperature: Double)

val timeStampEvents = raw.withColumn("timestamp", $"ts".cast(TimestampType))
                         .withWatermak("timestamp", "5 minutes")
```

Time-Based Window Aggregations

A natural question that we want to pose to streams of data is aggregated information at regular intervals of time. As streams are potentially never-ending, instead of asking "how many X are there?" in a stream-processing context, we are more interested in knowing "how many X were there in 15-minute intervals."

With the use of event-time processing, Structured Streaming removes the usual complexity of dealing with intermediate state in the face of the event delivery challenges that we have discussed in this chapter. Structured Streaming takes care of keeping partial aggregates of data and of updating the downstream consumer using the semantics corresponding to the chosen output mode.

Defining Time-Based Windows

We discussed the concept of window-based aggregations in "Window Aggregations" on page 19, in which we presented the definitions of *tumbling* and *sliding* windows. In Structured Streaming, the built-in event-time support makes it easy to define and use such window-based operations.

From the API perspective, window aggregations are declared using a `window` function as grouping criteria. The `window` function must be applied to the field that we want to use as event time.

Continuing with our weather station scenario, in Example 12-1 we can compute the average pressure each 10 minutes totalized across all reporting stations.

Example 12-1. Computing totalized averages

```
$>val perMinuteAvg = timeStampEvents
  .withWatermak("timestamp", "5 minutes")
  .groupBy(window($"timestamp", "1 minute"))
  .agg(avg($"pressure"))

$>perMinuteAvg.printSchema // let's inspect the schema of our window aggregation

root
 |-- window: struct (nullable = true)
 |    |-- start: timestamp (nullable = true)
 |    |-- end: timestamp (nullable = true)
 |-- pressureAvg: double (nullable = true)
 |-- tempAvg: double (nullable = true)

$>perMinuteAvg.writeStream.outputMode("append").format("console").start()
// after few minutes
+---------------------------------------------+------------+------------+
|window                                       |pressureAvg |tempAvg     |
+---------------------------------------------+------------+------------+
|[2018-06-17 23:27:00.0,2018-06-17 23:28:00.0]|101.515516867|5.19433723603|
|[2018-06-17 23:28:00.0,2018-06-17 23:29:00.0]|101.481236804|13.4036089642|
|[2018-06-17 23:29:00.0,2018-06-17 23:30:00.0]|101.534757332|7.29652790939|
|[2018-06-17 23:30:00.0,2018-06-17 23:31:00.0]|101.472349471|9.38486237260|
|[2018-06-17 23:31:00.0,2018-06-17 23:32:00.0]|101.523849943|12.3600638827|
|[2018-06-17 23:32:00.0,2018-06-17 23:33:00.0]|101.531088691|11.9662189701|
|[2018-06-17 23:33:00.0,2018-06-17 23:34:00.0]|101.491889383|9.07050033207|
+---------------------------------------------+------------+------------+
```

In this example, we observe that the resulting schema of a windowed aggregation contains the window period, indicated with `start` and `end` timestamp for each resulting window, together with the corresponding computed values.

Understanding How Intervals Are Computed

The window intervals are aligned to the start of the second/minute/hour/day that corresponds to the next upper time magnitude of the time unit used. For example, a window($"timestamp", "15 minutes") will produce 15-minute intervals aligned to the start of the hour.

The start time of the first interval is in the past to adjust the window alignment without any data loss. This implies that the first interval might contain only a fraction of the usual interval worth of data. So, if we are receiving about 100 messages per second, we expect to see about 90,000 messages in 15 minutes, whereas our first window might be just a fraction of that.

The time intervals in a window are inclusive at the start and exclusive at the end. In *interval notation*, this is written as [start-time, end-time). Using the 15-minute intervals as defined earlier, a data point that arrives with timestamp 11:30:00.00 will belong to the 11:30-11:45 window interval.

Using Composite Aggregation Keys

In Example 12-1, we calculated globally aggregated values for the pressure and temperature sensors. We are also interested in computing aggregated values for each weather station. We can achieve that by creating a composite aggregation key where we add the stationId to the aggregation criteria in the same way that we would do that with the static DataFrame API. Example 12-2 illustrates how we do this.

Example 12-2. Computing averages per station

```
$>val minuteAvgPerStation = timeStampEvents
  .withWatermak("timestamp", "5 minutes")
  .groupBy($"stationId", window($"timestamp", "1 minute"))
  .agg(avg($"pressure") as "pressureAvg", avg($"temp") as "tempAvg")

// The aggregation schema now contains the station Id
$>minuteAvgPerStation.printSchema
root
 |-- stationId: string (nullable = true)
 |-- window: struct (nullable = true)
 |    |-- start: timestamp (nullable = true)
 |    |-- end: timestamp (nullable = true)
 |-- pressureAvg: double (nullable = true)
 |-- tempAvg: double (nullable = true)

$>minuteAvgPerStation.writeStream.outputMode("append").format("console").start

+---------+---------------------------------------------+-----------+-----------+
|stationId|window                                       |pressureAvg|tempAvg    |
+---------+---------------------------------------------+-----------+-----------+
```

```
|d60779f6 |[2018-06-24 18:40:00,2018-06-24 18:41:00]|101.2941341|17.305931400|
|d1e46a42 |[2018-06-24 18:40:00,2018-06-24 18:41:00]|101.0664287|4.1361759034|
|d7e277b2 |[2018-06-24 18:40:00,2018-06-24 18:41:00]|101.8582047|26.733601007|
|d2f731cc |[2018-06-24 18:40:00,2018-06-24 18:41:00]|101.4787068|9.2916271894|
|d2e710aa |[2018-06-24 18:40:00,2018-06-24 18:41:00]|101.7895921|12.575678298|
   ...
|d2f731cc |[2018-06-24 18:41:00,2018-06-24 18:42:00]|101.3489804|11.372200251|
|d60779f6 |[2018-06-24 18:41:00,2018-06-24 18:42:00]|101.6932267|17.162540135|
|d1b06f88 |[2018-06-24 18:41:00,2018-06-24 18:42:00]|101.3705194|-3.318370333|
|d4c162ee |[2018-06-24 18:41:00,2018-06-24 18:42:00]|101.3407332|19.347538519|
+---------+----------------------------------------------+----------+-----------+
// ** output has been edited to fit into the page
```

Tumbling and Sliding Windows

window is a SQL function that takes a timeColumn of TimestampType type and additional parameters to specify the duration of the window:

```
window(timeColumn: Column,
       windowDuration: String,
       slideDuration: String,
       startTime: String)
```

Overloaded definitions of this method make slideDuration and startTime optional.

This API lets us specify two kinds of windows: tumbling and sliding windows. The optional startTime can delay the creation of the window, for example, when we want to allow the stream throughput to stabilize after a ramp-up period.

Tumbling windows

Tumbling windows segment the time in nonoverlapping, contiguous periods. They are the natural window operation when we refer to a "total count each 15 minutes" or "production level per generator each hour." We specify a tumbling window by only providing the windowDuration parameter:

```
window($"timestamp", "5 minutes")
```

This window definition produces one result every five minutes.

Sliding windows

In contrast with tumbling windows, sliding windows are overlapping intervals of time. The size of the interval is determined by the windowDuration time. All values from the stream in that interval come into consideration for the aggregate operation. For the next slice, we add the elements arriving during slideDuration, remove the elements corresponding to the oldest *slice*, and apply the aggregation to the data within the window, producing a result at each slideDuration:

```
window($"timestamp", "10 minutes", "1 minute")
```

This window definition uses 10 minutes' worth of data to produce a result every minute.

It's worth noting that a tumbling window is a particular case of a sliding window in which `windowDuration` and `slideDuration` have equal values:

```
window($"timestamp", "5 minutes", "5 minutes")
```

It is illegal to use a `slideInterval` larger than the `windowDuration`. Structured Streaming will throw an `org.apache.spark.sql.AnalysisException` error if such a case occurs.

Interval offset

The third parameter in the window definition, called `startTime`, provides a way to offset the window alignment. In "Understanding How Intervals Are Computed" on page 163 we saw that the window intervals are aligned to the upper-next time magnitude. `startTime` (a misnomer in our opinion) lets us offset the window intervals by the indicated time.

In the following window definition, we offset a 10-minute window with a slide duration of 5 minutes by 2 minutes, resulting in time intervals like `00:02-00:12`, `00:07-00:17`, `00:12-00:22`, ...

```
window($"timestamp", "10 minutes", "5 minute", "2 minutes")
```

`startTime` must strictly be less than `slideDuration`. Structured Streaming will throw an `org.apache.spark.sql.AnalysisException` error if an invalid configuration is provided. Intuitively, given that `slideDuration` provides the periodicity at which the window is reported, we can offset that period for only a time that is less than the period itself.

Record Deduplication

Structured Streaming offers a built-in function that removes duplicate records in the stream. It is possible to specify a watermark that determines when it is safe to discard previously seen keys.

The base form is quite simple:

```
val deduplicatedStream = stream.dropDuplicates(<field> , <field>, ...)
```

Nevertheless, this base method is discouraged, as it requires you to store all received values for the set of fields defining a unique record, which can potentially be unbounded.

A more robust alternative involves specifying a watermark on the stream before the `dropDuplicates` function:

```
val deduplicatedStream = stream
  .withWatermark(<event-time-field>, <delay-threshold>)
  .dropDuplicates(<field> , <field>, ...)
```

When using a watermark, keys older than the watermark become eligible for deletion, allowing the state store to keep its storage needs bounded.

Summary

In this chapter we explored how Structured Streaming implements the concept of event time and the facilities the API offers to make use of time embedded in the event data:

- We learned how to use event time and how to fall back on processing time, when needed.
- We explored watermarks, an important concept that lets us determine which events are too late and when state-related data might be evicted from the store.
- We saw the different configuration for window operations and their link with event time.
- Finally, we learned about the deduplication function in how it uses watermarks to keep its state bounded.

Event-time processing is a powerful set of features built into Structured Streaming that encapsulates the complexity of dealing with time, ordering, and lateness into an easy-to-use API.

Nevertheless, there are cases when the built-in functions are not sufficient to implement certain stateful processes. For those cases, Structured Streaming offers advanced functions to implement arbitrary stateful processes, as we see in the next chapter.

## CHAPTER 13

Advanced Stateful Operations

Chapter 8 demonstrated how easy it is to express an aggregation in Structured Streaming using the existing aggregation functions in the *structured* Spark APIs. Chapter 12 showed the effectiveness of Spark's built-in support for using the embedded time information in the event stream, the so-called *event-time processing*.

However, there are cases when we need to meet custom aggregation criteria that are not directly supported by the built-in models. In this chapter, we explore how to conduct advanced stateful operations to address these situations.

Structured Streaming offers an API to implement arbitrary stateful processing. This API is represented by two operations: `mapGroupsWithState` and `flatMapGroupsWithState`. Both operations allow us to create a custom definition of a state, set up the rules of how this state evolves as new data comes in over time, determine when it expires, and provide us with a method to combine this state definition with the incoming data to produce results.

The main difference between `mapGroupsWithState` and `flatMapGroupsWithState` is that the former must produce a single result for each processed group, whereas the latter might produce zero or more results. Semantically, this means that `mapGroupsWithState` should be used when new data always results in a new state, whereas `flatMapGroupsWithState` should be used in all other cases.

Internally, Structured Streaming takes care of managing state between operations and ensures its availability and fault-tolerant preservation during and across executions of the streaming process over time.

Example: Car Fleet Management

Let's imagine a car fleet management solution in which the vehicles of the fleet are enabled with wireless network capabilities. Each vehicle regularly reports its geographical location and many operational parameters like fuel level, speed, acceleration, bearing, engine temperature, and so on. The stakeholders would like to exploit this stream of telemetry data to implement a range of applications to help them manage the operational and financial aspects of the business.

Using the Structured Streaming features we know so far, we could already implement many use cases, like monitoring kilometers driven per day using event-time windows or finding vehicles with a low-fuel warning by applying filters.

Now, we would like to have the notion of a trip: the driven road segment from a start to a stop. Individually, the notion of a trip is useful to compute fuel efficiency or monitor compliance to geo-fencing agreements. When analyzed in groups, trip information might reveal transportation patterns, traffic hotspots, and, when combined with other sensor information, they can even report road conditions. From our stream-processing perspective, we could see trips as an arbitrary window that opens when the vehicle starts moving and closes when it finally stops. The event-time window aggregations we saw in Chapter 12 use fixed time intervals as windowing criteria, so they are of no help to implement our trip analysis.

We can appreciate that we need a more powerful definition of state that is not purely based on time, but also on arbitrary conditions. In our example, this condition is that the vehicle is driving.

Understanding Group with State Operations

The arbitrary state operations, `mapGroupsWithState` and `flatMapGroupWithState`, work exclusively on the typed `Dataset` API using either the Scala or the Java bindings.

Based on the data that we are processing and the requirements of our stateful transformation, we need to provide three type definitions, typically encoded as a `case class` (Scala) or a `Java Bean` (Java):

- The input event (`I`)
- The arbitrary state to keep (`S`)
- The output (`O`) (this type might be the same as the state representation, if suitable)

All of these types must be encodable into Spark SQL types. This means that there should be an `Encoder` available. The usual import statement

```
import spark.implicits._
```

is sufficient for all basic types, tuples, and `case classes`.

With these types in place, we can formulate the state transformation function that implements our custom state handling logic.

`mapGroupsWithState` requires that this function returns a single mandatory value:

```
def mappingFunction(key: K, values: Iterator[I], state: GroupState[S]): O
```

`flatMapGroupsWithState` requires that this function returns an `Iterator`, which might contain zero or more elements:

```
def flatMappingFunction(
    key: K, values: Iterator[I], state: GroupState[S]): Iterator[O]
```

`GroupState[S]` is a wrapper provided by Structured Streaming and used internally to manage the state S across executions. Within the function, `GroupState` provides mutation access to the state and the ability to check and set timeouts.

> The implementation of the `mappingFunction/flatMappingFunc`
> `tion` *must be* `Serializable`.
>
> At runtime, this function is distributed to the executors of the cluster using Java Serialization. This requirement also has the consequence that we *must not* include any local state like counters or other mutable variables in the body of the function. All managed state *must be* encapsulated in the `State` representation class.

Internal State Flow

In Figure 13-1, we illustrate the process that combines the incoming data, in the form of events, with the state maintained internally, to produce a result. In this chart, the `mappingFunction` (denoted with a Σ) uses the custom logic to process this group of elements, that when combined with the state managed by `GroupState[S]`, leads to a result. In this illustration, we used the stop symbol to indicate a timeout. In the case of `MapGroupsWithState`, a timeout also triggers the production of an event and *should* evict the state. Given that the eviction logic is under the control of the programmed logic, the complete state management is under the responsibility of the developer. Structured Streaming provides only the building blocks.

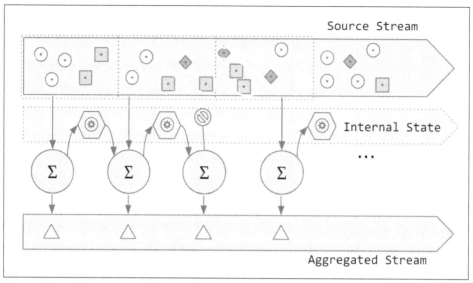

Figure 13-1. Map groups with state dynamics

Using MapGroupsWithState

In "Sliding windows" on page 164, we saw how we can compute a moving average based on a time window. This time-based window would produce a result independently of the number of elements found in the window.

Now, suppose that our requirement is to compute a moving average of the last 10 elements received per key. We cannot use a time window, because we don't know how long it will take us to have the number of elements we need. Instead, we can define our own count-based window using a custom state with MapGroupsWithState.

Online Resources

For this example, we will use the map_groups_with_state notebook in the online resources for the book, located on *http://github.com/stream-processing-with-spark*.

Let's begin with the same streaming Dataset that we used in "Sliding windows" on page 164. The WeatherEvent case class becomes our input type (I):

```
// a representation of a weather station event
case class WeatherEvent(stationId: String,
  timestamp: Timestamp,
  location:(Double,Double),
  pressure: Double,
  temp: Double)
```

```
val weatherEvents: Dataset[WeatherEvents] = ...
```

Next, we define the state (S). What we want is to keep the latest n elements in our state and drop anything older. This seems a natural application of a FIFO (First In, First Out) collection, such as a Queue. Newer elements are added to the front of the queue, we keep the most recent n, and drop any older element.

Our state definition becomes a FIFOBuffer backed by a Queue with few helper methods to facilitate its usage:

```
import scala.collection.immutable.Queue
case class FIFOBuffer[T](
    capacity: Int, data: Queue[T] = Queue.empty
    ) extends Serializable {

  def add(element: T): FIFOBuffer[T] =
    this.copy(data = data.enqueue(element).take(capacity))

  def get: List[T] = data.toList

  def size: Int = data.size
}
```

Then, we need to define the output type (O) that results from the stateful computation. The desired result of our stateful computation is the moving average of the sensor values present in the input WeatherEvent. We also would like to know the time span of the values used for the computation. With this knowledge, we design our output type, WeatherEventAverage:

```
import java.sql.Timestamp
case class WeatherEventAverage(stationId: String,
                              startTime: Timestamp,
                              endTime:Timestamp,
                              pressureAvg: Double,
                              tempAvg: Double)
```

With these types defined, we can proceed to create the mappingFunction that combines the existing state and the new elements into a result. We can see the implementation of the mapping function in Example 13-1. Remember that this function is also responsible for updating the internal state through the functions provided by the GroupState wrapper. It's important to note that the state cannot be updated with a null value. An attempt to do so will throw an IllegalArgumentException. To remove a state, use the method state.remove().

Example 13-1. Using mapGroupsWithState for a count-based moving average

```
import org.apache.spark.sql.streaming.GroupState
def mappingFunction(
```

```scala
    key: String,
    values: Iterator[WeatherEvent],
    state: GroupState[FIFOBuffer[WeatherEvent]]
  ): WeatherEventAverage = {

  // the size of the window
  val ElementCountWindowSize = 10

  // get current state or create a new one if there's no previous state
  val currentState = state.getOption
    .getOrElse(
      new FIFOBuffer[WeatherEvent](ElementCountWindowSize)
    )

  // enrich the state with the new events
  val updatedState = values.foldLeft(currentState) {
    case (st, ev) => st.add(ev)
  }

  // update the state with the enriched state
  state.update(updatedState)

  // if we have enough data, create a WeatherEventAverage from the state
  // otherwise, make a zeroed record
  val data = updatedState.get
  if (data.size > 2) {
    val start = data.head
    val end = data.last
    val pressureAvg = data
      .map(event => event.pressure)
      .sum / data.size
    val tempAvg = data
      .map(event => event.temp)
      .sum / data.size
    WeatherEventAverage(
      key,
      start.timestamp,
      end.timestamp,
      pressureAvg,
      tempAvg
    )
  } else {
    WeatherEventAverage(
      key,
      new Timestamp(0),
      new Timestamp(0),
      0.0,
      0.0
    )
  }
}
```

Now, we use the `mappingFunction` to declare the stateful transformation of the streaming `Dataset`:

```
import org.apache.spark.sql.streaming.GroupStateTimeout
val weatherEventsMovingAverage = weatherEvents
  .groupByKey(record => record.stationId)
  .mapGroupsWithState(GroupStateTimeout.ProcessingTimeTimeout)(mappingFunction)
```

Note that we first create *groups* out of the key identifiers in our domain. In this example, this is the `stationId`. The `groupByKey` operation creates an intermediate structure, a `KeyValueGroupedDataset` that becomes the entry point for the [map|flatMap]GroupWithState operations.

Besides the mapping function, we also need to provide a timeout type. A timeout type can be either a `ProcessingTimeTimeout` or an `EventTimeTimeout`. Because we are not relying on the timestamp of the events for our state management, we chose the `ProcessingTimeTimeout`. We discuss timeout management in detail later in this chapter.

Finally, we can easily observe the results of the query by using the Console sink:

```
val outQuery = weatherEventsMovingAverage.writeStream
  .format("console")
  .outputMode("update")
  .start()
```

```
+---------+-------------------+-------------------+-----------+-----------+
|stationId|startTime          |endTime            |pressureAvg |tempAvg    |
+---------+-------------------+-------------------+-----------+-----------+
|d1e46a42 |2018-07-08 19:20:31|2018-07-08 19:20:36|101.33375295|19.753225782|
|d1e46a42 |2018-07-08 19:20:31|2018-07-08 19:20:44|101.33667584|14.287718525|
|d60779f6 |2018-07-08 19:20:38|2018-07-08 19:20:48|101.59818386|11.990002708|
|d1e46a42 |2018-07-08 19:20:31|2018-07-08 19:20:49|101.34226429|11.294964619|
|d60779f6 |2018-07-08 19:20:38|2018-07-08 19:20:51|101.63191940|8.3239282534|
|d8e16e2a |2018-07-08 19:20:40|2018-07-08 19:20:52|101.61979385|5.0717571842|
|d4c162ee |2018-07-08 19:20:34|2018-07-08 19:20:53|101.55532969|13.072768358|
+---------+-------------------+-------------------+-----------+-----------+
// (!) output edited to fit in the page
```

Using FlatMapGroupsWithState

Our previous implementation has a flaw. Can you spot it?

When we start processing the stream, and before we have collected all the elements that we deem required to compute the moving average, the operation of `mapGroups WithState` produces zeroed-out values:

```
+---------+-------------------+-------------------+-----------+-------+
|stationId|startTime          |endTime            |pressureAvg|tempAvg|
+---------+-------------------+-------------------+-----------+-------+
|d2e710aa |1970-01-01 01:00:00|1970-01-01 01:00:00|0.0        |0.0    |
```

```
|d1e46a42 |1970-01-01 01:00:00|1970-01-01 01:00:00|0.0       |0.0    |
|d4a11632 |1970-01-01 01:00:00|1970-01-01 01:00:00|0.0       |0.0    |
+---------+-------------------+-------------------+----------+-------+
```

As we mentioned earlier, `mapGroupsWithState` requires the state handling function to produce a single record for each group processed at every trigger interval. This is fine when the arrival of new data corresponding to each key naturally updates its state.

But there are cases for which our state logic requires a series of events to occur before we can produce a result. In our current example, we need *n* elements before we can start producing an average over them. In other scenarios, it might be that a single incoming event might complete several temporary states and therefore produce more than one result. For example, the arrival of a single mass transport to its destination might update the traveling state of all of its passengers, potentially producing a record for each of them.

`flatMapGroupsWithState` is a generalization of `mapGroupsWithState` in which the state handling function produces an `Iterator` of results, which might contain zero or more elements.

Let's see how we can use this function to improve our moving average computation over *n*-elements.

Online Resources

For this example, we will use the `mapgroupswithstate-n-moving-average` notebook in the online resources for the book, located at *https://github.com/stream-processing-with-spark*.

We need to update the mapping function to return an `Iterator` of results. In our case, this `Iterator` will contain zero elements when we don't have enough values to compute the average, and a value otherwise. Our changed function looks like Example 13-2.

Example 13-2. Using FlatMapGroupsWithState for a count-based moving average

```
import org.apache.spark.sql.streaming._
def flatMappingFunction(
    key: String,
    values: Iterator[WeatherEvent],
    state: GroupState[FIFOBuffer[WeatherEvent]]
  ): Iterator[WeatherEventAverage] = {

  val ElementCountWindowSize = 10

  // get current state or create a new one if there's no previous state
  val currentState = state.getOption
```

```scala
      .getOrElse(
        new FIFOBuffer[WeatherEvent](ElementCountWindowSize)
      )

    // enrich the state with the new events
    val updatedState = values.foldLeft(currentState) {
      case (st, ev) => st.add(ev)
    }

    // update the state with the enriched state
    state.update(updatedState)

    // only when we have enough data, create a WeatherEventAverage from the state
    // before that, we return an empty result.
    val data = updatedState.get
    if (data.size == ElementCountWindowSize) {
      val start = data.head
      val end = data.last
      val pressureAvg = data
        .map(event => event.pressure)
        .sum / data.size
      val tempAvg = data
        .map(event => event.temp)
        .sum / data.size
      Iterator(
        WeatherEventAverage(
          key,
          start.timestamp,
          end.timestamp,
          pressureAvg,
          tempAvg
        )
      )
    } else {
      Iterator.empty
    }
}

val weatherEventsMovingAverage = weatherEvents
  .groupByKey(record => record.stationId)
  .flatMapGroupsWithState(
    OutputMode.Update,
    GroupStateTimeout.ProcessingTimeTimeout
  )(flatMappingFunction)
```

Using `flatMapGroupsWithState`, we no longer need to produce artificial zeroed records. In addition to that, our state management definition is now strict in having *n* elements to produce a result.

Output Modes

Although the cardinality difference in the results between the `map` and the `flatMap GroupsWithState` operations might seem like a small practical API difference, it has deeper consequences beyond the obvious variable production of results.

As we can appreciate in the example, `flatMapGroupsWithState` requires the additional specification of an output mode. This is needed to provide information about the record production semantics of the stateful operation to the downstream process. In turn, this helps Structured Streaming to compute the allowed output operation for the downstream sink.

The output mode specified in `flatMapGroupsWithState` can be either of the following:

update

> This indicates that the records produced are nonfinal. They are intermediate results that might be updated with new information later on. In the previous example, the arrival of new data for a key will produce a new data point. The downstream sink must use `update` and no aggregations can follow the `flatMap GroupsWithState` operation.

append

> This designates that we have collected all of the information we need to produce a result for a group, and no further incoming events will change that outcome. The downstream sink must use `append` mode to write. Given that the application of `flatMapGroupsWithState` produces a final record, it's possible to apply further aggregations to that result.

Managing State Over Time

A critical requirement of managing state over time is to ensure that we have a stable working set.[1] That is, the memory required by our process is bounded over time and remains at a safe distance under the available memory to allow for fluctuations.

In the managed stateful aggregations, such as the time-based windows that we saw in Chapter 12, Structured Streaming internally manages mechanisms to evict state and events that are deemed expired in order to limit the amount of memory used. When we use the custom state management capabilities offered by `[map|flatMap]Group sWithState`, we must also assume the responsibility of removing old state.

---

1 *Working set* is a concept that refers to the amount of memory used by a process to function over a period of time.

Luckily, Structured Streaming exposes time and timeout information that we can use to decide when to expire certain state. The first step is to decide the time reference to use. Timeouts can be based on event time or processing time and the choice is global to the state handled by the particular [map|flatMap]GroupsWithState being configured.

The timeout type is specified when we call [map|flatMap]GroupsWithState. Recalling the moving average example, we configured the mapGroupsWithState function to use processing time like this:

```
import org.apache.spark.sql.streaming.GroupStateTimeout
val weatherEventsMovingAverage = weatherEvents
  .groupByKey(record => record.stationId)
  .mapGroupsWithState(GroupStateTimeout.ProcessingTimeTimeout)(mappingFunction)
```

To use event time, we also need to declare a watermark definition. This definition consists of the timestamp field from the event and the configured lag of the watermark. If we wanted to use event time with the previous example, we would declare it like so:

```
val weatherEventsMovingAverage = weatherEvents
  .withWatermark("timestamp", "2 minutes")
  .groupByKey(record => record.stationId)
  .mapGroupsWithState(GroupStateTimeout.EventTimeTimeout)(mappingFunction)
```

The timeout type declares the global source of the time reference. There is also the option GroupStateTimeout.NoTimeout for the cases in which we don't need timeouts. The actual value of the timeout is managed per individual group, using the methods available in GroupState to manage timeout: state.setTimeoutDuration or state.setTimeoutTimestamp.

To determine whether a state has expired, we check state.hasTimedOut. When a state has timed out, the call to the (flat)MapFunction will be issued with an empty iterator of values for the group that has timed out.

Let's put the timeout feature to use. Continuing with our running example, the first thing we want to do is extract the transformation of state into event:

```
def stateToAverageEvent(
    key: String,
    data: FIFOBuffer[WeatherEvent]
  ): Iterator[WeatherEventAverage] = {
  if (data.size == ElementCountWindowSize) {
    val events = data.get
    val start = events.head
    val end = events.last
    val pressureAvg = events
      .map(event => event.pressure)
      .sum / data.size
    val tempAvg = events
```

```
        .map(event => event.temp)
        .sum / data.size
      Iterator(
        WeatherEventAverage(
          key,
          start.timestamp,
          end.timestamp,
          pressureAvg,
          tempAvg
        )
      )
    } else {
      Iterator.empty
    }
  }
```

Now, we can use that new abstraction to transform our state in the case of a timeout as well as in the usual scenario where data is coming in. Note in Example 13-3 how we use the timeout information to evict the expiring state.

Example 13-3. Using timeouts in flatMapGroupsWithState

```
import org.apache.spark.sql.streaming.GroupState
def flatMappingFunction(
    key: String,
    values: Iterator[WeatherEvent],
    state: GroupState[FIFOBuffer[WeatherEvent]]
  ): Iterator[WeatherEventAverage] = {
  // first check for timeout in the state
  if (state.hasTimedOut) {
    // when the state has a timeout, the values are empty
    // this validation is only to illustrate the point
    assert(
      values.isEmpty,
      "When the state has a timeout, the values are empty"
    )
    val result = stateToAverageEvent(key, state.get)
    // evict the timed-out state
    state.remove()
    // emit the result of transforming the current state into an output record
    result
  } else {
    // get current state or create a new one if there's no previous state
    val currentState = state.getOption.getOrElse(
      new FIFOBuffer[WeatherEvent](ElementCountWindowSize)
    )
    // enrich the state with the new events
    val updatedState = values.foldLeft(currentState) {
      case (st, ev) => st.add(ev)
    }
    // update the state with the enriched state
```

```
    state.update(updatedState)
    state.setTimeoutDuration("30 seconds")
    // only when we have enough data,
    // create a WeatherEventAverage from the accumulated state
    // before that, we return an empty result.
    stateToAverageEvent(key, updatedState)
  }
}
```

When a timeout actually times out

The semantics of the timeouts in Structured Streaming gives the guarantee that no event will be timed out before the clock advances past the watermark. This follows our intuition of a timeout: our state does not timeout before the set expiration time.

Where the timeout semantics depart from the common intuition is *when* the timeout event actually happens after the expiration time has passed.

Currently, the timeout processing is bound to the receiving of new data. So, a stream that goes silent for a while and does not generate new triggers to process will not generate timeouts either. The current timeout semantics are defined in terms of an eventuality: The timeout event will be eventually triggered after the state has expired, without any guarantees about how long the timeout event will fire after the actual timeout has happened. Stated formally: there is a no strict upper bound on when the timeout would occur.

There is work in progress to make timeouts fire even when no new data is available.

Summary

In this chapter, we learned about the arbitrary stateful processing API in Structured Streaming. We explored the details of and differences between the mapGroupsWith State and flatMapGroupsWithState with relation to the events produced and the output modes supported. At the end, we also learned about the timeout settings and became aware of its semantics.

Although this API is more complex to use than the regular SQL-like constructs of the structured APIs, it provides us with a powerful toolset to implement arbitrary state management to address the development of the most demanding streaming use cases.

## CHAPTER 14

Monitoring Structured Streaming Applications

Application monitoring is an integral part of any robust deployment. Monitoring provides insights on the application performance characteristics over time by collecting and processing metrics that quantify different aspects of the application's performance, such as responsiveness, resource usage, and task-specific indicators.

Streaming applications have strict requirements regarding response times and throughput. In the case of distributed applications like Spark, the number of variables that we need to account for during the application's lifetime are multiplied by the complexities of running on a cluster of machines. In the context of a cluster, we need to keep tabs on resource usage, like CPU, memory, and secondary storage across different hosts, from the perspective of each host, as well as a consolidated view of the running application.

For example, imagine an application running on 10 different executors. The total memory usage indicator shows a 15% increase, which might be within the expected tolerance for this application, but then, we notice that the increase comes from a single node. Such imbalance needs investigation because it will potentially cause a failure when that node runs out of memory. It also implies that there is potentially an unbalanced distribution of work that's causing a bottleneck. Without proper monitoring, we would not observe such behavior in the first place.

The operational metrics of Structured Streaming can be exposed through three different channels:

- The Spark metrics subsystem
- The `StreamingQuery` instance returned by the `writeStream.start` operation

- The `StreamingQueryListener` interface

As we detail in the following sections, these interfaces offer different levels of detail and exposure to cater for different monitoring needs.

The Spark Metrics Subsystem

Available through the Spark core engine, the Spark metrics subsystem offers a configurable metrics collection and reporting API with a pluggable sink interface—not to be confused with the streaming sinks that we discussed earlier in this book. Spark comes with several such sinks, including HTTP, JMX, and comma-separated values (CSV) files. In addition to that, there's a Ganglia sink that needs additional compilation flags due to licensing restrictions.

The HTTP sink is enabled by default. It's implemented by a servlet that registers an endpoint on the driver host on the same port as the Spark UI. The metrics are accessible at the `/metrics/json` endpoint. Other sinks can be enabled through configuration. The choice of a given sink is driven by the monitoring infrastructure with which we want to integrate. For example, the JMX sink is a common option to integrate with Prometheus, a popular metric collector in the Kubernetes cluster scheduler.

Structured Streaming Metrics

To acquire metrics from a Structured Streaming job, we first must enable the internal reporting of such metrics. We achieve that by setting the configuration flag `spark.sql.streaming.metricsEnabled` to `true`, as demonstrated here:

```
// at session creation time
val spark = SparkSession
  .builder()
  .appName("SparkSessionExample")
  .config("spark.sql.streaming.metricsEnabled", true)
  .config(...)
  .getOrCreate()

// by setting the config value
spark.conf.set("spark.sql.streaming.metricsEnabled", "true")

// or by using the SQL configuration
spark.sql("SET spark.sql.streaming.metricsEnabled=true")
```

With this configuration in place, the metrics reported will contain three additional metrics for each streaming query running in the same `SparkSession` context:

inputRate-total
    The total number of messages ingested per trigger interval

latency
> The processing time for the trigger interval

processingRate-total
> The speed at which the records are being processed

The StreamingQuery Instance

As we have seen through previous Structured Streaming examples, the call to start a *streaming query* produces a `StreamingQuery` result. Let's zoom in on the `weatherE ventsMovingAverage` from Example 13-1:

```
val query = scoredStream.writeStream
        .format("memory")
        .queryName("memory_predictions")
        .start()

query: org.apache.spark.sql.streaming.StreamingQuery =
  org.apache.spark.sql.execution.streaming.StreamingQueryWrapper@7875ee2b
```

The result we obtain from that call in the `query` value is a `StreamingQuery` instance. A `StreamingQuery` is a handler to the actual streaming query that is running continuously in the engine. This handler contains methods to inspect the execution of the query and control its life cycle. Some interesting methods are:

`query.awaitTermination()`
> Blocks the current thread until the query ends, either because it's stopped or because it encountered an error. This method is useful to block the `main` thread and prevent it from terminating early.

`query.stop()`
> Stops the execution of the query.

`query.exception()`
> Retrieves any fatal exception encountered by the execution of the query. This method returns `None` when the query is operating normally. After a query stops, inspecting this value informs us as to whether it failed and for what reason.

`query.status()`
> Shows a brief snapshot of what the query is currently doing.

For example, retrieving the `query.status` of a running query shows a result similar to this:

```
$query.status
res: org.apache.spark.sql.streaming.StreamingQueryStatus =
{
  "message" : "Processing new data",
```

```
    "isDataAvailable" : true,
    "isTriggerActive" : false
}
```

Even though the status information is not very revealing when everything is working correctly, it can be useful when developing a new job. `query.start()` is silent when an error occurs. Consulting `query.status()` might reveal that there is a problem, in which case, `query.exception` will return the cause.

In Example 14-1, we used an incorrect schema as input for a Kafka sink. If we recall from "The Kafka Sink" on page 144, a Kafka sink requires a mandatory field in the output stream: `value` (even `key` is optional). In this case, `query.status` provided relevant feedback to solve that issue.

Example 14-1. `query.status` shows the reason for a stream failure

```
res: org.apache.spark.sql.streaming.StreamingQueryStatus =
{
  "message": "Terminated with exception: Required attribute 'value' not found",
  "isDataAvailable": false,
  "isTriggerActive": false
}
```

The methods in `StreamingQueryStatus` are *thread-safe*, meaning that they can be called concurrently from another thread without risking corruption of the query state.

Getting Metrics with StreamingQueryProgress

For the purpose of monitoring, we are more interested in a set of methods that provide insights into the query execution metrics. The `StreamingQuery` handler offers two such methods:

`query.lastProgress`
    Retrieves the most recent `StreamingQueryProgress` report.

`query.recentProgress`
    Retrieves an array of the most recent `StreamingQueryProgress` reports. The maximum number of *progress* objects retrieved can be set using the configuration parameter `spark.sql.streaming.numRecentProgressUpdates` in the Spark Session. If you do not set this configuration, it defaults to the last 100 reports.

As we can appreciate in Example 14-2, each `StreamingQueryProgress` instance offers a comprehensive snapshot of the query performance produced at each trigger.

Example 14-2. StreamingQueryProgress sample

```
{
  "id": "639503f1-b6d0-49a5-89f2-402eb262ad26",
  "runId": "85d6c7d8-0d93-4cc0-bf3c-b84a4eda8b12",
  "name": "memory_predictions",
  "timestamp": "2018-08-19T14:40:10.033Z",
  "batchId": 34,
  "numInputRows": 37,
  "inputRowsPerSecond": 500.0,
  "processedRowsPerSecond": 627.1186440677966,
  "durationMs": {
    "addBatch": 31,
    "getBatch": 3,
    "getOffset": 1,
    "queryPlanning": 14,
    "triggerExecution": 59,
    "walCommit": 10
  },
  "stateOperators": [],
  "sources": [
    {
      "description": "KafkaSource[Subscribe[sensor-office-src]]",
      "startOffset": {
        "sensor-office-src": {
          "0": 606580
        }
      },
      "endOffset": {
        "sensor-office-src": {
          "0": 606617
        }
      },
      "numInputRows": 37,
      "inputRowsPerSecond": 500.0,
      "processedRowsPerSecond": 627.1186440677966
    }
  ],
  "sink": {
    "description": "MemorySink"
  }
}
```

From the perspective of monitoring the job's performance, we are particularly interested in `numInputRows`, `inputRowsPerSecond`, and `processedRowsPerSecond`. These self-describing fields provide key indicators about the job performance. If we have more data than our query can process, `inputRowsPerSecond` will be higher than `processedRowsPerSecond` for sustained periods of time. This might indicate that the cluster resources allocated for this job should be increased to reach a sustainable long-term performance.

The StreamingQueryListener Interface

Monitoring is a "day 2 operations" concern, and we require an automated collection of performance metrics to enable other processes such as capacity management, alerting, and operational support.

The inspection methods made available by the `StreamingQuery` handler that we saw in the previous section are useful when we work on an interactive environment such as the *Spark shell* or a notebook, like we use in the exercises of this book. In an interactive setting, we have the opportunity to manually sample the output of the `StreamingQueryProgress` to get an initial idea about the performance characteristics of our job.

Yet, the `StreamingQuery` methods are not automation friendly. Given that a new progress record becomes available at each streaming trigger, automating a method to collect information from this interface needs to be coupled to the internal scheduling of the streaming job.

Luckily, Structured Streaming provides the `StreamingQueryListener`, a *listener-based* interface that provides asynchronous callbacks to report updates in the life cycle of a streaming job.

Implementing a StreamingQueryListener

To hook up to the internal event bus, we must provide an implementation of the `StreamingQueryListener` interface and register it to the running `SparkSession`.

`StreamingQueryListener` consists of three methods:

`onQueryStarted(event: QueryStartedEvent)`
> Called when a streaming query starts. The `event` provides a unique id for the query and a `runId` that changes if the query is stopped and restarted. This callback is called synchronously with the start of the query and should not be blocked.

`onQueryTerminated(event: QueryTerminatedEvent)`
> Called when a streaming query is stopped. The `event` contains id and `runId` fields that correlate with the start event. It also provides an `exception` field that contains an `exception` if the query failed due to an error.

`onQueryProgress(event: StreamingQueryProgress)`
> Called at each query trigger. The `event` contains a `progress` field that encapsulates a `StreamingQueryProgress` instance that we know already from "Getting Metrics with StreamingQueryProgress" on page 184. This callback provides us with the events that we need to monitor the query performance.

Example 14-3 illustrates the implementation of a simplified version of such a listener. This chartListener, when instantiated from a notebook, plots the input and processing rates per second.

Example 14-3. Plotting streaming job performance

```
import org.apache.spark.sql.streaming.StreamingQueryListener
import org.apache.spark.sql.streaming.StreamingQueryListener._
val chartListener = new StreamingQueryListener() {
  val MaxDataPoints = 100
  // a mutable reference to an immutable container to buffer n data points
  var data: List[Metric] = Nil

  def onQueryStarted(event: QueryStartedEvent) = ()

  def onQueryTerminated(event: QueryTerminatedEvent) = ()

  def onQueryProgress(event: QueryProgressEvent) = {
    val queryProgress = event.progress
    // ignore zero-valued events
    if (queryProgress.numInputRows > 0) {
      val time = queryProgress.timestamp
      val input = Metric("in", time, event.progress.inputRowsPerSecond)
      val processed = Metric("proc", time, event.progress.processedRowsPerSecond)
      data = (input :: processed :: data).take(MaxDataPoints)
      chart.applyOn(data)
    }
  }
}
```

After a listener instance has been defined, it must be attached to the event bus, using the addListener method in the SparkSession:

```
sparkSession.streams.addListener(chartListener)
```

After running this chartListener against one of the notebooks included in this book's online resources, we can visualize the input and processing rates, as shown in Figure 14-1.

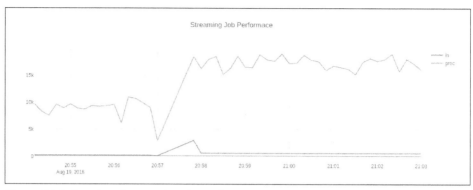

Figure 14-1. Input and processing streaming rates

Similar listener implementations can be used to send metric reports to popular monitoring systems, such as Prometheus, Graphite, or queryable databases like InfluxDB, which can be easily integrated with dashboard applications such as Grafana.

## CHAPTER 15

Experimental Areas: Continuous Processing and Machine Learning

Structured Streaming first appeared in Spark 2.0 as an experimental API, offering a new streaming model aimed at simplifying the way we think about streaming applications. In Spark 2.2, Structured Streaming "graduated" to *production-ready*, giving the signal that this new model was all set for industry adoption. With Spark 2.3, we saw further improvements in the area of streaming joins, and it also introduced a new experimental continuous execution model for low-latency stream processing.

As with any new successful development, we can expect Structured Streaming to keep advancing at a fast pace. Although industry adoption will contribute evolutionary feedback on important features, market trends such as the increasing popularity of machine learning will drive the roadmap of the releases to come.

In this chapter, we want to provide insights into some of the areas under development that will probably become mainstream in upcoming releases.

Continuous Processing

Continuous processing is an alternative execution mode for Structured Streaming that allows for low-latency processing of individual events. It has been included as an experimental feature in Spark v2.3 and is still under active development, in particular in the areas of delivery semantics, stateful operation support, and monitoring.

Understanding Continuous Processing

The initial streaming API for Spark, Spark Streaming, was conceived with the idea of reusing the batch capabilities of Spark. In a nutshell, the data stream is split into small chunks that are given to Spark for processing, using the core engine in its native batch execution mode. Using a scheduled repetition of this process at short time intervals, the input stream is constantly consumed and results are produced in a streaming fashion. This is called the *microbatch model*, which we discussed early on in Chapter 5. We study the application of this model in more detail when we talk about Spark Streaming in the next part of the book. The important part to remember for now, is that the definition of that interval of time, called *batch interval*, is the keystone of the original microbatch implementation.

Microbatch in Structured Streaming

When Structured Streaming was introduced, a similar evolution took place. Instead of introducing an alternative processing model, Structured Streaming was embedded into the `Dataset` API and reused the existing capabilities of the underlying Spark SQL engine. As a result, Structured Streaming offers a unified API with the more traditional batch mode and fully benefits from the performance optimizations introduced by Spark SQL, such as query optimization and Tungsten's code generation.

In that effort, the underlying engine received additional capabilities to sustain a streaming workload, like incremental query execution and the support of resilient state management over time.

At the API surface level, Structured Streaming avoided making the notion of time an explicit user-facing parameter. This is what allows for the implementation of event-time aggregations, as the notion of time is inferred from the data stream, instead. Internally, the execution engine still relies on a microbatch architecture, but the abstraction of time allows for the creation of engines with different models of execution.

The first execution model that departs from the fixed-time microbatch is the *best-effort* execution in Structured Streaming, which is the default mode when no `trigger` is specified. In best-effort mode, the next microbatch starts as soon as the previous one ends. This creates the observable continuity of the resulting stream and improves the usage of the underlying computing resources.

The microbatch execution engine uses a task-dispatching model. Task dispatching and coordination over the cluster is rather expensive and the minimal latency possible is roughly 100 ms.

In Figure 15-1, you can observe how the process of filtering the incoming "circles" and transforming them to "triangles" works with the microbatch model. We collect all elements that arrive in a certain interval and apply our function *f* to all of them at the same time.

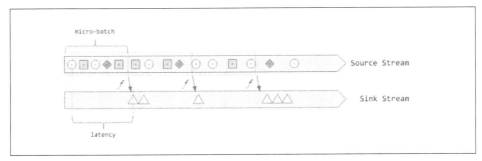

Figure 15-1. Microbatch latency

The processing latency is the time duration between the arrival of the event in the *source* stream and the production of a result in the *sink*. As we can appreciate, in the microbatch model, the latency upper limit is the batch interval plus the time it takes to process the data, which consists of the computation itself and the coordination needed to execute such computation in some executor of the cluster.

Introducing continuous processing: A low-latency streaming mode

Taking advantage of the time abstraction in Structured Streaming, it is possible to introduce new modes of execution without changing the user-facing API.

In the continuous processing execution mode, the data-processing query is implemented as a long-running task that executes *continuously* on the executors. The parallelism model is simple: for each input partition, we will have such a task running on a node of the cluster. This task subscribes to the input partition and continuously processes incoming individual events. The deployment of a query under continuous processing creates a topology of tasks in the cluster.

As illustrated in Figure 15-2, this new execution model eliminates the microbatch delay and produces a result for each element as soon as it's processed. This model is similar to Apache Flink.

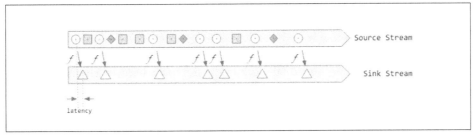

Figure 15-2. Continuous processing latency

Using Continuous Processing

All that is required to use the continuous processing execution mode is to specify `Trigger.Continuous` as a `trigger` and provide it with the time interval for the asynchronous checkpoint function, like we show in this minimalistic example:

```
import org.apache.spark.sql.streaming.Trigger

val stream = spark.readStream
    .format("rate")
    .option("rowsPerSecond", "5")
    .load()

val evenElements = stream.select($"timestamp", $"value").where($"value" % 2 === 0)

val query = evenElements.writeStream
    .format("console")
    .trigger(Trigger.Continuous("2 seconds"))
    .start()
```

 Do not confuse the time interval provided in `Trigger.Continuous(<time-interval>)` with a microbatch interval. This is the time interval of the asynchronous checkpoint operation, done by the *continuous query* executor.

Limitations

Although there are no changes at the API level, there are a number of restrictions on the type of queries that are supported in continuous mode. The intuition is that continuous mode works with queries that can be applied on a per-element basis. In SQL terms, we can use selections, projections, and transformations, including SQL functions except for aggregations. In functional terms, we can use `filter`, `map`, `flatMap`, and `mapPartitions`.

When using aggregations and window functions, in particular with event-based data, we have much longer deadlines to wait for late and out-of-order data. The very nature of a time period in a window and related concepts such as *watermarks* do not benefit from the low-latency characteristics of this execution model. In such cases, the recommended approach is to fall back to the microbatch-based engine, replacing `Trigger.Continuous(<checkpoint-interval>)` with a microbatch trigger definition: `Trigger.ProcessingTime(<trigger-interval>)`.

The support of arbitrary stateful processing such as `[flat]mapGroupsWithState` is currently under development.

Machine Learning

As the amount of available data and its rate of arrival increases, traditional techniques of understanding signals in the data become a major block to extract actionable insights from it.

Machine learning is, in essence, the combination of algorithms and statistical analysis techniques to *learn* from the data and use that learning to provide an answer to certain questions. Machine learning uses data to estimate a model, a mathematical representation of some aspect of the world. Once a model has been determined, it can be queried on existing or new data to obtain an answer.

The nature of the answer we want from the data divides the aim of the machine learning algorithms into three groups:

Regression
> We want to predict a value in a continuous range. Example: using data about a student's number of absences and hours of study for a given class, predict the score in their final exam.

Classification
> We want to separate data points into one of several categories. Example: given a text sample, we want to estimate the language.

Clustering
> Given a set of elements, we want to divide it into subsets using some notion of similarity. Example: in an online wine store, we want to group customers with similar purchase behavior.

In the learning process, we also have the notion of *supervision*. We talk about *supervised learning* when the algorithm being trained requires data that maps a number of observations to an outcome. Regression and classification techniques fall under the category of *supervised learning*. Using our previous example of the exam score, to build our regression model, we require a dataset of historical student performance that contains the exam scores along with the number of absences and hours of study reported by the students. Obtaining *good* data is the most challenging aspect of a machine learning task.

Learning Versus Exploiting

We can identify two phases in the application of machine learning techniques:

- A learning phase, in which data is prepared and used to estimate a model. This is also known as *training* or *learning*.

- An exploit phase, in which the estimated model is queried on new data. This phase is known as *prediction* or *scoring*.

The training phase in machine learning is typically done using historical datasets. These datasets are usually cleaned and prepared for the target application. The machine learning methodology also calls for a validation phase in which the resulting model is evaluated against a dataset of known results, usually called the *testing* or *validation* set. The result of the testing phase are metrics that report how well the learned model performs on data that it didn't see during the training.

Spark MLLib: Machine Learning Support in Spark

As part of the effort to offer a unified data-processing API based on the concepts of *structured data*, Spark MLLib, the machine learning library in Spark, also adopted the `DataFrame` API, through the introduction of the *ML Pipelines* concept.

ML Pipelines is a high-level API for MLLib built on top of `DataFrames`. It combines the idea of dynamic `DataFrame` transformations with the schema-driven capability of addressing specific fields in the data, as the values that participate in the machine learning process. This reduces the typical burden of preparing separate data artifacts in specific formats, such as *vectors*, to be used as input to the MLLib implementation of the algorithm used.

For an in-depth coverage of machine learning using Apache Spark, we recommend reading *Advanced Analytics with Spark, 2nd Edition* by Sean Owen, Sandy Ryza, et al. (O'Reilly).

Applying a Machine Learning Model to a Stream

As we mentioned earlier, creating a machine learning model is usually a batch-based process that uses historical data to train a statistical model. As soon as that model is available, it can be used to *score* new data to obtain an estimate of the specific aspect for which the model was trained.

The unified *structured* APIs of Apache Spark across batch, machine learning, and streaming make it straightforward to apply a previously trained model to a streaming `DataFrame`.

Assuming that the model is stored on disk, the process consists of two steps:

1. Load the model.
2. Use its `transform` method to apply the model to the streaming `DataFrame`.

Let's see the API in action with an example.

Example: Estimating Room Occupancy by Using Ambient Sensors

During the development of this part of the book, we have been using sensor information as a running theme. Up to now, we have used the sensor data to explore the data processing and analytic capabilities of Structured Streaming. Now, imagine that we have such ambient sensors in a series of rooms, but instead of keeping track of temperature or humidity data over time, we want to use that information to drive a novel application. We would like to estimate whether the room is occupied at a certain moment by using the sensor data. Although temperature or humidity alone are probably not sufficient to determine whether a room is in use, maybe a combination of these factors is able to predict occupancy to a certain degree of accuracy.

Online Resources

For this example, we will use the `occupancy_detection_model` and `occupancy_streaming_prediction` notebooks in the online resources for the book, located at *https://github.com/stream-processing-with-spark*.

For this example, we are going to use an occupancy dataset that was collected with the intention of answering that question. The dataset (*http://bit.ly/2PH7De8*) consists of the following schema:

```
|-- id: integer (nullable = true)
|-- date: timestamp (nullable = true)
|-- Temperature: double (nullable = true)
|-- Humidity: double (nullable = true)
|-- Light: double (nullable = true)
|-- CO2: double (nullable = true)
|-- HumidityRatio: double (nullable = true)
|-- Occupancy: integer (nullable = true)
```

The occupancy information in the training dataset was obtained using camera images of the room to detect with certainty the presence of people in it.

Using this data, we trained a logistic regression model that estimates the occupancy, represented by the binomial outcome [0,1], where 0 – not occupied and 1 – occupied.

For this example, we assume that the trained model is already available on disk. The complete training phase of this example is available in the book's online resources.

The first step is to load the previously trained model:

```
$ import org.apache.spark.ml._
$ val pipelineModel = PipelineModel.read.load(modelFile)
>pipelineModel: org.apache.spark.ml.PipelineModel = pipeline_5b323b4dfffd
```

This call results in a model that contains information over the stages of our pipeline.

With the call to model.stages, we can visualize these stages:

```
$ model.stages
res16: Array[org.apache.spark.ml.Transformer] =
    Array(vecAssembler_7582c780b304, logreg_52e582f4bdb0)
```

Our pipeline consists of two stages: a VectorAssembler and a LogisticRegression classifier. The VectorAssembler is a transformation that selectively transforms the chosen fields in the input data into a numeric Vector that serves as input for the model. The LogisticRegression stage is the trained logistic regression classifier. It uses the learned parameters to transform the input Vector into three fields that are added to the streaming DataFrame: rawPrediction, probability, and prediction.

For our application, we are interested in the prediction value that will tell us whether the room is in use (1) or not (0).

The next step, shown in Example 15-1, is to apply the model to the streaming Data Frame.

Example 15-1. Using a trained machine learning model in Structured Streaming

```
// let's assume an existing sensorDataStream
$ val scoredStream = pipeline.transform(sensorDataStream)

// inspect the schema of the resulting DataFrame
$ scoredStream.printSchema
root
  |-- id: long (nullable = true)
  |-- timestamp: timestamp (nullable = true)
  |-- date: timestamp (nullable = true)
  |-- Temperature: double (nullable = true)
  |-- Humidity: double (nullable = true)
  |-- Light: double (nullable = true)
  |-- CO2: double (nullable = true)
  |-- HumidityRatio: double (nullable = true)
  |-- Occupancy: integer (nullable = true)
  |-- features: vector (nullable = true)
  |-- rawPrediction: vector (nullable = true)
  |-- probability: vector (nullable = true)
  |-- prediction: double (nullable = false)
```

At this point, we have a streaming DataFrame that contains the prediction of our original streaming data.

The final step in our streaming prediction is to do something with the prediction data. In this example, we are going to limit this step to querying the data using the memory sink to access the resulting data as a SQL table:

```
import org.apache.spark.sql.streaming.Trigger
val query = scoredStream.writeStream
        .format("memory")
        .queryName("occ_pred")
        .start()

// let the stream run for a while first so that the table gets populated
sparkSession.sql("select id, timestamp, occupancy, prediction from occ_pred")
        .show(10, false)
```

```
+---+-----------------------+---------+----------+
|id |timestamp              |occupancy|prediction|
+---+-----------------------+---------+----------+
|211|2018-08-06 00:13:15.687|1        |1.0       |
|212|2018-08-06 00:13:16.687|1        |1.0       |
|213|2018-08-06 00:13:17.687|1        |1.0       |
|214|2018-08-06 00:13:18.687|1        |1.0       |
|215|2018-08-06 00:13:19.687|1        |1.0       |
|216|2018-08-06 00:13:20.687|1        |0.0       |
|217|2018-08-06 00:13:21.687|1        |0.0       |
|218|2018-08-06 00:13:22.687|0        |0.0       |
|219|2018-08-06 00:13:23.687|0        |0.0       |
|220|2018-08-06 00:13:24.687|0        |0.0       |
+---+-----------------------+---------+----------+
```

Given that we are using a test dataset to drive our stream, we also have access to the original occupancy data. In this limited sample, we can observe that the actual occupancy and the prediction are accurate most but not all of the time.

For real-world applications, we will typically be interested in offering this service to other applications. Maybe in the form of an HTTP-based API or through pub/sub messaging interactions. We can use any of the available sinks to write the results to other systems for further use.

The challenge of model serving

Trained machine learning models are seldom perfect. There are always opportunities to train a model with more or better data, or tweak its parameters to improve the prediction accuracy. With ever-evolving trained models, the challenge becomes to upgrade our streaming scoring process with a new model whenever it becomes available.

This process of managing the life cycle of machine learning models from the training stage to their exploitation in an application is usually known by the broad concept of *model serving*.

Model serving comprises the process of transitioning trained models into a production platform and keeping those online *serving* processes up to date with the most recent trained models.

Model serving in Structured Streaming

In Structured Streaming, updating a running query is not possible. Like we saw in Example 15-1, we include the model scoring step as a transformation in our streaming process. After we start the corresponding streaming query, that declaration becomes part of the query plan that is deployed and will run until the query is stopped. Hence, updating machine learning models in Structured Streaming is not directly supported. It is, nevertheless, possible to create a managing system that calls the Structured Streaming APIs to stop, update, and restart a query for which a new model becomes available.

The topic of model serving is an ongoing discussion in the Spark community and will certainly see an evolution in future versions of Spark and Structured Streaming.

Online Training

In the machine learning process we described earlier, we made a distinction between the learning and scoring phases, in which the learning step was mainly an offline process. In the context of a streaming application, it is possible to train a machine learning model as data arrives. This is also called *online learning*. Online learning is particularly interesting when we want to adapt to evolving patterns in the data, such as the changing interests of a social network or trend analysis in financial markets.

Online learning poses a new set of challenges because its implementation mandates that each data point is observed only once and that should take into consideration that the total amount of data observed might be endless.

In its current form, Structured Streaming does not offer support for *online training*. There are efforts to implement some (limited) form of online learning on Structured Streaming, the most notable being Holden Karau and Seth Hendrickson (*https://oreil.ly/2IZwIQU*) and Ram Sriharsha and Vlad Feinberg (*http://bit.ly/2VFUV4J*).

It would seem that early initiatives to implement online learning on top of Structured Streaming have lost momentum. This might change in the future, so check new releases of Structured Streaming for potential updates in this area.

APPENDIX B

References for Part II

- [Akidau2017_2] Akidau, Tyler, Reuven Lax, and Slava Chernyak. *Streaming Systems*. O'Reilly, 2017.

- [Armbrust2016] Armbrust, Michael, and Tathagata Das. *Apache Spark 2.0*. O'Reilly, 2016.

- [Armbrust2017] Armbrust, Michael. "Making Apache Spark the Fastest Open Source Streaming Engine," Databricks Engineering blog, June 6, 2017. *http://bit.ly/2EbyN8q*.

- [Armbrust2017b] Armbrust, Michael, and Tathagata Das. "Easy, Scalable, Fault Tolerant Stream Processing with Structured Streaming in Apache Spark," YouTube, Jun 12, 2017. *https://youtu.be/8o-cyjMRJWg*.

- [Chambers2017] Chambers, Bill, and Michael Armbrust. "Taking Apache Spark's Structured Streaming to Production," Databricks Engineering blog, May 18, 2017. *http://bit.ly/2E7LDoj*.

- [Damji2017] Damji, Jules. "Apache Spark's Structured Streaming with Amazon Kinesis on Databricks," Databricks Engineering blog, August 9, 2017. *http://bit.ly/2LKTgat*.

- [Damji2017b] Damji, Jules. "Bay Area Apache Spark Meetup Summary," Databricks Engineering blog, May 26, 2017. *http://bit.ly/2YwDuRW*.

- [Das2017] Das, T., M. Armbrust, T. Condie. "Real-time Streaming ETL with Structured Streaming in Apache Spark 2.1," Databricks Engineering blog, February 23, 2017. *http://bit.ly/30nCmBX*.

- [Das2017b] Das, Tathagata. "Event-time Aggregation and Watermarking in Apache Spark's Structured Streaming," Databricks Engineering blog, May 8, 2017. *http://bit.ly/2VtcAZi*.

- [Karau2016] Karau, Holden, and Seth Hendrickson. "Spark Structured Streaming for Machine Learning," StrataNY, November 22, 2016. *http://bit.ly/2LXSFSG*.

- [Karau2017_2] Karau, Holden. "Extend Structured Streaming for Spark ML," O'Reilly Radar, September 19, 2016. *https://oreil.ly/2IZwIQU*.

- [Khamar2017] Khamar, Kunal, Tyson Condie, and Michael Armbrust. "Processing Data in Apache Kafka with Structured Streaming in Apache Spark 2.2," Databricks Engineering blog, April 26, 2017. *http://bit.ly/2VwOxso*.

- [Koeninger2015_2] Koeninger, Cody, Davies Liu, and Tathagata Das. "Improvements to Kafka Integration of Spark Streaming," Databricks Engineering blog, March 30, 2015. *http://bit.ly/2Hn7dat*.

- [Lorica2016] Lorica, Ben. "Structured Streaming Comes to Apache Spark 2.0," O'Reilly Data Show, May 19, 2016. *https://oreil.ly/2Jq7s6P*.

- [Medasani2017] Medsani, Guru, and Jordan Hambleton. "Offset Management For Apache Kafka With Apache Spark Streaming," Cloudera Engineering blog, June 21, 2017. *http://bit.ly/2w05Yr4*.

- [Narkhede2016] Narkhede, Neha, Gwen Shapira, and Todd Palino. *Kafka: The Definitive Guide*. O'Reilly, 2016.

- [Pointer2016] Pointer, Ian. "What Spark's Structured Streaming really means," InfoWorld, April 7, 2016. *http://bit.ly/2w3NEgW*.

- [Sitaula2017] Sitaula, Sunil. "Real-Time End-to-End Integration with Apache Kafka in Apache Spark's Structured Streaming," Databricks Engineering blog, April 4, 2017. *http://bit.ly/2JKkCeb*.

- [Woodie2016] Woodie, Alex. "Spark 2.0 to Introduce New 'Structured Streaming' Engine," Datanami, February 25, 2016. *http://bit.ly/2Yu5XYE*, *http://bit.ly/2EeuRnl*.

- [Yavuz2017] Yavuz, Burak and Tyson Condie. "Running Streaming Jobs Once a Day For 10x Cost Savings," Databricks Engineering blog, May 22, 2017. *http://bit.ly/2BuQUSR*.

- [Yavuz2017b] Yavuz, B., M. Armbrust, T. Das, T. Condie. "Working with Complex Data Formats with Structured Streaming in Apache Spark 2.1," Databricks Engineering blog, February 23, 2017. *http://bit.ly/2EeuRnl*.

- [Zaharia2016] Zaharia, Matei, Tathagata Das, Michael Armbrust, and Reynold Xin. "Structured Streaming in Apache Spark: A New High-Level API for Streaming," Databricks Engineering blog, July 28, 2016. *http://bit.ly/2bM8UAw*.

- [Zaharia2016b] Zaharia, Matei. "Continuous Applications: Evolving Streaming in Apache Spark 2.0," Databricks Engineering blog, July 28, 2016. *http://bit.ly/2bvecOm*.

- [Zaharia2017] Zaharia, Matei, Tim Hunter, and Michael Armbrust. "Expanding Apache Spark Use Cases in 2.2 and Beyond," YouTube, June 6, 2017. *https://youtu.be/qAZ5XUz32yM*.

## PART III

Spark Streaming

In this part, we are going to learn about Spark Streaming.

Spark Streaming was the first streaming API offered on Apache Spark and is currently used in production by many companies around the world. It provides a powerful and extensible functional API based on the core Spark abstractions. Nowadays, Spark Streaming is mature and stable.

Our exploration of Spark Streaming begins with a practical example that provides us with an initial feeling of its API usage and programming model. As we progress through this part, we explore the different aspects involved in the programming and execution of robust Spark Streaming applications:

- Understanding the *Discretized Stream* (DStream) abstraction
- Creating applications using the API and programming model
- Consuming and producing data using streaming sources and *Output Operations*
- Combining *SparkSQL* and other libraries into streaming applications
- Understanding the fault-tolerance characteristics and how to create robust applications
- Monitoring and managing streaming applications

After this part, you will have the knowledge required to design, implement, and execute stream-processing applications using Spark Streaming. We will also be prepared for Part IV, in which we cover more advanced topics like the application of probabilistic data structures for stream processing and online machine learning.

## CHAPTER 16

Introducing Spark Streaming

Spark Streaming was the first stream-processing framework built on top of the distributed processing capabilities of Spark. Nowadays, it offers a mature API that's widely adopted in the industry to process large-scale data streams.

Spark is, by design, a system that is really good at processing data distributed over a cluster of machines. Spark's core abstraction, the *Resilient Distributed Dataset* (RDD), and its fluent functional API permits the creation of programs that treat distributed data as a collection. That abstraction lets us reason about data-processing logic in the form of transformation of the distributed dataset. By doing so, it reduces the cognitive load previously required to create and execute scalable and distributed data-processing programs.

Spark Streaming was created upon a simple yet powerful premise: apply Spark's distributed computing capabilities to stream processing by transforming a continuous stream of data into discrete data collections on which Spark could operate.

As we can see in Figure 16-1, the main task of Spark Streaming is to take data from the stream, package it down into small batches, and provide them to Spark for further processing. The output is then produced to some downstream system.

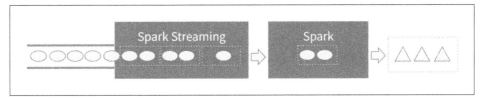

Figure 16-1. Spark and Spark Streaming in action

The DStream Abstraction

Whereas Structured Streaming, which you learned in Part II, builds its streaming capabilities on top of the *Spark SQL* abstractions of `DataFrame` and `Dataset`, Spark Streaming relies on the much more fundamental Spark abstraction of RDD. At the same time, Spark Streaming introduces a new concept: the *Discretized Stream* or DStream. A DStream represents a stream in terms of discrete blocks of data that in turn are represented as RDDs over time, as we can see in Figure 16-2.

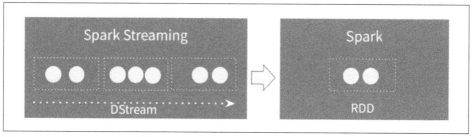

Figure 16-2. DStreams and RDDs in Spark Streaming

The DStream abstraction is primarily an execution model that, when combined with a functional programming model, provides us with a complete framework to develop and execute streaming applications.

DStreams as a Programming Model

The code representation of DStreams give us a functional programming API consistent with the RDD API and augmented with stream-specific functions to deal with aggregations, time-based operations, and stateful computations. In Spark Streaming, we consume a stream by creating a DStream from one of the native implementations, such as a `SocketInputStream` or using one of the many connectors available that provide a DStream implementation specific to a stream provider (this is the case of Kafka, Twitter, or Kinesis connectors for Spark Streaming, just to name a few):

```
// creates a dstream using a client socket connected to the given host and port
val textDStream = ssc.socketTextStream("localhost", 9876)
```

After we have obtained a DStream reference, we can implement our application logic using the functions provided by the `DStream` API. For example, if the `textDStream` in the preceding code is connected to a log server, we could count the number of error occurrences:

```
// we break down the stream of logs into error or info (not error)
// and create pairs of `(x, y)`.
// (1, 1) represents an error, and
// (0, 1) a non-error occurrence.
val errorLabelStream = textDStream.map{line =>
```

```
    if (line.contains("ERROR")) (1, 1) else (0, 1)
  }
```

We can then count the totals and compute the error rate by using an aggregation function called reduce:

```
// reduce by key applies the provided function for each key.
val errorCountStream = errorLabelStream.reduce {
    case ((x1,y1), (x2, y2))  => (x1+x2, y1+y2)
  }
```

To obtain our error rate, we perform a safe division:

```
// compute the error rate and create a string message with the value
val errorRateStream = errorCountStream.map {case (errors, total) =>
    val errorRate = if (total > 0 ) errors.toDouble/total else 0.0
    "Error Rate:" + errorRate
  }
```

It's important to note that up until now, we have been using transformations on the DStream but there is still no data processing happening. All transformations on DStreams are lazy. This process of defining the logic of a stream-processing application is better seen as the set of transformations that will be applied to the data after the stream processing is started. As such, it's a plan of action that Spark Streaming will recurrently execute on the data consumed from the source DStream. DStreams are immutable. It's only through a chain of transformations that we can process and obtain a result from our data.

Finally, the DStream programming model requires that the transformations are ended by an output operation. This particular operation specifies how the DStream is materialized. In our case, we are interested in printing the results of this stream computation to the console:

```
// print the results to the console
errorRateStream.print()
```

In summary, the DStream programming model consists of the functional composition of transformations over the stream payload, materialized by one or more *output operations* and recurrently executed by the Spark Streaming engine.

DStreams as an Execution Model

In the preceding introduction to the Spark Streaming programming model, we could see how data is transformed from its original form into our intended result as a series of lazy functional transformations. The Spark Streaming engine is responsible for taking that chain of functional transformations and turning it into an actual execution plan. That happens by receiving data from the input stream(s), collecting that data into batches, and feeding it to Spark in a timely manner.

The measure of time to wait for data is known as the *batch interval*. It is usually a short amount of time, ranging from approximately two hundred milliseconds to minutes depending on the application requirements for latency. The batch interval is the central unit of time in Spark Streaming. At each batch interval, the data corresponding to the previous interval is sent to Spark for processing while new data is received. This process repeats as long as the Spark Streaming job is active and healthy. A natural consequence of this recurring microbatch operation is that the computation on the batch's data has to complete within the duration of the batch interval so that computing resources are available when the new microbatch arrives. As you will learn in this part of the book, the batch interval dictates the time for most other functions in Spark Streaming.

In summary, the DStream model dictates that a continuous stream of data is discretized into microbatches using a regular time interval defined as the batch interval. At each batch interval, Spark Streaming delivers to Spark the corresponding data for that period, together with the functional transformations to be applied to it. In turn, Spark applies the computation to the data and produces a result, usually to an external system. Spark has—at most—the same batch interval of time to process the data. Otherwise, bad things could happen, as you will learn later on.

The Structure of a Spark Streaming Application

To gain intuition into the structure and programming model of Spark Streaming applications, we are going to begin with an example.

Any Spark Streaming application needs to do the following four things:

- Create a *Spark Streaming Context*
- Define one or several DStreams from data sources or other DStreams
- Define one or more output operations to materialize the results of these DStream operations
- Start the Spark Streaming Context to get the stream processing going

For the sake of our example, we will stop the process after is has run for a while.

The behavior of the job is defined in the operations defined between the moment that the instance for the Streaming Context is defined and the moment it is started. In that sense, the manipulation of the context before it is started defines the scaffolding for the streaming application, which will be its behavior and execution for the duration of the streaming application.

It is during this definition phase that all the DStreams and their transformations will be defined and the behavior of the Spark Streaming application will be "wired," so to speak.

Note that after the Spark Streaming Context has started, no new DStream can be added to it nor can any existing DStream can be structurally modified.

Creating the Spark Streaming Context

The Spark Streaming Context has as a goal to keep tabs on the creation, provisioning, and processing of DStreams in the Spark cluster. As such, it creates jobs based on the Spark RDDs produced at each interval, and it keeps track of the DStream lineage.

To gain a clearer idea of this picture, we are going to have a look at how to create a Streaming Context to host our stream. The simplest way is, in the Spark shell, to wrap a streaming context around the Spark Context, which in the shell is available under the name sc:

```scala
scala> import org.apache.spark.streaming._
import org.apache.spark.streaming._

scala> val ssc = new StreamingContext(sc, Seconds(2))
ssc: org.apache.spark.streaming.StreamingContext =
    org.apache.spark.streaming.StreamingContext@77331101
```

The Streaming Context is in charge of starting the ingestion process, which is deferred until the start() method is called on the corresponding streamingContext instance.

A frequent beginner's mistake is to attempt to test Spark Streaming either by allocating a single core in local mode (--master "local[1]") or by launching it in a virtual machine with a single core: the consumption of data by the receiver would block any Spark processing on the same machine, resulting in a streaming job that does not progress.

Defining a DStream

Let's now declare a DStream that will listen for data over an arbitrary local port. A DStream on its own does not do anything. In the same way that RDDs need actions to materialize a computation, DStreams require the declaration of output operations in order to trigger the scheduling of the execution of the DStream transformations. In this example, we use the count transformation, which counts the number of elements received at each batch interval:

```scala
scala> val dstream = ssc.socketTextStream("localhost", 8088)
dstream: org.apache.spark.streaming.dstream.ReceiverInputDStream[String] =
    org.apache.spark.streaming.dstream.SocketInputDStream@3042f1b

scala> val countStream = dstream.count()
```

```
countStream: org.apache.spark.streaming.dstream.DStream[Long] =
        org.apache.spark.streaming.dstream.MappedDStream@255b84a9
```

Defining Output Operations

For this example, we use `print`, an output operation that outputs a small sample of elements in `DStream` at each batch interval:

```
scala> countStream.print()
```

Now, in a separate console, we can loop through our file of common last names and send it over a local TCP socket by using a small Bash script:

```
$ { while :; do cat names.txt; sleep 0.05; done; } | netcat -l -p 8088
```

This iterates through the file we have and continuously loops over it, sending it infinitely over the TCP socket.

Starting the Spark Streaming Context

At this point, we have created a DStream, declared a simple `count` transformation, and used `print` as an output operation to observe the result. We also started our server socket data producer, which is looping over a file of names and sending each entry to a network socket. Yet, we don't see any results. To materialize the transformations declared on the DStream into a running process, we need to start the Streaming Context, represented by `ssc`:

```
scala> ssc.start()

...
\-------------------------------------------
Time: 1491775416000 ms
\-------------------------------------------
1086879


\-------------------------------------------
Time: 1491775420000 ms
\-------------------------------------------
956881


\-------------------------------------------
Time: 1491775422000 ms
\-------------------------------------------
510846


\-------------------------------------------
Time: 1491775424000 ms
\-------------------------------------------
0


\-------------------------------------------
```

```
Time: 1491775426000 ms
\-------------------------------------------
932714
```

Stopping the Streaming Process

The final step in our initial Spark Streaming exploration is to stop the stream process. After the `streamingContext` is stopped, all DStreams declared within its scope are stopped and no further data is consumed:

```
scala> ssc.stop(stopSparkContext = false)
```

You cannot restart a stopped `streamingContext`. To restart a stopped job, the complete setup, from the point of creating the `streamingContext` instance needs to be re-executed.

Summary

In this chapter, we introduced Spark Streaming as the first and most mature stream-processing API in Spark.

- We learned about DStreams: the core abstraction in Spark Streaming
- We explored the DStream functional API and applied it in our first application
- We got a notion of the DStream model and how microbatches are defined by a time measure known as the interval

In the next chapters, you gain a deeper understanding of the programming model and execution aspects in Spark Streaming.

## CHAPTER 17

The Spark Streaming Programming Model

In Chapter 16, you learned about Spark Streaming's central abstraction, the DStream, and how it blends a microbatch execution model with a functional programming API to deliver a complete foundation for stream processing on Spark.

In this chapter, we explore the API offered by the DStream abstraction that enables the implementation of arbitrarily complex business logic in a streaming fashion. From an API perspective, DStreams delegate much of their work to the underlying data structure in Spark, the Resilient Distributed Dataset (RDD). Before we delve into the details of the DStream API, we are going to take a quick tour of the RDD abstraction. A good understanding of the RDD concept and API is essential to comprehend how DStreams work.

RDDs as the Underlying Abstraction for DStreams

Spark has one single data structure as a base element of its API and libraries: RDD. This is a polymorphic collection that represents a bag of elements, in which the data to be analyzed is represented as an arbitrary Scala type. The dataset is distributed across the executors of the cluster and processed using those machines.

Since the introduction of Spark SQL, the `DataFrame` and `Dataset` abstractions are the recommended programming interfaces to Spark. In the most recent versions, only library programmers are required to know about the RDD API and its runtime. Although RDDs are not often visible at the interface level, they still drive the core engine's distributed computing capabilities.

To understand how Spark works, some basic knowledge of RDD-level programming is highly recommended. In the following section, we cover only the most notable elements. For a more in-depth treatment of the RDD programming model, we refer you to [Karau2015].

Using those RDDs involves (mostly) calling functions on the RDD collection type. The functions in this API are higher-order functions. In that sense, programming in Spark involves functional programming at its core: indeed, a programming language is considered to be functional when, in particular, it's able to define a function anywhere: as an argument, as a variable, or more generally as a syntax element. But, more importantly, on the programming languages theory level, a language becomes a functional programming language only when it is able to pass functions as arguments. In the example that follows, we see how Spark lets you use an implementation of map to transform all of the values of a collection by applying an arbitrary function to every single element.

In the following example, we read a text file containing frequent last names from census data as an `RDD[String]` (read as *RDD of Strings*). Then, we obtain the length of those names using a map operation that transforms the initial name, represented as a `String` into its length:

```
scala> val names = sc.textFile("/home/learning-spark-streaming/names.txt")
names: org.apache.spark.rdd.RDD[String] =
      MapPartitionsRDD[1] at textFile at <console>:24
scala> names.take(10)
res0: Array[String] =
      Array(smith, johnson, williams, jones, brown, davis, miller,
            wilson, moore, taylor)
scala> val lengths = names.map(str => str.length )
lengths: org.apache.spark.rdd.RDD[Int] =
      MapPartitionsRDD[3] at map at <console>:27
scala> lengths.take(10)
res3: Array[Int] = Array(6, 6, 6, 8, 9, 7, 7, 7, 6, 6)
```

Spark also provides us with a `reduce` function, which lets us aggregate key elements of a collection into another result, obtained through iterative composition. We are also going to use the `count` operation, which computes the number of elements in an RDD. Let's have a look:

```
scala> val totalLength = lengths.reduce( (acc, newValue) => acc + newValue )
totalLength: Int = 606623
scala> val count = lengths.count()
count: Int = 88799
scala> val average = totalLength.toDouble / count
average: Double = 6.831417020461942
```

It's worth noting that reduce requires that the RDD is not empty. Otherwise, it will throw a java.lang.UnsupportedOperationException exception with the message: empty collection. This might seem like an extreme case given that we are in the midst of a discussion about processing large datasets, but it becomes necessary when we want to process incoming data in real-time.

To overcome this limitation, we could use fold, an aggregator similar to reduce. Besides the reduction function, fold lets us define an initial "zero" element to use with the aggregation function, therefore working properly even with empty RDDs.

fold and reduce both use an aggregation function closed over the RDD type. Hence, we could sum an RDD of Ints or calculate the min or max of an RDD of cartesian coordinates according to a measure. There are cases for which we would like to return a different type than the data represented by the RDD. The more general aggregate function lets you determine how to combine disparate input and output types in an intermediate step:

```
scala> names.aggregate[TAB]
def aggregate[U](zeroValue: U)
  (seqOp: (U, T) => U, combOp: (U, U) => U)(implicit scala.reflect.ClassTag[U]): U

scala> names.fold[TAB]
    def fold(zeroValue: T)(op: (T, T) => T): T
```

It is the ease of use of this API that has won Spark RDDs the nickname of *"the ultimate Scala collections."* This reference to Spark's original implementation programming language points at the collections library of Scala, which already lets us benefit from functional programming on a single machine with a rich API. It lets us expand our data-processing vocabulary from the basic map and reduce from the original MapReduce model.

The real genius of Spark is that it reproduces the ease of use of the Scala API, and scales it up to operate over a cluster of computing resources. The RDD API defines two broad families of functions: transformations and actions. Transformations, like map or filter, let us work on the immutable data contained by the RDD by creating new RDDs as the result of applying a transformation to its *parent*. This chain of RDD transformations forms a directed acyclic graph or DAG that informs Spark where the raw data is and how it needs to be transformed into the desired result. All transformations are declarative and lazy. That means that they do not result in data being actually processed. To obtain results, we need to materialize the chain of transformations by issuing an *action*. Actions trigger the distributed execution of data operations and produce a tangible result. It can be writing to a file or printing samples on the screen.

Additional functional operations, such as `flatMap`, `groupBy`, and `zip` are also available. You can also find RDD combinators, like `join` and `cogroup`, that allow you to merge two or more existing RDDs.

Understanding DStream Transformations

The DStream programming API consists of transformations or higher-order functions that take another function as an argument. At the API level, a `DStream[T]` is a strongly typed data structure that represents a stream of data of type `T`.

DStreams are immutable. This means that we cannot mutate their contents in place. Instead, we implement our intended application logic by applying a series of *transformations* to the input DStream. Each transformation creates a new DStream that represents the transformed data from the parent DStream. DStream transformations are lazy, meaning that the underlying data is not actually processed until the system needs to materialize a result. In the case of DStreams, this materialization process is triggered when we want to produce results to a stream sink through a particular operation known as an *output operation*.

> For readers coming from a functional programming background, it is evident that DStream transformations can be considered pure functions, whereas output operations are side-effecting functions that produce a result to an external system.

Let's review these concepts using the code we used earlier in the introduction:

```
val errorLabelStream = textDStream.map{ line =>
    if (line.contains("ERROR")) (1, 1) else (0, 1)
}
```

Here, the `textDStream` contains lines of text. Using a `map` transformation, we apply a fairly naive error-counting function to each line in the original `DStream[String]`, resulting in a new `DStream[(Long, Long)]` of long tuples. In this case, `map` is a DStream transformation and it takes a function applicable to its contents, `Strings` in this case, to produce another DStream with the transformed contents.

DStreams are a streaming abstraction in which the elements of the stream are grouped into microbatches over a time dimension, as we illustrate in Figure 17-1. In turn, each microbatch is represented by an RDD. At the execution level, the main task of Spark Streaming is to schedule and manage the timely collection and delivery of data

---

blocks to Spark. In turn, the Spark core engine will apply the programmed sequence of operations to the data that constitute our application logic.

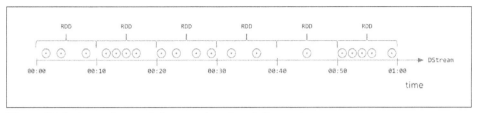

Figure 17-1. Streaming model mapped on Spark Streaming

Going back to how this is reflected in the API, we see that there are operators, like the classical map, filter, and so on that operate on a single element. These operations follow the same principles of distributed execution and abide by the same serialization constraints as their batch Spark counterparts.

There are also operators, like transform and foreachRDD, that operate on an RDD instead of an element. These operators are executed by the Spark Streaming scheduler and the functions provided to them run in the context of the driver. It is within the scope of these operators that we can implement logic that crosses the boundary of microbatches, like bookkeeping history or maintaining application-level counters. They also provide access to all the Spark execution contexts. Within these operators, we can interact with Spark SQL, Spark ML, or even manage the life cycle of the streaming application. These operations are true bridges between the recurrent streaming microbatch scheduling, the element-level transformations, and the Spark runtime context.

Using this distinction, we can observe two broad groups of transformations:

Element-centric DStream transformations
    Transformations that apply to a single element of the stream.

RDD-centric DStream transformations
    Transformations that apply to the underlying RDD of each microbatch.

Besides this general classification, we also find two other classes of transformations in the DStream API:

Counting transformations
    Dedicated operations to count elements in a stream.

Structure-modifying transformations
    Transformations that change the internal structure or organization of the DStream but do not change the contents.

In the rest of this chapter, we study these transformations in detail.

Element-Centric DStream Transformations

In general, the element-centric transformations on the DStream API mirror functions also available in the RDD API, unifying the development experience among batch and streaming modes in Spark.

The most commonly used transformations follow:

 The signature of each transformation has been simplified by removing implicit parameters to make the signature more concise, where applicable.

map

```
map[U](mapFunc: (T) => U): DStream[U]
```

The map function on a DStream takes a function T => U and applies it to every element of a DStream[T], leaving the RDD structure unchanged. As in RDDs, it is the appropriate choice to make for a massively parallel operation, for which it is of no importance whether its input is in a particular position with respect to the rest of the data.

flatMap

```
flatMap[U](flatMapFunc: (T) => TraversableOnce[U]): DStream[U]
```

flatmap is the usual companion of map, which instead of returning elements of type U, returns the type of a TraversableOnce container of U. These containers are coalesced in a single one before returning. All Scala collections implement the TraversableOnce interface, making them all usable as target types for this function.

The common use cases for flatMap are when we want to create zero or more target elements from a single element. We can use flatMap to explode a record into many elements or, when used in combination with the Option type, it can be applied to filter out input records that do not meet certain criteria.

An important remark is that this version of flatMap does not follow the strict monadic definition, which would be: flatMap[U](flatMapFunc: (T) => DStream[U]): DStream[U]. This is often a cause of confusion to newcomers with a functional programming background.

mapPartitions

```
mapPartitions[U](mapPartFunc: (Iterator[T]) => Iterator[U],
                 preservePartitioning: Boolean = false): DStream[U]
```

This function, like the homonymous function defined on RDD, allows us to directly apply a map operation on each of the partitions of an RDD. The result is a new DStream[U] where the elements are mapped. As with the mapPartitions call as defined on an RDD, this function is useful because it allows us to have executor-specific behavior; that is, some logic that will *not* be repeated for every element but will rather be executed once for each executor where the data is processed.

One classic example is initializing a random number generator that is then used in the processing of every element of the partition, accessible through the Itera tor[T]. Another useful case is to amortize the creation of expensive resources, such as a server or database connection, and reuse such resources to process every input element. An additional advantage is that the initialization code is run directly on the executors, letting us use nonserializable libraries in a distributed computing process.

filter

```
filter(filterFunc: (T) => Boolean): DStream[T]
```

This function selects some elements of the DStream according to the predicate passed as an argument. As for map, the predicate is checked on every element of the DStream. Beware that this can generate empty RDDs if no element verifying the predicate is received during a particular batch interval.

glom

```
glom(): DStream[Array[T]]
```

This function, like the homonymous function defined on RDD, allows us to coalesce elements in an array. In fact, as the glom call on an RDD returns arrays of elements—as many as there are partitions—the DStream equivalent returns the result of calling the glom function on each of its constituent RDDs.

reduce

```
reduce(reduceFunc: (T, T) => T): DStream[T]
```

This is the equivalent of the reduce function on an RDD. It allows us to aggregate the elements of an RDD using the provided aggregation function. reduce takes a function of two arguments, the *accumulator* and a new element of the RDD, and returns the new value for the accumulator. The result of applying reduce to a DStream[T] is hence a DStream of the same type T of which each batch inter val will contain an RDD with only one element: the final value of the accumulator. Note in particular that you should use reduce with care: it cannot deal with an empty RDD on its own, and in a streaming application, an empty batch of data can always happen, like when data production or ingestion is stalled.

We can summarize these various transformations in the following way, according to what type of action they have on the source DStream. In Table 17-1 we can see whether any operation works on a whole RDD rather than element-wise, and whether it has constraints on the output RDD.

Table 17-1. The computation model and output of some essential DStream operations

Operation	Effect	Output RDD's structure
map,filter	element-wise	Unchanged (as many elements as original)
glom	partition-wise	As many arrays as there are partitions in the original
mapPartitions	partition-wise	As many partitions as original RDD
reduce,fold	aggregating	One element
flatMap	element-wise	As many elements as the size of the output container

RDD-Centric DStream Transformations

These operations give us direct access to the underlying RDD of a DStream. What makes these operations special is that they execute in the context of the Spark driver. Therefore, we can have access to the facilities provided by the Spark Session (or Spark context) as well as to the execution context of the driver program. In this local execution context, we can have access to local variables, data stores, or API calls to external services that may influence the way you want to process the data.

The most commonly used transformations follow:

transform

```
transform[U](transformFunc: (RDD[T]) => RDD[U]): DStream[U]
transform[U](transformFunc: (RDD[T], Time) => RDD[U]): DStream[U]
```

transform allows us to reuse a transformation function of type RDD[T] => RDD[U] and apply it on each constituent RDD of a DStream. It is often used to take advantage of some processing written for a batch job—or more simply in another context—to yield a streaming process.

transform also has a timed version, with signature (RDD[T], Time) => RDD[U]. As we will remark soon for the foreachRDD action, this can be very useful for tagging the data in a DStream with the time of the batch of which this data was part.

transformWith

```
transformWith[U,V](
  other: DStream[U], transformFunc: (RDD[T], RDD[U]) => RDD[V]
): DStream[V]
transformWith[U,V](
  other: DStream[U], transformFunc: (RDD[T], RDD[U], Time) => RDD[V]
): DStream[V]
```

transformWith lets us combine this DStream with another DStream using an arbitrary transformation function. We can use it to implement custom join functions between the two DStreams where the join function is not based on the key. For example, we could apply a similarity function and combine those elements that are *close enough*. Like transform, transformWith offers an overload that provides access to the batch time to provide a differentiation of timestamp mechanism to the incoming data.

Counting

Because the contents of a stream often comprise data whose cardinality is important, such as counting errors in a log, or hashtags in a tweet, counting is a frequent operation that has been optimized enough in Spark to warrant a specific API function.

It is interesting to note that although count is a materializing action in the RDD API because it directly produces a result, in the DStream API, it is a transformation that produces a new DStream with the counts at each microbatch interval.

Spark Streaming has several counting functions for a given DStream, which are better seen with an example.

Let's assume that we have a DStream consisting of names keyed by their first letter and that this DStream "repeats" itself: each RDD, on each batch interval, consists of 10 distinct such names per alphabet letter:

```
val namesRDD: RDD[(Char, String)] = ...
val keyedNames: DStream[(Char, String)] =
    ConstantInputDStream(namesRDD, 5s)
```

This would lead to the results shown in Table 17-2.

Table 17-2. Count operations

Operation	Return type	Result
keyedNames.count()	DStream[Long]	260
keyedNames.countByWindow(60s)	DStream[Long]	260 (because the same RDD repeats each time)
keyedNames.countByValue()	DStream[((Char, String), Long)]	1 for each of the 260 distinct (1st character, name) pairs
keyedNames.countByKey()	DStream[(Char, Long)]	10 for each of the 26 letters
keyednames.countByValueAndWindow(60s)	DStream[((Char, String), Long)]	12 for each of the 260 distinct (1st character, name) pairs

Structure-Changing Transformations

The previous operations are all transformations; that is, they always return a DStream after applying a function to the content of the stream. There are other transformations that do not transform the data in the stream but rather the structure of the DStream and in some cases, the flow of data through the Spark cluster:

`repartition`

```
repartition(int numPartitions): DStream[T]
```

> `repartition` results in a new DStream with an increased or decreased partitioning of the underlying RDDs in this DStream. Repartitioning allows us to change the parallelism characteristics of some streaming computation. For example, we might want to increase partitioning when a few input streams deliver a high volume of data that we want to distribute to a large cluster for some CPU-intensive computation. Decreasing the partitioning might be interesting when we want to ensure that we have a few partitions with a large number of elements before writing to a database, for example. Note that the parameter provided is the absolute number of the target number of partitions. Whether this operation results in creating or reducing the partitioning depends on the original number of partitions of this DStream, which in turn might be dependent on the source parallelism.

> Unlike data-oriented transformations, correct usage of `repartition` requires knowledge of the input parallelism, the complexity of the distributed computation, and the size of the cluster where the streaming job will be running.

`union`

```
union(other: DStream[T]): DStream[T]
```

union adds two DStreams of the same type into a single stream. The result is a DStream that contains the elements found on both input DStreams. An alternative usage form is calling union on the `streamingContext` instance with a collection of the DStreams to be joined. This second form allows us to unite many DStreams at once:

```
union[T](streams: Seq[DStream[T]]): DStream[T]
```

Summary

In this chapter, we have learned about the API offered by the DStream to implement streaming applications. We saw the following:

- DStreams are immutable and we operate on them using transformations.
- Transformations are lazy. They need to be materialized by a special output operation.

- DStreams offer a rich functional API that allows the transformation of elements.

- Some transformations expose the underlying RDD, providing access to the full extent of the rich Spark core API.

In the next chapters, you learn how to source data from external systems by creating DStreams. You also learn about a particular set of operations, called output operations in Spark Streaming jargon, that trigger the execution of transformations over our data streams and are able to produce data to other systems or secondary storage.

## CHAPTER 18

The Spark Streaming Execution Model

When we began our Spark Streaming journey in Chapter 16, we discussed how the DStream abstraction embodies the programming and the operational models offered by this streaming API. After learning about the programming model in Chapter 17, we are ready to understand the execution model behind the Spark Streaming runtime.

In this chapter, you learn about the bulk synchronous architecture and how it provides us with a framework to reason about the microbatch streaming model. Then, we explore how Spark Streaming consumes data using the receiver model and the guarantees that this model provides in terms of data-processing reliability. Finally, we examine the direct API as an alternative to receivers for streaming data providers that are able to offer reliable data delivery.

The Bulk-Synchronous Architecture

In Chapter 5 we discussed the *bulk-synchronous parallelism* or *BSP* model as a theoretical framework that allows us to reason how distributed stream processing could be done on microbatches of data from a stream.

Spark Streaming follows a processing model similar to bulk-synchronous parallelism:

- All of the Spark executors on the cluster are assumed to have a synchronous clock; for example, synchronized through a network time protocol (NTP) server.

- In the case of a receiver-based source, one or several of the executors runs a special Spark job, a *receiver*. This receiver is tasked with consuming new elements of the Stream. It receives two clock ticks:

  — The most frequent clock tick is called the *block interval*. It signals when elements received from the stream should be allocated to a block; that is, the portion of the stream that should be processed by a single executor, for this current interval. Each such block becomes a partition of the Resilient Distributed Dataset (RDD) produced at each batch interval.

— The second and less frequent is the *batch interval*. It marks when the receiver should assemble the data from the stream collected since the last clock tick and produces an RDD for distributed processing on the cluster.

- When using the direct approach, only the batch interval tick is relevant.

- During all processing, as is the case with a regular (batch) Spark job, blocks are signaled to the block manager, a component that ensures any block of data put into Spark is replicated according to the configured persistence level, for the purpose of fault tolerance.

- On each batch interval, the RDD from which data was received during the previous batch interval becomes available, and is thus scheduled for processing during this batch.

Figure 18-1 illustrates how these elements come together to conceptually form a DStream.

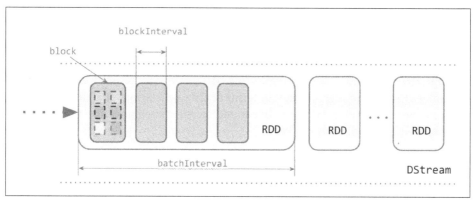

Figure 18-1. The DStream structure: blocks and batches

To achieve the concurrent execution with a strict bulk-synchronous model, the barrier here would be the arrival of a new *RDD* at the batch interval. Except that in Spark Streaming, this is not really a barrier because the data delivery happens independently of the state of the cluster at the moment of the arrival of the new batch: Spark's receivers do not wait for the cluster to be finished with receiving data to start on the new batch.

This is not a design fault; rather, it's a consequence of Spark Streaming trying to do real stream processing at its most honest: despite having a microbatching model, Spark Streaming acknowledges that a stream has no predefined end, and that the system is required to receive data continuously.

The consequence of this relatively simple model is that the Spark Streaming job tasked with receiving data—the receiver—needs to be a job scheduled in the cluster to continuously work. If it ever were to crash, it would be restarted on another executor, continuing the ingestion of data without further interruption.

The Receiver Model

As we previously hinted, in Spark Streaming, the receiver is a process able to continuously collect data from the input stream regardless of the state of processing of the Spark cluster.

This component is an adaptor between the data delivered by the stream source and the data-processing engine in Spark Streaming. As an adaptor, it implements the specific API and semantics of the external stream and delivers that data using an internal contract. Figure 18-2 shows the role of the receiver in the DStream data flow.

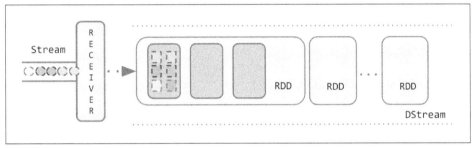

Figure 18-2. Receiver model

The Receiver API

The most fundamental receiver consists of three methods:

`def onStart()`
> Starts the reception of data from the external sources. In practice, `onStart` should asynchronously initiate the inbound data collection process and return immediately.

`def store(...)`
> Delivers one or several data elements to Spark Streaming. `store` must be called from the asynchronous process initiated by `onStart` whenever there is new data available.

`def stop(...)`
> Stops the receiving process. `stop` must take care of properly cleaning up any resources used by the receiving process started by `onStart`.

This model provides a generic interface that can be implemented to integrate a wide range of streaming data providers. Note how the genericity abstracts over the data delivery method of the streaming system. We can implement an always-connected push-based receiver, like a TCP client socket, as well as a request-based pull connector, like a REST/HTTP connector to some system.

How Receivers Work

The task of the receiver is to collect data from the stream source and deliver it to Spark Streaming. Intuitively, it's very easy to understand: as data comes in, it's collected and packaged in blocks during the time of the batch interval. As soon as each batch interval period of time is completed, the collected data blocks are given to Spark for processing.

Figure 18-3 depicts how the timing of this sequence of events takes place. At the start of the streaming process, the receiver begins collecting data. At the end of the *t0* interval, the first collected block #0 is given to Spark for processing. At time *t2*, Spark is processing the data block collected at *t1*, while the receiver is collecting the data corresponding to block #2.

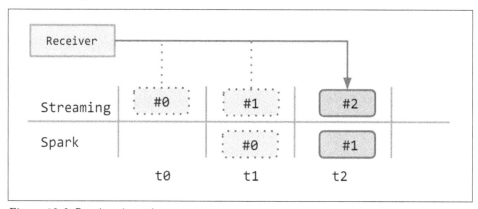

Figure 18-3. Receiver in action

We can generalize that, at any point in time, Spark is processing the previous batch of data, while the receivers are collecting data for the current interval. After a batch has been processed by Spark (like #0 in Figure 18-3), it can be cleaned up. The time when that RDD will be cleaned up is determined by the `spark.cleaner.ttl` setting.

The Receiver's Data Flow

Figure 18-4 illustrates the data flow of a Spark application in this case.

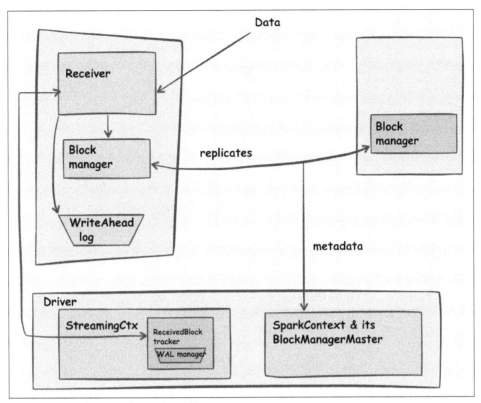

Figure 18-4. The data flow of Spark's receiver

In this figure, we can see that data ingestion occurs as a job that is translated into a single task on one executor. This task deals with connecting to a data source and initiates the data transfer. It is managed from the Spark Context, a bookkeeping object that resides within the driver machine.

On each block interval tick (as measured on the executor that is running the receiver), this machine groups the data received for the previous block interval into a block. The block is then registered with the Block Manager, also present in the bookkeeping of the Spark Context, on the driver. This process initiates the replication of the data that this block represents, to ensure that the source data in Spark Streaming is replicated the number of times indicated by the storage level.

On each batch interval tick (as measured on the driver), the driver groups the data received for the previous batch interval, which has been replicated the correct number of times, into an RDD. Spark registers this RDD with the JobScheduler, initiating the scheduling of a job on that particular RDD—in fact, the whole point of Spark Streaming's microbatching model consists of repeatedly scheduling the user-defined program on successive batched RDDs of data.

The Internal Data Resilience

The fact that receivers are independent jobs has consequences, in particular for the resource usage and data delivery semantics. To execute its data collection job, the receiver consumes one core on an executor regardless of the amount of work it needs to do. Therefore, using a single streaming receiver will result in data ingestion done in sequence by a single core in an executor, which becomes the limiting factor to the amount of data that Spark Streaming can ingest.

The base unit of replication for Spark is a block: any block can be on one or several machines (up to the persistence level indicated in the configuration, so at most two by default), and it is only when a block has reached that persistence level that it can be processed. Therefore, it is only when an RDD has every block replicated that it can be taken into account for job scheduling.

At the Spark engine side, each block becomes a partition of the RDD. The combination of a partition of data and the work that needs to be applied to it becomes a task. Each task can be processed in parallel, usually on the executor that contains the data locally. Therefore, the level of parallelism we can expect for an RDD obtained from a single receiver is exactly the ratio of the batch interval to the block interval, as defined in Equation 18-1.

Equation 18-1. Single receiver partitioning

$$numberpartitions = \frac{batchinterval}{blockinterval}$$

In Spark, the usual rule of thumb for task parallelism is to have two to three times ratio of the number of tasks to the number of available executor cores. Taking a factor of three for our discussion, we should set the block interval to that shown in Equation 18-2.

Equation 18-2. Block interval tuning

$$blockinterval = \frac{batchinterval}{3 * Sparkcores}$$

Receiver Parallelism

We mentioned that a single receiver would be a limiting factor to the amount of data that we can process with Spark Streaming.

A simple way to increase incoming data throughput is to declare more DStreams at the code level. Each DStream will be attached to its own consumer—and therefore each will have its own core consumption—on the cluster. The DStream operation union allows us to merge those streams, ensuring that we produce a single pipeline of data from our various input streams.

Let's assume that we create DStreams in parallel an put them in a sequence:

```
val inputDstreams: Seq[DStream[(K,V)]] = Seq.fill(parallelism: Int) {
... // the input Stream creation function
}
val joinedStream  = ssc.union(inputDstreams)
```

 The union of the created DStreams is important because this reduces the number of transformation pipelines on the input DStream to one. Not doing this will multiply the number of stages by the number of consumers, resulting in unnecessary overhead.

In this way, we can exploit the receiver parallelism, here represented by the #paral lelism factor of concurrently created DStreams.

Balancing Resources: Receivers Versus Processing Cores

Given that each created receiver consumes its own core in a cluster, increasing consumer parallelism has consequences in the number of cores available for processing in our cluster.

Let's imagine that we have a 12-core cluster that we want to dedicate to our streaming analytics application. When using a single receiver, we use one core for receiving and nine cores for processing data. The cluster might be underutilized because a single receiver might not receive enough data to give work to all of the available processing cores. Figure 18-5 illustrates that situation, in which the green nodes are being used for processing, and the gray nodes remain idle.

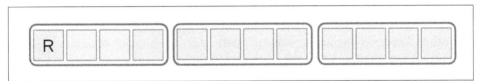

Figure 18-5. Single-receiver allocation

To improve cluster utilization, we increase the number of receivers, as we just discussed. In our hypothetical scenario, using four receivers provides us with a much better resource allocation, as shown in Figure 18-6.

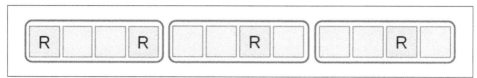

Figure 18-6. Multiple-receiver allocation

The batch interval is fixed by the needs of the analysis and remains the same. What should the block interval be? Well, four DStreams ingesting in parallel will necessarily create four times as many blocks per block interval as one single DStream would. Therefore, with the same block interval, the number of partitions of the unionized DStream will be four times what it was in the original case. Hence, we can't use the same block interval. Instead, we should use the following:

$$blockinterval = \frac{4 * batchinterval}{3 * Sparkcores}$$

Because we want *at least* three partitions, we round this number *down* to the nearest millisecond.

Generalizing, with an arbitrary set of characteristics, we should use this:

$$blockinterval = \frac{receivers * batchinterval}{partitionspercore * Sparkcores}$$

Where the total number of cores used in the system is as follows:

total system cores = # of receivers + # of spark cores

Achieving Zero Data Loss with the Write-Ahead Log

The original receiver design, previous to Spark v1.2, had a major design flaw. While the receiver is collecting data for the current block, that data is only found in a memory buffer in the receiver process. Only when the block is completed and delivered does it become replicated in the cluster. In case of failure of the receiver, the data in that buffer gets lost and cannot be recovered, causing data loss.

To prevent data loss, data collected by the receiver is additionally appended to a log file on a reliable filesystem. This is known as the write-ahead log (WAL), a component commonly used in database design to guarantee reliable and durable data reception.

The WAL is an append-only structure in which data is written before it is delivered for processing. When data is known to be correctly processed, its entry in the log is marked as processed. In the database world, the equivalent process is the commit of the transaction in which the data is involved, making this log also known as the *commit log*.

In case of failure, data from the WAL is replayed from the record following the last registered commit, compensating in that way for the potential loss of data of the receiver. The combination of the WAL and the receiver is known as the reliable receiver. Streaming sources based on the reliable receiver model are known as *reliable sources*.

Enabling the WAL

To enable the WAL-backed data delivery to ensure zero data loss, we need to apply the following settings:

`streamingContext.checkpoint(dir)`
    This directory is used for both checkpoints and the write-ahead logs.

`spark.streaming.receiver.writeAheadLog.enable` *(default:* `false`*)*
    Set to `true` to enable the write-ahead process.

Note that due to the increased work of writing to the log, the overall throughput of the streaming job might lower and the overall resource usage might increase. As the WAL writes to a reliable filesystem, the infrastructure of that filesystem needs to have enough resources to accept the continuous write stream to the log, in terms of storage and processing capacity.

The Receiverless or Direct Model

Spark Streaming aims to be a generic stream-processing framework. Within that premise, the receiver model provides a general, source-agnostic contract that enables the integration of any streaming source. But some sources allow for a direct consumption model in which the role of the receiver as an intermediary in the data delivery process becomes unnecessary.

The increasing popularity of Kafka as a streaming backend for Spark Streaming jobs made it a focus of additional consideration. In the previous section, we learned about the WAL as a solution to achieve zero data loss for the receiver model in face of failure.

Kafka is, at its core, an implementation of a distributed commit log. When the Kafka reliable receiver was implemented, it became evident that the use of the WAL was duplicating the same functionality already present in Kafka. Moreover, consuming data from Kafka into a receiver was not even necessary. Let us recall that the receiver takes care of data redundancy through duplication of the blocks in the Spark memory. Kafka already replicates data reliability and provides equivalent data durability guarantees. To consume data from Kafka, all that was required was to track the *offset* of the data already processed and compute the offset of the new data received in a batch interval. Using these two offsets for each partition consumed would be sufficient to launch a Spark job that would directly consume the data segment determined by these two offsets and operate on it. When the processing of the microbatch succeeds, the consumed offset is committed.

The direct connector model is more of a manager than a data broker. Its role is to compute data segments to be processed by Spark and maintain the bookkeeping of data to be processed versus data already handled. Given the high-performance and low-latency data delivery characteristics of Kafka, this method turned out to be much faster and requires fewer resources than the receiver-based implementation.

> For the specific usage of the *direct* connector for Kafka, refer to Chapter 19.

Summary

So far, we have seen a primer on the Spark Streaming execution model and the fundamentals of how it treats stream processing:

- Streams are aggregated data seen over time on a data source. On every block interval, a new partition of data is produced and replicated. In every batch interval (a multiple of the block interval), the resulting data is assembled into an RDD and a job can be scheduled on it.

- Scheduling is done by user-defined functions in a script, but can also be the byproduct of some built-in functionality (e.g., checkpointing). The scheduling itself has a fixed core.

- The most generic way of creating a DStream is the receiver model, which creates a job connecting to the input source on an executor, consuming one core. Parallelism can be increased in some cases by creating several DStreams.

- Factors such as resource allocation and configuration parameters affect the overall performance of a streaming job, and there are options to tune such behavior.

- Enabling the WAL prevents potential data loss at the expense of additional resource usage.

- For particular systems, such as Kafka, that provide high-performance and durable data delivery guarantees, it's possible to reduce the responsibilities of the receiver to minimal bookkeeping that computes microbatch intervals in terms native to the streaming system. This model, known as the direct model, is both more resource efficient and performant than having to copy and replicate the data into the memory of the Spark cluster.

## CHAPTER 19

Spark Streaming Sources

As you learned earlier in Chapter 2, a streaming source is a data provider that continuously delivers data. In Spark Streaming, *sources* are adaptors running within the context of the Spark Streaming job that implement the interaction with the external streaming source and provide the data to Spark Streaming using the DStream abstraction. From the programming perspective, consuming a streaming data source means creating a DStream using the appropriate implementation for the corresponding source.

In the "The DStream Abstraction" on page 206, we saw an example of how to consume data from a network socket. Let's revisit that example in Example 19-1.

Example 19-1. Creating a text stream from a socket connection

```
// creates a DStream using a client socket connected to the given host and port
val textDStream: DStream[String] = ssc.socketTextStream("localhost", 9876)
```

In Example 19-1, we can see that the creation of a streaming source is provided by a dedicated implementation. In this case, it is provided by the `ssc` instance, the *streaming context*, and results in a `DStream[String]` that contains the text data delivered by the socket typed with the content of the DStream. Although the implementation for each source is different, this pattern is the same for all of them: creating a source requires a `streamingContext` and results in a DStream that represents the contents of the stream. The streaming application further operates on the resulting DStream to implement the logic of the job at hand.

Types of Sources

As a generic stream-processing framework, Spark Streaming can integrate with a wide variety of streaming data sources.

When classified by their mode of operation, there are three different types of sources:

- Basic
- Receiver based
- Direct source

Basic Sources

Basic sources are natively provided by the `streamingContext`. They are provided primarily as examples or test sources and do not offer failure-recovery semantics. Therefore, they are not recommended to be used in production systems.

Following are the basic sources:

The File source

Used to monitor directories of a filesystem and read new files. Files are a widespread mechanism of communicating data between systems, especially in systems evolving from a batch-based integration model, such as data warehouses and many data lake implementations.

The Queue source

A producer-consumer queue local to the `streamingContext` that can be used to inject data into Spark Streaming. Typically used for testing.

We are going to talk about the `ConstantInputDStream`, which is not officially a source, but it performs a function similar to the *Queue* source, and it's much easier to use.

Receiver-Based Sources

As we discussed in Chapter 18, receivers are special processes in Spark Streaming that are in charge of accepting data from a streaming source and delivering it in a reliable way to Spark in the form of RDDs. Receivers are responsible for implementing data delivery reliability, even if the backing source cannot provide such guarantees. For that purpose, they receive and replicate the data within the cluster before making it available to Spark for processing.

Within this class of sources, we also have the reliable receivers, which improve the data reception guarantees through the use of a write-ahead log (WAL).

From the perspective of the programming model, each receiver is linked to a single DStream that represents the data delivered by its receiver to the Spark Streaming application.

To scale-up the number of receivers in a distributed context, we create several instances of a DStream that will consume its data.

Given that the receiver model was the original interaction model implemented in Spark Streaming, all sources that were supported since the initial versions are available as receiver-based sources, although many of them are deprecated in favor of the direct sources. The most commonly used receivers are: Socket, Kafka, Kinesis, Flume, and Twitter.

The receiver API also allows for the creation of custom sources. This enabled the proliferation of third-party sources for Spark Streaming and also let us create our own custom source, to connect to legacy enterprise systems, for example.

Direct Sources

As we discussed previously in Chapter 18, the realization that some sources, such as Kafka, could natively provide strong data delivery guarantees, rendered the data reliability of the receiver model irrelevant for those sources.

The direct model, also known as the *receiverless model*, is a lightweight controller that keeps track of the metadata related to data consumption from the corresponding source and computes microbatches from it, leaving the actual data transfer and processing to the core Spark engine. This simplified process relies directly on the data delivery semantics of the streaming source backend and the reliable computing model of Spark.

The most popular sources implemented using the direct approach are Kafka and Kinesis.

Commonly Used Sources

Given the widespread adoption of Spark Streaming, there are many open source and proprietary sources available. In the rest of this chapter, we cover the most popular sources delivered by the Spark project.

We begin with the basic sources, the *File* and the *Queue* sources, because they are quite easy to use and can provide a low-threshold entrance to start developing some examples in Spark Streaming.

After reviewing the built-in basic sources, we move to one example of a receiver-based source: the *socket* source, a source that implements a TCP client socket that can connect to and receive data from a TCP server on a network port.

Next, we discuss the Kafka source, given that Apache Kafka is probably the most popular open source event broker currently used to build streaming systems. Given the widespread use of Kafka, it has a detailed, up-to-date online coverage of its integration with Spark Streaming. In this discussion, we highlight the usage patterns as the starting point of adoption.

We close this chapter with a note about Apache Bahir, where you can find many more sources for Spark Streaming.

The File Source

The File source monitors a given directory in a filesystem and processes new files as they are discovered in the directory. The target filesystem must be Hadoop compatible and addressable from the distributed environment where Spark Streaming is running. A common storage choice is Hadoop Distributed File System (HDFS). Cloud block-storage systems, like Simple Storage Service (Amazon S3), are also supported, although they require additional testing regarding their behavior with respect to when new files are reported. This source is useful to bridge legacy systems, which usually deliver their results in batches of files.

The File source comes in the form of dedicated methods in the `StreamingContext`. The `StreamingContext` provides several versions with increasing levels of configuration options.

The most simple method is used to load a stream of text files from a filesystem directory path:

```
val stream: DStream[String] = ssc.textFileStream(path)
```

And a similar method is used to load a stream of binary files, containing fixed-length records:

```
val stream: DStream[Array[Byte]] = ssc.binaryRecordsStream(path, recordLength)
```

For custom data formats, the general form of the File source takes types K for the `KeyClass`, V for the `ValueClass`, and F as the `InputFormatClass`. All these types are defined using the Hadoop API, which provides many available implementations for commonly used types. The result is a DStream of key–value pairs that correspond to the provided type definition:

```
val stream: DStream[(K,V)] = ssc.fileStream[K,V,F] (
    directory: String,
    filter: Path => Boolean,
    newFilesOnly: Boolean,
    conf: Configuration)
```

Where the parameters are the following:

directory: String
: The directory to monitor for new files.

filter: Path => Boolean
: A predicate used to evaluate the files to be processed. An example of a filter predicate to select only .log files would be:

```
filter = (p:Path) => p.getFileName.toString.endsWith(".log")
```

newFilesOnly: Boolean
: A flag used to indicate whether existing files in the monitored directory should be considered at the beginning of the streaming process. When newFilesOnly is true, files present in the directory are considered using the time rules specified in the example that follows. When false, all files present in the monitored folder at the start of a job will be selected for processing.

conf : Configuration
: This is a Hadoop Configuration instance. We can use it to set up particular behavior, like end-of-line characters or credentials for a specific storage provider. For example, we could manually specify an implementation provider and credentials to access a given Amazon S3 bucket, like this:

```
val s3Conf = new Configuration()
s3Conf.set("fs.s3.impl","org.apache.hadoop.fs.s3native.NativeS3FileSystem")
s3Conf.set("fs.s3.awsAccessKeyId",awsAccessKeyId)
s3Conf.set("fs.s3.awsSecretAccessKey", awsSecretAccessKey)

val stream = ssc.fileStream[K,V,F] (directory, filter, newFilesOnly, s3Conf)
```

How It Works

At each batch interval, the File source checks the listing of the monitored directory. All new files found in the directory are selected for processing, read as an RDD, and given to Spark for processing.

How the File source defines new files deserves particular attention:

- At each batch interval, the directory listing is evaluated.
- The age of the file is determined by its last-modified timestamp.
- Files with a modified timestamp within the processing window interval are considered for processing and added to a list of processed files.
- Processed files are remembered for the length of the processing window interval so that files already processed are not selected again.

- Files older than the processing window interval are ignored. If the file was previously remembered, it is removed from the *remembered* list, becoming *forgotten*. We illustrate that process in Figure 19-1.

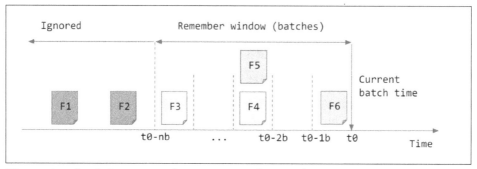

Figure 19-1. Spark Streaming File source remember window at t0

Let's examine more closely what's happening in Figure 19-1:

- The current batch time is indicated as *t0*.
- The remember window consists of *n* microbatches.
- Files F1 and F2 are in the *Ignored* area. They might have been processed in the past, but Spark Streaming has no knowledge of that.
- Files F3 and F4 have been processed already and are currently remembered.
- Files F5 and F6 are new. They become selected for processing and are included in the remembered list.

When time advances to the next batch interval, as shown in Figure 19-2, we can observe how F3 has aged to become part of the ignored list. The new file F7 is selected for processing and included in the remembered list.

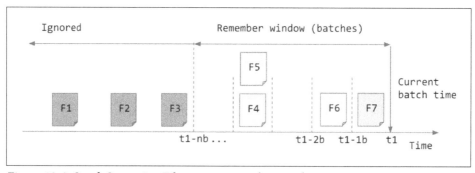

Figure 19-2. Spark Streaming File source remember window at t1

This process goes on for as long as the Spark Streaming process is operational. We can configure the length of the remember window by using the setting `spark.stream ing.minRememberDuration`, which defaults to 60 seconds. Note that this process assumes that the clock of the filesystem is synchronized with the clock of the executor running the Spark Streaming job.

The remember window is calculated in terms of microbatches. Even though the configuration parameter `spark.streaming.minRememberDuration` is provided as a time duration, the actual window will be computed as the `ceiling(remember_duration/ batch_interval)`.

For example, using the default remember duration of 60 seconds and a batch interval of 45 seconds, the number of remember batches will be `ceil(60/45) = 2`. This means that the actual duration of the remember period is 90 seconds.

The File source does not offer any data reliability guarantees. Upon restart of a streaming process that uses the File source, the recovery semantics will be based on the clock time and the dynamics of the remember window depicted in Figure 19-2. This means that a quick recovery might incur in duplicated records as files already processed become eligible again, while if the recovery time is long, unprocessed files might age past the point of the remember window and become ineligible, resulting in lost data.

For a robust file-based stream integration we recommend the use of Structured Streaming and its File source.

The Queue Source

The Queue source is a programmatic source. It does not receive data from an external system. Instead, it provides a producer-consumer queue that allows the creation of a DStream as the consumer, which can be fed with data from within the process itself acting as the producer.

As a basic source, the Queue source is provided by the `streamingContext` instance:

```
// ssc is an instance of SparkContext
val queueStream: InputDStream[T] = queueStream[T](
    queue,
    oneAtATime,
    defaultRDD
  )
```

Here are the parameters:

`queue: Queue[RDD[T]]`

> A `scala.collection.mutable.Queue` of the type `RDD[T]`. This queue must be created beforehand. It might already be populated with data or data can be pushed at a later stage.

`oneAtATime: Boolean`

> A flag to indicate how the data from the queue is to be dosed. When `oneAtATime` = `true` a single RDD element from the queue will be taken at each batch interval for processing. When `oneAtATime` = `false`, all RDD elements available in the queue at each batch interval will be consumed at once.

`defaultRDD: RDD[T]`

> An RDD instance to be offered for processing in the case that the queue is empty. This option may be used to ensure that there's always data at the consumer side independently of the producer. There's an available overload with this parameter omitted, in which case, there is no data when the queue is empty.

How It Works

The Queue source implements a producer-consumer pattern using the `queue` as an intermediary. A programmatic producer adds RDDs of data to the queue. The consumer side implements the DStream interface and presents the data to the streaming system.

The primary use case of the Queue source is the creation of unit tests for Spark Streaming programs. Test data is prepared and added to the queue. The test execution uses the DStream attached to the Queue source and the result is asserted against expectations.

Using a Queue Source for Unit Testing

For example, let's assume that we want to test `streamWordCount`, a streaming implementation of the now famous word count program that counts instances of words in a dataset.

A streaming version of word count could look like this:

```
val streamWordCount: DStream[String] => DStream[(String, Long)] = stream =>
    stream.flatMap(sentence => sentence.split(","))
        .map(word => (word.trim, 1L))
        .reduceByKey((count1: Long, count2:Long) => count1 + count2)
```

This is a functional representation of the word count computation. Note that instead of starting with a given DStream implementation, we expect it as a parameter to the function. In this way, we separate the DStream instance from the process, allowing us to use the queueDStream as input.

To create the queueDStream, we require a queue and some data, where the data must already be in RDDs:

```
import scala.collection.mutable.Queue
val queue = new Queue[RDD[String]]() // the mutable queue instance
val data = List(
    "Chimay, Ciney, Corsendonck, Duivel, Chimay, Corsendonck ",
    "Leffe, Ciney, Leffe, Ciney, Grimbergen, Leffe, La Chouffe, Leffe",
    "Leffe, Hapkin, Corsendonck, Leffe, Hapkin, La Chouffe, Leffe"
  )
// we create a list of RDDs, each one containing a String of words
val rdds = data.map(sentence => sparkContext.parallelize(Array(sentence)))
// we enqueue the rdds
queue.enqueue(rdds:_*)
```

With the data and queue in place, we can create the queueDStream:

```
val testStream  = ssc.queueStream(queue = queue, oneAtATime = true)
```

The next step involves a method to extract the results from the streaming output. Because we are in the mood for queues, we also use one to capture the results:

```
val queueOut = new Queue[Array[(String, Long)]]()
```

At this point, we are ready to define the execution of our test:

```
streamWordCount(testStream).foreachRDD(rdd => queueOut.enqueue(rdd.collect))
ssc.start()
ssc.awaitTerminationOrTimeout(3000) // 3 batch intervals of 1 second
```

Finally, we can assert that we received the results that we expect:

```
// first batch
assert(queueOut.dequeue.contains("Chimay" -> 2), "missing an expected element")
// second batch
assert(queueOut.dequeue.contains("Leffe" -> 4), "missing an expected element")
```

A Simpler Alternative to the Queue Source: The ConstantInputDStream

The ConstantInputDStream allows us to provide a single RDD value to the stream on each batch interval. Although not officially a *source*, the ConstantInputDStream provides functionality similar to the Queue source and it is much easier to set up. While the Queue source allows us to programmatically provide microbatches of custom data to a streaming job, the ConstantInputDStream lets us provide a single RDD that will constantly be replayed for each batch interval:

```
// ssc is an instance of SparkContext
val constantStream: InputDStream[T] = new ConstantInputDStream[T](ssc, rdd)
```

Here are the parameters:

ssc: StreamingContext
> This is the active StreamingContext instance.

rdd: RDD[T]
> This is the RDD to replay at each batch interval.

How it works

The RDD instance provided to the ConstantInputDStream at creation time will be replayed at each batch interval. This creates a constant source of data that can be used for testing purposes.

ConstantInputDStream as a random data generator

Oftentimes, we need to generate a random dataset for tests or simulation purposes. As we just learned, the ConstantInputDStream repeats the same RDD over and over again. The clue of this technique is that functions are values. Instead of creating a data RDD, we create an RDD of random data generator functions. These functions are evaluated at each batch interval, creating in this way a continuous flow of random data into our streaming application.

For this technique, we need to first create a random data generator, which is a function from Unit into our desired type: () => T. In this example, we are going to generate a stream of sensor records. Each record is a comma-separated String that contains an id, a timestamp, and the value:

```scala
import scala.util.Random

val maxSensorId = 1000
// random sensor Id
val sensorId: () => Int = () =>  Random.nextInt(maxSensorId)
// random sensor value
val data: () => Double = () => Random.nextDouble
// current time as timestamp in milliseconds
val timestamp: () => Long = () => System.currentTimeMillis
// Generates records with Random data, with 10% of invalid records

val recordGeneratorFunction: () => String = { () =>
  if (Random.nextDouble < 0.9) {
    Seq(sensorId().toString, timestamp(), data()).mkString(",")
  } else {
    // simulate 10% crap data as well… real world streams are seldom clean
    "!!~corrupt~^&##$"
  }
}
```

With this recordGeneratorFunction, we can create an RDD of functions:

```
// we assume `n` as the number of records delivered by each RDD
val n = 100
val nGenerators = Seq.fill(n)(recordGeneratorFunction)
val sensorDataGeneratorRDD = sparkContext.parallelize(nGenerators )
```

 The rationale behind this method is that, in Scala, functions are values. RDDs are collections of values, and hence we can create collections of functions.

We can now create our `ConstantInputDStream` using the `sensorDataGeneratorRDD`:

```
import org.apache.spark.streaming.dstream.ConstantInputDStream
// ssc is an active streaming context
val stream: DStream[() => String] =
    new ConstantInputDStream(ssc, sensorDataGeneratorRDD)
```

Note the type signature of the `DStream[() => String]`. To make the values concrete, we need to evaluate that function. Given that this transformation is part of the DStream lineage, it will happen at each batch interval, effectively generating new values each time:

```
val materializedValues = stream.map(generatorFunc => generatorFunc())
```

If we are using the Spark Shell, we can observe these values by using the `print` output operation and starting the `streamingContext`:

```
materializedValues.print() // output operation
ssc.start

-------------------------------------------
Time: 1550491831000 ms
-------------------------------------------
581,1550491831012,0.22741105530053118
112,1550491831012,0.636337819187351
247,1550491831012,0.46327133256442854
!!~corrupt~^&##$
65,1550491831012,0.5154695043787045
634,1550491831012,0.8736169835370479
885,1550491831012,0.6434156134252232
764,1550491831012,0.03938150372641791
111,1550491831012,0.05571238399267886
!!~corrupt~^&##$
```

This technique is very useful to have test data at early stages of the development phase, without requiring the time and effort to set up an external streaming system.

The Socket Source

The Socket source acts as a TCP client and is implemented as a receiver-based source, where the receiver process instantiates and manages the TCP client connection. It connects to a TCP server running on a network location, identified by its `host:port` combination.

The Socket source is available as a method of the `sparkContext`. Its general form is as follows:

```
// ssc is an instance of SparkContext
val stream: DStream[Type] =
  ssc.socketStream[Type](hostname, port, converter, storageLevel)
```

It has the following parameters:

`hostname: String`
> This is the network host of the server to which to connect.

`port: Int`
> The network port to which to connect.

`converter: (InputStream) => Iterator[Type]`
> A function able to decode the input stream into the target type specified.

`storageLevel: StorageLevel`
> The `StorageLevel` to use for the data received by this source. A recommended starting point is `StorageLevel.MEMORY_AND_DISK_SER_2`, which is the common default for other sources.

There is also a simplified version for a text stream encoding using the UTF-8 charset. This alternative is the most commonly used, given its simplicity:

```
// ssc is an instance of SparkContext
val stream: DStream[String] = ssc.socketTextStream(host, port)
```

How It Works

The Socket source is implemented as a receiver-based process that takes care of the socket connection and related logic to receive the stream of data.

The Socket source is commonly used as a test source. Given the simplicity of creating a network server using command-line utilities like `netcat`, the Socket source has been the go-to source for many of the available basic examples of Spark Streaming. In this scenario, it's common to run the client and the server in the same machine, leading to the use of `localhost` as the *host* specification, like in the following snippet:

```
// ssc is an instance of SparkContext
val textStream = ssc.socketTextStream("localhost", 9876)
```

It's worth noting that the use of `localhost` works only when Spark is running in local mode. If Spark runs in a cluster, the Socket source receiver process will be hosted in an arbitrary executor. Therefore, in a cluster setup, proper use of IP addresses or DNS names is required for the Socket source to connect to the server.

 The Socket source implementation in the Spark project at SocketInputDStream.scala (*http://bit.ly/2vqPRCv*) is a good example of how to develop a custom receiver.

The Kafka Source

When it comes to streaming platforms, Apache Kafka is one of the most popular choices for a scalable messaging broker. Apache Kafka is a highly scalable distributed streaming platform based on the abstraction of a distributed commit log.

Kafka implements a publish/subscribe pattern: clients, called *producers* in Kafka terminology, publish data to the brokers. The consumers use a pull-based subscription, making it possible that different subscribers consume the available data at different rates. One subscriber might consume the data as it becomes available for real-time use cases, whereas another might choose to pick larger chunks of data over time; for example, when we want to generate a report over the last hour of data. This particular behavior makes Kafka an excellent match for Spark Streaming because it is complementary to the microbatch approach: longer microbatches naturally hold more data and can increase the throughput of the application, whereas a shorter batch interval improves the latency of the application at the expense of lower throughput.

The Kafka source is available as a separate library that needs to be imported in the dependencies of the project to use it.

For Spark 2.4, this is the dependency to use:

```
groupId = org.apache.spark
artifactId = spark-streaming-kafka-0-10_2.11
version = 2.4.0
```

 Note that Kafka integration for Structured Streaming is a different library. Make sure you use the correct dependency for the API in use.

To create a Kafka direct stream, we call `createDirectStream` in `KafkaUtils`, the implementation provider for this source:

```
val stream: InputDStream[ConsumerRecord[K, V]] =
  KafkaUtils.createDirectStream[K, V](ssc, locationStrategy, consumerStrategy)
```

Following are the type parameters:

K
   The type of the message key.

V
   The type of the message value.

And here are the expected parameters:

`ssc: StreamingContext`
   The active streaming context.

`locationStrategy: LocationStrategy`
   The strategy to use to schedule consumers for a given (`topic`, `partition`) on an executor. The choices are as follows:

   `PreferBrokers`
      Attempts to schedule the consumer on the same executor as the Kafka brokers. This works only in the unlikely scenario that Spark and Kafka run on the same physical nodes.

   `PreferConsistent`
      Attempts to preserve the consumer-executor mapping for a given (`topic`, `partition`). This is important for performance reasons because the consumers implement message prefetching.

   `PreferFixed(map: java.util.Map[TopicPartition, String])`
      Place a particular (`topic`, `partition`) combination on the given executor. The preferred strategy is `LocationStrategies.PreferConsistent`. The other two options are to be used in very specific cases. Note that the location preference is a hint. The actual consumer for a partition can be placed somewhere else, depending on the availability of resources.

`consumerStrategy: ConsumerStrategy[K, V]`
   The consumer strategy determines how (`topics`, `partitions`) are selected for consumption. There are three different strategies available:

   `Subscribe`
      Subscribes to a collection of named topics.

   `SubscribePattern`
      Subscribes to a collection of topics matching the provided `regex` pattern.

   `Assign`
      Provides a fixed list of (`topics`, `partitions`) to consume. Note that when using this method, arbitrary partitions of a given topic might be skipped. Use

only when the requirements call for such strict strategy. In such a case, prefer to compute the (`topic`, `partition`) assignment instead of relying on static configuration. The most common `consumerStrategy` is `Subscribe`. We illustrate the use of the Kafka source with this strategy in the next example.

Using the Kafka Source

Setting up a Kafka source requires us to define a configuration and use that configuration in the creation of the source. This configuration is provided as a `map` of `configuration-name, value`. Here are the mandatory elements in the configuration:

`bootstrap.servers`
> Provide the location of the Kafka broker as a comma-separated list of `host:port`.

`key.deserializer`
> The class used to deserialize the binary stream into the expected key type. Kafka comes with the most common types already implemented.

`value.deserializer`
> Analogous to the `key.deserializer` but for the values.

`group.id`
> The Kafka consumer group name to use.

`auto.offset.reset`
> The starting point in a partition when a new consumer group subscribes. `earliest` starts consuming all of the data available in the topic, whereas `latest` ignores all existing data and starts consuming records from the last offset at the moment the group joins.

There are many knobs that can be tuned on the underlying Kafka consumer. For a list of all configuration parameters, consult the online documentation (*http://bit.ly/2vrUH2n*):

```
import org.apache.spark.streaming.kafka010._

val preferredHosts = LocationStrategies.PreferConsistent
val topics = List("random")
import org.apache.kafka.common.serialization.StringDeserializer
val kafkaParams: Map[String, Object] = Map(
  "bootstrap.servers" -> "localhost:9092",
  "key.deserializer" -> classOf[StringDeserializer],
  "value.deserializer" -> classOf[StringDeserializer],
  "group.id" -> "randomStream",
  "auto.offset.reset" -> "latest",
  "enable.auto.commit" -> Boolean.box(true)
)
```

With the configuration in place, we can proceed to create the direct Kafka source:

```
import org.apache.kafka.common.TopicPartition
val offsets = Map(new TopicPartition("datatopic", 0) -> 2L)

val dstream = KafkaUtils.createDirectStream[String, String](
  ssc,
  preferredHosts,
  ConsumerStrategies.Subscribe[String, String](topics, kafkaParams, offsets))
```

In this example, we specify initial offsets for our `topic` using the `offsets` parameters for the purpose of illustrating the usage of this option.

How It Works

The Kafka direct stream functions based on offsets, which are indexes of positions of elements in the stream.

The gist of data delivery is that the Spark driver queries offsets and decides offset ranges for every batch interval from Apache Kafka. After it receives those offsets, the driver dispatches them by launching a task for each partition, resulting in a 1:1 parallelism between the Kafka partitions and the Spark partitions at work. Each task retrieves data using its specific offset ranges. The driver does not send data to the executors; instead, it simply sends a few offsets they use to directly consume data. As a consequence, the parallelism of data ingestion from Apache Kafka is much better than the legacy receiver model, where each stream was consumed by a single machine.

This is also more efficient for fault tolerance because the executors in that `Direct Stream` acknowledge the reception of data for their particular offsets by committing the offsets. In case of a failure, the new executor picks up the partition data from the latest known committed offsets. This behavior guarantees an at-least-once data delivery semantic because output operators can still be offered a replay of data that they have already seen. To achieve effectively exactly-once semantics, we require the output operations to be idempotent. That is, executing the operation more than once has the same result as executing the operation once. For example, writing a record on a database using a unique primary key that ensures that if the record is inserted, we will find only one instance of it.

Where to Find More Sources

A few sources that started their life as part of the Spark codebase, as well as some additional contributions, moved under Apache Bahir (*https://bahir.apache.org*), a project that serves as an umbrella repository for a number of Apache Spark and Apache Flink extensions.

Among these extensions, we find a series of Spark Streaming connectors for the following:

Apache CouchDB/Cloudant
    A NoSQL database

Akka
    An actor system Google Cloud Pub/Sub: A cloud-based pub/sub system proprietary to Google

MQTT
    A lightweight machine-to-machine/Internet of Things (IoT) pub/sub protocol

Twitter
    A source to subscribe to tweets from this popular social network

ZeroMQ
    An asynchronous messaging library

To use a connector from the Apache Bahir library, add the corresponding dependency to the project build definition and use the dedicated method provided by the library to create a stream.

## CHAPTER 20

Spark Streaming Sinks

After acquiring data through a source represented as a DStream and applying a series of transformations using the DStream API to implement our business logic, we would want to inspect, save, or produce that result to an external system.

As we recall from Chapter 2, in our general streaming model, we call the component in charge of externalizing the data from the streaming process a sink. In Spark Streaming, sinks are implemented using the so-called *output operations*.

In this chapter, we are going to explore the capabilities and modalities of Spark Streaming to produce data to external systems through these output operations.

Output Operations

Output operations play a crucial role in every Spark Streaming application. They are required to trigger the computations over the DStream and, at the same time, they provide access to the resulting data through a programmable interface.

In Figure 20-1 we illustrate a generic Spark Streaming job that takes two streams as input, transforms one of them, and then joins them together before writing the result to a database. At execution time, the chain of DStream transformations that end on that *output operation* becomes a Spark job.

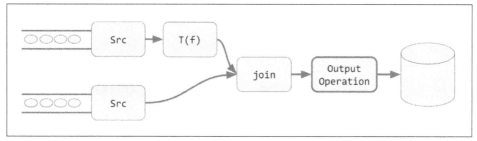

Figure 20-1. A Spark Streaming job

This job is attached to the Spark Streaming scheduler. In turn, the scheduler triggers the execution of the defined job at each batch interval, shown in Figure 20-2.

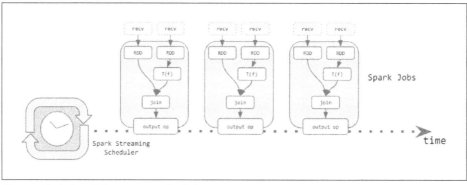

Figure 20-2. Spark Streaming scheduler

Output operations provide the link between the following:

- The sequence of lazy transformations on DStreams
- The Spark Streaming scheduler
- The external systems we produce data to

From the execution model perspective, every output operation declared in the streaming program is attached to the Spark Streaming scheduler in the same order in which they were declared in the program. This ordering guarantees a sequencing semantic in which later output operations will be triggered after the previous operation has finished execution. For example, in the following code snippet, we are storing media assets in a database before they are added to the searchable index. The guaranteed order of execution of output operations in Spark Streaming will ensure that the new media is added to the main database before it becomes searchable through the search index:

```
// assume a mediaStream is a DStream[Media],
// Media is the type that contains the meta-data for new audio/video assets
```

```
// Save to the assets database
mediaStream.foreachRDD{mediaRDD => assetsDB.store(mediaRDD)}

// Add the new media to an ElasticSearch Index
mediaStream.saveToEs("assets/media")
```

Every Spark Streaming job must have, at least, one output operation. This is a logical requirement; otherwise, there's no way to materialize transformations or obtain results. This requirement is enforced at runtime, at the moment that the sparkStrea mingContext.start() operation is called. A streaming job that does not provide at least one output operation will fail to start, and throw the following error:

```
scala> ssc.start()

17/06/30 12:30:16 ERROR StreamingContext:
    Error starting the context, marking it as stopped
java.lang.IllegalArgumentException:
    requirement failed: No output operations registered, so nothing to execute
```

Output operations, as the name suggests, provide access to the data that results from the computations declared on the DStream. We use them to observe the resulting data, save it to disk, or feed it to other systems, like storing it in a database for later querying or directly sending it to an online monitoring system for observation.

In general terms, the function of output operations is to schedule the provided action at the intervals dictated by the batch interval. For output operations that take a closure, the code in the closure executes once at each batch interval on the Spark driver, not distributed in the cluster. All output operations return Unit; that is, they execute only side-effecting actions and are not composable. A streaming job can have as many output operations as necessary. They are the endpoints for the transformation DAG of DStreams.

Built-In Output Operations

There are a few output operations provided by the Spark Streaming core library. We take a look at them in the following subsections.

print

print() outputs the first elements of a DStream to the standard output. When used without arguments, it will print the first 10 elements of the DStream at every streaming interval, including the timestamp when the operation runs. It's also possible to call print(num: Int) with an arbitrary number, to obtain that given maximum of elements at each streaming interval.

Given that the results are written only to the standard output, the practical use of print is limited to exploration and debugging of a streaming computation, where we can see on the console a continuous log of the first elements of a DStream.

For example, calling print() in the network stream of names that we used in Chapter 2, we see the following:

```
namesDStream.print()
ssc.start()


-------------------------------------------
Time: 1498753595000 ms
-------------------------------------------
MARSHALL
SMITH
JONES
BROWN
JOHNSON
WILLIAMS
MILLER
TAYLOR
WILSON
DAVIS
...
```

saveAsxyz

The saveAsxyz family of output operations provides a file-based sink for the stream output. Here are the available options:

saveAsTextFiles(prefix, suffix)
  Stores the content of the DStream as files in the filesystem. The prefix and optional suffix are used to locate and name the file in the target filesystem. One file is generated at each streaming interval. The name of each generated file will be prefix-<timestamp_in_milliseconds>[.suffix].

saveAsObjectFiles(prefix, suffix)
  Saves a DStream of serializable objects to files using standard Java serialization. The file generation dynamic is the same as for saveAsTextFiles.

saveAsHadoopFiles(prefix, suffix)
  Saves the DStream as Hadoop files. The file generation dynamic is the same as for saveAsTextFiles.

Hadoop Distributed File System Disk Usage and Streaming Files

It is important to highlight that, depending on the data throughput and chosen streaming interval, saveAsxxx operations often result in many small files, one generated at each interval. This is potentially detrimental when used in combination with filesystems that have large allocation blocks. Such is the case with Hadoop Distributed File System (HDFS), for which the default block size is of 128 MB. Doing a back-of-the-envelope calculation, a DStream with a throughput of 150 Kb and with a batch interval of 10 seconds will generate files of approximately 1.5 MB at each interval. After a day, we should have stored about 12.65 GB of data in 8,640 files. The actual usage in an HDFS with a block size of 128 Mb will be 8,640 x 128 Mb, or roughly 1 TB of data. If we take into account a replication factor of 3, which is a typical HDFS setting, our initial 12.65 GB of data occupies 3 TB of raw disk storage. This is a waste of resources that we would like to avoid.

When using saveAsxxx output operations, one approach to consider is to make tumbling windows of a suitable size to match the characteristics of the secondary storage. Continuing with the previous example, we could make a window of 850 seconds (almost 15 minutes) to create files of about 127 MB that are suitable for optimized storage in those conditions. As we discuss in detail in Chapter 21, we should also consider reducing the data before any storage step, although it is understood that this is a use-case–dependent requirement.

Finally, note that the new Hadoop API makes use of Hadoop sequence files to alleviate the issues tied to HDFS storage space consumption. This is reflected in the explicit mentioning of newAPI in the name of the methods that access these better implementations. To learn more about Sequence files and their impact on disk usage, see [White2009].

foreachRDD

foreachRDD(func) is a general-purpose output operation that provides access to the underlying RDD within the DStream at each streaming interval.

All other output operations mentioned earlier use foreachRDD to back their implementations. We could say that foreachRDD is the native output operator for Spark Streaming, and all other output operations are derived from it.

It is our workhorse to materialize Spark Streaming results and arguably the most useful native output operation. As such, it deserves its own section.

Using foreachRDD as a Programmable Sink

`foreachRDD` is the primary method to interact with the data that has been processed through the transformations declared on the DStream. `foreachRDD` has two method overloads:

`foreachRDD(foreachFunc: RDD[T] => Unit)`
> The function passed as a parameter takes an RDD and applies side-effecting operations on it.

`foreachRDD(foreachFunc: (RDD[T], Time) => Unit)`
> This is an alternative in which we also have access to the time when the operation takes place, which can be used to differentiate the data from the time-of-arrival perspective.

> It's important to note that the time provided by the `foreachRDD` method refers to processing time. As we discussed in "The Effect of Time" on page 25, this is the time when the streaming engine handles the event. The event of type T, contained in the `RDD[T]`, might or might not include additional information about the time when the event was produced, the time domain we understand as event time.

Within the closure of the `foreachRDD`, we have access to the two abstraction layers of Spark Streaming:

The Spark Streaming scheduler
> Functions applied within the `foreachRDD` closure that does not operate on the RDD execute locally in the driver program within the scope of the Spark Streaming scheduler. This level is useful for bookkeeping of iterations, accessing external web services to enrich the streaming data, local (mutable) variables, or the local filesystem. It's important to remark that at this level we have access to the `SparkContext` and the `SparkSession`, making it possible to interact with other subsystems of Spark, such as Spark SQL, DataFrames, and Datasets.

RDD operations
> Operations applied to the RDD provided to the closure function will be executed distributedly in the Spark cluster. All usual RDD-based operations are allowed in this scope. These operations will follow the typical Spark-core process of serialization and distributed execution in the cluster.

A common pattern is to observe two closures in `foreachRDD`: an outer scope, containing the local operations, and an inner closure applied to the RDD that executes in the cluster. This duality is often a source of confusion and is best learned by way of a code example.

Let's consider the code snippet in Example 20-1, in which we want to sort the incoming data into a set of *alternatives* (any concrete classification). These alternatives change dynamically and are managed by an external service that we access through an external web service call. At each batch interval, the external service is consulted for the set of alternatives to consider. For each alternative, we create a `formatter`. We use this particular `formatter` to transform the corresponding records by applying a distributed `map` transformation. Lastly, we use a `foreachPartition` operation on the filtered RDD to get a connection to a database and store the records. The `DB` connection is not serializable, and therefore we need this particular construct on the RDD to get a local instance on each executor.

 This is a simplified version of an actual Spark Streaming production job that took care of sorting Internet of Things (IoT) data for devices of many different customers.

Example 20-1. RDD operations within foreachRDD

```
dstream.foreachRDD{rdd => ❶
    rdd.cache() ❷
    val alternatives = restServer.get("/v1/alternatives").toSet ❸
    alternatives.foreach{alternative =>   ❹
      val filteredRDD = rdd.filter(element => element.kind == alternative) ❺
      val formatter = new Formatter(alternative) ❻
      val recordRDD = filteredRDD.map(element => formatter(element))
      recordRDD.foreachPartition{partition => ❼
          val conn = DB.connect(server) ❽
          partition.foreach(element => conn.insert(alternative, element) ❾
      }
    }
    rdd.unpersist(true) ❿
}
```

At first glance, a lot is going on in this DStream output operation. Let's break it down into more digestible pieces:

❶ We declare a `foreachRDD` operation on a DStream and use the closure notation `f{ x => y }` to provide an inline implementation.

❷ We begin our implementation by caching the provided `RDD` because we are going to iterate multiple times over its content. (We discuss caching in detail in "Caching" on page 342).

❸ We access the web service. This happens once at each batch interval and the execution takes place on the driver host. This is also important from the networking perspective, because executors might be "enclosed" in a private network, whereas the driver might have firewall access to other services in the infrastructure.

❹ We start a loop over the values contained in the received set, letting us iteratively filter over the values contained by the RDD.

❺ This declares a `filter` transformation over the RDD. This operation is lazy and will take place in a distributed manner in the cluster when some action would call for materialization.

❻ We obtain a local reference to a serializable Formatter instance that we use in line 7 to format the records filtered in the previous step.

❼ We use a `foreachPartition` action on our filtered RDD.

❽ We need a local instance of the database driver at the executor.

❾ We issue parallel insertion of the records into the database.

❿ Finally, we `unpersist` the RDD to free up the memory for the next iteration.

In Figure 20-3, we highlight the different execution scopes of the code within the closure of a `foreachRDD` call. In a nutshell, all code that is not backed by an RDD operation executes locally in the context of the driver. Functions and closures called on RDDs are executed in a distributed manner in the cluster. We must pay extra attention to avoid passing nonserializable code from the local context to the RDD execution context. This is an often-named source of issues in Spark Streaming applications.

```
                                                              Executes on the Driver

         dstream.foreachRDD{rdd =>
              rdd.cache()
              val alternatives = restServer.get("/v1/alternatives").toSet
              alternatives.foreach{alternative =>
  ⊢                 val byAlternativeRDD = rdd.filter(element => element.kind == alternative)
  closure             val asRecordRDD = byAlternativeRDD.map(element => asRecord(element))
  foreachRDD          asRecordRDD.foreachPartition{partition =>
                          val conn = DB.connect(server)
                          partition.foreach(element => conn.insert(element))
                      }
                  }
              rdd.unpersist(true)                              Executes distributed on
                                                               the Workers
         }
```

Figure 20-3. Scope of foreachRDD closure

As we can see, `foreachRDD` is a versatile output operation with which we can mix and match local and distributed operations to obtain results of our computations and push data to other systems after it has been processed by the streaming logic.

Third-Party Output Operations

Several third-party libraries add Spark Streaming support for specific target systems by using the library enrichment pattern in Scala to add output operations to DStreams.

For example, the Spark-Cassandra Connector (*http://bit.ly/2IPiUIL*) by Datastax enables a `saveToCassandra` operation on DStreams to directly save the streaming data to a target Apache Cassandra keyspace and table. The spark-kafka-writer (*http://bit.ly/2ZNLrnw*) by Ben Fradet enables a similar construct, `dStream.writeToKafka`, to write a DStream to a Kafka topic.

Elasticsearch provides support for Spark Streaming using the same pattern. The Spark support for the Elasticsearch library enriches the `DStream` API with a `saveToEs` call. You can find more information in Elastic's Spark Integration Guide (*http://bit.ly/2V3DyLL*).

Those library implementations make use of Scala implicits and `foreachRDD` behind the scenes to offer user-friendly, high-level APIs toward specific third-party systems, saving the users from the sometimes intricate details that deal with the multilevel abstractions within the `foreachRDD` explained previously.

For more connectors, see SparkPackages (*https://spark-packages.org*).

## CHAPTER 21

Time-Based Stream Processing

As we have hinted at previously, and as we have shown in previous transformations, Spark Streaming offers the capability of building time-based aggregates of data. In contrast with Structured Streaming, the out-of-the-box capabilities of Spark Streaming in this area are limited to processing time, which, if you recall from "The Effect of Time" on page 25, is the time when the streaming engine processes the events.

In this chapter, we are going to look into the different aggregation capabilities of Spark Streaming. Although they are constrained to the processing-time domain, they provide rich semantics and can be helpful to process data in a scalable and resource-constrained way.

Window Aggregations

Aggregation is a frequent pattern in stream data processing, reflecting the difference in concerns from the producers of the data (at the input) and the consumers of data (at the output).

As discussed in "Window Aggregations" on page 19, the concept of a *window* of data over time can help us to create aggregates that span large periods of time. The Spark Streaming API offers definitions for the two generic window concepts presented in that section, *tumbling* and *sliding windows*, and provides specialized reduce functions that operate over windows to limit the amount of intermediate memory required to execute a given aggregation over a period of time.

In the next pages, we are going to explore the windowing capabilities of Spark Streaming:

- Tumbling windows
- Sliding windows
- Window-based reductions

Tumbling Windows

In Spark Streaming, the most basic window definition is the `window(<time>)` operation on DStreams. This DStream transformation creates a new *windowed* DStream that can further transform to implement our desired logic.

Assuming a DStream of hashtags, we can do this with tumbling windows:

```
val tumblingHashtagFrequency = hashTags.window(Seconds(60))
                                       .map(hashTag => (hashTag,1))
                                       .reduceByKey(_ + _)
```

In the `window` operation, before the `map` and `reduceByKey` steps—that we now know do a simple counting—we are reprogramming the segmentation of our DStream into RDDs. The original stream, `hashTags`, follows a strict segmentation according to the batch interval: one RDD per batch.

In this case, we are configuring the new DStream, `hashTags.window(Seconds(60))`, to contain one RDD per 60 seconds. Every time the clock ticks 60 seconds, a new RDD is created on the cluster's resources, independently of the previous elements of the same windowed DStream. In that sense, the window is *tumbling* as explained in "Tumbling Windows" on page 20: every RDD is 100% composed of new "fresh" elements read on the wire.

Window Length Versus Batch Interval

Because the creation of a windowed stream is obtained by coalescing the information of several RDDs of the original stream into a single one for the windowed stream, the window interval *must be* a multiple of the batch interval.

Naturally, any window length that's a multiple of the initial `batch interval` can be passed as an argument. Hence, this kind of grouped stream allows the user to ask questions of the last minute, 15 minutes, or hour of data—more precisely, of the k-th interval of the windowed streaming computation runtime.

One important observation that takes new users by surprise: the window interval is aligned with the start of the streaming application. For example, given a 30-minute window over a DStream with a batch interval of two minutes, if the streaming job starts at 10:11, the windowed intervals will be computed at 10:41, 11:11, 11:41, 12:11, 12:41, and so on.

Sliding Windows

Although the information of "what were the most popular hashtags each 10 minutes during a famous sporting event" is interesting for forensics or future predictions, it is not the kind of question one usually asks during that event. Neither is a tumbling window the relevant time frame when detecting anomalies. In that case, aggregates are usually necessary because the values being observed have frequent but often small, and therefore meaningless fluctuations, that require the context provided by additional data points for analysis. The price of a stock or the temperature of a component have small fluctuations that should not be observed individually. The actual trends become visible by observing a series of recent events.

It is often useful to look at a different type of aggregate that presents data over a relatively large period, while keeping part of it fresh—sliding windows:

```
val slidingSums = hashTags.window(Seconds(60), Seconds(10))
                          .map(hashTag => (hashTag, 1))
                          .reduceByKey(_ + _)
```

In this example, we are describing a different type of DStream to compute the most frequent hashtags on: this time, a new RDD is produced every 10 seconds. In this alternative of the `window` function, the first argument, named `windowDuration`, determines the length of the window, whereas the second argument, called `slideDura tion`, dictates how often we want to observe a new window of data.

Coming back to the example, the resulting windowed DStream will contain RDDs that present the result of the computation over the latest 60 seconds of data, produced every 10 seconds.

This sliding view makes it possible to implement a monitoring application, and it is not infrequent to see the data produced by such a stream be sent to a dashboard after processing. In that case, naturally, the refresh rate of the dashboard is linked to the slide interval.

Sliding Windows Versus Batch Interval

Again, because the RDDs of the output function are obtained by coalescing the input RDDs of the original DStream, it is clear that the slide interval needs to be a multiple of the batch interval, and that the window interval needs to be a multiple of the slide interval.

For example, using a *streaming context* with a batch interval of 5 seconds, and a base DStream called `stream`, the expression `stream.window(30, 9)` is illegal because the slide interval is not a multiple of the batch interval. A correct window specification would be `stream.window(30, 10)`. The expression `stream.window(Seconds(40), Seconds(25))` is equally invalid, despite the window duration and slide interval being a multiple of the batch interval. That's because the window interval must be a multiple of the slide interval. In this case, `stream.window(Seconds(50), Seconds(25))` is a correct window duration and sliding interval definition.

In a nutshell, the batch interval can be seen as an "indivisible atom" of the time interval of windowed DStreams.

Finally, note that the sliding window needs to be smaller than the window length for the computation to make sense. Spark will output runtime errors if one of these constraints is not respected.

Sliding Windows Versus Tumbling Windows

The trivial case of a sliding window is that one in which the slide interval is equal to the window length. In this case, you'll notice that the stream is the equivalent to the tumbling windows case presented earlier, in which the `window` function has only the `windowDuration` argument. This corresponds precisely to the semantics implemented internally by the `window` function.

Using Windows Versus Longer Batch Intervals

You could wonder, looking at the simple tumbling windows, why it would be necessary to use windowed streams in tumbling mode rather than simply increase the batch interval: after all, if a user wants the data aggregated per minute, isn't that exactly what the batch interval is made for? There are several counterarguments to this approach:

Multiple aggregation needs
> It sometimes happens that users want to see data computed upon in different increments, which would require extracting two particular frequencies of looking at the data. In that case, because the batch interval is indivisible and is the source of the aggregation for other windows, it is best set to the smallest of the necessary latencies. In mathematical terms, if we want multiple windows of our data, say of durations *x, y, and z*, we want to set our `batch interval` to the *greatest common divisor* (`gcd`) of them: `gcd(x,y,z)`.

Safety and locality
> The batch interval is not only the source of the division of a DStream into RDDs. For receiver-based sources, the batch interval also plays a role in how its data is replicated and moved across the network. If, for example, we have a cluster of eight machines, each with four cores, because we might want to have on the order of two partitions per core, we want to set the block interval so that there are 32 block intervals per batch. It is the block interval that determines the clock tick at which data received in Spark is considered for replication by the block

manager. Hence, when the batch interval grows, the block interval, which should be configured to a fraction of the batch interval, can grow, as well, and would make the system more susceptible to a crash that would compromise data ingestion (e.g., if a receiver machine dies). For example, with a large batch interval of one hour, and a block interval of two minutes, the potential data loss in case of a receiver crash is of maximum two minutes, which depending on the data frequency, might be inappropriate. We can mitigate this risk by using reliable receivers that use the write-ahead log (WAL) to avoid data loss, yet that comes at the cost of extra overhead and storage.

For the case in which we would want an aggregation of one hour, a tumbling window of one hour, based on a source DStream with batch intervals of five minutes, gives a block interval a little bit under 10 seconds, which would make for a lesser potential data loss.

In sum, keeping a batch interval of a reasonable size increases the resiliency of the cluster's setup.

Window Reductions

Toward the end of building a complex pipeline, we often want to see indicators of our data that are inherently something that depends on various notions of time. We expect to see, for example, the count of visitors on our website or cars passing through a crossroad during the past 15 minutes, during the past hour, and during the previous day.

Those three pieces of information can all be computed based on counts on a windowed DStream, which we have already seen in this chapter. Although the window-based functions provide us with the primitives that we need to produce aggregates over different periods of time, they also require us to maintain all of the data for the specified period. For example, to produce a 24-hour aggregation, the window functions we know so far would require us to keep 24 hours' worth of data in storage (memory and/or disk—depending on the DStream configuration).

Imagine that we want the total of user visits to our site during that 24-hour period. We don't really need to keep each individual record for 24 hours to then count. Instead, we can have a running count and add new data as it comes in. This is the intuition behind window-based reductions. The provided function—which is assumed to be associative—is applied to each new microbatch of data and then, the result is added to the aggregation maintained by the window DStream. Instead of keeping potentially large amounts of data around, we aggregate it as it comes into the system, providing a scalable aggregation that uses minimal memory resources.

The windowed reducers family of functions in Spark Streaming take a reducer function together with the parameters for a window definition that we learned earlier. The following sections discuss a few such reducers:

reduceByWindow

reduceByWindow takes a reduce function, the window duration, and the slide duration. The reduce function must combine two elements of the original DStream and produce a new combined element of the same type. slideDuration can be omitted to produce a tumbling window of windowDuration length:

```
def reduceByWindow(
    reduceFunc: (T, T) => T,
    windowDuration: Duration,
    slideDuration: Duration
): DStream[T]
```

reduceByKeyAndWindow

reduceByKeyAndWindow is defined only in pair DStreams—a DStream of (Key,Value) tuples. It requires similar parameters as reduceByWindow but the reduce function applies to the values of the DStream. This operation is potentially more useful than its sibling reduceByWindow because we can have keys to indicate what values we are dealing with:

```
def reduceByKeyAndWindow(
    reduceFunc: (V, V) => V,
    windowDuration: Duration,
    slideDuration: Duration
): DStream[(K, V)]
```

Coming back to our example of hashtags, we could implement a daily aggregate of hashtag frequency by using the reduceByKeyAndWindow function:

```
val sumFunc: Long => Long => Long = x => y => x+y
val reduceAggregatedSums = hashTags.map(hashTag => (hashTag, 1))
                    .reduceByKeyAndwindow(sumFunc, Seconds(60), Seconds(10))
```

countByWindow

countByWindow is a specialized form of reduceByWindow in which we are interested only in the count of elements in the DStream over a window of time. It answers the question: *how many events were received in the given window?*

```
def countByWindow(
    windowDuration: Duration,
    slideDuration: Duration): DStream[Long]
```

countByWindow uses the same windowDuration and slideDuration parameters that we saw defined in "Sliding Windows" on page 267.

countByValueAndWindow

countByValueAndWindow is a grouped variant of the countByWindow operation just mentioned.

```
def countByValueAndWindow(
      windowDuration: Duration,
      slideDuration: Duration,
      numPartitions: Int = ssc.sc.defaultParallelism)
      (implicit ord: Ordering[T] = null) : DStream[(T, Long)]
```

countByValueAndWindow uses the values in the original DStream as keys for counting. It makes our hashtag example rather trivial:

```
val sumFunc: Long => Long => Long = x => y => x+y
val reduceAggregatedSums =
  hashTags.countByValueAndWindow(Seconds(60), Seconds(10))
```

Internally, it is doing similar steps to our earlier example: creating tuples with the form (value, 1L) and then using reduceByKeyAndWindow over the resulting DStream. As the name gives away, we use countByValueAndWindow to count the occurrences of each value in the original DStream for each window specified.

It uses the same windowDuration and slideDuration parameters that we saw defined in "Sliding Windows" on page 267

Invertible Window Aggregations

The reduceByWindow and reduceByKeyAndWindow functions contain an additional fourth argument as an optional parameter. That argument is called the *inverse reduce function*. It matters only if you happen to use an aggregation function that is invertible, meaning you can "take away" an element from the aggregate.

Formally, the inverse function invReduceFunc is such that for any accumulated value y, and an element x: invReduceFunc(reduceFunc(x, y), x) = y.

Behind the scenes, this invertible notion lets Spark simplify the computation of our aggregates by letting Spark compute over the elements of a couple of slide intervals on each new sliding window rather than of the full contents of the window.

For example, suppose that we aggregate integer counts that we see with a batch interval of one minute, over a window of 15 minutes, sliding every minute. If you are not specifying an inverse reduce function, you need to add every new count over 15 minutes for summarizing the data that you have seen on your DStream. We sketch this process in Figure 21-1.

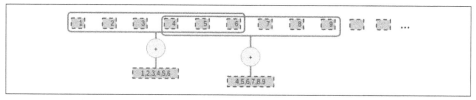

Figure 21-1. The aggregation of a reduceByWindow with a noninvertible function

This works, but if we see 100,000 elements in a minute, we are summing 1.5 million data points in the window for every minute—and, more important, we need to store those 1.5 million elements in memory. Can we do better?

We could remember the count over the previous 15 minutes and consider that we have a new minute of data incoming. Taking the count over those previous 15 minutes, we could subtract the count for the oldest minute of that 15-minute aggregate, because a counting (summation) function is invertible. We subtract the count for the oldest minute, resulting in a 14-minute aggregate, to which we just need to add the newest one minute of data, giving us the last 15 minutes of data. Figure 21-2 shows this process at work.

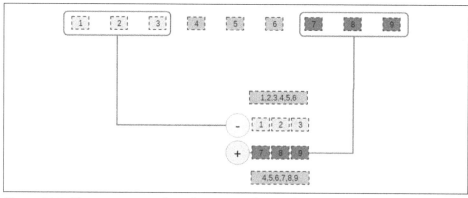

Figure 21-2. The aggregation of a reduceByWindow with an invertible function

The interesting part of this is that we do not need to store 1.5 million data points; rather, we only need the intermediate counts for every minute—that is, 15 values.

As you can see, having an invertible function for reduction can be tremendously useful in the case of windowed aggregations. It is also something that we can make the generation of various DStreams created by reduceByWindow inexpensive, giving us an excellent way to share information and aggregates on the values that we want to consider when analyzing our stream even over long aggregation periods.

The inverse of the aggregation function is useless for tumbling windows, since every aggregation interval is entirement disjoint from the others. It is therefore not worth bothering with this option if you do not use a slide interval!

Slicing Streams

Finally, note Spark's DStreams also have a selection function called `slice`, which returns the particular subpart of a DStream that was included between two bounds. You can specify the bounds using a beginning and end `Time`, which corresponds to Spark's `org.apache.spark.streaming.Time` or as an `org.apache.spark.streaming.Interval`. Both are simple reimplementations of time arithmetic using milliseconds as the base unit—leaving the user with a decent expressivity.

Spark will produce sliced DStreams by letting through the elements that carry the correct timestamp. Note also that `slice` produces as many RDDs as there are batch intervals between the two boundaries of the DStream.

What If Your Slice Specification Doesn't Fit Neatly into Batches?

The timing of an RDD's original batch and the output of the slice might not exactly match if the beginning and end time are not aligned with the original DStream's batch interval *ticks*. Any change in timings will be reflected in logs at the `INFO` level:

```
INFO Slicing from [fromTime] to [toTime]
     (aligned to [alignedFromTime] and [alignedToTime])
```

Summary

In this chapter, we looked at the capabilities of Spark Streaming to create and process windows of data from a DStream. You are now able to do the following:

- Express a tumbling and a sliding window using the DStream API
- Count elements in a window, including using keys in the data to group the counts
- Create window-based counts and aggregations
- Use the optimized `reduce` versions that exploit function inversibility to drastically reduce the amount of internal memory used

Window aggregations let us observe trends in the data as it unfolds over periods of time much longer than a batch interval. The tools you just learned empower you to apply these techniques in Spark Streaming.

## CHAPTER 22

Arbitrary Stateful Streaming Computation

So far, we have seen how Spark Streaming can work on the incoming data independently of past records. In many applications, we are also interested in analyzing the evolution of the data that arrives with respect to older data points. We could also be interested in tracking changes generated by the received data points. That is, we might be interested in building a stateful representation of a system using the data that we have already seen.

Spark Streaming provides several functions that let us build and store knowledge about previously seen data as well as use that knowledge to transform new data.

Statefulness at the Scale of a Stream

Functional programmers like functions without statefulness. These functions return values that are independent of the state of the world outside their function definition, caring only about the value of their input.

However, a function can be stateless, care only about its input, and yet maintain a notion of a managed value along with its computation, without breaking any rules about being functional. The idea is that this value, representing some intermediate state, is used in the traversal of one or several arguments of the computation, to keep some record simultaneously with the traversal of the argument's structure.

For example, the `reduce` operation discussed in Chapter 17 keeps one single value updated along the traversal of whichever RDD it was given as an argument:

```
val streamSums = stream.reduce {
  case (accum, x) => (accum + x)
}
```

Here, the computation of the intermediate sums for each RDD along the input DStream is made by iterating over the elements of the RDD, from left to right, and keeping an accumulator variable updated—an operation specified thanks to the update operation that returns the new value of the accumulator (between brackets).

updateStateByKey

Sometimes it is useful to compute some result that depends on the previous elements of the stream, which took place more than one batch before the current one. Examples of such cases include the following:

- The running sum of all elements of the stream
- The number of occurrences of a specific, marker value
- The highest elements encountered in the stream, given a particular ordering of the elements of the stream

This computation can often be thought of as the result of a big reduce operation, that would update some representation of the state of a computation, all along the traversal of the stream. In Spark Streaming, this is offered by the updateStateByKey function:

```
def updateStateByKey[S: ClassTag](
    updateFunc: (Seq[V], Option[S]) => Option[S]
): DStream[(K, S)]
```

updateStateBykey is an operation that is defined only on DStreams of key–value pairs. It takes a state update function as an argument. This state update function should have the following type:

```
`Seq[V] -> Option[S] -> Option[S]`
```

This type reflects how the update operation takes a set of new values for type V, which corresponds to all *values* for a given *key* that arrive during the operation of the current batch, and an optional state represented with type S. It then computes and returns a new value for the state S as Some(state) if there is one to return or None if there's no new state, in which case, the stored state corresponding to this key is deleted from the internal representation:

```
def updateFunction(Values: Seq[Int], runningCount: Option[Int]): Option[Int] = {
    val newCount = runningCount.getOrElse(0) + Values.filter(x => x >5).length
    if (newCount > 0)
      Some(newCount)
    else
      None
}
```

The update state function is called, on each batch, on all of the keys that the executor encounters since the beginning of processing this stream. In some cases, this is on a new key that was never previously seen. This is the case in which the second argument of the update function, the state, is None. In other cases, it will be on a key for which no new values have come in this batch, in which case the first argument of the update function, the new value, is Nil.

Finally, the updateStateByKey function returns a value (that is, a snapshot of the new state for a particular key), only when the user's updates mandate it should. This explains the Option in the return type of the function: in the previous example, we update the state only when we actually encounter integers greater than five. If a particular key encounters only values less than five, there will be no state created for this key, and correspondingly no update.

Figure 22-1 depicts the dynamics of the internal state preserved when using a stateful computation such as updateStateByKey. The intermediate state of the stream is kept in an internal state store. At each batch interval, the internal state is combined with the new data coming from the stream using the updateFunc function, producing a secondary stream with the current results of the stateful computation.

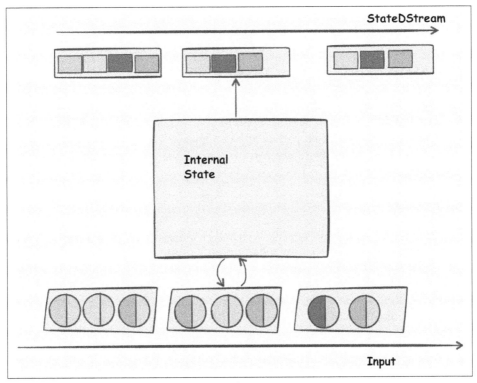

Figure 22-1. The data flow produced by updateStateByKey

Mandatory Checkpointing on Stateful Streams

Note that when starting a Spark Streaming Context for this application, Spark might output the following error:

java.lang.IllegalArgumentException: requirement failed: The checkpoint directory has not been set. Please set it by StreamingContext.checkpoint()

The reason for this is that the StateStream created under the hood by updateStateByKey has RDDs that inherently each have a dependency on the previous ones, meaning that the only way to reconstruct the chain of partial sums at each batch interval for each hashtag is to replay the entire stream. This does not play well with fault tolerance because we would need to preserve every record received to be able to recreate the state at some arbitrary point in time. Instead of preserving all records, we save the intermediary result of state to disk. In case one of the executors working on this stream crashes, it can recover from this intermediate state.

Luckily, the error tells us exactly how to do so, using ssc.check point("path/to/checkpoint/dir"). Replace the content of the String passed as an argument with a directory in a shared filesystem, accessible by the driver and all executors that are part of the job.

Limitation of updateStateByKey

The updateStateByKey function that we have described so far allows us to do stateful programming using Spark Streaming. It allows us to encode, for example, the concept of user sessions—for which no particular batch interval is a clear match to the application at hand. However, there are two problems with this approach. Let's look at those a bit more closely.

Performance

The first problem is related to performance: this updateStateByKey function is run on every single key encountered by the framework of the application since the beginning of the run. This is problematic because, even on a dataset that is somewhat sparse—provided there is a long tail to the variety of the data and in particular, in the variety of its keys—there is a clear argument that the total amount of data represented in memory grows indefinitely.

For example, if a key or a particular user is seen on a website at the beginning of the run of the application, what is the relevance of updating the state of that user to signify that we have not seen a session from this particular individual since the beginning of the application (e.g., since last month)? The benefits to the application are not clear.

Memory Usage

The second issue is that because the state should not grow indefinitely, the programmer must do the bookkeeping of memory by themselves—writing code for every key, to figure out whether it is still relevant to keep data in state for that particular element. This is a complexity that requires manual accounting for memory management.

Indeed, for most stateful computations, dealing with state is a simple operation: either a key is still relevant, such as a user who has visited a website within a certain time frame, or it hasn't been refreshed in a while.

Introducing Stateful Computation with mapwithState

mapWithState is a better model for stateful updates in Spark, which overcomes the two aforementioned shortcomings: updating every key and setting default timeouts to limit the size of the state objects created along with the computation. It was introduced in Spark 1.5:

```
def mapWithState[StateType: ClassTag, MappedType: ClassTag](
    spec: StateSpec[K, V, StateType, MappedType]
): MapWithStateDStream[K, V, StateType, MappedType]
```

mapWithState requires you to write a StateSpec function that operates on a state specification containing a key, an optional value, and a State object. Even though this is apparently more complex, because it involves a few explicit types, it simplifies a number of elements:

- The programmer operates on values one by one rather than as a list
- The update function has access to the key itself
- This update is run only on keys that have a new value in the current batch
- Updating the state is an imperative call to a method of the state object, rather than the implicit act of producing an output
- The programmer can now produce an output independently of state management
- The function has an automatic timeout

Figure 22-2 presents the data flow when using the mapWithState function.

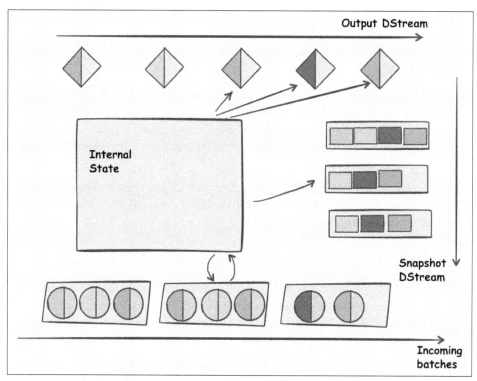

Figure 22-2. The dataflow produced by mapWithState

If you want to see a snapshot of the state for each and every key on each and every batch interval, call the .snapshots function on your particular DStream created by mapWithState.

mapWithState and updateStateByKey: When to Use Which

mapWithState is more performant and nicer to use than the upda teStateByKey function, and the former is indeed a good default choice for stateful computation. However, one caveat is that the model for pushing data out of the state representation (aka flushing State data) is specifically a timeout, and no longer user controlled. As a consequence, mapWithState is particularly appropriate if you want to keep state under a freshness condition (e.g., the number of clicks on a time-bound session of a web user). We would prefer updateStateByKey for the niche cases for which we absolutely want to guarantee maintaining a small state over a long period of time.

An example is flood watching: if we are dealing with sensors reporting water heights at specific locations near a river, and if we want to keep the largest values ever observed over the length of our observation, it might make sense to use updateStateBykey rather than mapWithState.

With mapWithState, the computation on elements of our stream can start as events are being received and, ideally, completes shortly after the last few structural events are received. We are going to see an example of this in the next few pages.

Using mapWithState

mapWithState requires the user to provide a StateSpec object, which describes the workings of the state computation. The core piece of this is, naturally, the function that takes in new values for a given key and returns an output as well as updates the state for this key. In fact, the builder object for this StateSpec makes this function mandatory.

This StateSpec is parameterized by four types:

- Key type K
- Value type V
- State type S, representing the type used to store the state
- Output type U

In its most general form, the StateSpec builder, StateSpec.function, requires a (Time, K, Option[V], State[S]) => Option[U] argument, or a (K, Option[V], State[S]) => Option[U] if you don't need the timestamp of the batch that mapWith State comes with.

The state type that intervenes in the definition of this function can be seen as a mutable cell with support for timeout. You can query it by using state.exists() and state.get(), or even treat it like an option with state.getOption(), you can check whether it's timing out by using state.isTimingOut(), erase it using state.remove(), or update it using state.update(newState: S).

Let's assume that we're monitoring a plant with sensors and we want both the average temperature over the last batch and a straightforward way of detecting anomalous temperatures. For this exercise, let's define an anomalous temperature to be higher than 80 degrees:

```
import org.apache.spark.streaming.State

case class Average(count: Int, mean: Float){
  def ingest(value: Float) =
    Average(count + 1, mean + (value - mean) / (count + 1))
}

def trackHighestTemperatures(sensorID: String,
    temperature: Option[Float],
    average: State[Average]): Option[(String, Float)] = {
  val oldMax = average.getOption.getOrElse(Average(0, 0f))
  temperature.foreach{ t => average.update(oldMax.ingest(t)) }
  temperature.map{
    case Some(t) if t >= (80) => Some(sensorID, t)
    case _ => None
  }
}

val highTempStateSpec = StateSpec.function(trackHighestTemperatures)
                          .timeout(Seconds(3600))
```

In this function, we extract the old maximum value and run both an aggregation of the latest value with the mean and with the threshold value, routing the results to, correspondingly, the state update and our output value. This lets us exploit two streams:

- temperatureStream.mapWithState(highTempStateSpec), which tracks high temperatures as they occur
- temperatureStream.mapWithState(highTempStateSpec).stateSnapshots(), which tracks the mean temperatures for each sensor

If a sensor stops emitting for 60 minutes, its state is removed automatically, preventing the state storage explosion that we feared. Note that we could have used the explicit remove() function for this, as well.

There is, however, an issue with this: in the first few values of a sensor, we compare the sensor's value to a low default, which might not be appropriate for each sensor.

We might detect temperature spikes reading values that might be perfectly appropriate for this particular sensor, simply because we do not have values for it yet.

In this case, we have the opportunity to provide initial values for our sensor, using `highTempStateSpec.initialState(initialTemps: RDD[(String, Float)])`.

Event-Time Stream Computation Using mapWithState

An auxiliary benefit of `mapWithState` is that it lets us efficiently and explicitly store data about the past in its `State` object. This can be very useful in order to accomplish event-time computing.

Indeed, elements seen "on the wire" in a streaming system can arrive out of order, be delayed, or even arrive exceptionally fast with respect to other elements. Because of this, the only way to be sure that we are dealing with data elements that have been generated at a very specific time is to timestamp them at the time of generation. A stream of temperatures in which we are trying to detect spikes, as in our previous example, could confuse temperature increases and temperature decreases if some events arrive in inverse order, for example.

 Although event-time computation is supported natively by Structured Streaming as we saw in Chapter 12, you can programmatically implement it in Spark Streaming using the technique described here.

However, if we aim to process events in order, we need to be able to detect and invert the misordering by reading the timestamps present on data elements seen on our stream. To perform this reordering, we need to have an idea of the order of magnitude of the delays (in one direction or another) that we can expect to see on our stream. Indeed, without this boundary on the scope of the reordering, we would need to wait indefinitely to be able to compute a final result on a particular period of time: we could always receive yet another element that would have been delayed.

To deal with this practically, we are going to define a *watermark*, or the highest duration of time for which we are going to wait for straggler elements. In the spirit of Spark Streaming's notion of time, it should be a multiple of the batch interval. After this watermark, we are going to "seal" the result of the computation and ignore elements that are delayed by more than the watermark.

The spontaneous approach to dealing with this misordering could be windowed streams: define a window interval equal to the watermark, and make it slide by exactly one batch, defining a transformation that orders elements by their timestamp.

This is correct insofar as it will result in a correct view of the ordered elements, as soon as they're past the first watermark interval. However, it requires the user to accept an initial delay equal to the watermark to see the results of the computation. It's plausible, however, to see a watermark that's one order of magnitude higher than the batch interval, and such latency would not be acceptable for a system like Spark Streaming, which already incurs high latency because of its microbatching approach.

A good event-time streaming solution would allow us to compute based on a provisional view of the events of the stream and then update this result if and when delayed elements arrive.

Suppose that we have a notion of a circular buffer, a fixed-size vector of size k, that contains the last k elements it has received:

```
import scala.collection.immutable

object CircularBuffer {
  def empty[T](): CircularBuffer[T] = immutable.Vector.empty[T]
}

implicit class CircularBuffer[T](v: Vector[T]) extends Serializable {
  val maxSize = 4
  def get(): Vector[T] = v
  def addItem(item : T) : CircularBuffer[T]  =
    v.drop(Math.min(v.size, v.size - maxSize + 1)) :+ item
}
```

This object keeps an inner vector of at least one, and at most maxSize of elements, selecting its most recent additions.

Let's now assume that we are tracking the average temperature for the last four batches, assuming a batch interval of five milliseconds:

```
import org.apache.spark.streaming.State

def batch(t:Time): Long = (t.milliseconds % 5000)

def trackTempStateFunc(
  batchTime: Time,
  sensorName: String,
  value: Option[(Time, Float)],
  state: State[CB]): Option[(String, Time, Int)] = {

  value.flatMap { (t: Time, temperature: Float) =>
```

```
          if ( batch(t) <= batch(batchTime)) { // this element is in the past
            val newState: CB =
              state.getOption.fold(Vector((t, Average(1, temperature))): CB){ c =>
                val (before, hereOrAfter) =
                  c.get.partition{case (timeStamp, _) => batch(timeStamp) < batch(t) }
                (hereOrAfter.toList match {
                  case (tS, avg: Average) :: tl if (batch(tS) == batch(t)) =>
                    (tS, avg.ingest(temperature)) ::tl
                  case l@_ => (t, Average(1, temperature)) :: l
                }).toVector.foldLeft(before: CB){ case (cB, item) => cB.addItem(item)}
              }
            state.update(newState) // update the State
            // output the new average temperature for the batch that was updated!
            newState.get.find{ case (tS, avg) => batch(tS) == batch(t) }.map{
              case (ts, i) => (key, ts, i)
            }
          }
          else None // this element is from the future! ignore it.
        }
      }
```

In this function, our State is a set of four cells containing averages for each of the batches. Here we are using mapWithState in the variant that takes the current batch time as an argument. We use the batch function in order to make batch comparisons sensible, in that if t1, t2 are within the same batch, we expect that batch(t1) == batch(t2).

We begin by examining our new value and its event time. If that event time's batch is beyond the current batch time, there is an error in our wall clock or the event time. For this example, we return None, but we could log an error as well. If the event is in the past, we need to find which batch it belongs to. For that, we use Scala's partition function on the batches of each cell of our CircularBuffer State and separate the elements coming from before our element's batch from those coming from the same batch or after.

We then look at whether there was already an average initialized for the batch of our event that we should find at the head of the latter list (thanks to our partition). If there is one, we add the new temperature to it; otherwise, we make an average out of our single element. Finally, we take the batches from before the current element's time and add all the posterior batches to it in order. The CircularBuffer natively ensures that we retain only the latest elements if there are more than our threshold (four).

As the last step, we look up the updated average on the cell that we updated with our new element (if there indeed was one, we might have updated a stale element), and we output the new average if so. As a consequence, the mapWithState stream we can create on an RDD of (String, (Time, Float)) elements (with the sensor name as a key, and the timestamped temperature as a value) updates the averages for the last updates we received, from the very first batch.

Naturally, it uses a linear time in processing the content of our `CircularBuffer`, a consequence of the simplicity that we wanted to reach through this example. Note, however, how we are dealing with a structure that is ordered by timestamp and how a different data structure such as a skip list would let us gain a lot in processing speed and let us make this scalable.

In sum, `mapWithState`, with its powerful state update semantics, its parsimonious timeout semantics, and the versatility brought by `snapshots()`, gives us a powerful tool to represent basic event-time processing in a few lines of Scala.

## CHAPTER 23

Working with Spark SQL

So far, we have seen how Spark Streaming can work as a standalone framework to process streams of many sources and produce results that can be sent or stored for further consumption.

Data in isolation has limited value. We often want to combine datasets to explore relationships that become evident only when data from different sources are merged.

In the particular case of streaming data, the data we see at each batch interval is merely a sample of a potentially infinite dataset. Therefore, to increase the value of the observed data at a given point in time, it's imperative that we have the means to combine it with the knowledge we already have. It might be historical data that we have in files or a database, a model that we created based on data from the previous day, or even earlier streaming data.

One of the key value propositions of Spark Streaming is its seamless interoperability with other Spark frameworks. This synergy among the Spark modules increases the spectrum of data-oriented applications that we can create, resulting in applications with a lower complexity than combining arbitrary—and often incompatible—libraries by ourselves. This translates to increased development efficiency, which in turn improves the business value delivered by the application.

In this chapter, we explore how you can combine Spark Streaming applications with Spark SQL.

As we saw in Part II, Structured Streaming is the native approach in Spark to use the Spark SQL abstractions for streaming. The techniques described in this chapter apply when we have a Spark Streaming job that we would like to complement with Spark SQL functions for a specific purpose.

For a pure Spark SQL approach to stream processing, consider Structured Streaming first.

Spark SQL

Spark SQL is the Spark module that works with structured data. It implements functions and abstractions traditionally found in the realms of databases, such as a query analyzer, optimizer, and an execution planner, to enable a table-like manipulation of arbitrarily structured data sources on top of the Spark engine.

Spark SQL introduces three important features:

- The use of the SQL query language to represent data operations
- Datasets, a type-safe data-processing *domain specific language* (DSL) that resembles SQL
- DataFrames, the dynamically typed counterpart of Datasets

For the purpose of this chapter, we assume the reader's familiarity with Spark SQL, Datasets, and DataFrames. For a more in-depth Spark SQL discussion, we refer the reader to [Karau2015].

With the combination of Spark Streaming and Spark SQL, we get access to the significant data wrangling capabilities of Spark SQL from the context of a Spark Streaming job. We could efficiently enrich an incoming stream using reference data loaded from a database through DataFrames. Or apply advanced summary computations using the available SQL functions. We could also write the incoming or resulting data to one of the supported writer formats, such as Parquet, ORC, or to an external database through Java Database Connectivity (JDBC). The possibilities are endless.

As we saw in Part II, Apache Spark offers a native streaming API that uses the Dataset/DataFrame API abstractions and concepts. Structured Streaming should be our first option when it comes to tapping into the native SQL capabilities of Spark. But there are cases for which we want to access those capabilities from the context of Spark Streaming. In this chapter, we explore techniques that you can use when you need to combine Spark Streaming with Spark SQL.

Accessing Spark SQL Functions from Spark Streaming

The most common use case of augmenting Spark Streaming with Spark SQL is to gain access to the query capabilities and write access to the structured data formats supported, such as relational databases, comma-separated values (CSV), and Parquet files.

Example: Writing Streaming Data to Parquet

Our streaming dataset will consist of our running sensor information, containing the sensorId, a timestamp, and a value. For the sake of simplicity in this self-contained example, we are going to generate a randomized dataset, using a scenario that simulates a real Internet of Things (IoT) use case. The timestamp will be the time of execution, and each record will be formatted as a string coming from "the field" of comma-separated values.

Online Resources

For this example, we will use the enriching-streaming-data notebook in the online resources for the book, located at *https:// github.com/stream-processing-with-spark*.

We also add a bit of real-world chaos to the data: due to weather conditions, some sensors publish corrupt data.

We begin by defining our data-generation functions:

```scala
import scala.util.Random
// 100K sensors in our system
val sensorId: () => Int = () =>  Random.nextInt(100000)
val data: () => Double = () => Random.nextDouble
val timestamp: () => Long = () => System.currentTimeMillis
val recordFunction: () => String = { () =>
  if (Random.nextDouble < 0.9) {
    Seq(sensorId().toString, timestamp(), data()).mkString(",")
  } else {
    "!!~corrupt~^&##$"
  }
}

> import scala.util.Random
> sensorId: () => Int = <function0>
> data: () => Double = <function0>
> timestamp: () => Long = <function0>
> recordFunction: () => String = <function0>
```

We use a particular trick that requires a moment of attention. Note how the values in the preceding example are functions. Instead of creating an RDD of text records, we create an RDD of record-generating functions. Then, each time the RDD is evaluated, the record function will generate a new random record. This way we can simulate a realistic load of random data that delivers a different set on each batch.

```
val sensorDataGenerator = sparkContext.parallelize(1 to 100)
                                    .map(_ => recordFunction)
val sensorData = sensorDataGenerator.map(recordFun => recordFun())
```

```
> sensorDataGenerator: org.apache.spark.rdd.RDD[() => String] =
  MapPartitionsRDD[1] at map at <console>:73
> sensorData: org.apache.spark.rdd.RDD[String] =
  MapPartitionsRDD[2] at map at <console>:74
```

We sample some data:

```
sensorData.take(5)
```

```
> res3: Array[String] = Array(
            !!~corrupt~^&##$,
            26779,1495395920021,0.13529198017496724,
            74226,1495395920022,0.46164872694412384,
            65930,1495395920022,0.8150752966356496,
            38572,1495395920022,0.5731793018367316
)
```

And we create the Streaming Context:

```
import org.apache.spark.streaming.StreamingContext
import org.apache.spark.streaming.Seconds

val streamingContext = new StreamingContext(sparkContext, Seconds(2))
```

Our stream source will be a `ConstantInputDStream` fed by a record-generating RDD. By combining a `ConstantInputDStream` with the record-generating RDD, we create a self-generating stream of fresh, random data to process in our example. This method makes the example self-contained. It removes the need for an external stream-generating process:

```
import org.apache.spark.streaming.dstream.ConstantInputDStream
val rawDStream = new ConstantInputDStream(streamingContext, sensorData)
```

We must provide the schema information for our streaming data.

Now that we have a DStream of fresh data processed in a two-second interval, we can begin focusing on the gist of this example. First, we want to define and apply a schema to the data that we are receiving. In Scala, we define a schema with a `case class`, as shown here:

```
case class SensorData(sensorId: Int, timestamp: Long, value: Double)
```

```
> defined class SensorData
```

Now, we need to apply the schema to the DStream using the `flatMap` function:

We use `flatMap` instead of a `map` because there might be cases for which the incoming data is incomplete or corrupted.

If we use `map`, we would need to provide a resulting value for each transformed record. This is something that we cannot do for invalid records. With `flatMap` in combination with `Option`, we can represent valid records as `Some(recordValue)`, and invalid records as `None`. By the virtue of `flatMap` the internal `Option` container is flattened and our resulting stream will contain only valid `record` `Values`.

During the parsing of the comma-separated records, we not only protect ourselves against missing fields, but also parse the numeric values to their expected types. The surrounding `Try` captures any `NumberFormatException` that might arise from invalid records.

```
import scala.util.Try
val schemaStream = rawDStream.flatMap{record =>
  val fields = record.split(",")
  // this Try captures exceptions related to corrupted input values
  Try {
    SensorData(fields(0).toInt, fields(1).toLong, fields(2).toDouble)
  }.toOption
}
```

```
> schemaStream: org.apache.spark.streaming.dstream.DStream[SensorData] =
    org.apache.spark.streaming.dstream.FlatMappedDStream@4c0a0f5
```

Saving DataFrames

With the schema stream in place, we can proceed to transform the underlying RDDs into DataFrames. We do this in the context of the general-purpose action `foreachRDD`. It's impossible to use transformation at this point because a `DStream[DataFrame]` is undefined. This also means that any further operations we would like to apply to the DataFrame (or Dataset) need to be contained in the scope of the `foreachRDD` closure, as demonstrated here:

```
import org.apache.spark.sql.SaveMode.Append
schemaStream.foreachRDD{rdd =>
  val df = rdd.toDF()
  df.write.format("parquet").mode(Append).save("/tmp/iotstream.parquet")
}
```

Finally, we start the stream process:

```
streamingContext.start()
```

We then can inspect the target directory to see the resulting data streaming into the Parquet file.

Now, let's head to the URL `http://<spark-host>:4040` to inspect the Spark Console. There, you can see that both the SQL and Streaming tabs are present, as depicted in Figure 23-1. In particular, the Streaming tab is of interest to us.

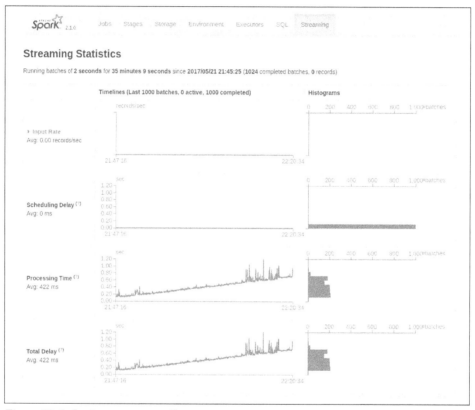

Figure 23-1. Saving a stream to Parquet

In Figure 23-1, you can see how the writing time of Parquet quickly increases with time. Appending operations to Parquet files becomes more expensive with time. For long-lived processes like a Spark Streaming job, one way to work around this limitation is to append to a fresh file every so often.

In Example 23-1, we change the suffix of the file every hour (3,600 seconds), measuring from the moment the streaming job started.

Example 23-1. Timestamping a file destination

```
def ts: String = ((time.milliseconds - timeOrigin)/(3600 * 1000)).toString
df.write.mode(SaveMode.Append).format("parquet").save(s"${outputPath}-$ts")
```

In the Streaming UI, you might notice that the Input Rate chart remains flat on zero. This chart collects its information from the receiver implementation. Because we are using a `ConstantInputD Stream`, there's no actual incoming record count for this chart.

Dealing with Data at Rest

A typical question that arises during the design and implementation of streaming applications is how to use existing data to enrich the events in the stream. This data "at rest" could be historical records in files, lookup tables, tables on a database, or any other static data that we can use to enhance to the data "in flight."

We can use the capabilities of Spark SQL to load "resting" datasets that can be combined with the incoming streaming data. A key advantage of Spark SQL in this scenario is that the loaded data is structured. This reduces the effort that the streaming developer needs to invest in preparing the data into the right format before performing a join operation.

This example illustrates the use of `join` on a fixed dataset in the form of a DataFrame and the streaming data that is consumed continuously by our application.

Using Join to Enrich the Input Stream

In our previous example, we processed an incoming stream of sensor data, parsed it into valid records, and stored it directly into a Parquet file. But to interpret the values in the reported data points, we first need to know the sensor type, its working range, and the units of each recorded value.

In our IoT application, sensors are initially registered before they are deployed. The registration process captures the information that we require. Luckily for us, this information is available as a CSV file export that we can import in our streaming application, as we can see in Figure 23-2.

For this example, we are going to discuss only the relevant differences with the previous program. The complete notebook is available online (*https://github.com/LearningSparkStreaming/notebooks*) for your own exploration.

Let's define some constants with the locations of our data:

```
val sensorCount = 100000
val workDir = "/tmp/learningsparkstreaming/"
val referenceFile = "sensor-records.parquet"
val targetFile = "enrichedIoTStream.parquet"
```

Now, we load the reference data from a Parquet file (see Figure 23-2). We also cache the data to keep it in memory and improve the performance of our streaming application:

```
val sensorRef = sparkSession.read.parquet(s"$workDir/$referenceFile")
sensorRef.cache()
```

sensorId	sensorType	unit	minRange	maxRange
25001	"noise"	"dB"	0	200
25002	"luminosity"	"Lux"	0	100000
25003	"noise"	"dB"	0	200
25004	"humidity"	"Rel%"	0	100
25005	"radiation"	"mSv"	0	100000
25006	"temp"	"C"	-100	100
25007	"radiation"	"mSv"	0	100000
25008	"radiation"	"mSv"	0	100000
25009	"temp"	"C"	-100	100
25010	"temp"	"C"	-100	100
25011	"noise"	"dB"	0	200
25012	"pressure"	"kPa"	0	140
25013	"pressure"	"kPa"	0	140
25014	"luminosity"	"Lux"	0	100000
25015	"radiation"	"mSv"	0	100000
25016	"luminosity"	"Lux"	0	100000

Figure 23-2. Sample reference data

Next, we enrich the streaming data. With the schema stream in place, we can proceed to transform the underlying RDDs into DataFrames. This time, we are going to use the reference data to add the specific sensor information. We are also going to denormalize the recorded value according to the sensor range so that we don't need to repeat that data in the resulting dataset.

As before, we do this in the context of the general-purpose action `foreachRDD`:

```
val stableSparkSession = sparkSession
import stableSparkSession.implicits._
import org.apache.spark.sql.SaveMode.Append
schemaStream.foreachRDD{ rdd =>
  val sensorDF = rdd.toDF()
```

```
val sensorWithInfo = sensorDF.join(sensorRef, "sensorId")
val sensorRecords =
  sensorWithInfo.withColumn(
    "dnvalue", $"value"*($"maxRange"-$"minRange")+$"minRange"
  ).drop("value", "maxRange", "minRange")
sensorRecords.write
            .format("parquet")
            .mode(Append)
            .save(s"$workDir/$targetFile")
}
```

 The seemingly weird construct for the stableSparkSession is necessary because in the SparkNotebook, the sparkSession reference is a mutable variable, and we cannot issue an import from a non-stable reference.

Go ahead and inspect the result. We can use the current Spark Session concurrently with the running Spark Streaming job in order to inspect the resulting data, as shown in Figure 23-3:

```
val enrichedRecords = sparkSession.read.parquet(s"$workDir/$targetFile")
enrichedRecords
```

enrichedRecords

res31: org.apache.spark.sql.DataFrame = [sensorId: int, timestamp:

1   >>

sensorId	timestamp	sensorType	unit	dnvalue
26140	1495402992211	"radiation"	"mSv"	8529.460065196548
84739	1495402992212	"luminosity"	"Lux"	40891.46792556275
82070	1495402992212	"temp"	"C"	14.345990752880283
10484	1495402992212	"noise"	"dB"	91.61852200516864
70760	1495402992212	"radiation"	"mSv"	53155.29779322772
75464	1495402992212	"luminosity"	"Lux"	18450.203608756743
3970	1495402992212	"radiation"	"mSv"	833.5520188078372
52765	1495402992212	"humidity"	"Rel%"	33.70152466216159
99686	1495402992212	"noise"	"dB"	16.095900641350113
64578	1495402992212	"pressure"	"kPa"	81.47635868016002
65802	1495402992213	"radiation"	"mSv"	25745.591428913216

Figure 23-3. Sample from the enrichedRecords DataFrame

At this point, we can see the record count evolving. We can issue a count on the resulting dataset to see how the streaming process increments the dataset. We wait a few moments between the two executions to observe the difference:

```
enrichedRecords.count
>res33: Long = 45135
// ... wait few seconds ...
enrichedRecords.count
>res37: Long = 51167
```

Join Optimizations

Our current solution has a major drawback: it will drop incoming data from unregistered sensors. Because we are loading the reference data only once at the start of our process, sensors registered after that moment will be silently dropped. We can improve this situation by using a different kind of join operation. Let's remember that within the foreachRDD, we have full access to the capabilities of other Spark libraries. In this particular case, the join operation we are using comes from Spark SQL, and we can make use of options in that package to enhance our streaming process. In particular, we are going to use an *outer* join to differentiate between the IoT sensor IDs that are known to the system from those that are unknown. We can then write the data from the unknown devices to a separate file for later reconciliation.

The rest of the program remains the same except for the foreachRDD call, in which we add the new logic, as demonstrated in Example 23-2.

Example 23-2. Using broadcast optimization with an outer join

```
val stableSparkSession = sparkSession
import stableSparkSession.implicits._
import org.apache.spark.sql.SaveMode.Append
schemaStream.foreachRDD{ rdd =>
  val sensorDF = rdd.toDF()
  val sensorWithInfo = sensorRef.join(
    broadcast(sensorDF), Seq("sensorId"), "rightouter"
  )
  val sensorRecords =
    sensorWithInfo.withColumn(
      "dnvalue", $"value"*($"maxRange"-$"minRange")+$"minRange"
    ).drop("value", "maxRange", "minRange")
  sensorRecords.write
              .format("parquet")
              .mode(Append)
              .save(s"$workDir/$targetFile")
}
```

Sharp eyes will notice that we have introduced two changes to the join operation. Example 23-3 focuses on them.

Example 23-3. Detail of the join operation

```
val sensorWithInfo = sensorRef.join(
  broadcast(sensorDF), Seq("sensorId"), "rightouter"
)
```

The difference is that we changed the order of the join. Instead of joining the incoming data with the reference dataset, we do the opposite. We need that change in direction for a particular reason: we are adding a `broadcast` hint to the join expression to instruct Spark to perform a *broadcast join*.

Broadcast joins, also known as *map-side joins* in Hadoop jargon, are useful when there's a large difference in size between the two datasets participating in the join and one of them is small enough to be sent to the memory of every executor. Instead of performing an I/O-heavy shuffle-based join, the small dataset can be used as an in-memory lookup table on each executor, in parallel. This results in lower I/O overhead and hence faster execution time.

In our scenario, we swap the order of the participating datasets because we know that our reference dataset is much larger than the received device data at each interval. Whereas our reference dataset contains a record for every device known to us, the streaming data contains only a sample of the total population. Therefore, in terms of performance, it's better to broadcast the data from the stream to execute the broadcast join with the reference data.

The last remark in this code fragment is the join direction, given by the join type `rightouter`. This join type preserves all records from the right side, our incoming sensor data, and adds the fields from the left side if the join condition matches. In our case, that is a matching `sensorId`.

We store the results in two files: one with the enriched sensor data for the known `SensorIds` (see Figure 23-4), and another with the raw data of the sensors that we don't know at this time (see Figure 23-5).

```
enrichedRecords
res31: org.apache.spark.sql.DataFrame = [sensorId: int, timestamp:
                                                          1   >>
```

sensorId	timestamp	sensorType	unit	dnvalue
26140	1495402992211	"radiation"	"mSv"	8529.460065196548
84739	1495402992212	"luminosity"	"Lux"	40891.46792556275
82070	1495402992212	"temp"	"C"	14.345990752880283
10484	1495402992212	"noise"	"dB"	91.61852200516864
70760	1495402992212	"radiation"	"mSv"	53155.29779322772
75464	1495402992212	"luminosity"	"Lux"	18450.203608756743
3970	1495402992212	"radiation"	"mSv"	833.5520188078372
52765	1495402992212	"humidity"	"Rel%"	33.70152466216159
99686	1495402992212	"noise"	"dB"	16.095900641350113
64578	1495402992212	"pressure"	"kPa"	81.47635868016002
65802	1495402992213	"radiation"	"mSv"	25745.591428913216

Figure 23-4. Sample of enriched records

sensorId	sensorType	unit	minRange	maxRange	timestamp	value
100200					1498867518294	0.4296108409658099
100275					1498867506376	0.3535681531311208
100855					1498867506366	0.6230050066156928
100920					1498867530329	0.30692198074148225
100562					1498867510248	0.05377385469435081

Figure 23-5. Sample of records from unknown devices

For an in-depth discussion of the different join options in Spark and their particular characteristics, read [Karau2017].

Updating Reference Datasets in a Streaming Application

In the previous section, you saw how we could load a static dataset to enrich an incoming stream.

Although some datasets are fairly static, like last year's synthetic profile for Smart Grids, calibration data for IoT sensors, or population distribution following a census, oftentimes we will also find that the dataset that we need to combine with our streaming data changes, as well. Those changes might be at a different, much slower pace than our streaming application and hence do not need to be considered a stream on their own.

In their digital evolution, organizations often have a mix of processes of different cadences. Slow-paced output processes such as data exports or daily reports are valid inputs of our streaming system that require regular, but not continuous updates.

We are going to explore a Spark Streaming technique to integrate a static dataset ("slow data") into our streaming ("fast data") track.

At its core, Spark Streaming is a high-performance scheduling and coordination application. To ensure data integrity, Spark Streaming schedules the different output operations of a streaming job in sequence. The order of declaration in the application code becomes the execution sequence at runtime.

Chapter 18 looks at the `batch interval` and how it provides the synchronization point between the collection of data and the submission of previously collected data to the Spark engine for further processing. We can hook onto the Spark Streaming scheduler in order to execute Spark operations other than stream processing.

In particular, we will use a `ConstantInputDStream` with an empty input as the essential building block to schedule our additional operations within the streaming application. We combine the empty DStream with the general-purpose operation `foreachRDD` to have Spark Streaming take care of the regular execution of those additional operations we require in the context of our application.

Enhancing Our Example with a Reference Dataset

To better understand the dynamics of this technique, let's continue with our running example.

In the previous section, we used a reference dataset that contained the description of each sensor known to the system. That data was used to enrich the streaming sensor data with the parameters needed for its further processing. A critical limitation of that approach is that after the streaming application is started, we cannot add, update, or remove any sensor present in that list.

In the context of our example, we get an update of that list every hour. We would like that our streaming application would use the new reference data.

Loading the reference data from a Parquet file

As in the previous example, we load the reference data from the Parquet file. We also cache the data to keep it in memory and improve the performance of our streaming application. The only difference that we observe in this step is that we now use a `vari able` instead of a `value` to keep the reference to our reference data. We need to make this reference mutable because we will be updating it with new data as the streaming application runs:

```
var sensorRef: DataFrame = sparkSession.read.parquet(s"$workDir/$referenceFile")
sensorRef.cache()
```

Setting up the refreshing mechanism

To periodically load the reference data, we are going to *hook* onto the Spark Streaming scheduler. We can do that only in terms of the batch interval, which serves as the internal tick of the clock for all operations. Hence, we express the refresh interval as a window over the base batch interval. In practical terms, every x batches, we are going to refresh our reference data.

We use a ConstantInputDStream with an empty RDD. This ensures that at all times we have an empty DStream whose only function will be to give us access to the scheduler through the foreachRDD function. At each window interval, we update the variable that points to the current DataFrame. This is a safe construction because the Spark Streaming scheduler will linearly execute the scheduled operations that are due at each batch interval. Therefore, the new data will be available for the upstream operations that make use of it.

We use caching to ensure that the reference dataset is loaded only once over the intervals that it's used in the streaming application. It's also important to unpersist the expiring data that was previously cached in order to free up resources in the cluster and ensure that we have a stable system from the perspective of resource consumption:

```
import org.apache.spark.rdd.RDD
val emptyRDD: RDD[Int] = sparkContext.emptyRDD
val refreshDStream  = new ConstantInputDStream(streamingContext, emptyRDD)
val refreshIntervalDStream = refreshDStream.window(Seconds(60), Seconds(60))
refreshIntervalDStream.foreachRDD{ rdd =>
  sensorRef.unpersist(false)
  sensorRef = sparkSession.read.parquet(s"$workDir/$referenceFile")
  sensorRef.cache()
}
```

We use a tumbling window of 60 seconds for our refresh process.

Runtime implications

Loading a large dataset incurs a cost in time and resources and therefore it has an operational impact. Figure 23-6 depicts the recurrent spikes in processing time that correspond to the loading of the reference dataset.

Figure 23-6. Loading reference data has a visible effect on the runtime

By scheduling the load of reference data at a rate much lower than the cadence of the streaming application, the cost is amortized over a relatively large number of micro-batches. Nevertheless, you need to take this additional load into consideration when planning for cluster resources in order to have a stable execution over time.

Summary

Even though SQL capabilities are native to Structured Streaming, in this chapter you saw how to use Spark SQL features from Spark Streaming and the possibilities that this combination opens up. You learned about the following:

- Accessing the Spark SQL Context from output operations in Spark Streaming
- Loading and reloading data at rest to enrich our streaming data
- How to join data with different join modes

## CHAPTER 24

Checkpointing

The act of checkpointing consists of regularly saving the information necessary to restart a stateful streaming application without losing information and without requiring the reprocessing of all of the data seen up to that point.

Checkpointing is a subject that merits particular attention when dealing with stateful Spark Streaming applications. Without checkpointing, restarting a stateful streaming application would require us to rebuild the state up to the point where the application previously stopped. In the case of a window operation, that rebuild process might potentially consist of hours of data, which would require more massive intermediate storage. The more challenging case is when we are implementing arbitrary stateful aggregation, as we saw in Chapter 22. Without checkpoints, even a simple stateful application, like counting the number of visitors to each page of a website, would need to reprocess all data ever seen to rebuild its state to a consistent level; a challenge that might range from very difficult to impossible, as the data necessary might no longer be available in the system.

However, checkpoints are not free. The checkpoint operation poses additional requirements to the streaming application concerning the storage required to maintain the checkpoint data and the impact that this recurrent operation has on the performance of the application.

In this chapter, we discuss the necessary considerations to set up and use checkpointing with our Spark Streaming application. We begin with an example to illustrate the practical aspects of setting up checkpoints in a program. Thereafter, we see how to recover from a checkpoint, the operational cost that checkpointing introduces and, finally, we discuss some techniques to tune checkpointing's performance.

Understanding the Use of Checkpoints

Let's consider the following streaming job that keeps track of the number of times a video has been played per hour in an online video store. It uses `mapWithState` to keep track of the `videoPlayed` events coming through the stream and processes the time-stamp embedded in the event to determine the time-based aggregation.

In the code snippet that follows, we make the following assumptions:

- The data stream consists of the structure `VideoPlayed(video-id, client-id, timestamp)`
- We have a `videoPlayedDStream` available of type `DStream[VideoPlayed]`
- We have a `trackVideoHits` function with this signature:

```
// Data Structures
case class VideoPlayed(videoId: String, clientId: String, timestamp: Long)
case class VideoPlayCount(videoId: String, day: Date, count: Long)

// State Tracking Function
def trackVideoHits(videoId: String,
                   timestamp:Option[Long],
                   runningCount: State[VideoPlayCount]
                   ): Option[VideoPlayCount]
```

Online Resources

We have reduced the code to the elements needed to understand checkpointing. To explore the complete example, go to the stand-alone project `checkpointed-video-stream` in the online resources for the book, located at *https://github.com/stream-processing-with-spark*.

Example 24-1. Stream checkpointing

```
import org.apache.spark.streaming.State
import org.apache.spark.streaming._

val streamingContext = new StreamingContext(spark.sparkContext, Seconds(10))
streamingContext.checkpoint("/tmp/streaming")

val checkpointedVideoPlayedDStream = videoPlayedDStream.checkpoint(Seconds(60))


// create the mapWithState spec
val videoHitsCounterSpec = StateSpec.function(trackVideoHits _)
                                    .timeout(Seconds(3600))

// Stateful stream of videoHitsPerHour
```

```
val statefulVideoHitsPerHour = checkpointedVideoPlayedDStream.map(videoPlay =>
  (videoPlay.videoId, videoPlay.timestamp)
).mapWithState(videoHitsCounterSpec)

// remove the None values from the state stream by "flattening" the DStream
val videoHitsPerHour = statefulVideoHitsPerHour.flatMap(elem => elem)

// print the top-10 highest values
videoHitsPerHour.foreachRDD{ rdd =>
  val top10 = rdd.top(10)(Ordering[Long].on((v: VideoPlayCount) => v.count))
  top10.foreach(videoCount => println(videoCount))
}

streamingContext.start()
```

If we run this example, we should see an output similar to this:

```
Top 10 at time 2019-03-17 21:44:00.0
==========================
video-935, 2019-03-17 23:00:00.0, 18
video-981, 2019-03-18 00:00:00.0, 18
video-172, 2019-03-18 00:00:00.0, 17
video-846, 2019-03-18 00:00:00.0, 17
video-996, 2019-03-18 00:00:00.0, 17
video-324, 2019-03-18 00:00:00.0, 16
video-344, 2019-03-17 23:00:00.0, 16
video-523, 2019-03-18 00:00:00.0, 16
video-674, 2019-03-18 00:00:00.0, 16
video-162, 2019-03-18 00:00:00.0, 16
==========================
```

The more interesting aspect to observe while this job is executing is the Spark UI, where we can see how the dependency of each batch execution on previous stages unfolds.

Figure 24-1 illustrates how the first iteration (Job #0) depends only on the initial batch of data, identified by the makeRDD operation.

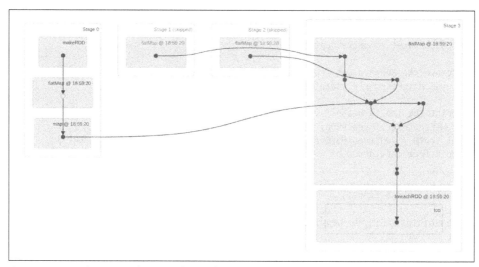

Figure 24-1. Observing the initial stateful job lineage

To see this representation on your own setup, go to the Spark UI at
`<host>:4040` (or 4041, 4042, and so on if there is more than one
job running on the same host).

Then, click the job details, leading to the page `http://<host>:`
`4040/jobs/job/?id=0` where you can expand the *DAG Visualiza-*
tion to display the visualization.

As the job makes progress, we can inspect the DAG visualization of the next job executed, job #1, which we show in Figure 24-2. There, we can see that the results are dependent on the previous makeRDD and the current batch of data, brought together by the stateful computation embodied by the mapWithState stage.

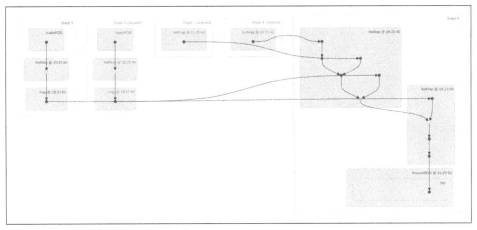

Figure 24-2. Evolving stateful job lineage

If we look at the details of `stage 8` in `job #1`, in Figure 24-3, we can appreciate how the combination the current results depend on previous and new data combined.

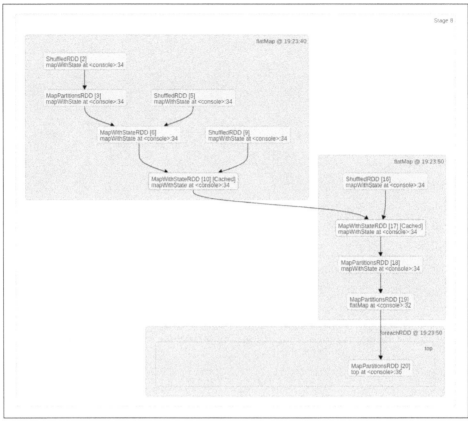

Figure 24-3. Evolving stateful job lineage: detail

This process repeats with each new batch of data, creating an ever more complex dependency graph on each iteration. In the same charts, we can see older stages skipped because the results are still available in memory. But we cannot keep all previous results around forever.

Checkpointing provides us with a solution to bound this complexity. At each checkpoint, Spark Streaming stores the intermediate state of the stream computation so that results previous to the checkpoint are no longer required to process new data.

In Figure 24-4, we can see the state of the same streaming job after more than 300 iterations. Instead of keeping the previous 300 results in memory, the stateful computation combines the checkpoint information with the most recent batches of data to obtain a result for the latest microbatch.

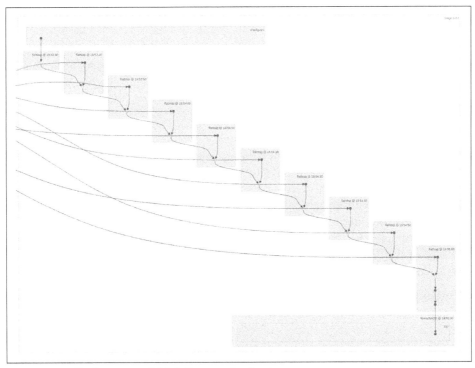

Figure 24-4. Evolving stateful job lineage: checkpoint

Checkpointing DStreams

To enable checkpointing, you need to set two parameters:

`streamingContext.checkpoint(<dir>)`
Sets the checkpoint directory for this streaming context. This directory should be on a resilient filesystem, such as Hadoop Distributed Files System (HDFS).

`dstream.checkpoint(<duration>)`
Sets the checkpoint frequency of the DStream to the specified `duration`.

Setting the duration on the DStream is optional. If not set, it defaults to a specific value, depending on the DStream type. For `MapWithStateDStream`, it defaults to 10x the duration of the batch interval. For all other DStreams, it defaults to 10 seconds or the batch interval, whichever is largest.

The checkpoint frequency *must* be a multiple of the batch interval, or the job will fail with an initialization error. Intuitively, what we want is the interval frequency to be each *n* batch intervals, where the choice of *n* depends on the volume of the data and how critical the requirements are for failure recovery of the job. A rule of thumb, advised in the Spark documentation, is to do checkpointing every five to seven batch intervals as a start.

 Note that if you have a batch interval longer than 10 seconds, leaving the default value will create a checkpoint on every batch, which might negatively affect the performance of the streaming job.

Checkpointing is required for stateful processing when the streaming operation depends on a previous state, and therefore, it might be computationally expensive or simply impossible to keep all of the necessary data around. The idea here is that Spark Streaming implements computations that depend possibly on a number of prior RDDs, either from intermediate results or prior source data. As we have seen in the previous example, this constitutes the lineage of the computation. However, as we also observed, that lineage can grow long or even indefinitely in cases in which a stateful computation is used.

For example, the reasoning to compute the length of the maximal lineage obtained out of a windowed computation is to consider what kind of data we would need to recover if we were to perform the entire computation due to partial data loss in the worst case. Given a batch interval of duration t and a window interval of $n \times t$, we will need the last n RDDs of data to recompute the window. In the case of windowed computation, the length of the lineage might be long but bounded by a fixed factor.

The use of checkpointing jumps from convenient to necessary when the lineage of our computation might be arbitrarily long. In the case of arbitrary stateful streams, the length of the state dependence on a prior RDD can go as far back as the beginning of the runtime of our application, making the use of checkpoints on stateful streams mandatory.

Recovery from a Checkpoint

In our discussion so far, we have considered the role that checkpointing plays in saving the intermediate state of a stateful streaming job so that further iterations can refer to that intermediate result instead of depending on the complete lineage of the job, that might go as far as the first element ever received.

There is another equally important aspect to checkpointing when we deal with failure and recovering from it. Let's go back to our initial example and think for a minute: "What would happen if my job fails at any point?" Without checkpoints, we would need to replay the data for at least the past hour to recover the partial totals for every video played. Now imagine that we were counting daily totals. Then, we would need to replay a day's worth of data while new data is still arriving for processing.

The information contained in a checkpoint lets us recover our stream-processing application from the last known state, when the last checkpoint was taken. This implies that a full recovery will require only the replay of a few batches of data instead of hours' or days' worth of records.

Recovery from a checkpoint must be supported by the Spark Streaming application in its implementation. In particular, we need to use a particular method to obtain an active `streamingContext`. The `streamingContext` provides a `getActiveOr Create(<dir>, <ctx-creation-function>)` method that permits an application to start from an existing checkpoint stored at `<dir>`, and if it's not available, to create a new `streamingContext` using the `<ctx-creation-function>` function.

If we update our earlier example with checkpoint recovery, our `streamingContext` creation should look like this:

```
def setupContext(
  checkpointDir : String,
  sparkContext: SparkContext
  ): StreamingContext = {
// create a streamingContext and setup the DStream operations we saw previously
}

val checkpointDir = "/tmp/streaming"
val streamingContext = StreamingContext.getOrCreate(
  CheckpointDir,
  () => setupContext(CheckpointDir, spark.sparkContext)
)

streamingContext.start()
streamingContext.awaitTermination()
```

Limitations

Checkpoint recovery is supported only for packaged applications into a JAR file and submitted using `spark-submit`. Recovering from a checkpoint is limited to the same application logic that wrote the checkpoint data and cannot be used to perform upgrades from a running streaming application. Changes in the application logic will affect the possibility to rebuild the application state from its serialized form in the checkpoint and will fail to restart.

Checkpoints seriously hamper the possibility to upgrade streaming applications to newer versions and require particular architectural considerations to restore stateful computations when new versions of the application become available.

The Cost of Checkpointing

The added cost of checkpointing to the execution time of a streaming application is of particular concern in Spark Streaming because we consider our batch interval as a computation budget. The writing of a potentially large state to a disk can be expensive, especially if the hardware that is backing this application is relatively slow, which is often the case when using Hadoop Distributed File System (HDFS) as a backing store. Note that this is the most common case of checkpointing: HDFS is a reliable filesystem and magnetic drives offer replicated storage at a manageable cost.

Checkpointing should ideally operate on a reliable filesystem so that in the case of a failure, it will be able to recover the state of the stream rapidly, by reading the data from that reliable storage. However, considering that writing to HDFS can be slow, we need to face the fact that checkpointing will periodically require more runtime, possibly even more time than the batch interval. And as we have explained previously, having a batch processing time longer than the batch interval can be problematic.

Checkpoint Tuning

Thanks to the Spark user interface, you can measure on average how much more time you will need for a batch interval computation that includes checkpointing compared to the batch processing time that you observe in RDDs that do not require checkpointing. Suppose that our batch processing time is about 30 seconds for a batch interval that is one minute. This is a relatively favorable case: at every batch interval, we spend only 30 seconds computing, and we have 30 seconds of "free" time during which our processing system is sitting idle while receiving data.

Given our application requirements, we decide to checkpoint every five minutes. Now that we've decided to do that checkpointing every five minutes, we run some measurements and observe that our checkpointing batches require four minutes of actual batch processing time. We can conclude that we will need about three and a half minutes to write to disk, considering that during that same batch we have also expanded 30 seconds in computation. It means that in this case, we will require four batches to checkpoint once again. Why is that?

This is because when we spend three and a half minutes actually writing our files to disk, we are in fact still receiving data when those three and a half minutes elapse. In those three and a half minutes, we have received three and a half new batches that we did not have time to process because our system was blocked waiting for the checkpoint operation to end. As a consequence, we now have three and a half—that is, four batches of data that are stored on our system—that we need to process to catch up and reach stability again. Now, we have a computation time on a normal batch of 30 seconds, which means that we will be able to catch up by one new batch on every batch interval of one minute, so that in four batches we will be caught up with the received data. We will be able to checkpoint again at the fifth batch interval. At a checkpointing interval of five batches, we are in fact just at the stability limit of the system.

That is, of course, if the state encoded in your stateful stream does reflect a size that is more or less constant with respect to the amount of data received from the input source over time. The relationship between the size of the state and the amount of data received over time might be more complex and dependent on the particular application and computation, which is why it is often very useful to proceed experimentally with checkpointing length. The idea is that a larger checkpointing interval will give more time to our cluster to catch up with time lost during checkpointing, and the equally important concern that if we set a checkpoint interval that is too high, we might have a cluster that will have some trouble catching up if we incur some kind of data loss through a crash. In that case, we will indeed require the system to load the checkpoint and to reprocess all the RDDs that have been seen since that checkpoint.

Finally, note that any Spark user should consider changing the default checkpoint interval on any DStream because it is set to 10 seconds. This means that on each batch, Spark will checkpoint if the interval elapsed since the last checkpoint is greater than the checkpointing interval. As a consequence, if you have a batch interval larger than 10 seconds, this leads to the "sawtooth" pattern in processing times, shown in Figure 24-5, depicting checkpointing on every other batch (which is probably too frequent for most applications).

There exists another alternative to this discipline of checkpoint interval tuning, which consists of writing to a persistent directory that accepts data at a very high speed. For that purpose, you can choose to point your checkpoint directory to a path of an HDFS cluster that is backed by very fast hardware storage, such as solid-state drives (SSDs). Another alternative is to have this backed by memory with a decent offload to disk when memory is filled, something performed by Alluxio, for example—a project that was initially developed as Tachyon, some module of Apache Spark. This simple method for reducing the checkpointing time and the time lost in checkpointing is often one of the most efficient ways to reach a stable computation under Spark Streaming; that is, if it is affordable, of course.

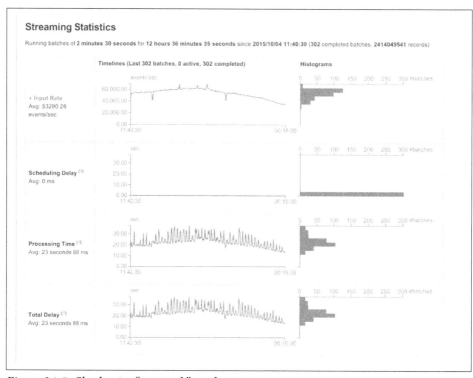

Figure 24-5. Checkpoint "sawtooth" performance pattern

## CHAPTER 25

Monitoring Spark Streaming

Monitoring in streaming applications is required to gain operational confidence of the deployed applications and should include a holistic view of the resources used by the application, such as CPU, memory, and secondary storage. As a distributed application, the number of factors to monitor is multiplied by the number of nodes that are part of a clustered deployment.

To manage this complexity, we need a comprehensive and smart monitoring system. It needs to collect metrics from all the key *moving parts* that participate in the streaming application runtime and, at the same time, it needs to provide them in an understandable and consumable form.

In the case of Spark Streaming, next to the general indicators just discussed, we are mainly concerned with the relationship between the amount of data received, the batch interval chosen for our application, and the actual execution time of every microbatch. The relation between these three parameters is key for a stable Spark Streaming job in the long run. To ensure that our job performs within stable boundaries, we need to make performance monitoring an integral part of the development and production process.

Spark offers several monitoring interfaces that cater to the different stages of that process:

The Streaming UI
> A web interface that provides charts of key indicators about the running job

The Monitoring REST API
> A set of APIs that can be consumed by an external monitoring system to obtain metrics through an HTTP interface

The Metrics Subsystem
> A pluggable Service Provider Interface (SPI) that allows for tight integration of external monitoring tools into Spark

The Internal Event Bus
> A pub/sub subsystem in Spark in which programmatic subscribers can receive events about different aspects of the application execution on the cluster

In this chapter, we explore these monitoring interfaces and how they apply to the different phases of the life cycle of a streaming application. We begin with the Streaming UI, in which we survey the functionality provided by this interface and its links to the different aspects of a running Spark Streaming job. The Streaming UI is a powerful visual tool that we can use in the initial development and deployment phase to better understand how our application behaves from a pragmatic perspective. We dedicate a section to detailing the use of the Streaming UI with this particular focus on performance.

In the rest of the chapter, we cover the different monitoring integration capabilities of Spark Streaming. We explore the APIs offered by the REST API and the Metrics Subsystem SPI to expose internal metrics to external monitoring clients. To finalize, we describe the data model and interactions of the *Internal Event Bus*, which we can use to programmatically access all the metrics offered by Spark Streaming for cases in which maximal flexibility is required to integrate a custom monitoring solution.

The Streaming UI

The SparkUI is a web application available on the Spark driver node, usually running on port 4040, unless there are other Spark processes running on the same node, in which case, the port used will increase (4041, 4042, and so on) until one free port is found. We can also configure this port by using the configuration key `spark.ui.port`.

What we refer to as the *Streaming UI* is a tab in the Spark UI that becomes active whenever a `StreamingContext` is started, as illustrated in Figure 25-1.

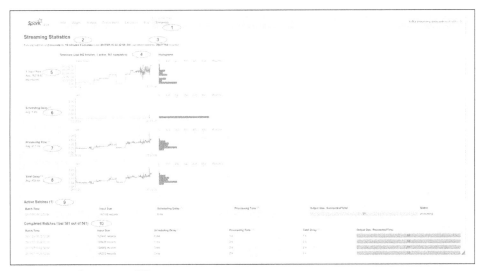

Figure 25-1. Streaming UI

The Streaming UI comprises several visual elements that provide an at-a-glance view of the performance of a Spark Streaming job. Following the numerical clues in the image, these are the elements that make up the UI:

(1) Streaming UI tab
 This is the Streaming tab on the Spark UI. Clicking it opens that Streaming UI.

(2) Time-based stats
 The overall statistics line includes that batch interval, the time this application has been up, and the start timestamp.

(3) Summary of batches and records
 Next to the timing information, we find the total number of batches completed and the grand total of records processed.

(4) Performance charts
 The title in the table of charts reports what data is used in the charts displayed. The data represented in the charts is preserved in circular buffers. We see only the thousand (1,000) most recent data points received.

(5) The Input Rate chart
 A time-series representation of the number of records received at each batch interval with a distribution histogram next to it.

(6) The Scheduling Delay chart
 This chart reports the difference between the moment when the batch is scheduled and when it's processed.

(7) The Processing Time chart
   A time-series of the amount of time (duration) needed to process each batch.

(8) Total Delay chart
   A time-series of the sum of the scheduling delay and the processing time. It provides a view of the joint execution of Spark Streaming and the Spark core engine.

(9) Active batches
   Provides a list of the batches currently in the Spark Streaming queue. It shows the batch or batches currently executing as well as the batches of any potential backlog in case of an overload. Ideally, only batches in status processing are in this list. This list might appear empty if at the time of loading the Streaming UI, the current batch had finished processing and the next one is not yet due for scheduling.

(10) Completed batches
   A list of the most recent batches processed with a link to the details of that batch.

Understanding Job Performance Using the Streaming UI

As discussed in "The Streaming UI" on page 316, the four charts that comprise the main screen of the Streaming UI provide a snapshot of the current and most recent performance of our streaming job. By default, the last 1,000 processing intervals are presented in the UI, meaning that the period of time we are able to view is intervals x batch interval, so for a job with a two-second batch interval, we see the metrics of roughly the last half hour (2 x 1,000 = 2,000 seconds, or 33,33 minutes). We can configure the number of remembered intervals by using the `spark.ui.retainedJobs` configuration parameter.

Input Rate Chart

The Input Rate chart, on top, gives a view of the input load that the application is sustaining. All charts share a common timeline. We can imagine a vertical line through all of them that would serve as a reference to correlate the different metrics to the input load, as illustrated in Figure 25-2. The data points of chart lines are clickable and will link to the corresponding job detail line that appears underneath the charts. As we will explore later on, this navigation feature is very helpful to track back the origins of certain behaviors that we can observe on the charts.

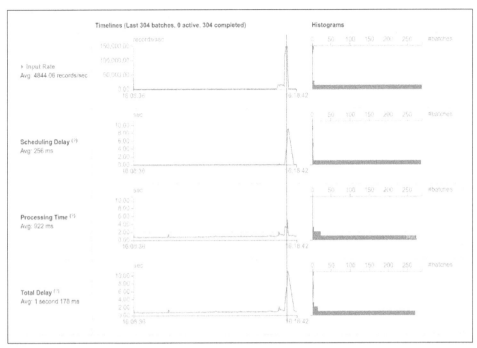

Figure 25-2. Streaming UI: correlation of metrics

Scheduling Delay Chart

The next chart in the UI is the Scheduling Delay chart. This is a key health indicator: for an application that is running well within its time and resource constraints, this metric will be constantly flat on zero. Small periodic disturbances might point to regular supporting processes such as snapshots.

Window operations that create exceptional load will potentially also affect this metric. It's important to note that the delay will show on the batches that immediately follow a batch that took longer than the batch interval to complete. These delays will not show a correlation with the input rate. Delays introduced by peaks in data input will correlate with a high peak in the Input Rate with an offset. Figure 25-3 depicts how the peak in the Input Rate chart happens earlier than the corresponding increase in the Scheduling Delay. Because this chart represents a delay, we see the effects of the peak in input rate after the system has begun to "digest" the data overload.

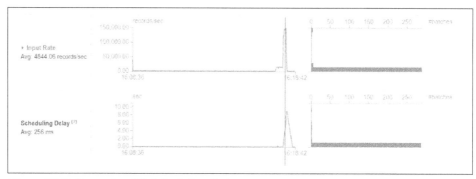

Figure 25-3. Streaming UI: Scheduling Delay

Processing Time Chart

This chart, shown in Figure 25-4, represents the time that the data-processing part of the streaming job takes to execute. This execution takes place on the Spark cluster, so this is the main indicator of how the actual data crunching is performing on the (potentially) distributed environment. An important aspect of this chart is the high watermark line at the level corresponding to the batch interval time. Let's quickly recall that the batch interval is the time of each microbatch and also the time we have to process the data that arrived at the previous interval. A processing time below this watermark is considered stable. An occasional peak above this line might be acceptable if the job has enough room to recover from it. A job that is constantly above this line will build a backlog using storage resources in memory and/or disk. If the available storage is exhausted, the job will eventually crash. This chart usually has a high correlation with the Input Rate chart because it's common that the execution time of the job is related to the volume of data received on each batch interval.

Figure 25-4. Streaming UI: Processing Time

Total Delay Chart

The Total Delay chart is a graphical representation of the end-to-end latency of the system. Total delay comprises the length of time that Spark Streaming takes to collect, schedule, and submit each microbatch for processing and the amount of time it takes for Spark to apply the job's logic and produce a result. This chart provides a holistic view of the system performance and reveals any delays that might happen during the execution of the job. As for the Scheduling Delay chart, any sustained increase in the

---

total delay metric is a reason of concern and might indicate high load or other conditions such as increasing storage latency that negatively affect the job's performance.

Batch Details

When we scroll below the charts that constitute the main screen of the Streaming UI, we find two tables: Active Batches and Completed Batches. These tables have columns that correspond to the charts that we just studied: Input Size, Scheduling Delay, Processing Time, and an Output Operations counter. In addition to these fields, Completed Batches also shows the Total Delay of the corresponding microbatch.

 Output Ops relates to the number of output operations registered to execute on the microbatch. This refers to the job's code structure and should not be confused with a parallelism indicator. As we recall, output operations, such as print() or foreachRDD, are the operations that trigger the lazy execution of a DStream.

Active Batches

Contains information about the microbatches in the Spark Streaming scheduler queue. For a healthy job, this table contains at most one row: the batch currently executing. This entry indicates the number of records contained in the microbatch and any delay before the start of execution. Processing Time is unknown until the microbatch has been completed, so this metric is never present on the Active Batches table.

When more than one row is present in this table, it indicates that the job has a delay beyond the batch interval and new microbatches queue awaiting execution, forming an execution backlog.

Completed batches

Right after a batch execution completes, its corresponding entry in the Active Batches table transitions to the Completed Batches table. In this transition, the Processing Time field is filled with its execution time and the Total Delay is finally known and also included.

Each entry is identified by the timestamp, labeled as batch time. This label also provides a link to the details of the corresponding Spark job that provided the execution for this batch.

The link to the batch details deserves further exploration. As explained in earlier chapters, the Spark Streaming model is based on microbatches. The Batch Detail page provides insights in the execution of each batch, broken down into the different jobs that constitute the batch. Figure 25-5 presents the structure. A batch is defined as a sequence of output operations that are executed in the same order as they were defined in the application code. Each output operation contains one or more jobs.

This page summarizes this relationship, displays the duration per job, and the parallelism level in the task overview.

Figure 25-5. Streaming UI: batch details

The jobs are listed by job ID and provide a link to the job page in the Spark UI. These are *normal* Spark jobs executed by the core engine. By clicking through, we can explore the execution, in terms of stages, assigned executor, and execution time statistics.

> To exercise the use of the Streaming UI locally, there are two notebooks provided in the online resources of this book:
>
> *kafka-data-generator.snb*
> This notebook is used to produce a configurable number of records per second that are sent to a local Kafka topic.
>
> *kafka-streaming-data.snb*
> This notebook consumes from that same topic, joins the data with a reference dataset, and writes the result to a local file.
>
> By experimenting with the producer rate, we can observe the behavior of the Streaming UI and experience what stable and overload situations look like. This is a good exercise to put into practice when moving a streaming application to production because it helps in understanding its performance characteristics and in determining the load thresholds where the application performs correctly.

The Monitoring REST API

The Monitoring REST API exposes the job's streaming metrics as a set of predefined HTTP endpoints that deliver the data as JSON-formatted objects. These objects can be consumed by external monitoring and alerting applications to integrate the Spark Streaming jobs with some external monitoring system.

Using the Monitoring REST API

The Monitoring REST API is served by the Spark driver node, on the same port as the Spark UI, and mounted at the `/api/v1` endpoint: `http://<driver-host>:<ui-port>/api/v1`.

The `/api/v1/applications/:app-id` resource offers information about the application ID `app-id` provided. This `id` first must be queried by calling `/api/v1/applica tions` to construct the application-specific URL. In the following URLs, we refer to this variable application ID as `app-id`.

Note that for a running Spark Streaming context, there will be only one current application ID.

 The Monitoring REST API introduced support for Spark Streaming only from Spark version 2.2 onward. For earlier versions of Spark, consider the metrics servlet, further explained in the next section.

Information Exposed by the Monitoring REST API

The resources corresponding to the running Spark Streaming context are available at `/api/v1/applications/:app-id/streaming`.

Table 25-1 summarizes the subresources provided by this endpoint.

Table 25-1. Subresources of the streaming resource

Resource	Meaning	Corresponding UI element
`/statistics`	A set of summarized metrics (see the sections that follow for details)	Streaming UI charts
`/receivers`	A list of all receivers instantiated in this streaming job	Receivers summary on the Input Rate chart
`/receivers/:stream-id`	Details of the receiver indexed by the provided `stream-id`	Click-open receivers on the Input Rate chart
`/batches`	A list of all the currently kept batches	List of batches underneath the charts
`/batches/:batch-id/operations`	The output operations	Click-through a batch in the batch list
`/batches/:batch-id/ operations/:output-op-id`	Detailed information of the corresponding output operation in the given batch	Click-through in the operations details under the batch detail page

From a monitoring perspective, we should pay some additional attention to the `sta tistics` object. It contains the key performance indicators that we need to monitor in order to ensure a healthy streaming job: `/api/v1/applications/:app-id/ stream ing/statistics`.

Table 25-2 presents a listing of the different data delivered by the `statistics` end-point, their type, and a brief description of the metric involved.

Table 25-2. Statistics object of the streaming resource

Key	Type	Description
startTime	String	Timestamp encoded in ISO 8601 format
batchDuration	Number (Long)	Batch interval duration in milliseconds
numReceivers	Number (Long)	Count of registered receivers
numActiveReceivers	Number (Long)	Count of the currently active receivers
numInactiveReceivers	Number (Long)	Count of the currently inactive receivers
numTotalCompletedBatches	Number (Long)	Count of the completed batches since the start of this streaming job
numRetainedCompletedBatches	Number (Long)	Count of the currently kept batches from which we still store information
numActiveBatches	Number (Long)	Count of the batches in the execution queue of the streaming context
numProcessedRecords	Number (Long)	Totalized sum of the records processed by the currently running job
numReceivedRecords	Number (Long)	Totalized sum of the records received by the currently running job
avgInputRate	Number (Double)	Arithmetic mean of the input rate over the last kept batches
avgSchedulingDelay	Number (Double)	Arithmetic mean of the scheduling delay over the last kept batches
avgProcessingTime	Number (Double)	Arithmetic mean of the processing time over the last kept batches
avgTotalDelay	Number (Double)	Arithmetic mean of the total delay over the last kept batches

When integrating a monitoring tool with Spark Streaming, we are particularly interested in `avgSchedulingDelay` and making sure that it does not grow over time. Many monitoring applications use a *grow rate* (or similar) gauge to measure change over time. Given that the value provided by the API is an average over the last kept batches (1,000 by default), setting up alarms on this metric should take into consideration small increasing changes.

The Metrics Subsystem

In Spark, the Metrics Subsystem is an SPI that allows the implementation of metric sinks to integrate Spark with external management and monitoring solutions.

It offers a number of built-in implementations such as the following:

Console
Logs metric information to the standard output of the job

HTTP Servlet
Delivers metrics using HTTP/JSON

CSV
Delivers the metrics to files in the configured directory using a comma-separated values (CSV) format

JMX
Enables reporting of metrics through Java Management Extensions (JMX)

Log
Delivers metric information to the logs of the application

Graphite, StatsD
Forwards metrics to a Graphite/StatsD service

Ganglia
Delivers metrics to an existing Ganglia deployment (note that due to license restrictions, using this option requires recompilation of the Spark binaries)

The Metrics Subsystem reports the most recent values of Spark and Spark Streaming processes. This gives us raw access to performance metrics that can feed remote performance monitoring applications and also enable accurate and timely alerting on abnormalities in a streaming process.

The specific metrics for the streaming job are available under the key `<app-id>.driver.<application name>.StreamingMetrics.streaming`.

These are as follows:

- `lastCompletedBatch_processingDelay`
- `lastCompletedBatch_processingEndTime`
- `lastCompletedBatch_processingStartTime`
- `lastCompletedBatch_schedulingDelay`
- `lastCompletedBatch_submissionTime`
- `lastCompletedBatch_totalDelay`
- `lastReceivedBatch_processingEndTime`
- `lastReceivedBatch_processingStartTime`
- `lastReceivedBatch_records`

- `lastReceivedBatch_submissionTime`
- `receivers`
- `retainedCompletedBatches`
- `runningBatches`
- `totalCompletedBatches`
- `totalProcessedRecords`
- `totalReceivedRecords`
- `unprocessedBatches`
- `waitingBatches`

Although not readily offered, you can obtain the `lastCompletedBatch_processing Time` by simple arithmetic: `lastCompletedBatch_processingEndTime - lastComple tedBatch_processingStartTime`.

In this API, the key indicator to track for job stability is `lastCompletedBatch_proces singDelay`, which we expect to be zero or close to zero and stable over time. A moving average of the last 5 to 10 values should remove the noise that small delays sometimes introduce and offer a metric that we can rely on to trigger alarms or pager calls.

The Internal Event Bus

All the metrics interfaces discussed in this chapter have a single source of truth in common: they are all consuming data from an internal Spark event bus though dedicated `StreamingListener` implementations.

Spark uses several internal event buses to deliver life cycle events and metadata about the executing Spark jobs to subscribed clients. This interface is mostly used by internal Spark consumers that offer the data in some processed form. The Spark UI is the most significant example of such interaction.

For those cases in which the existing high-level interfaces are not sufficient to fulfill our requirements, it's possible to develop custom listeners and register them to receive events. To create a custom Spark Streaming listener, we extend the `org.apache.spark.streaming.scheduler.StreamingListener` trait. This trait has a no-op default implementation for all of its callback methods, so that extending it requires only to override the desired callbacks with our custom metric processing logic.

Note that this internal Spark API is marked as `DeveloperApi`. Hence, its definitions, such as classes and interfaces, are subject to change without public notice.

You can explore a custom Spark Streaming listener implementation in the online resources. The notebook *kafka-streaming-with-listener* extends the Kafka notebook that we used earlier with a custom notebook listener that delivers all events to a `TableWidget` that can be directly displayed in the notebook.

Interacting with the Event Bus

The `StreamingListener` interface consists of a trait with several callback methods. Each method is called by the notification process with an instance of a subclass of `StreamingListenerEvent` that contains the relevant information for the callback method.

The StreamingListener interface

In the following overview, we highlight the most interesting parts of those data events:

onStreamingStarted

```
def onStreamingStarted(
    streamingStarted:StreamingListenerStreamingStarted):Unit
```

This method is called when the streaming job starts. The `StreamingListener StreamingStarted` instance has a single field, `time`, that contains the timestamp in milliseconds when the streaming job started.

Receiver events

All callback methods that relate to the life cycle of receivers share a common `ReceiverInfo` class that describes the receiver that is being reported. Each event-reporting class will have a single `receiverInfo: ReceiverInfo` member. The information contained in the attributes of the `ReceiverInfo` class will depend on the relevant receiver information for the reported event.

onReceiverStarted

```
def onReceiverStarted(
    receiverStarted: StreamingListenerReceiverStarted): Unit
```

This method is called when a receiver has been started. The `StreamingListener ReceiverStarted` instance contains a `ReceiverInfo` instance that describes the receiver started for this streaming job. Note that this method is only relevant for the receiver-based streaming model.

onReceiverError

```
def onReceiverError(
    receiverError: StreamingListenerReceiverError): Unit
```

This method is called when an existing receiver reports an error. Like for the onReceiverStarted call, the provided StreamingListenerReceiverError instance contains a ReceiverInfo object. Within this Receiver Info instance, we will find detailed information about the error, such as the error message and the timestamp of the occurrence.

onReceiverStopped

```
def onReceiverStopped(
    receiverStopped: StreamingListenerReceiverStopped): Unit
```

This is the counterpart of the onReceiverStarted event. It fires when a receiver has been stopped.

Batch events

These events relate to the life cycle of batch processing, from submission to completion. Recall that each output operation registered on a DStream will lead to an independent job execution. Those jobs are grouped in batches that are submitted together and in sequence to the Spark core engine for execution. This section of the listener interface fires events following the life cycle of submission and execution of batches.

As these events will fire following the processing of each microbatch, their reporting rate is at least as frequent as the batch interval of the related StreamingContext.

Following the same implementation pattern as the receiver callback interface, all batch-related events report a container class with a single BatchInfo member. Each BatchInfo instance reported contains the relevant information corresponding to the reporting callback.

BatchInfo also contains a Map of the output operations registered in this batch, represented by the OutputOperationInfo class. This class contains detailed information about the time, duration, and eventual errors for each individual output operation. We could use this data point to split the total execution time of a batch into the time taken by the different operations that lead to individual job execution on the Spark core engine:

onBatchSubmitted

```
def onBatchSubmitted(
    batchSubmitted: StreamingListenerBatchSubmitted)
```

This method is called when a batch of jobs is submitted to Spark for processing. The corresponding BatchInfo object, reported by the StreamingListenerBatch Submitted contains the timestamp of the batch submission time. At this point, the optional values processingStartTime and processingEndTime are set to None because those values are unknown at this stage of the batch-processing cycle.

onBatchStarted

```
def onBatchStarted(batchStarted: StreamingListenerBatchStarted): Unit
```

This method is called when the processing of an individual job has just started. The `BatchInfo` object, embedded in the `StreamingListenerBatchStarted` instance provided, contains a populated `processingStartTime`.

onBatchCompleted

```
def onBatchCompleted(batchCompleted: StreamingListenerBatchCompleted): Unit
```

This method is called when the processing of a batch has been completed. The provided `BatchInfo` instance will be fully populated with the overall timing of the batch. The map of `OutputOperationInfo` will also contain the detailed timing information for the execution of each output operation.

Output operation events

This section of the `StreamingListener` callback interface provides information at the level of each job execution triggered by the submission of a batch. Because there might be many output operations registered into the same batch, this interface might fire at a much higher rate than the batch interval of the `StreamingContext`. Any receiving client of the data provided by this interface should be dimensioned to receive such a load of events.

The events reported by these methods contain an `OutputOperationInfo` instance that provides further timing details about the output operation being reported. This `OutputOperationInfo` is the same data structure contained by the `outputOperationInfo` of the `BatchInfo` object we just saw in the batch-related events. For cases in which we are interested only in the timing information of each job, but we don't need to be informed in real time about the execution life cycle, you should consult the event provided by `onBatchCompleted` (as just described).

Here are the callbacks you can use to inject your own processing during a job's execution.

onOutputOperationStarted

```
def onOutputOperationStarted(
    outputOperationStarted: StreamingListenerOutputOperationStarted): Unit
```

This method is called when the processing of a job, corresponding to an output operation, starts. Individual jobs can be related back into their corresponding batch, by the `batchTime` attribute.

onOutputOperationCompleted

```
def onOutputOperationCompleted(
    outputOperationCompleted: StreamingListenerOutputOperationCompleted): Unit
```

This method is called when the processing of an individual job has completed. Note that there are no callbacks to notify individual job failures. The `OutputOper ationInfo` instance contains an attribute, `failureReason`, which is an `Option[String]`. In case of a job failure, this option will be populated with `Some(error message)`.

StreamingListener registration

After we have developed our custom `StreamingListener`, we need to register it to consume events. The streaming listener bus is hosted by the `StreamingContext`, which exposes a registration call to add custom implementations of the `StreamingLis tener` trait.

Suppose that we implemented a `LogReportingStreamingListener` that forwards all events to a logging framework. Example 25-1 shows how to register our custom listener in a `StreamingContext`.

Example 25-1. Custom listener registration

```
val streamingContext = new StreamingContext(sc, Seconds(10))
val customLogStreamingReporter = new LogReportingStreamingListener(...)
streamingContext.addStreamingListener(customLogStreamingReporter)
```

Summary

In this chapter, you learned about the different methods to observe and continuously monitor your running Spark Streaming applications. Given that the performance characteristics of a job are a critical aspect to guarantee its stable deployment to a production environment, performance monitoring is an activity that you should perform from the early phases of the development cycle.

The Streaming UI, a tab in the Spark UI, is ideal for the interactive monitoring of your streaming application. It provides high-level charts that track the key performance indicators of a streaming job and provides links to detailed views where you can investigate down to the level of the individual jobs that make up a batch. This is an active process that leads to actionable insights into the performance characteristics of the streaming job.

After the job is put to a continuous execution, it's clear that we cannot keep human monitoring on a 24/7 basis. You can achieve integration with existing monitoring and alerting tools by consuming the REST-based interface that reports data equivalent to that available in the Streaming UI or through the Metrics Subsystem, which offers standard pluggable external interfaces that monitoring tools can consume.

For the particular use cases that require a fully customizable solution that can get the finest-grained resolution of execution information in real time, you can implement a custom `StreamingListener` and register it to the `StreamingContext` of your application.

This broad spectrum of monitoring alternatives ensures that your Spark Streaming application deployments can be deployed and coexist in a production infrastructure with a common monitoring and alerting subsystem, following the internal quality processes of the enterprise.

## CHAPTER 26

Performance Tuning

The performance characteristics of a distributed streaming application are often dictated by complex relationships among internal and external factors involved in its operation.

External factors are bound to the environment in which the application executes, like the hosts that constitute the cluster and the network that connects them. Each host provides resources like CPU, memory, and storage with certain performance characteristics. For example, we might have magnetic disks that are typically slow but offer low-cost storage or fast solid-state drive (SSD) arrays that provide very fast access at a higher cost per storage unit. Or we might be using cloud storage, which is bound to the capacity of the network and the available internet connection. Likewise, the data producers are often outside of the control of the streaming application.

Under internal factors, we consider the complexity of the algorithms implemented, the resources assigned to the application, and the particular configuration that dictates how the application must behave.

In this chapter, we first work to gain a deeper understanding of the performance factors in Spark Streaming. Then, we survey several strategies that you can apply to tune the performance of an existing job.

The Performance Balance of Spark Streaming

Performance tuning in Spark Streaming can sometimes be complex, but it always begins with the simple equilibrium between the batch interval and the batch processing time. We can view the batch processing time as the time cost we have to complete the processing of all the received data and any other related bookkeeping, whereas the batch interval is the budget we have allocated. Much like the financial analogy, a healthy application will fit its processing cost within the allocated budget. Although it might happen that in some particular moments when the pressure goes up, we go beyond the budget, we must see that in the longer term, our balance is preserved. An application that exceeds this time-budget balance over a long period will result in a systemic failure, usually resulting in the crash of the application due to resource exhaustion.

The Relationship Between Batch Interval and Processing Delay

A strong constraint with streaming applications, in general, is that data ingestion does not stop. In Spark Streaming, the ingestion of data occurs at regular intervals, and there are no facilities to turn it off arbitrarily. Hence, if the job queue is not empty by the time that the new batch interval starts, and new data is inserted into the system, Spark Streaming needs to finish processing the prior jobs before getting to the new data that is just entering the queue.

With only one job running at a time, we can see the following:

- If the batch processing time is only temporarily greater than the batch interval but, in general, Spark is able to process a batch in less than the batch interval, Spark Streaming will eventually catch up and empty the job (RDD) queue.

- If, on the other hand, the lateness is systemic and on average the cluster takes more than a batch interval to process a microbatch, Spark Streaming will keep accepting on average more data than it can remove from its storage management on every batch interval. Eventually, the cluster will run out of resources and crash.

We need then to consider what happens when that accumulation of excess data occurs for a stable amount of time. By default, RDDs that represent the data fed into the system are put into the memory of the cluster's machines. Within that memory, the origin data—a source RDD—requires a replication, meaning that as the data is fed into the system, a second copy is created for fault tolerance, progressively, on every block interval. As a consequence, for a temporary amount of time, and until the data of this RDD is processed, that data is present in two copies in the memory of executors of the system. In the receiver model, because the data is always present in one copy on the receiver, this machine bears most of the memory pressure.

The Last Moments of a Failing Job

Eventually, if we add too much data into a spot in the system, we end up overflowing the memory of a few executors. In the receiver model, this might well be the receiver executor that happens to crash with an `OutOfMemoryError`. What happens next is that another machine on the cluster will be designated as the new receiver and will begin receiving new data. Because some of the blocks that were in the memory of that receiver have now been lost due to the crash, they will now be present in only the cluster in one single copy, meaning that this will trigger a reduplication of this data before processing of that data can occur. So, the existing executors in the cluster will pick up the prior memory pressure—there is no inherent relief from data lost during the crash. A few executors will be busy copying the data, and one new executor will be accepting data once again. But remember that if prior to the crash our cluster included *N* executors, it is now composed of *N − 1* executors, and it is potentially slower in processing the same rhythm of data ingestion—not to mention that most executors are now busy with data replication instead of processing as usual. The batch-processing times we observed before the crash can now only be higher, and, in particular, higher than the batch interval.

In conclusion, having a batch-processing time that is, on average, higher than the batch interval has the potential of creating cascading crashes throughout your cluster. It is therefore extremely important to maintain Spark's equilibrium in considering the batch interval as a time budget for all of the things that we might want to do during the normal functioning of the cluster.

> You can remove the constraint that only one job can execute at a given time by setting `spark.streaming.concurrent.jobs` to a value greater than the one in your Spark configuration. However, this can be risky in that it can create competition for resources and can make it more difficult to debug whether there are sufficient resources in the system to process the ingested data fast enough.

Going Deeper: Scheduling Delay and Processing Delay

Many factors can have an influence on the batch-processing time. Of course, the first and foremost constraint is the analysis that is to be performed on the data—the logic of the job itself. The running time of that computation might or might not depend on the size of the data, and might or might not depend on the values present in the data.

This purely computational time is accounted for under the name of *processing delay*, which is the difference between the time elapsed running the job and the time elapsed setting it up.

Scheduling delay, on the other hand, accounts for the time necessary in taking the job definition (often a *closure*), serializing it, and sending it to an executor that will need to process it. Naturally, this distribution of tasks implies some overhead—time that is not spent computing—so it's wise not to decompose our workload into too many small jobs and to tune the parallelism so that it is commensurate with the number of executors on our cluster. Finally, the *scheduling delay* also accounts for job lateness, if our Spark Streaming cluster has accumulated jobs on its queue. It is formally defined as the time between the entrance of the job (RDD) in the job queue, and the moment Spark Streaming actually begins computation.

Another important factor influencing scheduling delay are the locality settings, in particular `spark.locality.wait`, which dictates how long to wait for the most local placement of the task with relation to the data before escalating to the next locality level. The following are the locality levels:

PROCESS_LOCAL

Same process Java virtual machine (JVM). This is the highest locality level.

NODE_LOCAL

Same executor machine.

NO_PREF

No locality preference.

RACK_LOCAL

Same server rack.

ANY

This is the lowest locality level, usually as a result of not being able to obtain a locality at any level above.

Checkpoint Influence in Processing Time

There are other factors that, perhaps counterintuitively, can contribute to the batch processing time, in particular checkpointing. As is discussed in Chapter 24, checkpointing is a safeguard that is necessary in the processing of stateful streams to avoid data loss while recovering from failure. It uses the storage of intermediate computation values on the disk so that in the event of a failure, data that depends on values seen in the stream since the very beginning of processing do not need to be recomputed from the data source, but only from the time of the last checkpoint. The checkpointing operation is structurally programmed by Spark as a periodic job, and, as such, the time making the checkpoint is actually considered as part of the processing delay, not the scheduling delay.

The usual checkpointing on a stateful stream for which checkpoints are usually significant, in terms of semantics and in the size of the safeguarded data, can take an amount of time much larger than a batch interval. Checkpointing durations on the order of 10 batch intervals is not unheard of. As a consequence, when making sure that the average batch-processing time is less than the batch interval, it's necessary to take checkpointing into account. The contribution of checkpointing to the average batch-processing time is as follows:

$$\frac{checkpointing delay}{batch interval} * checkpointing duration$$

This should be added to the average computation time observed during a noncheck-pointing job to have an idea of the real batch-processing time. Alternatively, another way to proceed is to compute how much time we have left in our budget (the difference between batch interval and batch-processing time) without checkpointing and tune the checkpointing interval in a function:

$$checkpointingdelay \geq checkpointingduration/(batchinterval - batchprocessingtime^*)$$

Where * marks the measure of the batch-processing time without checkpointing.

External Factors that Influence the Job's Performance

Finally, if all those factors have been taken into account and you are still witnessing spikes in the processing delay of your jobs, another aspect that we really need to pay attention to is the changing conditions on the cluster.

For example, other systems colocated on our cluster may impact our shared processing resources: the Hadoop Distributed File System (HDFS) is known to have had bugs in its older versions that constrained concurrent disk writes.[1] Therefore, we might be running a cluster at a very stable rate, while simultaneously, a different job —that might not even be Spark related—can require heavy use of the disk. This can affect the following:

- Data ingestion in the reliable receiver model, when using a write-ahead log (WAL)
- Checkpointing time
- Actions of our stream processing that involve saving data to the disk

To alleviate this issue of external impacts on our job through disk usage, we could do the following:

- Use a distributed in-memory cache such as Alluxio[2]
- Reduce disk pressure by saving structured, small data in a NoSQL database rather than on files
- Avoid colocating more disk-intensive applications with Spark than is strictly necessary

---

1 You can refer to HDFS-7489 (*https://issues.apache.org/jira/browse/HDFS-7489*) for an example of one of those subtle concurrency issues.

2 Alluxio was originally named Tachyon and was part of the Spark code base, which hints at how complementary its features are to data processing with Spark.

Disk access is only one of the possible bottlenecks that could affect our job through resource sharing with the cluster. Another possibility can be network starvation or, more generally, the existence of workloads that cannot be monitored and scheduled through our resource manager.

How to Improve Performance?

In the previous section, we discussed the intrinsic and extrinsic factors that can influence the performance of a Spark Streaming job.

Let's imagine that we are in a situation in which we developed a job and we observe certain issues that affect the performance and, hence, the stability of the job. The first step to take would be to gain insights in the different performance indicators of our job, perhaps using the techniques outlined in "Understanding Job Performance Using the Streaming UI" on page 318.

We use that information as a comparison baseline as well as guidance to use one or more of the different strategies that follow.

Tweaking the Batch Interval

A strategy that is mentioned frequently is to lengthen the batch interval. This approach might help to improve some parallelism and resource usage issues. For example, if we increase a batch interval from one minute to five minutes, we have to serialize only the tasks that are the components of our job once every five minutes instead of once every minute—a five-fold reduction.

Nonetheless, the batches of our stream will represent five minutes' worth of data seen "over the wire" instead of one, and because most of the instability issues are caused by an inadequate distribution of our resources to the throughput of our stream, the batch interval might change little to this imbalance. More important the batch interval that we seek to implement is often of high semantic value in our analysis; if only because, as we have seen in Chapter 21, it constrains the windowing and sliding intervals that we can create on an aggregated stream. Changing these analysis semantics to accommodate processing constraints should be envisioned only as a last resort.

A more compelling strategy consists of reducing general inefficiencies, such as using a fast serialization library or implementing algorithms with better performance characteristics. We can also accelerate disk-writing speeds by augmenting or replacing our distributed filesystem with an in-memory cache, such as Alluxio (*https://www.alluxio.com/*). When that's not sufficient, we should consider adding more resources to our cluster, letting us distribute the stream on more executors by correspondingly augmenting the number of partitions that we use through, for example, block interval tuning.

Limiting the Data Ingress with Fixed-Rate Throttling

If getting more resources is absolutely impossible, we need to look at reducing the number of data elements that we must deal with.

Since version 1.3, Spark includes a fixed-rate throttling that allows it to accept a maximum number of elements. We can set this by adding `spark.stream ing.receiver.maxRate` to a value in elements per second in your Spark configuration. Note that for the receiver-based consumers, this limitation is enforced at block creation and simply refuses to read any more elements from the data source if the throttle limit has been reached.

For the Kafka direct connector, there's a dedicated configuration `spark.stream ing.kafka.maxRatePerPartition` that sets the max rate limit per partition in the topic in records per second. When using this option, be mindful that the total rate will be as follows:

$$maxRatePerPartition * partitionspertopic * batchinterval$$

Note that this behavior does not, in and of itself, include any signaling; Spark will just let a limited amount of elements, and pick up the reading of new elements on the next batch interval. This has consequences on the system that is feeding data into Spark:

- If this is a pull-based system, such as in Kafka, Flume, and others, the input system could compute the number of elements read and manage the overflow data in a custom fashion.
- If the input system is more prosaically a buffer (file buffer, TCP buffer), it will overflow after a few block intervals (because our stream has a large throughput than the throttle) and will periodically be flushed (deleted) when this happens.

As a consequence, throttled ingestion in Spark can exhibit some "jitter" in the elements read, because Spark reads every element until an underlying TCP or file buffer, used as a queue for "late" elements, reaches capacity and is flushed as a whole. The effect of this is that the input stream is separated in large intervals of processed elements interspersed with "holes" (dropped elements) of a regular size (e.g., one TCP buffer).

Backpressure

The queue-based system we have described with fixed-rate throttling has the disadvantage that it makes it obscure for our entire pipeline to understand where inefficiencies lie. Indeed, we have considered a *data source* (e.g., a TCP socket) that consists of *reading data from an external server* (e.g., an HTTP server), into a *local system-level queue* (a TCP buffer), before Spark feeds this data in an *application-level buffer* (Spark Streaming's RDDs). Unless we use a listener tied to our Spark Streaming receiver, it is challenging to detect and diagnose that our system is congested and, if so, where the congestion occurs.

The external server could perhaps decide, if it was aware that our Spark Streaming cluster is congested, to react on that signal and use its own approach to either delay or select the incoming elements to Spark. More important, it could make the congestion information flow back up the stream to the data producers it depends on, calling every part of the pipeline to be aware of and help with the congestion. It would also allow any monitoring system to have a better view of how and where congestion happens in our system helping with resource management and tuning.

The *upstream-flowing, quantified signal* about congestion is called *backpressure*. This is a continuous signaling that explicitly says how many elements the system in question (here, our Spark Streaming cluster) can be expected to process at this specific instant. Backpressure signaling has an advantage with respect to throttling because it is set up as a dynamic signal that varies in function to the influx of elements and the state of the queue in Spark. As such, it does not affect the system if there is no congestion, and it does not require tuning of an arbitrary limit, avoiding the associated risks in misconfiguration (underused resources if the limit is too restrictive; overflow if the limit is too permissive).

This approach has been available in Spark since version 1.5 and can, in a nutshell, provide dynamic throttling.

Dynamic Throttling

In Spark Streaming, dynamic throttling is regulated by default with a *Proportional-Integral-Derivative* (PID) controller, which observes an error signal as the difference between the latest *ingestion rate*, observed on a batch interval in terms of number of elements per second, and the *processing rate*, which is the number of elements that have been processed per second. We could consider this error as the imbalance between the number of elements coming in and the number of elements going out of Spark at the current instant (with an "instant" rounded to a full batch interval).

The PID controller then aims at regulating the number of ingested elements on the *next* batch interval by taking into account the following:

- A proportional term (the error at this instant)
- An integral or "historic" term (the sum of all errors in the past; here, the number of unprocessed elements lying in the queue)

- A derivative or "speed" term (the rate at which the number of elements has been diminishing in the past)

The PID then attempts to compute an ideal number depending on these three factors.

Backpressure-based dynamic throttling in Spark can be turned on by setting `spark.streaming.backpressure.enabled` to `true` in your Spark configuration. Another variable `spark.streaming.backpressure.initialRate` dictates the number of elements per second the throttling should initially expect. You should set it slightly above your best estimate of the throughput of your stream to allow the algorithm to "warm up."

 The approach of focusing on backpressure to deal with congestion in a pipelined system is inspired by the Reactive Streams specification (*http://www.reactive-streams.org/*), an implementation-agnostic API intended to realize a manifesto on the advantages of this approach, backed by numerous industry players with a stake in stream processing, including Netflix, Lightbend, and Twitter.

Tuning the Backpressure PID

PID tuning is a well-established and vast subject, the scope of which is beyond this book, but the Spark Streaming user should have an intuition of what this is used for. The *proportional term* helps with dealing with the current snapshot of the error, the *integral term* helps the system to deal with the accumulated error until now, and the *derivative term* helps the system either avoid overshooting for cases in which it is correcting too fast, or undercorrection in case we face a brutal spike in the throughput of stream elements.

Each of the terms of the PID has a weight factor attached to it, between 0 and 1, as befits a classical implementation of PIDs. Here are the parameters that you need to set in your Spark configuration:

```
spark.streaming.backpressure.pid.proportional
spark.streaming.backpressure.pid.integral
spark.streaming.backpressure.pid.derived
```

By default, Spark implements a proportional–integral controller, with a proportional weight of 1, an integral weight of 0.2, and a derivative weight of 0. This offers a sensible default in Spark Streaming applications where the stream throughput varies relatively slowly with respect to the batch interval, and is easier to interpret: Spark aims to ingest no more than the last rate of processing allowed, with a "buffer" for processing one-fifth of the late elements on each batch. Note, however, that if you are faced with a fast-changing stream with an irregular throughput, you might consider having a nonzero derivative term.

Custom Rate Estimator

The PID estimator is not the only rate estimator that we can implement in Spark. It is an implementation of the `RateEstimator` trait, and the particular implementation can be swapped by setting the value of `spark.streaming.backpressure.rateEstima` `tor` to your class name. Remember that you will need to include the class in question in the Spark classpath; for example, through the `--jars` argument to `spark-submit`.

The `RateEstimator` trait is a serializable trait that requires a single method:

```
def compute(
    time: Long,
    elements: Long,
    processingDelay: Long,
    schedulingDelay: Long): Option[Double]
}
```

This function should return an estimate of the number of records the stream attached to this `RateEstimator` should ingest per second, given an update on the size and completion times of the latest batch. You should feel free to contribute an alternative implementation.

A Note on Alternative Dynamic Handling Strategies

Throttling in Spark, dynamic or not, is expressed in the `InputDStream` classes, which include `ReceiverInputDStream` for the receiver model and `DirectKafkaInputD` `Stream` for the Kafka direct receiver. These implementations currently both have a simple way of dealing with excess elements: they are neither read from the input source (`ReceiverInputDStream`) nor consumed from the topic (`DirectKafkaInputD` `Stream`).

But it would be reasonable to propose several possible alternative implementations based on the backpressure signal received at the `InputDStream`. We could imagine policies such as taking the first, largest, or smallest elements, or a random sample.

Sadly, the `rateController: RateController` member of these classes is `protected[streaming]`, but this member has a `getLatestRate` function that lets the DStream implementation receive the relevant limit at any instant. Any implementation of a custom DStream could thus take inspiration from the nonpublic but open source methods of rate control to help dealing with congestion in a better way.

Caching

Caching in Spark Streaming is a feature that, when well manipulated, can significantly speed up the computation performed by your application. This seems to be counterintuitive given that the base RDDs representing the data stored in the input of a computation are actually replicated twice before any job runs on them.

However, over the lifetime of your application, there might be a very long pipeline that takes your computation from those base RDDs to some very refined and structured representations of the data that usually involves a key–value tuple. At the end of the computation performed by your application, you are probably looking at doing some distribution of the output of your computation into various outlets: data stores or databases such as Cassandra, for example. That distribution usually involves looking at the data computed during the previous batch interval and finding which portions of the output data should go where.

A typical use case for that is to look at the keys in the RDD of the structured output data (the last DStream in your computation), to find exactly where to put the results of your computation outside of Spark, depending on these keys. Another use case would be to look for only some specific elements on the RDD received during the last batch. Indeed, your RDD might actually be the output of a computation that depends not only on the last batch of data, but on many prior events received since the start of the application. The last step of your pipeline might summarize the state of your system. Looking at that RDD of output structured results, we might be searching for some elements that pass certain criteria, comparing new results with previous values, or distributing data to different organizational entities, to name a few cases.

For example, think of anomaly detection. You might compute some metrics or features on values (users or elements that you are monitoring on a routine basis). Some of those features might reveal some problems or that some alerts need to be produced. To output those to an alerting system, you want to find elements that pass some criteria in the RDD of data that you're currently looking at. To do that, you are going to *iterate* over the RDD of results. Beside the alerting, you might also want to publish the state of your application to, for example, feed a data visualization or a dashboard, informing you on more general characteristics of the system that you are currently surveying.

The point of this thought exercise is to envision that computing on an output DStream involves several operations for each and every RDD that composes the final result of your pipeline, despite it being very structured and probably reduced in size from the input data. For that purpose, using the cache to store that final RDD before several iterations occur on it is extremely useful.

When you do several iterations on a cached RDD, while the first cycle takes the same time as the noncached version, while each subsequent iteration takes only a fraction of the time. The reason for that is that although the base data of Spark Streaming is cached in the system, intermediate steps need to be recovered from that base data along the way, using the potentially very long pipeline defined by your application.

Retrieving that elaborated data takes time, in every single iteration that is required to process the data as specified by your application, as shown here:

```
dstream.foreachRDD{ (rdd)  =>
  rdd.cache()
  keys.foreach{ (key) =>
    rdd.filter(elem=> key(elem) == key).saveAsFooBar(...)
  }
  rdd.unpersist()
}
```

As a consequence, if your DStream or the corresponding RDDs are used multiple times, caching them significantly speeds up the process. However, it is very important to not overtax Spark's memory management and assume RDDs of a DStream will naturally fall out of cache when your DStream moves to the next RDD, after a batch interval. It is very important that at the end of the iteration over every single RDD of your DStream you think of unpersisting the RDD to let it fall out of cache.

Otherwise, Spark will need to do some relatively clever computation to try to understand which pieces of data it should retain. That particular computation might slow down the results of your application or limit the memory that would be accessible to it.

One last point to consider is that you should not use cache eagerly and everywhere. The cache operation has a cost that might outweigh the benefits if the cached data is not used enough times. In summary, cache is a performance-boosting function that should be used with care.

Speculative Execution

Apache Spark deals with straggler jobs, whether in streaming or batch execution, using *speculative execution*. This mechanism uses the fact that Spark's processing puts the same task in the queue of every worker at the same time. As such, it seems reasonable to estimate that workers should require more or less the same amount of time to complete one task. If that is not the case, it's most often because of one of two reasons:

- Either our dataset is suffering from data skew, in which a few tasks concentrate most of the computation. This is in some cases normal,[3] but in most instances a bad situation, that we will want alleviate (e.g., via shuffling our input).

---

3 For example, in anomaly detection inference, the executor detecting an anomalous value sometimes has duties of alerting that are an additional burden on top of the regular node duties.

- Or a particular executor is slow because it's *that* executor, presenting a case of bad hardware on the node, or if the node is otherwise overloaded in the context of a shared cluster.

If Spark detects this unusually long execution time and has resources available, it has the ability to relaunch on another node the task that is currently running late. This speculative task (which *speculates* that something has gone wrong with the original) will either finish first and cancel the old job, or be canceled as soon as the former one returns. Overall, this competition between the "tortoise and the hare" yields a better completion time and usage of available resources.

Speculative execution is responsive to four configuration parameters, listed in Table 26-1.

Table 26-1. Speculative execution configuration parameters

Option	Default	Meaning
spark.speculation	false	If set to "true," performs speculative execution of tasks
spark.speculation.interval	100ms	How often Spark will check for tasks to speculate
spark.speculation.multiplier	1.5	How many times slower a task is than the median to be considered for speculation
spark.speculation.quantile	0.75	Fraction of tasks that must be complete before speculation is enabled for a particular stage

References for Part III

- [Armbrust2015] Armbrust, Michael, Reynold S. Xin, Cheng Lian, Yin Huai, Davies Liu, Joseph K. Bradley, Xiangrui Meng, et al. "Spark SQL: Relational Data Processing in Spark," SIGMOD, 2015. *http://bit.ly/2HSljk6*.

- [Chintapalli2015_3] Chintapalli, S., D. Dagit, B. Evans, R. Farivar, T. Graves, M. Holderbaugh, Z. Liu, et al. "Benchmarking Streaming Computation Engines at Yahoo!" Yahoo! Engineering, December 18, 2015. *http://bit.ly/2HSkpnG*.

- [Das2016] Das, T. and S. Zhu. "Faster Stateful Stream Processing in Apache Spark Streaming," Databricks Engineering blog, February 1, 2016. *http://bit.ly/2wyLw0L*.

- [Das2015_3] Das, T., M Zaharia, and P. Wendell. "Diving into Apache Spark Streaming's Execution Model," Databricks Engineering blog, July 30, 2015. *http://bit.ly/2wBkPZr*.

- [Greenberg2015_3] Greenberg, David. *Building Applications on Mesos*. O'Reilly, 2015.

- [Hammer2015] Hammer Lab team, "Monitoring Spark with Graphite and Grafana," Hammer Lab blog, February 27, 2015. *http://bit.ly/2WGdLJE*.

- [Karau2017] Karau, Holden, and Rachel Warren. *High Performance Spark* 1st Ed. O'Reilly, 2017.

- [Kestelyn2015_3] Kestelyn, J. "Exactly-once Spark Streaming from Apache Kafka," Cloudera Engineering blog, March 16, 2015. *http://bit.ly/2IetkPA*.

- [Koeninger2015_3] Koeninger, Cody, Davies Liu, and Tathagata Das. "Improvements to Kafka integration of Spark Streaming," Databricks Engineering Blog. March 30, 2015. *http://bit.ly/2QPEZIB*.

- [Krishnamurthy2010] Krishnamurthy, Sailesh. "Continuous Analytics Over Discontinuous Streams," SIGMOD, 2010. *http://bit.ly/2wyMES3*.

- [Medasani2017_3] Medasani, Guru, and Jordan Hambleton. "Offset Management For Apache Kafka With Apache Spark Streaming," Cloudera Engineering blog, June 21, 2017. *http://bit.ly/2EOEObs*.

- [Noll2014] Noll, Michael. "Integrating Kafka and Spark: and Spark Streaming: Code Examples and State of the Game," personal blog, October 1, 2014. *http://bit.ly/2wz4QLp*.

- [SparkMonDocs] "Monitoring and Instrumentation," Apache Spark Online Documentation. *http://bit.ly/2EPY889*.

- [Valiant1990_3] Valiant, L.G. "Bulk-synchronous parallel computers." *Communications of the ACM* 33:8 (August 1990). *http://bit.ly/2IgX3ar*.

- [Vavilapalli2013_3] Vavilapalli, et al. "Apache Hadoop YARN: Yet Another Resource Negotiator," SOCC 2013. *http://bit.ly/2Xn3tuZ*.

- [White2009] White, Tom. "The Small Files Problem," Cloudera Engineering blog, February 2, 2009. *http://bit.ly/2WF2gSJ*.

- [White2010_3] White, Tom. *Hadoop: The Definitive Guide.* O'Reilly, 2010.

## PART IV

Advanced Spark Streaming Techniques

In this part, we examine some of the more advanced applications that you can create using Spark Streaming, namely approximation algorithms and machine learning algorithms.[1]

Approximation algorithms offer a window into pushing the scalability of Spark to the edge and offer a technique for graceful degradation when the throughput of data is more than what the deployment can endure. In this part, we cover:

- Hashing functions and their use for the building block of sketching
- The HyperLogLog algorithm, for counting distinct elements
- The Count-Min-Sketch algorithm, for answering queries about top elements of a structure

We also cover the T-Digest, a useful estimator that allows us to store a succinct representation of a distribution of values using clustering techniques.

Machine learning models offer novel techniques for producing relevant and accurate results on an ever-changing stream of data. In the following chapters, we see how to

---

[1] Although we focus our presentation on Spark Streaming, some of the algorithms we describe, such as the HyperLogLog, are present in built-in functions of Spark as part of the DataFrames API, such as `approxCount Distinct`.

adapt well-known batch algorithms, such as naive Bayesian classification, decision trees, and K-Means clustering for streaming. This will lead us to cover, respectively:

- Online Naive Bayes
- Hoeffding Trees
- Online K-Means clustering

These algorithms will form a streaming complement of their treatment for Spark in batch form in [Laserson2017]. This should equip you with powerful techniques for classifying or clustering elements of a data stream.

## CHAPTER 27

Streaming Approximation and Sampling Algorithms

Stream processing poses particular challenges when it comes to producing summaries of the observed data over time. Because we only get one chance at observing the values in a stream, even queries considered simple on a bounded dataset become challenging when you want to answer the same question over a data stream.

The crux of the issue lies in how those queries ask for a form of global summary, or a *supremum*, result that requires observing the entire dataset, for example:

- The count of all the distinct elements in the stream (summary)
- The k highest elements of the stream (global supremum)
- The k most frequent elements of the stream (global supremum)

Naturally, when data comes from a stream, the difficulty is in seeing the entire data set at once. These sorts of queries can be answered naively by storing the whole stream, and then treating it as a batch of data. But not only is this storage not always possible, it's a heavy-handed approach. As you will see, we can construct succinct data representations that reflect the main numerical and characteristics of our stream. This succinctness has a cost, measured in the accuracy of the answer they return: those data structures and the algorithms that operate them return approximative results, with specific error bounds. In summary:

- Exact algorithms are more accurate, but very resource intensive
- Approximation algorithms are less accurate, but we're willing to accept a bit less accuracy rather than take on the extra resource cost.

In this section, we study the application of approximation algorithms and sampling techniques to help us sort out global questions over the elements observed in the stream over time using a limited amount of resources. To begin, we explore the tension between real-time responses and the exactness of those responses in the face of large amounts of data. Then, we introduce the concepts of hashing and sketching that we need to understand three covered approximation methods:

HyperLogLog (HLL)
For counting distinct elements

CountMinSketch (CMS)
For counting the frequency of elements

T-Digest
For approximating the frequency histogram of observed elements

We end the chapter with an overview of different sampling methods and how are they supported in Spark.

Exactness, Real Time, and Big Data

Distributed computing, when operating on a continuous flow of data is often considered a special beast in that it's constrained by a triangle of concepts:

- The exactness of the produced results
- Computation occurring in real time
- Computation on big data

Let's look at these concepts in detail:

Exactness

First, we can see exact computation as the reflection of the need to produce a precise numerical result answering a question that we ask from our data. For example, if we are monitoring the data coming from a website, we might want to understand the number of *distinct* current users by analyzing interactions, events, and logs that the website produces.

Real-Time Processing

The second aspect is the freshness or latency of that analysis. In this context, latency relates to the time between the moment when data is first available and when we can get some insights from it. Coming back to the website visitor example, we could ask the *distinct users* question at the end of the day. We would analyze the logs that the website produced during the last 24 hours and try to compute the value of how many unique users have been visiting during that period. Such a computation might take minutes to hours before we get a result, depending on the volume of data that we need to process. We consider that a *high-latency* approach. We could also ask "how many users are on the website" at any time of the day and expect an answer *right now*. Except, as browsers transact with web servers in punctual queries, what *right now* translates to is "how many distinct visitors have we had for *a short duration of time carefully chosen to represent the length of a browsing session?*"

Big Data

The third point that we need to address is, how voluminous is the data that we are dealing with? Are we looking at the website of a local sports club with but a few users at a given time, or are we looking at the website of a massive retailer such as Amazon, which welcomes thousands upon thousands of visitors at any given moment?

The Exactness, Real-Time, and Big Data triangle

The notions of exactness, real-time processing, and data size can be represented as a triangle as illustrated in Figure 27-1. This triangle reflects that achieving exactness and freshness (near-real-time results) are at odds as the volume of data increases: these three needs are rarely all met at the same time. The analysis of distributed data processing, up to fairly recently, has often focused on only two sides of this triangle.

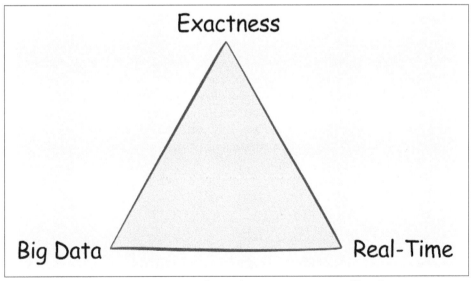

Figure 27-1. The triangle of exact results, real-time processing, and big data

For example, in the domain of website monitoring, we have focused in the past on exact and real-time processing, devising systems that allow us to understand very quickly how many users are visiting our website and that gives us an exact answer as to the number of distinct users.

This is the regular meat-and-potatoes work of stream processing. It has fallen behind in recent times because of the pull of the third vertex of the triangle: big data. Larger and larger online businesses have often put scalability first as an imperative: when a large website scales, its maintainers still want very precise results on how many users have been visiting, and therefore often end up asking the question of analyzing that number of visitors over a large amount of data. They then need to come to terms with the fact that the computation of the answer might require large amounts of time—sometimes longer than the time it took to be collected.

This often translates into processing the logs of a very voluminous website through analytics frameworks such as Apache Spark. Estimating based on periodic (e.g., monthly average) might be sufficient for long-term capacity planning, but as businesses need to react faster and faster to a changing environment, there is inherently more and more interest in getting quick answers to our questions. Nowadays, in the age of elastic cloud infrastructure, commercial website maintainers would like to understand in real time whether there is a change in conditions because they would be able to react to it, as we're about to see.

Big Data and Real Time

To solve this conundrum, we need to move to the third side of the triangle, between the big data and real-time vertices.

For example, Walmart is a commercial retail website that is accessed frequently by about 300 million distinct users per month in 2018 (*http://bit.ly/2Lm9Aye*). However, during Black Friday in 2012, the number of users that visited the Walmart website to benefit from sales on that particular day doubled in a matter of hours, as depicted in Figure 27-2, in a way that was not predictable from analyzing the traffic of the prior years. The resources needed in the website's infrastructure to process that new influx of users was suddenly much higher than what had been anticipated.

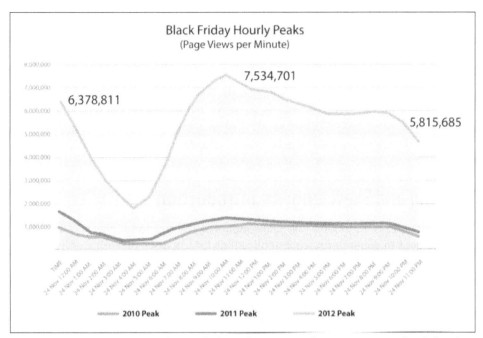

Figure 27-2. Walmart.ca traffic on Black Friday in 2012 (image courtesy of Lightbend, Inc.)

The scalability problem has an impact on our ability to produce real-time answers. It would take us a much longer time to count the web sessions of distinct users on the Walmart website on Black Friday than on any other day.

In this case, it is more useful to have an approximate answer to our question that comes in very fast rather than an exact answer that comes in delayed. The approximate answer is easier to compute, but still an operational value: a good website administrator will give resources to a website to match the ballpark of the number of website visits—a small imprecision in the number of users will create a cost (in unused resources) that will be more than covered for by the increase in revenue from users that will not have to face a sluggish responsiveness in the busiest online shopping day of the year.

In case more resources are not available, the administrator is also able to organize a more graceful degradation of service, using, for example, admission control (i.e., redirecting a percentage of users to a static page, and serving those users he or she can in an efficient fashion, rather than letting all users suffer through a slow, unusable website). All the administrator needs for this is a ballpark measure.

Approximation Algorithms

Approximation algorithms have much better scalability than the textbook exact algorithms, in a manner that we'll quantify precisely in the following pages.

In this section, we are going to introduce a number of approximation algorithms that compute a result on real-time data streams, including algorithms that allow us to count distinct users, algorithms that allow us to get an idea of the histogram of the values that we are seeing on the data stream, and algorithms that get us an approximation of the most frequently encountered values occurring over a stream of data.

Hashing and Sketching: An Introduction

A hash function is a function that maps inputs of any size to outputs of a fixed size. They are used in computer science applications for use cases including cryptography applications, hash tables, and databases. One of these uses is as a representative of the equality—or near equality—of several objects.

Let's go back to the definition of a hash function. The hash function maps an object of its input domain—for example, arbitrarily long `String` elements—to a fixed-size output domain. Let's consider this output domain to be the space of 32-bit integers. One interesting property that is that those integers are good *identifiers* of these strings: if we are able to work with integers of 32 bits, we have only a small amount of computation to do in order to determine whether two large strings are equal.

In the design of hash functions, we often say that we would like them to have *collision resistance*, meaning that it is improbable to hit the same hash for two distinct, randomly chosen input documents.

 Our definition of collision resistance is relaxed because *cryptographically secure* hash functions are not relevant to our context. In this context, we would require that it be difficult for an adversary to intentionally find two distinct documents that produce the same hash value.

Naturally, it is not trivial to give numbers to every possible string: there are only 4,294,967,295 integers of 32 bits that we can represent on the Java virtual machine (JVM) (or roughly four billion), and there are more `String` elements than that.

Indeed, if we are mapping more than five billion distinct documents to the space of 32-bit integers, which has a size of 4 billion, there are at least a billion documents for which our hash function, will reuse integers it already associated to previous documents. We call this mapping of two distinct documents to the same hash a *collision*.

They always occur, irrespective of the function when our function is used on an input set larger than its fixed-sized output domain.

However, as our application deals with documents extracted from a very large dataset, we would hope that we will either have a large enough hash function, or never compare those few elements that would result in a collision (i.e., a *false positive* for document equality).

We're going to consider hashes as a marker for the identity of a particular element, and as we pick good hash functions, it means that we will save a lot of computation comparing hashes rather than entire documents, and that collision probabilities are reduced to cardinality comparisons.

Hash Probability Collision

Rigorously, the probability of having a collision among k keys represented by a domain of size N is computed from the probability of generating k unique integers, as follows:

$$1 - \prod_{i=1}^{k-1} \frac{(N-i)}{N} \approx 1 - e^{\frac{-k(k-1)}{2N}}$$

In the next few sections, we look at how we can take advantage of this by having very small representations for the set of elements we're going to observe on a stream. However, it will always be useful to keep in mind the necessity to control for collisions in our hashes, and the pseudo-randomness of the mapping a good hash function creates between its domain and image.

Counting Distinct Elements: HyperLogLog

The necessity for counting distinct elements in a large amount of data exists in many analytics tasks, often because this unicity is the marker of discrete "cases" in the data: think of the different sessions of users in a website log, the number of transactions in a commerce registry, and so on. But it is also called in a statistic the first "moment" of the dataset, with "moments" designating various indicators of the distribution of the frequencies of the elements in the stream.

The naïve version of counting all of the distinct elements in a DStream would have us store a multiset of every single distinct element observed. For data that comes in a streaming fashion, however, this is not practical: the number of distinct elements might be unbounded.

Thankfully, since 1983, we know a probabilistic way of counting distinct elements of a stream, the Flageolet-Martin algorithm. It has since been extended successively into the LogLog counting, the HyperLogLog algorithms, and a particular hybrid implementation, HyperLogLog++, a version of which is used in Spark today under the `approxCountDistinct` API of DataSets and RDDs.

All of those algorithms inherit from the central idea of the Flajolet-Martin algorithm, which we will now explain. First, however, we begin with an example.

Role-Playing Exercise: If We Were a System Administrator

The first thing we can consider to count the elements of our DStream is to hash those elements. Let's assume that we are a system administrator counting the distinct URLs accessed by customers, to scope the size of a caching proxy. If we consider only the most common URLs in the modern web, which could have a plausible median length of 77 ASCII characters,[1] and if we actually store all the possibilities, we are looking at an average 616 bits per effectively accessed URL (one ASCII character is 1 byte or 8 bits).

Let's size our hash function correctly. We would have reached the 97th percentile of URL lengths by character 172,[2] which means that there's a possible dataset size of 8^{172}, something that is represented by $\log_2(8^{172}) = 516$ bits. But, of course, not all combinations of 172 ASCII characters are correct. According to the resource mentioned earlier, there are 6,627,999 publicly unique URLs from 78,764 domains, which means that we can expect a URL density of about 84 URLs per domain. Let's multiply this by 10 for good measure (the article we quote is from 2010) and compare this to the number of existing websites: about 1.2 billion, as of this writing.[3] Therefore, we can expect a dataset of a maximum of 960 billion possible URLs. This is adequately represented by a hash of about 40 bits. Hence, we can pick a hash of size 64 bits instead of the 600 bits we were considering earlier—a reduction of 10 times over storing every distinct element of the stream.

The way our counting method is going to work is by considering statistical properties of the binary representation of our hashes. As a general prelude, let's consider how unlikely it is to obtain four tails in a row in a repeated coin flip. Given that a coin flip has a binary outcome, the probability of obtaining such a flip is $1/2^4$. In general, to expect to hit a four-tails-in-a row, we expect to need to repeat the four-coin-flips experiment 2^4 times, which is 16 times (for a total of 64 flips). We note how this easily extrapolates to n tails in a row. The binary representation of our hashes functions in a similar way, because the spread of encountered distinct numbers is uniform. As a

---

1 This length, taken as a ballpark estimate, is the mean length of the URLs found in a large web crawl by Supermind (*http://www.supermind.org/blog/740/average-length-of-a-url-part-2*).

2 Ibid.

3 *http://www.internetlivestats.com/total-number-of-websites/*

consequence, if we pick a particular number of length k bits in the binary representation of our hashes, we can expect that we'll need to see 2^k samples (unique stream elements) to reach it.[4]

Let's now consider a particular sequence of bits. Arbitrarily, we can decide to consider a long sequence of zeros preceded by a nonzero higher-order bit.[5] Let's call the trailing (lower-order) zeros in the binary representation of a number its *tail*. For example, the tail of 12 (1100 in binary) is two, the tail of 8 (1000 in binary) is three, the tail of 10 (1010) is one. Therefore, we can infer that, if we observe a number of tail size at least k, 2^k is an expectation of the number of samples we've had to draw from the set to reach that tail length. Because the uniformity of our hash function lets us assimilate hashing our inputs to drawing independent samples, we can conclude that *if we observe a maximal tail of size* k *among the hashes of the elements of our stream, 2^k is a good estimate of the number of distinct elements in the stream*—if very unstable.

However, this has two problems:

- Because this is a randomized method toward computing the number of elements in the stream, it is sensitive to outliers. That is, though very improbable, we could encounter a stream element with a very long tail as the first element of the stream and vastly overestimate the number of distinct elements on the stream.

- Moreover, because the measure for the increase of our estimate of the longest tail in hashes of elements of the stream is used as an exponent of our estimate, we produce only estimates in powers of two: 2, 4, 8, …, 1,024, 2,048, and so on.

A way to alleviate this problem is to use several pairwise-independent hash functions *in parallel*: if those hash functions are independent, we can hedge the risks of one particular hash function giving out unusual results in one particular experiment. But it is costly in terms of computation time (we would need to compute several hashed values per element scanned), and, worse, it would require a large set of pairwise-independent hashing functions, which we don't necessarily know to construct. However, we can emulate this use of several hash functions by partitioning our input stream into p subsets, treated by the same function, using a fixed-size prefix of the hash of the element as an indicator of the bucket this hash falls in.

The subtleties of comparing the estimated tail sizes in each of these buckets are not to be underestimated; their impact on the accuracy of the estimate is significant. The HyperLogLog algorithm, shown in Figure 27-3 uses the harmonic mean to compen-

---

4 Note how important the uniformity of our hash function is—without it, the value of the bits in our hashes are no longer independent to that of the bits that precede or succeed it, and it will likely result in a loss of the independence of our coin flips. This means that we no longer can consider 2^k as a good estimate of the number of samples necessary to reach our chosen k-bit number.

5 In Big Endian notation, of course.

sate for the possible presence of outliers in each bucket while preserving the ability to return estimates that are not powers of 2. As a consequence, for a hash of 64 bits, we can use p buckets, each of $(64-p)$ bits. In each of these buckets, the only number to store is the size of the longest tail met so far, which can be represented in log2(64-p).

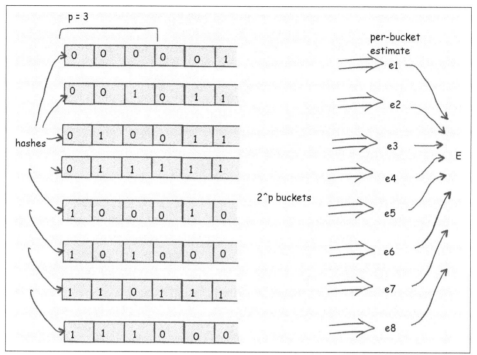

Figure 27-3. The dataflow of the HyperLogLog algorithm

In sum, our storage use is $2^p\left(log_2\left(log_2\left(N/2^p\right)\right)\right)$, where N is the cardinality that we are trying to measure. The striking gap between the cardinal we want to measure (potentially 960 billion URLs) and the actual amount of data stored 4 log2(60) = 24 bits is amazing.

The LogLog counting algorithm, on the one hand—and the specific variant, called HyperLogLog++—that is used by Spark and in the example that follows, while proceeding from the same ideas, are yet significantly different. In particular, HyperLogLog is a hybrid algorithm, that replaces the LogLog counting algorithm by linear counting for small cardinalities. Moreover, implementations often make choices of hash length and indexing length. We hope our explanation has helped convey the ideas of the basic algorithm, but using a more advanced implementation implies more parameters and choices.

For this reason, its always important to look at the documentation of the used implementation in detail, comparing it to the literature, to see if the parameters are what is right for your use case.

In the streamlib implementation that we are going to use, the relative accuracy is approximately $1.054/sqrt(2^p)$ where p is the number of bits of the input we are going to use for deciding the bucket in which an element should fall (our number of buckets is therefore 2^p). HyperLogLog++ has a second optional parameter, a nonzero $sp > p$ in HyperLogLogPlus(p, sp) that would trigger sparse representation of registers. For cases in which $n < m$, it might reduce the memory consumption and increase accuracy, but only when the cardinality is small, falling outside of the big data case.

Practical HyperLogLog in Spark

Let's now create a distinct element counter in Spark. We begin by importing the streamlib library, adding the following dependency:

```
groupId: com.clearspring.analytics
artifactId: stream
version: 2.7.0
```

When this is done, we can create an instance of an HyperLogLog++ counter in the following way:

```
val HLL = new HyperLogLogPlus(12, 0);
```

To understand this invocation, we need to consult the constructor of HyperLogLog, which tells us that:

> [this implementation] Has two representation modes: sparse and normal Has two procedures based on current mode. *Normal* mode works similar to HLL but has some new bias corrections. *Sparse* mode is linear counting.

The parameters to the constructor are HyperLogLog(p, sp), where p is the number of buckets for our hash function. If sp = 0, the Hyperloglog is in normal mode, and if sp > 0 it works in sparse mode for small cardinalities, as a hybrid algorithm. p should be between 4 and sp if sp is nonzero, and sp should be between p and 32, to determine the number of bits used for linear counting. If the cardinality being measured becomes too large, the representation of our set will be converted to a HyperLogLog.

The relative precision of our HyperLogLog is around $1.054/sqrt(2^p)$, which means that to reach a relative precision of 2%, we should be aiming at using 19 bits of indexing for our buckets. As a result, we can expect to have 2^{19} buckets, or 4,096.

We can add elements to the counter using `hll.offer()` and obtain the results using `hll.cardinality()`. Note, interestingly, that two `HyperLogLog` counters that are compatible (same *p* and *sp*) are mergeable using `hll.addAll(hll2)`, which means that they are a perfect match for many reduce functions in Spark, like the following:

- The `aggregateByKey` class of functions on our DStreams, their window counterparts

- Accumulators, which depend on the `merge` function to `reduce` the different local counts registered on each executor.

For a practical illustration of the use of HyperLogLog to calculate cardinality, we will consider the case of a simple website. Suppose that we have a media website and we want to know what is the current trendy content. Next to that, we also want to know the unique number of visitors at any time. Even though we can calculate the trends using a sliding window, as we learned in Chapter 21, we will make use of a custom accumulator to keep track of the unique visitors. Accumulators are mergeable data structures that let us keep tabs on particular metrics across the distributed execution of some logic. In Spark, there are built-in accumulators to count with integers and longs. We could use a `longAccumulator` if we wanted to know how many hits we received on our website across all content. There's also an API to create custom accumulators, and we will make use of it to create a HyperLogLog-based accumulator to keep a count of the unique users.

Online Resources

The functional code of this accumulator is available on this book's accompanying code repository, located at *https://github.com/ stream-processing-with-spark/HLLAccumulator*. In this section, we cover only the key characteristics of the implementation.

To create a new `HyperLogLogAccumulator`, we call the constructor using the parameter p explained earlier. Note that we have already provided a sensible default value. Also, note that the accumulator is typed. This type represents the kind of objects that we are going to track. Behind the scenes, all different types are treated as `Object` given that we are interested only in their hashcode:

```
class HLLAccumulator[T](precisionValue: Int = 12) extends AccumulatorV2[T, Long]
    with Serializable
```

To add an element to the accumulator, we call the method add with the object to be added. In turn, this will call the method offer in the HyperLogLog implementation to apply the hashing method already discussed.

```
override def add(v: T): Unit = hll.offer(v)
```

The last method that we would like to highlight is merge. The ability to merge is vital to reconcile partial calculations done in separate executors in parallel. Note that merging two HyperLogLog instances is like computing the union of a set, in that the resulting representation will contain the common and noncommon elements of both parts:

```
override def merge(other: AccumulatorV2[T, Long]): Unit = other match {
  case otherHllAcc: HLLAccumulator[T] => hll.addAll(otherHllAcc.hll)
  case _ => throw new UnsupportedOperationException(
      s"Cannot merge ${this.getClass.getName} with ${other.getClass.getName}")
}
```

After we have our HyperLogLogAccumulator, we can use it in our Spark Streaming job.

As we mentioned earlier, our streaming job tracks the popularity of content on a media website that contains blogs in different categories. The core logic is to track which articles are popular, by maintaining a register of the clicks received by URL, partitioned by path. To keep track of the unique visitors, we make use of accumulators, which are maintained as a parallel channel to the main streaming logic.

We use a simplified representation of a view stream, in the form of a schema that contains the timestamp of the click, the userId, and the path where the view was registered:

```
case class BlogHit(timestamp: Long, userId: String, path: String)
```

Our Stream context has a batch interval of two seconds to keep regular updates to our data:

```
@transient val ssc = new StreamingContext(sparkContext, Seconds(2))
```

The use of @transient in this declaration prevents the serialization of the nonserializable streaming context in case it gets captured by the closures used in the streaming application.

We are going to create and register our custom accumulator. The process differs slightly from the built-in accumulators available from the SparkContext. To use a custom accumulator, we first create a local instance and then we register it with the

SparkContext so that Spark can keep track of it as it's used in the distributed computation process:

```
import learning.spark.streaming.HLLAccumulator
val uniqueVisitorsAccumulator = new HLLAccumulator[String]()
sc.register(uniqueVisitorsAccumulator, "unique-visitors")
```

Here we use the knowledge we recently acquired about sliding windows to create a view of recent trends of our website traffic. Before decomposing the click info into a URL count, we also add the userId to our accumulator to register the userId of the click.

First, we offer the users to the accumulator. We might be tempted to think that we could get away with our count by using simple set operations here in order to calculate the unique users in a batch. But to do this, we would need to remember all users seen in a long period of time. This brings us back to the supporting arguments for the use of probabilistic data structures because we do not need to remember all seen users, but only the HyperLogLog combination of their hashes:

```
clickStream.foreachRDD{rdd =>
        rdd.foreach{
            case BlogHit(ts, user, url) => uniqueVisitorsAccumulator.add(user)
        }
        val currentTime =
            // get the hour part of the current timestamp in seconds
            (System.currentTimeMillis / 1000) % (60*60*24)
    val currentUniqueVisitors = uniqueVisitorsAccumulator.value
    uniqueUsersChart.addAndApply(Seq((currentTime, currentUniqueVisitors)))
}
```

 It's important to highlight again the differences in execution contexts within the foreachRDD in this case; the process of offering the data to the accumulator happens within an rdd.foreach operation, meaning that it will take place distributed in the cluster.

Right after, we access the value of the accumulator to update our charts. This call is executed in the driver. The driver is the exclusive execution context in which an accumulator can be read.

The charts used in this example are also local to the driver machine. Their backing data is also updated locally.

Next, we use a sliding window to analyze our website traffic trends. Here we use a fairly short window duration. This is for illustration purposes in the provided notebooks because we can observe the changes rather quickly. For a production environment, this parameter needs to be tuned according to the context of the application:

```
@transient val trendStream = clickStream
        .map{case BlogHit(ts, user, url) =>  (url,1)}
```

```
        .reduceByKeyAndWindow(
          (count:Int, agg:Int) => count + agg, Minutes(5), Seconds(2))

  trendStream.foreachRDD{rdd =>
        val top10URLs =
        // display top10URLs
        rdd.map(_.swap).sortByKey(ascending = false).take(10).map(_.swap)
  }
```

In the provided notebook, we can execute this example and observe how the two charts are updated, computing a rank of popular content at the same time that we keep track of unique users of our system.

 The Databricks blog contains a post on the implementation of approximate algorithms in Spark, including approximate counting. Even though we suggest using this algorithm on Streams and Spark provides it only as part of the Dataset API, the implementation chosen here is the same as the one used by Spark: the HyperLogLog++ of Streamlib. As a consequence, the insights provided in *Approximate Algorithms in Apache Spark: HyperLogLog and Quantiles (http://bit.ly/2UUQmiJ)* apply here:

> As a conclusion, when using approxCountDistinct, you should keep in mind the following:
>
> - When the requested error on the result is high (> 1%), approximate distinct counting is very fast and returns results for a fraction of the cost of computing the exact result. In fact, the performance is more or less the same for a target error of 20% or 1%.
>
> - For higher precisions, the algorithm hits a wall and starts to take more time than exact counting.

Note that irrespective of the run time, the HyperLogLog algorithm uses storage of size $\log\log(N)$, where N is the cardinality we want to report on. For streams of unbounded size, this is the main advantage.

Counting Element Frequency: Count Min Sketches

The problem of correctly determining the most frequent elements of a stream is useful in many applications, especially in problems relating to a "long tail" of elements, users or items. It encompasses the following:

- Determining the most popular items on a retail website
- Computing the most volatile stocks

- Understanding which TCP flows send the most traffic to our network, hinting at an attack

- Computing frequent web queries to populate a web cache

This problem can be solved easily by storing the count of every distinct element that we see on the stream, along with a copy of each element. We would then sort this dataset and output the first few elements. This works, but at the price of an $O(nlog(n))$ operations and a linear cost in storage. Can we do better?

Under the constraint of exactness, the answer is no, a theorem that is expressed formally as: there is no algorithm that solves the problem of finding the greatest elements with frequency greater than n/k, where n is the number of elements and k is a selector for the ratio of occurrences, in a single pass over the data and sublinear space in storage ([Alon1999] Prop.3.7). Nevertheless, committing a linear amount of space to computing frequencies is untractable for big data streams. This is, once again, where approximation can come to the rescue.

Introducing Bloom Filters

The principle of the count-min sketch is one inspired from a simpler approximate representation of a set called a *Bloom filter*. Which means that to learn how to rank elements with a count-min sketch, we begin by learning whether they are members of a set using a Bloom filter first.

Here's how a Bloom filter works: to represent a set, instead of using an *in extenso* representation of all of the objects in the set, we can choose to store hashes for each element. But this would still make storage linear in the size of the number of elements of the set. We are more ambitious in choosing to store only a constant number of indicator hashes, irrespective of the number of elements of the set. To achieve this, we hash each element into a word of m bits, and we superpose all such hashes for all the elements thus encountered. The i-th bit of the superposition S (the representant of the set) is set to one if any of the bits of the hashes of elements in the set was set to one.

This gives us an indicator with a large number of false positives, but no false negatives: if we take a new element z and wonder whether it was in the set, we'll look at $h(z)$ and check that in all the bit positions of $h(z)$ that are nonzero, the same bit position in S is nonzero, as well. If any such bit of S is zero (while the corresponding $h(z)$ is one), z could not have been part of the set, because any of its nonzero bits would have flipped the corresponding superposed bit to one. Otherwise, if all its nonzero bits are nonzero in S, as well, we know that there is a high probability that z was present in this set—though we can't guarantee it, any number z' which hash $h(z')$ contains one more than $h(z)$ in its binary notation could have been met instead of z.

The probability of a collision with this scheme is $1 - (1 - 1/m)^n$ if n is the number of inserted elements, which we improve into $1 - (1 - 1/m)^{kn}$ by using k such superpositions in parallel, to reduce the probability of a collision. This is done using independent hash functions to guarantee the product of independent probabilities, and yields to a controlled storage space of (km) bits in total for the filter scheme. The Bloom "filter" is called as such because it is used to create a query engine that answers with high probability whether a query is in some problematic set, with the intent of "returning" (or letting through) only the nonproblematic queries.

Bloom Filters with Spark

Though not specifically related to Streaming, Bloom filters are usable for various purposes with Spark, and they are particularly useful when trying to use them for their namesake purpose: filtering elements from a list, with a bias toward false positives.

You can use the streamlib library for this, as well:

```
import com.clearspring.analytics.stream.membership.BloomFilter

val numElements: Int = 10000
val maxFalsePosProbability: Double = 0.001

val bloom = BloomFilter(numElements, maxFalsePosProbability)
```

The library includes a helper that allows you to compute the best number of hash functions to use given the maximum false-positive probability you're ready to accept —and this ends up being the easiest constructor for the Bloom filter. After we have this filter of "undesirable" elements built, we can use it to filter stream elements:

```
val badWords = scala.io.Source.fromFile("prohibited.txt")
  .getLines
  .flatMap(_.split("\\W+"))

for (word <- badWords) bloom.add(word)

val filteredStream = myStream.filter{
    (w: String) => !bloom.isPresent(w)
}
```

If your goal is performance in the speed of hashing and you are comfortable with a Scala-only solution, have a look at Alexandr Nitkin's implementation ([Nitkin2016]), which compares favorably to the ones in Twitter's Algebird and Google's Guava.

Computing Frequencies with a Count-Min Sketch

Create an integer array initialized to zeros that is w wide and d deep. Take d pairwise independent hash functions, $h1, \ldots, h_d$ and associate one with each row of the table, these functions should produce a value in the range $[1..w]$. When a new value is seen, for each row of the table, hash the value with the corresponding hash function, and increment the counter in the indicated array slot. Figure 27-4 illustrates this process.

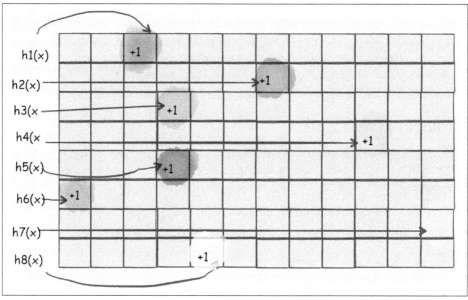

Figure 27-4. Building a count-min sketch

If you want to know the estimate of how many instances of a given value have been seen, hash the value as previously and look up the counter values that gives you in each row. Take the smallest of these as your estimate.

It's clear that in this way, we'll obtain a number that is greater than the real frequency count of the element x we are probing for, because each of its hashes indeed will have incremented each of the positions in the sketch we will be looking at. If we're lucky, x will be the only such element to have incremented these counters, and the estimate of each counter will be the frequency count of x. If we are not so lucky, there will be some collisions, and some counters will overestimate the number of occurrences of x. For this reason, we take the minimum of all counters: our estimates are biased, in that they only overestimate the real value we are seeking, and it is clear that the least biased estimate is the smallest one.

The count-min sketch has a relative error of ε with a probability of $(1 - \delta)$ provided we set $w = \lceil e/\varepsilon \rceil$ and $d = \lceil \ln 1/\delta \rceil$, where e is Euler's number ([Cormode2003]).

Using Spark, this is again part of the streamlib library:

```
import com.clearspring.analytics.stream.frequency.CountMinSketch

val sketch = new CountMinSketch(epsOfTotalCount, confidence)
```

```
// or val sketch = new CountMinSketch(depth, width)
```

The count-min sketch requires you to specify the relative error and the confidence (1 - δ) you are aiming with for in this construction, and tries to set the values of the width and depth for you, though you can specify the size of the sketch in explicit width and depth. In case you specify the width and depth, you are expected to provide integers, whereas with the probabilistic arguments, it's expected the constructor arguments will be doubles.

The conversion is given in the following table:

	Width of the sketch	Depth of the sketch	Relative error	Confidence level in the relative error
symbol	w	d	ε	$(1 - \delta)$
How to compute	$\lceil e/\varepsilon \rceil$	$\lceil \ln 1/\delta \rceil$	e / w	$1 - 1/2^d$
Streamlib's approximation	$\lceil 2 / \varepsilon \rceil$	$\lceil -\log(1 - \delta) / \log(2) \rceil$	$2 / w$	$1 - 1/2^d$

The count-min sketch is additive and mergeable, which makes it an ideal candidate for the `updateStateByKey` function:

```
dStream.updateStateByKey((
  elems: List[Long], optSketch: Option[CountMinSketch]) => {
  val sketch = optSketch.getOrElse(new CountMinSketch(16, 8))
  elems.foreach((e) => sketch.add(e))
  sketch
})
```

The sketch also has functions that allow you to add a `String` or `byte[]` argument.

Apache Spark has introduced a count-min sketch in Spark 2.0, under the package `org.apache.spark.util.sketch`.

This implementation is a pure reuse of the one from streamlib, with the exception of the hash function, for which a few convenience methods converting a Scala `Object` to one of the entry types for the `CountMinSketch` (`long`, `string`, `byte[]`) have been added, and that reuses the internal 32-bit `MurmurHash` hash function that is being used by Scala as the default.

The Spark count-min sketch is therefore interchangeable with the one we're exemplifying here.

Ranks and Quantiles: T-Digest

When evaluating the distribution of the values observed on a data stream one of the most useful things to focus on is a picture of the distribution of those values, as illustrated in Figure 27-5.

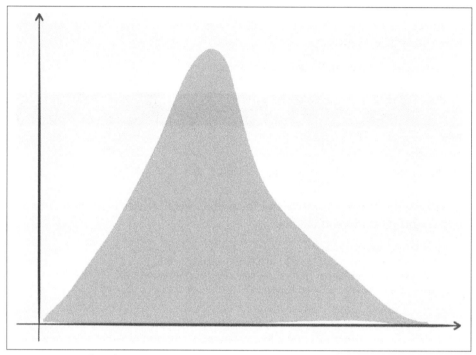

Figure 27-5. A distribution suitable for representation with a T-Digest

That distribution allows diagnoses of a change in the nature of data stream if it is computed over a recent sample of the stream, and exploratory analysis being a complete picture of various aggregate statistics (average, medium, etc.) delivered all in one. It is often easy to approach that distribution by looking at the cumulative distribution function (CDF), which represents for any value X how many of the data points observed on our stream were equal or lesser than X. An approximate way of looking at the cumulative distribution function is also easy to understand intuitively: the notion of *quantiles*.

Quantiles are a mapping between a percentage and a value, such that there is exactly that percentage of the values witness on the data stream that is inferior to the image of the percentage. For example, the 50th percentile (i.e., the median) is the value such that half of the data points are inferior.

Hence, it is useful to have as good a view of the CDF of the data points in our stream, even if this view is somewhat approximate. A compact way of representing the CDF that also allows us to quickly compute a representation of the CDF is a digest, in particular, the T-Digest, which answers the difficult problem of parallelizing the quantiles. Note this is not completely trivial. Because quantiles, contrary to averages, are not easily aggregable, whereas the average of a union can be computed using the sum and count of the number of elements of each component of the union, this is not true of the median. The T-Digest proceeds by approaching the representation of quantiles as a compression problem, instead of representing every point in the CDF of a data stream, it summarizes a set of points by a centroid which is the *barycenter* of these points chosen cleverly with respect to "compression rates" that we expect to see in various places in this CDF. Figure 27-6 depicts a possible distribution of centroids.

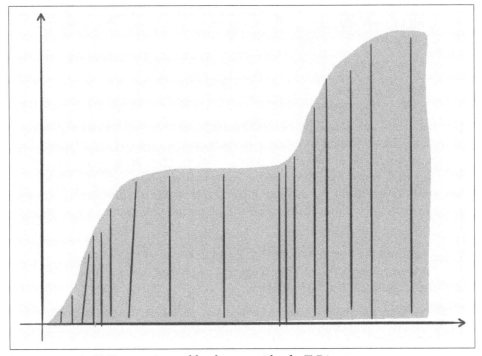

Figure 27-6. A CDF approximated by the centroids of a T-Digest

For example, under the assumption that our distribution respects the Gaussianity hypothesis or is a mixture of Guassians, it is very approximate of the value of the highest and lowest percentiles with a very low compression rate because the values reached at those percentiles have a very few representations. On the contrary, around the 50th percentile, we can expect that the values around that median will have many representations, and hence the approximation that we make replacing those with their average will not be particularly costly, neither in terms of information lost nor in terms of practical sense.

The T-Digest is a data structure invented by Ted Dunning ([Dunning2013]) that proceeds by first approximating the subset of a distribution using randomly placed centroids and then splitting those approximated subsets when too many points are attached to a particular centroid. However, the limits on how many points to reach are variable according to the value associated with this centroid. It is indeed a low on the edges of the CDF and relatively high around the median of the CDF. This ensures that this data structure is both compact and reflective of the values of our CDF to the degree that we are interested in a high precision.

T-Digest in Spark

Keeping with a common practice of this chapter, we point you to the implementation of the T-Digest found in the stream-lib library:

```
import com.clearspring.analytics.stream.quantile.TDigest

val compression: Double = 100
val digest = TDigest(compression)
```

The instantiation of a new T-Digest data structure requests a compression parameter that indicates how we want to balance accuracy and size for our compressed representation of the CDF of our distribution. Relative errors in accuracy are almost always less than thrice the inverse of the compression for any quantile, with much lower errors expected for the extreme quantiles. However, the number of centroids that we will use to track our distribution will be on the order of five times the compression.

The T-Digest has the base functions that let it be the core of either an Accumulator object (as seen earlier with the HyperLogLog), or an aggregate computation: addition of a single element and mergeability:

```
dStream.updateStateByKey((elems: List[Double], optSketch: Option[TDigest]) => {
  val digest = optSketch.getOrElse(new Digest(100))
  elems.foreach((e) => digest.add(e))
  digest
})
```

We can also invoke the merge function with a compression and a list of other TDigest instances to fuse them in a single one with the required compression. Of course, the sum of compressions of the argument digests should be greater or equal to that of the required final compression.

Finally, we can also use the two query functions of the TDigest. digest.cdf(value: Double) returns the approximate fraction of all samples that were less than or equal to value, and `digest.quantile(fraction: Double)` returns the minimum value v such that an approximate `fraction` of the samples is lesser than v.

Reducing the Number of Elements: Sampling

Spark offers a variety of methods that we can use to sample data, an operation that can be useful for data analytics as well as to guarantee the performance of our distributed application.

For data analytics under the constraints of time, sampling can enable the use of *heavier* algorithms on smaller datasets. Dominating trends of the original dataset will also appear on the sample, provided that the sampling technique used do not introduce any bias.

As a performance tuning tool, we can use sampling to reduce the load of specific applications that do not require to observe every element of the dataset.

The built-in sampling features of Spark, are expressed directly as functions of RDDs API. Therefore, within the semantics of stream processing, it can be applied at the microbatch level using DStream operations that provide access to the RDD-level of the stream, like `transform` or `foreachRDD`, which we saw in Chapter 17.

 As of this writing, `sampling` is not supported on Structured Streaming. Attempting to apply *sample* functions to a Streaming DataFrame or Dataset will result in an error:

```
org.apache.spark.sql.AnalysisException:
Sampling is not supported on streaming DataFrames/Datasets;
```

Random Sampling

The first and simplest option for sampling RDDs is the `RDD.sample` function, which can be tuned to sample a fraction of each microbatch RDD without or with replacement doing, respectively, Poisson or Bernoulli trials to implement this sampling:

```
// let's assume that dstream is a `DStream[Data]`
// create a random sampling
val sampledStream = dstream.transform{rdd =>
    rdd.sample(withReplacement, fraction,seed)
  }
```

Here are the parameters:

`withReplacement: Boolean`
A flag to indicate whether the sample elements can be sampled multiple times.

```
fraction: Double
```
A probability value in the range [0,1] that indicates the chance of one element being chosen in the sample.

```
seed: Long
```
The value to use as seed, in case we want repeatable results. Defaults to `Utils.random.nextLong` if not specified.

Random sampling is particularly useful in that it preserves the fairness of sampling and therefore a larger number of statistical properties when we consider the union of the sampled RDDs as being itself a single sample of the data stream.

If we would sample by percentage, unequally sized batches will contribute unequally to the final sample and therefore preserve the statistical properties of the data that we will try to tease out of the sample. Beware, however, that sampling without replacement, using the flag `withReplacement = false` can be done only within the scope of a single RDD, meaning that the notion of *without replacement* does not make sense for a DStream.

Stratified Sampling

Stratified sampling allows sampling of RDDs by class, where the different classes of data records are marked using the key of a key-value pair.

Spark Streaming can make use of stratified sampling using the RDD API, as we show in the following example:

```
// let's assume that dstream is a `DStream[(K,V)]`
// create a stratified sampling
val sampledStream = dstream.transform{rdd =>
    rdd.sampleByKey(withReplacement, fraction,seed)
  }
```

The API is identical to the *random sampling* function except that it operates only on `RDD[(K,V)]`s: RDDs containing key-value pairs.

However, sampling-by-class is particularly difficult to implement if we do not have an idea of the number of elements that exist in each class of our dataset. Therefore, we can either do two passes over the data set and provide the exact sample or use statistical laws over repeat samples, flipping a coin on each record to decide whether it will be sampled, a technique known as *stratified sampling*. This latter technique is what is used in the `sampleByKey` function, whereas the two-pass sampling bears the name, `sampleByKeyExact`.

`sampleByKeyExact` is not well defined on a DStream, because the *exact* class definition will be computed on each microbatch and won't be stable across the complete stream.

Note that class sampling has an equally important role in batch analytics as it does in streaming analytics; in particular, it is a valuable tool to fight the problem of class imbalance as well as to correct for biases in a dataset using methods such as boosting.

## CHAPTER 28

Real-Time Machine Learning

In this chapter, we explore how to build *online* classification and clustering algorithms. By online, we mean that these algorithms learn to produce an optimal classification and clustering result on the fly as new data is provided to them.

> This chapter assumes that you have a basic understanding of machine learning algorithms, including concepts such as supervised and unsupervised learning, and classification versus clustering algorithms. If you want a quick brush-up of fundamental machine learning concepts, we recommend reading [Conway2012].

In the following sections, we explain the training of several machine learning algorithms performed in an online fashion, with data coming from a stream. Before that, let's acknowledge that most industry implementations of machine learning models already have an online component: they perform training in a batch fashion—with data at rest—and link it with online inference, as examples are read over a stream of data and the previously trained models are used to score (or predict on) the streaming data.

In this sense, most machine learning algorithms are already deployed in a streaming context, and Spark offers features for making this task easier, whether it's the simple compatibility between Spark's batch and streaming APIs (which we've addressed in prior chapters) or external projects that aim to make deployment simpler, such as MLeap (*http://bit.ly/2PLbGGz*).

The challenge in making this architecture work—batch training followed by online inference—relies mostly on deploying copies of the model to sufficient machines to cope with the influx of requests. General horizontal scaling is an important engineering topic, but a broader one than what this book focuses on. We are rather interested in the challenge of training machine learning models when the conditions do not permit or encourage this pattern of batch training. This can happen for several reasons:

- The size of the data is such that batch training can occur only at low frequencies
- The data changes in nature frequently enough that models grow stale very fast
- As we'll see with Hoeffding trees, the training does not require seeing all the data to produce accurate results

In this chapter, we explore two online classification algorithms and one clustering algorithm. Those algorithms have clear batch alternatives, and as such form a good example of how the transformation from batch to streaming carries over to machine learning training.

The first classification algorithm that we approach is Multinomial Naive Bayes. It is the classifier most often used by basic spam filters and an appropriate classifier when you want to use discrete features (e.g., word counts for text classification).

We then study the Hoeffding trees, an online version of decision trees. The logic behind decision trees relies on classifying the dataset by repeatedly deciding on the most important feature to decide on an example. But in an online context, we should be able to learn what the most salient input features are to classify our dataset, despite just looking at a fragment of it. In this chapter, we demonstrate how, by relying on powerful statistical bounds, the algorithm is able to achieve this feat economically and quickly.

Finally, we see an online adaptation of the *K*-Means clustering algorithm offered in Spark Streaming natively, which buckets the data into a fixed set of groups. The online version uses a weight decay to reduce the impact of old examples, along with a technique for pruning irrelevant clusters, to ensure it constantly provides the most relevant results on fresh data.

This chapter should equip you with powerful online techniques that should form an initial point for applying machine learning techniques in an online learning context.

Streaming Classification with Naive Bayes

Naive Bayes methods are a set of supervised learning algorithms based on applying Bayes' theorem with the "naive" assumption of independence between every pair of features. In this section, we look in detail at a classifier for natural-language documents that use this technique, and we illustrate how an efficient classifier without any deep representation of language is realized.

Multinomial Naive Bayes implements the naive Bayes algorithm for a multiple-class distribution of data. It is one of the two classic naive Bayes variants used in text classification, the other being a Bernoulli model.

In our exploration of Multinomial Naive Bayes, we use a simple representation in which the data is represented as word count vectors. This means that a document is represented as a mixed bag of words, where a bag is a set that allows repeating elements and reflects only which words appear in the document and how many times they occur, while throwing away the word order.

Let's call the collection of these documents D, whose class is given by C. C represents the different classes in the classification. For example, in the classic case of email spam filtering there are two classes for C:

- S (spam) and
- H (ham, or not spam).

We classify D as the class that has the highest posterior probability $P(C|D)$, which we read as *the probability of the class C given the document D*. We can reexpressed this using Bayes' Theorem, which you can see in Equation 28-1.

Equation 28-1. Bayes' Theorem

$$P(C|D) = \frac{P(D|C)P(C)}{P(D)}$$

To select the best class C for our document D, we express $P(C|D)$ and try to choose the class that maximizes this expression. Using Bayes' Theorem, we come to Equation 28-1, which expresses this as a fraction with $P(D|C)P(C)$ as a numerator. This is the quantity we'll try to seek a maximum for, depending on C—and because it reaches a maximum when the initial fraction reaches a maximum, we can drop the constant denominator $P(D)$.

Our model represents documents using feature vectors whose components correspond to word types. If we have a vocabulary V, containing $|V|$ word types, then the feature vector has a dimension d = $|V|$. In a multinomial document model, a document is represented by a feature vector with integer elements whose value is the frequency of that word in the document. In that sense, representing word counts as $x_1...x_n$, we want to study $P(x1, x2, ..., xn|c)$. Assuming those features are independent from one another, this just amounts to computing each of the $P(x_i|c)$. In sum, we seek to find the class c_j, which reaches the maximum of $P(c_j)\prod P(x|c_j)$.

For each class, the probability of observing a word given that class is estimated from the training data by computing the relative frequency of each word in the collection of documents for that class. Of course, it seems that we'll have a problem if we have seen no training document for a particular (word, class) pair. In that case, we use something called a *Laplace smoothing factor* that represents a frequency for that word that is guaranteed to be minimal with respect to the size of the vocabulary. The classifier also requires the prior probabilities,[1] which are straightforward to estimate from the frequency of classes in the training set.

streamDM Introduction

Before we get into how to train a Bayesian model for classification, we want to get into the structure of the streamDM library that we will use for the purpose.

In streamDM, the model operates on a labeled `Example`. In other words, that internally, the streams are represented as Spark Streaming DStream, containing our internal instance data structure, the `Example`. An `Example` encompasses a tuple of input and output `Instance` and a weight; in turn, the `Instance` can contain a data structure depending on the input format of the streams (e.g., dense instances in comma-separated values [CSV] text format, sparse instances in LibSVM format, and text instances).

The `Example` class consists of the following:

- `input: Instance(data, x_j)`
- `output: Instance(labels, y_j)`
- `weight: Double`

In our example, we create the `Example` by using a convenience function called `Example.fromArff()`, which sets the default weight (=1) and reads our ARFF-formatted file. All operations are made on the `Example`; this allows for task design without the need for the model implementer to know the details of the implementation of the instances.

---

1 The prior probabilities, in this context, are the frequencies for the classes (e.g., spam, ham) implied by counting the supervised labels. They represent the larger notion of probability of an event based on established knowledge.

The ARFF File Format

ARFF is an acronym that stands for attribute-relation file format. It is an extension of the CSV file format in which a header is used that provides metadata about the data types in the columns, and is a staple of the Weka suite of machine learning software. Some of the ways of organizing the presentation of features is inspired from it. You can find more information on the Weka wiki (*https://bit.ly/ 30HHh0A*).

A task is a combination of blocks that are generally ordered, as in any learning process setup:

- A StreamReader (reads and parses Examples and creates a stream)
- A Learner (provides the train method from an input stream)
- A Model (data structure and set of methods used for Learner)
- An Evaluator (evaluation of predictions)
- A StreamWriter (manages the output of streams)

streamDM packages this flow into predefined tasks that it links through the method of *prequential evaluation*, which is something we're about to detail.

Naive Bayes in Practice

Multinomial Naive Bayes classifiers are properly a class of closely related algorithms. We'll focus on the one found in the streamDM library[2], which is an implementation of [McCallum1998].

It uses the streamDM implementation, which is based on a three-step prequential evaluation method. The prequential evaluation method, or interleaved test-then-train method, is an alternative to the traditional batch-oriented method that clearly separates these phases into training, validation, and scoring.

The prequential evaluation Figure 28-1 is designed specifically for stream-oriented settings in the sense that each sample serves two purposes, and that samples are analyzed sequentially, in order of arrival, and become immediately unavailable. Samples are effectively seen only once.

---

2 streamDM is sadly not published as a package, which is understandable given that it impinges on the org.apache.spark namespace, as we can see in the example.

This method consists of using each sample to test the model, which means to make a prediction, and then the same sample is used to train the model (partial fit). This way the model is always tested on samples that it hasn't seen yet.

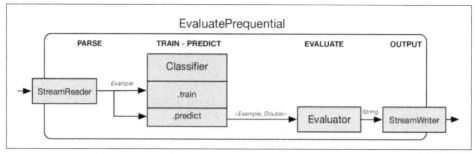

Figure 28-1. Model training and evaluation with prequential evaluation

streamDM integrates a `FileReader`, which is used to read data from one file of full data to simulate a stream of data. It works well with ARFF files.

Training a Movie Review Classifier

We can download a labeled version of the IMDB movie reviews dataset classified in movie genre categories from the MEKA project (*http://bit.ly/2VJJngU*).

The beginning of the files lists the included attributes, starting with the categories in binary form, followed by a word vector encoding of the review.

```
@relation 'IMDB: -C 28'

@attribute Sci-Fi {0,1}
@attribute Crime {0,1}
@attribute Romance {0,1}
@attribute Animation {0,1}
@attribute Music {0,1}
...
```

Here the nominal specifications within brackets correspond to the categories given to the movie by IMDB and then the word vector model follows. We can see the actual representation of one review later in the file:

```
{3 1,15 1,28 1,54 1,123 1,151 1,179 1,229 1,296 1,352 1,436 1,461 1,531 1,609
    1,712 1,907 1,909 1,915 1,968 1,1009 1,1018 1,1026 1}
```

The review gives an idea of the classification of the movie, followed by the word vectors indicating keywords in the review.

streamDM comes with a command-line feature that connects all of the classes in a task (which we detailed earlier) It makes calling our `MultinomialNaiveBayes` model a simple command, launched from the compiled checkout of the streamDM repository, at streamDM/scripts:

```
./spark.sh "EvaluatePrequential
  -l (org.apache.spark.streamdm.classifiers.bayes.MultinomialNaiveBayes
    -c 28 -f 1001 -l 1)
  -s (FileReader -f /<dowload-path>/IMDB-F.arff -k 100 -d 60)" 2> /tmp/error.log
```

The model constructor expects three arguments:

- The number of features in each example (by default 3), indicated by option -c

- The number of classes in each example (by default 2), indicated by option -c and

- A Laplace smoothing factor to handle the zero frequency issue, indicated by option -l.

The model outputs a confusion matrix of the generated data. On a reduced size example, we would obtain, for example:

```
2.159,0.573,0.510,0.241,0.328,0.589,104,100,327,469
2.326,0.633,0.759,0.456,0.570,0.574,243,77,290,390
2.837,0.719,NaN,0.000,NaN,0.719,0,0,281,719
3.834,0.490,0.688,0.021,0.041,0.487,11,5,505,479
4.838,0.567,0.571,0.018,0.036,0.567,8,6
```

Introducing Decision Trees

In a classification problem, we usually deal with a set of N training examples of the form (x, y), where y is a class label and x is a vector of attributes ($x = x_1, x_2, ...x_n$). The goal is to produce a model $y = f(x)$ from these examples, which will predict the classes y of future examples x with high accuracy.

One of the most effective and widely used classification methods is *decision-tree learning*. Learners of this type produce models in the form of decision trees, where each node contains a test on an attribute (a *split*), each branch from a node corresponds to a possible outcome of the test, and each leaf contains a class prediction. In doing so, the algorithm produces a series of splits, such as the one illustrated in Figure 28-2.

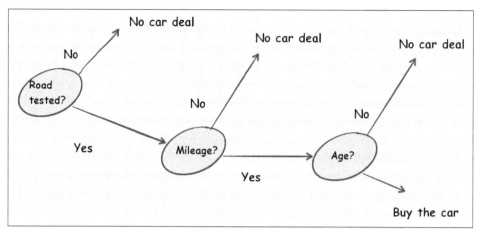

Figure 28-2. Decision tree for a car deal

The label $y = DT(x)$ for an example x results from passing the example down from the root to a leaf, testing the appropriate attribute at each node and following the branch corresponding to the attribute's value in the example. A decision tree is trained by recursively replacing leaves by test nodes, starting at the root. The attribute to test at a given node is chosen by comparing all of the available attributes and choosing the best one according to some heuristic measure, often one called *information gain*.

Information gain is, informally, a statistical indicator that measures how, while observing our potential decision variable ("does the input email contain the word *Viagra?*"), we learn something about the final classification variable ("is this email a spam email?"). It captures the best variables on which to base our decision, the first of those variables being the ones that give us the most information on the outcome of the classification.

The Spark implementation of decision trees relies on the *ID3 algorithm* (iterative dichotomizer, [Quinlan1986]) and relies on information gain.

Decision tree classifiers are a well-known decision algorithm in machine learning. Hoeffding trees are a streaming extension of decision trees that is well grounded in probability theory.

If you are unfamiliar with decision trees, we recommend you have a look at section 4 of *Advanced Analytics with Spark* ([Laserson2017]), which provides an extensive treatment.

These learners use every training example to select the best attribute at each split, a policy that requires all examples to be available during the entire training process. This makes those classic decision-tree learning procedures batch algorithms inapplicable to the streaming context for which data is available only in small increments.

Hoeffding Trees

Hoeffding trees,[3] ([Domingos2000]) address this problem and are able to learn from streaming data within tight time and memory constraints—without having to hold all previously seen data in memory. They accomplish this by remarking that it is mathematically sufficient to use only a small sample of the data when choosing the split attribute at any given node. Thus, only the first examples to arrive on the data stream need to be used to choose the split attribute at the root; subsequent examples are passed through the induced portion of the tree until they reach a leaf, are used to choose a split attribute there, and so on, recursively.

To determine the number of examples needed for each decision, this algorithm uses a statistical result known as a Hoeffding bound. A very informal description of the *Hoeffding bound* is that if you have a function on n random variables and if it doesn't change too much when you resample one of the variables, the function will be close to its mean with high probability. This result helps us understand in precise terms how the behavior of a sample of the values observed in a dataset is reflective of the entire distribution.

In concrete terms, this means that the values we observe one by one—a sample of the stream—will be reflective of the entire stream: we replace the *frequency counters* of decision trees by estimators. There is no need for windows of instances because sufficient statistics are kept by the estimators separately. In particular, the salience of some features is revealed from the data in the same way they would come out from examining the whole dataset.

This means that we have a clear idea of the number of values that we need to see in order to confidently make a decision on how our decision tree should be created—it tells us that learning a classification while having seen a few values is possible!

---

3 Sometimes also known as Very Fast Decision Trees (VFDT), after the name used in the paper that introduced them.

The Hoeffding Bound

After n independent observations of a real-valued random variable r with range R, the Hoeffding bound ensures that, with confidence $1 - \delta$, the true mean of r is at least $V - \varepsilon$, where V is the observed mean of the samples:

$$\epsilon = \sqrt{\frac{R^2 \ln (1/\delta)}{2n}}$$

The interesting part of this bound is that this is true irrespective of the probability distribution that generated the observations in the first place, which lets us apply this to any stream. The price of this generality is that the bound is more conservative than bounds that are distribution dependent (i.e., it will take more observations to reach the same δ and ε).[4]

As with any decision tree, we want to decide whether we should "expand" a leaf, making the decision on the subgroup of requests that end at this leaf split.

Let's call $G(Xi)$ the heuristic measure used to choose test attributes (e.g., information gain). After seeing n samples at a leaf, let Xa be the attribute with the best heuristic measure and Xb be the attribute with the second best. Let $\Delta G = G(Xa) - G(Xb)$ be a new random variable for the difference between the observed heuristic values. Applying the Hoeffding bound to ΔG, we see that if $\Delta G > \varepsilon$ (that we set with the bound using a δ that we choose), we can confidently say that the difference between $G(Xa)$ and $G(Xb)$ is larger than zero, and select Xa as the new split attribute.

The sketch of the algorithm then proceeds by sorting every example (x, y) into a leaf l using a provisional decision tree. For each value $x\_i\_$ in x such that $Xi \in Xl$, it then increments a counter of examples seen for this feature and class, and tries to label the leaf l with the majority class among the examples seen so far at l. If those are not all of the same class, it tries to split by computing a split heuristic _G_l(_X_i) for each attribute _X_i $\in$ _X_l, using the counters. If the difference in heuristic results between the first and second attribute is greater than an ε computed with the Hoeffding bound as just shown, we replace l by an internal node that splits on this first attribute, and update the tree we use then.

The counts are the sufficient statistics needed to compute most heuristic measures; this makes the algorithm frugal with memory.

---

4 The Hoeffding bound is also often called *additive Chernoff bound*. Note that it requires a bounded range of values R.

Hoeffding Trees Heuristics

The algorithm also implements a number of edge heuristics:

- Under memory pressure, Hoeffding trees deactivate the least promising leaves in order to make room for new ones; when data is readily available, these can be reactivated later.

- It also employs a tie mechanism that precludes it from spending inordinate time deciding between attributes whose practical difference is negligible. Indeed, it declares a tie and selects *Xa* as the split attribute any time $\Delta G < \varepsilon < \tau$ (where τ is a user-supplied tie threshold).

- Prepruning is carried out by considering at each node a "null" attribute *X_0 that consists of not splitting the node. Thus, a split will be made only if, with confidence 1 - δ, the best split found is better according to _G* than not splitting.

Notice that the tests for splits and ties are executed only once for every *m* (a user-supplied value) examples that arrive at a leaf. This is justified because that procedure is unlikely to make a decision after any given example, so it is wasteful to carry out these calculations for each one of them. This makes Hoeffding Trees particularly suitable for microbatching, as is done in Spark Streaming.

Hoeffding Trees in Spark, in Practice

The implementation of Hoeffding Trees for Spark can be found in the streamDM library. As is the case with the Naive Bayes classifier, it answers to a slightly different API than the usual Spark Streaming processing API. We could use the streamDM default task setup, as in the naive Bayes example. Such a setup for model evaluation is available in streamDM and is documented on GitHub (*https://huawei-noah.github.io/streamDM/docs/HDT.html*). Here, we sketch a manual construction of the training of the algorithm.

The Hoeffding Tree model requires a specification for initializing instances, named `ExampleSpecification`. An `ExampleSpecification` contains information about the input and output features in the data. It contains a reference to an input `InstanceSpecification` and an output `InstanceSpecification`. Those `InstanceSpecification` elements contain information about the features, differentiating between numerical and categorical features.

The Hoeffding Tree implementation presented here is made to work well with the ARFF file format. We can create features for the well-known Iris flower dataset, an Iris species classification dataset containing four features: length and width for petal and sepal parts of iris samples:

```
val inputIS = new InstanceSpecification()
val columnNames = List(
  "sepal length", "sepal width",
  "petal length", "petal width")
for (part <- range(0, columnNames.length))
  inputIS.addInput(part, columnNames(part), new NumericSpecification)
val outputIS = new InstanceSpecification()
val classFeature = new NominalFeatureSpecification(
  Array("setosa", "versicolor", "virginica"))
outputIS.setFeatureSpecification(0, classFeature)
outputIS.setName(0, "class")
```

The feature specification is done by separating numeric features to help the splitting algorithm organize how it should discriminate on this variable. The setup of the algorithm is then simpler:

```
val exampleSpec = new ExampleSpecification(inputIS, outputIS)

val hTree = new HoeffdingTree

hTree.init(exampleSpec)

hTree.trainIncremental(exampleStream: DStream[Example]): DStream[(Example, Double)]

hTree.predict(queryStream: DStream[Example]): DStream[(Example, Double)]
```

The training of the model comes first. After the model has been trained with the appropriate examples, we can query it with a single record by using the predict method, which operates on a String. Remember from the Naive Bayes example that the Example is a wrapper on top of the Instance class hierarchy. It contains a reference to an input Instance and an output Instance, and provides setters and getters for the features and labels.

Streaming Clustering with Online K-Means

In machine learning, clustering is the practice of grouping the elements of a set in an unsupervised manner, given a notion of similarity between those points. The most famous algorithm for clustering is K-means, and in this section, we study its online adaptation. The rest of this section is going to show you how to adapt an unsupervised algorithm to a streaming context.

K-Means Clustering

K-means clustering is a parametric, unsupervised algorithm for grouping data points in a metric space into specifically k clusters, where k is a predefined integer. The clus-

---

ters are each identified by a *centroid* (a point in this metric space) with the property that the centroid is the *barycenter*[5] of the data points that are assigned to it.

It functions by running through several epochs of alternatively caring about the attachment of points to a centroid on the one hand, and repositioning centroids on the other hand. In the first phase, each of the data points is associated with the centroid that is the closest to it—with the set of data points associated with a particular centroid forming *its cluster*. The later phase consists of selecting and resetting where the centroid is for each and every cluster by selecting the barycenter of all the points in the centroid's cluster. So for example, if we have 100 points and, say, 10 centroids, we can initially have the 10 centroids set at random positions in our space. We then assign all of our 100 points each to their closest centroid among the possible 10, and then we alternate and start for each group to recompute where the centroid should be. That recomputation is a barycenter calculation.

Now, the minimization of that overall distance is the core of the k-means algorithm. And if we want a convergence to an ideal clustering, the algorithm depends only on how many rounds will allow ourselves to execute before getting an error measure and the initial position of the centroids.

Online Data and *K*-Means

In the traditional *K*-means algorithm, we are given (and operate on) the total dataset before doing this ideal centroid computation. If, on the other hand, we need to operate in a sequential manner, considering points one by one and observing them only once, we will need to adopt a different approach.

Suppose, for example, that we consider points appearing on each RDD as being part of our dataset. We have fixed k, so that we know that we really want to separate our dataset into, say, 10 clusters. Yet we still don't want to understand precisely just the last RDD as being the complete epitome of our dataset. What we do to adapt this is that we let the most recent RDDs—that is the most recent batches of data—modify our centroid assignments and position with a stronger importance. We'll quantify this importance numerically using a notion of weight.

The online *K*-means algorithm ([Shindler2011]) consists of adapting *K*-means with a notion known as *forgetfulness*. This amounts to letting the oldest points that we have seen in the dataset have less impact over the centroid's position than the most recent points, reflecting the notion that our clustering should be an accurate snapshot of the best way to cluster the *most recent* points coming over the wire.

---

5 The barycenter is the point that minimizes the distance of each and every point existing in the cluster of attention at any given moment.

In practical terms, it means that the output of assignment of points under centroids is a fresh representation of the last few batches of the data that we have seen. To do this, we introduce a notion of weight ($w < 1$), or decay, that accompanies every single point. This is very relevant because the computation of a barycenter that we have seen in the vanilla batch interpretation of K-means is something that natively extends into a weighted computation. That weight reflects on every single batch for which we multiply points by decay factor. And because we do that on every batch, the weight of any particular point is exponentially decreased based on the number of batches elapsed since that point was read on the wire from our data source.

This factor can be expressed in Spark using the decay factor expressed as a float in the parametrization of the online K-means algorithm, or it can be expressed as a half-life. The half-life says how many batches a point should survive for before half of the dataset, in view of the algorithm, should be decreased. In fact, we're considering the number of batches after which the weight of each and every single point that was seen at that particular time diminishes by half.

 Another alternative in the parametrization of the algorithm consists in *counting the number of points* that we have seen of the entire stream. Indeed, the batch notion that Spark applies for determining the age of a particular point—and therefore the decay that should be applied to it in the algorithm—is something that is not always the most appropriate, because the simple amount and vastness of data for a stream of which we know the throughput varies a lot is a better indication of the recency of results than the timestamp at which the event arrived.

The Problem of Decaying Clusters

In any case, that forgetfulness lets us have centroids that carry the barycenter of lesser and lesser points. Now, since we have an assignment for those points, we can reposition the centroids based on the most recent points to arrive in that cluster. But how exactly are we going to deal with the fact that, after a given amount of time, it is often the case that some centroids can be completely forgotten? For example, let's consider a data stream that is operating on a cartesian, bounded plane. If we have, at the beginning, mostly points that hit the *upper-left* quadrant of our particular bounded plane or a particular zone of our space, we will probably assign, very early on, a centroid or several to that region.

After some time, let's then assume that the content of the point of our data stream moves to the *lower-right* quadrant of our space. In that case, the evolution of our online K-means is meant to play centroid in the new region rather than in the upper-left quadrant. As the points of a given cluster will move downward and rightward, the centroid will equally move but within the same cluster. What if, in any given point, we create such a gap in point location that we cannot assign a single point to the old cluster that was still in the upper left quadrant? Then, that cluster, while having a very small number of points, will still have "old" points associated to it. That is the total weight, being multiplied by a very small factor, will be negligible but strictly positive, meaning that there will still be a cluster "grouping" those old points. This is sub-optimal because it "consumes" a centroid to group points that are long past being relevant to our current stream.

The solution to this is to analyze decaying clusters that have such a small weight that they are in fact negligible. When using K-means, we have K possible centroids in the general formulation of the problem. Because of that invariant, we will need to examine "dying" (low-weight) clusters by comparing their total weight to the maximum weight witnessed at the "strongest" cluster. What lets us determine that a cluster is "dying," is to compare the total weight, in terms of number of points, multiplied by their decay factor for the lightest centroid to the total weight of the heaviest centroid, which is the centroid that has the most amount of weighted points. If the relative discrepancy between those centroids is higher than 10 million,[6] Spark will abandon the dying centroid and split the "heaviest" centroid in two.

In Figure 28-3, clusters A and B start at the upper-left corner and move progressively, downwards and rightwards, as the more recent points take over most of the weight of the cluster. However, when there is a discontinuous gap (in red) in the position of new point arrivals, the new points are assigned to another, distinct cluster C and begin disrupting the position of its centroid (in gray). We would instead like those new points to form a new cluster in the lower-left corner, with the red centroid. That is impossible as long as A stays in place as a cluster, regardless of how small its aggregated weight is (due to the decay factor).

---

6 This is a hardcoded constant in the current Streaming K-means implementation, unfortunately.

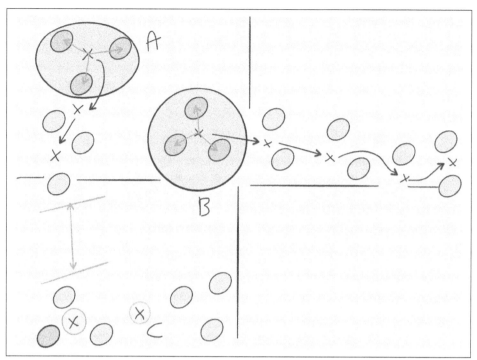

Figure 28-3. The effect of "dying" clusters

This operation occurring in every microbatch will help the algorithm find a newer location of centroids that well corresponds better to the exact allocation of points in our data stream irrelevant of whether large movements of points have occurred in space over the history of our data stream. The relative difference is not configurable, and, as a consequence, it would be advisable to make sure that we use large decay factors that will let Spark Streaming figure out across a stream with relatively long batteries that it should be very reactive in killing those decaying centroids and moving them around.

The practice of doing a test on a particular assignation of clusters separating a set of points, deleting a "bad" cluster (for some notion of goodness), and "splitting" the largest cluster in two is a powerful and systematic way of enhancing the basic *K*-means idea into more powerful algorithms.

Among those enhancements, we can cite the *G*-means algorithm, that consists of testing a candidate *K*-means cluster with a Gaussianity test, checking that the positions of the points in the cluster obey a Gaussian hypothesis, something that is valid for various kinds of data. If that Gaussianity assumption is not reached in data that should reflect it, *G*-means considers that it is looking for a number of clusters that is too low. The algorithm then splits this bad cluster and increases *k*, the number of clusters the algorithms seeks to find in the data.

You can find more references in [Hammerly2003] and an implementation in the SMILE library in [Li2017]

Streaming *K*-Means with Spark Streaming

A streaming *K*-means model is available in Spark Streaming since Spark 1.2. It works with two streams of data: one for training, and another one for prediction. The *K*-means model is initialized with a builder pattern:

```
val trainingData = ...
val testData = ...

val model = new StreamingKMeans()
  .setK(3)
  .setDecayFactor(1.0)
  .setRandomCenters(5, 0.0)

model.trainOn(trainingData)
model.predictOnValues(testData.map(lp => (lp.label, lp.features))).print()
```

In this example, we set out to determine three centers, with initial weighted random centers with a weight of 0, and points that are five-dimensional (a dimension we will need to find in the data). The decay factor of 1.0 indicates the forgetfulness of the previous centroids, marking the weight to assign to newer data in comparison to older ones. By default, this value of 1 does not operate any decay—assuming slow-moving values in the stream. We could also have passed the number of batch intervals after which the impact of a batch of points drops to half its value with `setHal fLife(batches: Double, durationUnit: String)`.

The training data should contain each point formatted as [x_1, $\_x\_2$, ..., $\_xn$], and each test data point should be formatted as (y, [x_1, $\_x\_2$, ..., $\_xn$]), where y is the label of this point. Note that `model.trainOn` does not, per se, create an output:

indeed, the process mutates the `model` object without further ado. This is why we use Spark Streaming's printing on the test dataset, which let us witness new classifications on updates of the test dataset. Note that the `latestModel()` function can be called on `StreamingKMeans` to access the latest version of the model.

References for Part IV

- [Alon1999] Alon, N., T. Matias, and M. Szegedy. "The space complexity of approximating the frequency moments." *Proceedings of the Twenty-Eighth Annual ACM Symposium on the Theory of Computing* (1999). *http://bit.ly/2W7jG6c*.

- [Bifet2015] Bifet, A., S. Maniu, J. Qian, G. Tian, C. He, W. Fan. "StreamDM: Advanced Data Mining in Spark Streaming," Data Mining Workshop (ICDMW), November 2015. *http://bit.ly/2XlXBSV*.

- [Carter1979] Carter, J. Lawrence, and Mark N. Wegman. "Universal Classes of Hash Functions," *Journal of Computer and System Sciences* 18 (1979). *http://bit.ly/2EQkkzf*.

- [Conway2012] Conway, D., and J. White. *Machine Learning for Hackers*. O'Reilly, 2012.

- [Cormode2003] Cormode, Graham, and S. Muthukrishnan. *An Improved Data Stream Summary: The Count-Min Sketch and its Applications*. Preprint submitted to Elsevier Science, December 2003. *http://bit.ly/2HSmSPe*.

- [Domingos2000] Domingos, Pedro, and Geoff Hulten. "Mining High-Speed Data Streams." *Proceedings of the Sixth ACM SIGKDD International Conference on Knowledge Discovery and Data Mining* (2000). *http://bit.ly/315nSqH*.

- [Dunning2013] Dunning, Ted, and Otmar Erti. "Computing Extremely Accurate Quantiles Using t-Digests." *http://bit.ly/2IlpZhs*.

- [Flajolet2007] Flajolet, Philippe, Éric Fusy, Olivier Gandouet, and Frédéric Meunier. "HyperLogLog: The Analysis of a Near-Optimal Cardinality Estimation Algorithm," *Discrete Mathematics and Theoretical Computer Science* (2007). *http://bit.ly/2MFI6V5*.

- [Freeman2015] Freeman, Jeremy. "Introducing Streaming k-means in Apache Spark 1.2, "Databricks Engineering blog, January 28, 2015. *http://bit.ly/2WlFn7k.*

- [Heule2013] Heule, Stefan, Marc Nunkesser, and Alexander Hall. "HyperLogLog in Practice: Algorithmic Engineering of a State-of-the-Art Cardinality Estimation Algorithm," EDBT/ICDT, March 2013. *http://bit.ly/2Wl6wr9.*

- [Hammerly2003] Hammerly, G., and G. Elkan. "Learning the k in k-means," *NIPS*, 2003. *http://bit.ly/2IbvfUY.*

- [Hulten2001] Hulten, Geoff, Laurie Spencer, and Pedro Domingos. "Mining Time-Changing Data Streams," *Proceedings of the seventh ACM SIGKDD International Conference on Knowledge Discovery and Data Mining (2001). http://bit.ly/2WqQIU0.*

- [Hunter2016] Hunter, Tim, Hossein Falaki, and Joseph Bradley. "Approximate Algorithms in Apache Spark: HyperLogLog and Quantiles," Databricks Engineering blog, May 19, 2016. *http://bit.ly/2EQFCg3.*

- [Kirsch2006] Kirsch, Adam, and Michael Mitzenmacher. "Less Hashing, Same Performance: Building a Better Bloom Filter" *LNCS* 4168 (2006). *http://bit.ly/2WFCyh2.*

- [Laserson2017] Laserson, U., S. Ryza, S. Owen, and J. Wills. *Advanced Analytics with Spark*, 2nd Ed. O'Reilly, 2017.

- [Li2017] Li, Haifeng. "Statistical Machine Intelligence and Learning Engine," Version 1.3. *http://bit.ly/2Xn1mY3.*

- [McCallum1998] McCallum, Andrew, and Kamal Nigam. "A Comparison of Event Models for Naive Bayes Text Classification," AAAI-98 Workshop on Learning for Text Categorization, 1998.

- [Ni2017] Ni, Yun, Kelvin Chu, and Joseph Bradley. "Detecting Abuse at Scale: Locality Sensitive Hashing at Uber Engineering," Databricks Engineering blog. *http://bit.ly/2KpSMnF.*

- [Nitkin2016] Nitkin, Alexandr. "Bloom Filter for Scala, the Fastest for JVM," personal blog, 2016. *http://bit.ly/2XlZT4t.*

- [Quinlan1986]] Quinlan, J. R. "Induction of Decision Trees," *Machine Learning* 1, 1 (March, 1986): 81–106. *http://bit.ly/2EPZKia.*

- [Shindler2011] Shindler, M., A. Wong, and A.W. Meyerson. "Fast and Accurate k-means for Large Datasets," *NIPS* (2011). *http://bit.ly/2WFGWww.*

- [Ziakas2018] Ziakas, Christos. "Implementation of Decision Trees for Data Streams in the Spark Streaming Platform," September, 2018. *http://bit.ly/2Z1gZow.*

## PART V

Beyond Apache Spark

In this part, we want to view Apache Spark's streaming engines within a broader scope. We begin with a detailed comparison with other relevant projects of the distributed stream-processing industry, explaining both where Spark comes from and how there is no alternative exactly like it.

We offer a brief description of and a focused comparison to other distributed processing engines, including the following:

Apache Storm
  A historical landmark of distributed processing, and a system that still has a legacy footprint today

Apache Flink
  A distributed stream processing engine that is the most active competitor of Spark

Apache Kafka Streams
  A reliable distributed log and stream connector that is fast developing analytical chops

We also touch on the cloud offerings of the main players (Amazon and Microsoft) as well as the centralizing engine of Google Cloud Dataflow.

After you are equipped with a detailed sense of the potential and challenges of Apache Spark's streaming ambitions, we'll touch on how you can become involved with the community and ecosystem of stream processing with Apache Spark, providing references for contributing, discussing, and growing in the practice of streaming analytics.

## CHAPTER 29

Other Distributed Real-Time Stream Processing Systems

As we have demonstrated throughout this book, stream processing is a crucial technology for every data-oriented enterprise. There are many stream-processing stacks out there that can help us in the task of processing streaming data, both proprietary and in the open source domain. They differ in capabilities, APIs, and offer different trade-offs in the balance between latency and throughput.

Following the principle of *the right tool for the job*, they should be compared and contrasted against the requirements of every new project to make the right choice.

Furthermore, the evolving importance of the cloud beyond being an infrastructure provider has created a new class of offerings, where the functionality of the system is offered as a managed service (Software as a Service [SAAS]).

In this chapter, we are going to briefly survey the most relevant open source stream processors currently maintained, such as Apache Storm, Apache Flink, Apache Beam, and Kafka Streams and offer an overview of the offering of the dominant cloud providers in the streaming arena.

Apache Storm

Apache Storm (*http://storm.apache.org/*) is an open source project created originally by Nathan Marz at BackType. It was then used at Twitter and open sourced in 2011, and consists of a mix of Java and Closure code. It's an open source, distributed, real-time computation system. It was the first "big data" streaming engine to be fast, scalable, and partially fault-tolerant, which, back then, meant it was considered the "Hadoop of Streaming." With this background, it has also inspired a lot of streaming systems and engines, including Apache Spark Streaming. Storm is programming-language agnostic and guarantees that data will be processed at least once, despite edge-case limitations in fault tolerance.

Storm is made for real-time analytics and stream processing at scale as well as online machine learning and continuous computation due to its very versatile programming model. It was the first real-time distributed streaming system that garnered a lot of adoption. Storm has a particular vocabulary of which the basics should be introduced to get an intuition of the level at which the programming API is placed. In particular, programming a Storm job embodies the concept of deploying a topology. But before we get to that topology, we need to have an idea of what is sent through a stream in Storm.

Processing Model

A stream in Storm is a stream of tuples, which is its main data structure. A Storm tuple is a named list of values, where each value can be any type. Tuples are dynamically typed: the types of the fields do not need to be declared. That unbounded sequence of tuples represents the stream that we are interested in. That stream's data flow is represented by the edges of a topology, where we are going to define what the vertexes consist of exactly. For those tuples to be meaningful, the content of what is in a stream is defined with a schema. That schema is tracked over a graph, which is the Storm topology and represents the computation. In that topology, the nodes of the graph can be of, roughly, two different types:

Spouts
Spouts are a source of a stream and are the origins of the data. This is where our directed graph presenting the topology always starts. An example of a spout could be a log file being replayed, a messaging system, a Kafka server, and so on. That spout creates tuples that are sent to other nodes. One of these other nodes could be, for example, a bolt.

Bolts
A bolt processes input streams and might produce new streams as an output. It can do anything, meaning that it can filter, do streaming joins, or accumulate an intermediate result. It can also receive several streams, do aggregations, read from and write to a database, among others. In particular, it can be an endpoint to the streaming system's computation, meaning that no other node consumes the output of that bolt. In which case, that final node is called a sink. Therefore, we can say that all sinks in the topology are bolts, but not all bolts are sinks.

The Storm Topology

The topology in Storm is a network of spouts and bolts, where the last layer of bolts are the sinks. They are a container for the application's logic and equivalent to a job in

Spark, but run forever. A Storm topology, therefore could be a couple of log file generators, such as web servers, which could each be sent to a splitter bolt that preprocesses and messages the data using some basic extract, transform, and load (ETL) rules, selecting interesting elements, for example. Of those two bolts, we could get a join that counts irregular elements and joins them by a time stamp to get an idea of the chronology of the events of those values web servers. That could be sent to a final bolt that sends its side effects to a particular dashboard, indicating errors and events, such as alerts that could have occurred in a distributed web service.

The Storm Cluster

In this context, a Storm Cluster is managed by three elements: the definition of the topology, which is the definition of the job itself is passed to a scheduler called Nimbus, which deals with Supervisors that deploy the topology. A Nimbus daemon is the scheduler of the cluster and manages the topologies that exist on the cluster. It's comparable to the idea of JobTracker in a YARN API. Besides this, a Supervisor daemon is a component that spawns workers. It's comparable to the idea of a Hadoop Task-Tracker and the workers that are spawned by Supervisors can receive an instance of one of the particular elements of the Storm topology.

Compared to Spark

When comparing Apache Spark to Apache Storm, we can see that Spark Streaming has been influenced by Apache Storm and its organization, notably in the deference to a resource manager for the purpose of spawning a job across a pool of Spark streaming executors.

Storm has the advantage that it deals with tuples *one by one* rather than in time-indexed *microbatches*. As they are being received, they are pushed immediately to bolts and new workers down the direct computation graph of a topology. On the other hand, to manage a topology, we need to describe the parallelism that we anticipate in the replication of bolts we expect to handle part of the stream. In this way, we have a lot more effort to perform in directly specifying the distribution that we want at each stage of the graph.

The simpler and straightforward *distribution* paradigm for a Spark Streaming job is its advantage, where Spark Streaming (especially in its dynamic allocation modes) will do its best to deploy successive stages of our program in a way that makes sense for very high throughput. This difference in paradigm will come up often as the main highlight of the comparison of Apache Spark's streaming approach with other systems, with the caveat that Spark is working on continuous processing.

It is also why several benchmarks ([Chintapallu2015]) have shown that although Storm usually delivers lower latencies than Spark Streaming, in general, the throughput of the equivalent Spark Streaming application is higher.

Apache Flink

Apache Flink (*https://flink.apache.org/*), originally named StratoSphere (*http://strato sphere.eu/*) ([Alexandrov2014]), is a streaming framework born from Technischen Universität Berlin and neighboring universities.

Flink ([Carbone2017]) is the first open source engine that supported out-of-order processing, given that the implementations of MillWheel and Cloud Dataflow are private Google offerings. It offers Java and Scala APIs that make it look similar to Apache Spark's RDD/DStream functional API:

```
val counts: DataStream[(String, Int)] = text
    // split up the lines in pairs (2-tuples) containing: (word,1)
    .flatMap(_.toLowerCase.split("\\W+"))
    .filter(_.nonEmpty)
    .map((_, 1))
    // group by the tuple field "0" and sum up tuple field "1"
    .keyBy(0)
    .sum(1)
```

Like Google Cloud Dataflow (which we mention late in the chapter), it uses the *dataflow programming model.*

Dataflow Programming

Dataflow programming (*http://bit.ly/2Wrnt3q*) is the conceptual name for a type of programming that models computation as a graph of data flowing between operations. It is closely related to functional programming in that it emphasizes the movement of data and models programs as a series of connections. Explicitly defined inputs and outputs are connected by operations, which are considered as black boxes from one another.

It was pioneered by Jack Dennis and his graduate students at MIT in the 1960s. Google then reused this name for its cloud programming API.

A Streaming-First Framework

Flink is a one-at-a-time streaming framework, and it also offers snapshots to armor computation against failures, despite its lack of a synchronous batch boundary. Nowadays, this very complete framework offers a lower-level API than Structured

Streaming, but it is a compelling alternative to Spark Streaming, if its low-latency focus is of interest. Flink has APIs in Scala and Java.[1]

Compared to Spark

Apache Spark, when compared to these alternative frameworks, retains its main advantage of a tightly integrated, high-level API for data processing with minimal changes between batch and streaming.

With the development of Structured Streaming, Apache Spark has caught up with the rich algebra of time queries (event-time, triggers, etc.) that Dataflow had and Spark Streaming used to lack. Yet Structured Streaming keeps a high degree of compatibility with the batch DataSet and Dataframe APIs well-established in Apache Spark.

This seamless extension of Spark's DataSet and Dataframe API with streaming functionality is the main value of Structured Streaming's approach: it is really possible to compute on streaming data with a minimum of purpose-specific training, and with little cognitive overload.

One of the most interesting aspects of this integration is the running of streaming dataset queries in Structured Streaming through the query planner of Catalyst, leading to consistent optimizations of the user's queries and making streaming computations less error prone than if they had to be written using a dataflow-like system. Note also that Flink has a system close to Apache Spark's Tungsten that allows it to manage its own memory segments off-heap, taking advantage of powerful low-level JIT optimizations ([Hueske2015], [Ewen2015]).

Finally, note that Apache Spark is also the subject of research on scheduling that hints at better low latency to come for a system such as Spark, reusing scheduling decisions across microbatches ([Venkataraman2016]).

In sum, Apache Spark exhibits, as an ecosystem, very strong arguments for its continued streaming performance, particularly in a context for which exchanging code with batch analytics is relevant, and Apache Beam, as an interface with other ways of developing streaming computations, seems an interesting platform for making this kind of development "write once, run on any cluster."

---

[1] To keep a fair amount of consistency between the Scala and Java APIs, some of the features that allow a high-level of expressiveness in Scala have been left out from the standard APIs for both batch and streaming. If you want to enjoy the full Scala experience you can choose to opt-in to extensions that enhance the Scala API via implicit conversions.

Kafka Streams

To continue this tour in other processing systems, we must mention the young Kafka Streams library.

Kafka Streams (*https://kafka.apache.org/documentation/streams/*) ([Kreps2016]), introduced in 2016, is an integrated stream-processing engine within the Apache Kafka project.

Kafka Streams provides a Java and a Scala API that we use to write client applications enriched with stream-processing capabilities. Whereas Spark, Storm, and Flink are *frameworks* that take a job definition and manage its execution on a cluster, Kafka Streams is a library. It's included in applications as a dependency and delivers an API that developers use to add streaming features to their application. Kafka Streams also provides backend support for a streaming SQL-like query language called KSQL.

Kafka Streams Programming Model

Kafka Streams exploits the stream–table duality by offering *views* of the streams that are backed by stateful data stores. It puts forward the observation that tables are aggregated streams. This insight is rooted in the same fundamental concepts present in the Structured Streaming model we saw in Part II. With Kafka Streams, you can benefit from one-event-at-a-time processing. Its processing support includes distributed joins, aggregations, and stateful processing. Windowing and event-time processing are also available as well as the rich distributed processing and fault tolerance guarantees that Kafka offers using offset-replay (reprocessing).

Compared to Spark

The key difference between Spark's model and Kafka Streams is that Kafka Streams is used as a client library within the scope of client applications whereas Spark is a distributed framework that takes the responsibility of coordinating the work among workers in a cluster. In terms of modern application architectures, Kafka Streams apps can be considered microservices that use Kafka as a data backend. Their scalability model is based on replicas—running several copies of the application—and it's bound to the number of partitions of the topic being consumed.

The main use of Kafka Streams is to "enrich" client applications with stream processing features or create simple stream processing applications that use Kafka as their source and sink.

However, Kafka Streams has the disadvantage of not having the rich ecosystem focused on streaming that is developed around Apache Spark, both around Spark Streaming and Structured Streaming, such as machine learning capabilities with MLlib or external interactions with the broad data source support that is available in

Spark. Moreover, Kafka Streams does not have the rich interplay with batch libraries and batch processing offered by Spark. As such, it becomes difficult to envision tomorrow's complex machine learning pipelines, taking advantage of a vast amount of scientific computation libraries, as deployed on Kafka Streams alone.

In the Cloud

Spark's expressive programming models and advanced analytics capabilities can be used on the cloud, including the offerings of the major players: Amazon, Microsoft, and Google. In this section, we provide a brief tour of the ways in which the streaming capabilities of Spark can be used on the cloud infrastructure and with native cloud functions, and, if relevant, how they compare with the cloud providers' own proprietary stream-processing system.

Amazon Kinesis on AWS

Amazon Kinesis (*https://aws.amazon.com/kinesis*) is the streaming delivery platform of Amazon Web Services (AWS). It comes with rich semantics for defining producers and consumers of streaming data, along with connectors for the pipelines created with those stream endpoints. We touched on Kinesis in Chapter 19, in which we described the connector between Kinesis and Spark Streaming.

There is a connector between Kinesis and Structured Streaming, as well, which is available in two flavors:

- One offered natively to users of the Databricks edition of Spark, itself available on the AWS and Microsoft Azure clouds
- The open source connector under JIRA Spark-18165 (*https://issues.apache.org/ jira/browse/SPARK-18165*), which offers a way to stream data out of Kinesis easily

Those connectors are necessary because Kinesis, by design, does not come with a comprehensive stream-processing paradigm besides a language of continuous queries on AWS analytics (*https://amzn.to/2QMPPyY*), which cover simpler SQL-based queries. Therefore, the value of Kinesis is to let clients implement their own processing from robust sources and sinks produced with the battle-tested clients of the Kinesis SDK. With Kinesis, it is possible to use the monitoring and throttling tools of the AWS platform, getting a production-ready stream delivery "out of the box" on the AWS cloud. You can find more details in [Amazon2017].

The open source connector between Amazon Kinesis and Structured Streaming is a contribution from Qubole engineers that you can find at [Georgiadis2018]. This library was developed and tested against Spark 2.2 and allows Kinesis to be a full citizen of the Spark ecosystem, letting Spark users define analytic processing of arbitrary complexity.

Finally, note that although the Kinesis connector for Spark Streaming was based on the older receiver model, which comes with some performance issues. This Structured Streaming client is much more modern in its implementation, but it has not yet migrated to the version 2 of the data source APIs, introduced in Spark 2.3.0. Kinesis is a region of the Spark ecosystem which would welcome easy contributions updating the quality of its implementations.

As a summary, Kinesis in AWS is a stream-delivery mechanism that introduces producing and consuming streams, and connects them to particular endpoints. However, it comes with limited built-in analytics capabilities, which makes it complementary to a streaming analytics engine, such as Spark's streaming modules.

Microsoft Azure Stream Analytics

Azure Streaming Analytics ([Chiu2014]) is a cloud platform available on Microsoft Azure that is inspired by DryadLINQ, a Microsoft research project on compiling language queries using logical processing plans, adapted to stream processing. It exposes a high-level SQL-like language to describe a user query, with experimental Javascript functions accessible as well for the user to define some custom processing. Its goal is to express advanced time-focused streaming queries using that SQL-like language.

In that respect, it is similar to Structured Streaming, supporting many temporal processing patterns. Besides the usual analytics functions—which include aggregates, last and first elements, conversions, date and time functions—Azure Stream Analytics supports window aggregates and temporal joins.

Temporal joins are SQL joins that include a temporal constraint in the matched events. This predicate on joining can allow a user to express, for example, that two joined events must have timestamps that follow each other but by a limited time delay. This rich query language is well supported by Microsoft, which attempted to reimplement it on Spark Streaming 1.4 around 2016 ([Chen2016]).

This work is not complete, and as such, it is not yet well integrated within Azure Streaming Analytics in production today. Structured Streaming has since caught up with those features and now offers temporal joins as a native feature as part of its inner join facility.

As a consequence, Azure Stream Analytics once had the upper hand in the ease of implementing complex time-based queries, but it is now offering fewer native facilities than Structured Streaming, which besides SQL-like queries offers rich processing capabilities in its Streaming Dataset API.

Hence, for an advanced stream-processing project on the Microsoft Cloud, it seems that deploying Spark on Azure is the more robust approach. The options include HDInsight managed Spark, Databricks on Azure, or using Azure's native resource provisioning capabilities, offering a managed Kubernetes (AKS) as well as virtual machines.

Apache Beam/Google Cloud Dataflow

Modern stream-processing systems are many and include among others, Apache Flink, Apache Spark, Apache Apex, Apache Gearpump, Hadoop MapReduce, JStorm, IBM Streams, and Apache Samza. Apache Beam, an open source project led by Google, is a way to manage the existence of this cottage industry of streaming systems while offering good integration with the Google Cloud Dataflow computing engine. Let's explain how this works.

In 2013, Google had another internal cloud stream-processing system called MillWheel [Akidau2013]. When the time had come to give it a new coat of paint and link it to a mature cloud offering that would open it to the public, MillWheel became the Google Cloud Dataflow [Akidau2014], adding several key streaming concepts in the area of fault tolerance and event triggers. There is more to it, which you can find in [Akidau2017].

But why offer yet another alternative to all of the others that we have listed, when it would possible to implement one system under one API, that runs stream processing under all of those computation engines?

That API turned into an open source project, Apache Beam, which aims at offering a single programming API for stream processing that can be plugged to any stream computation engine among the ones that we cited earlier, as well as Apex, Gearpump, MapReduce, JStorm, IBM Streams, and Samza. All of these computational engines are exposed as backend plug-ins (or "runners") of Apache Beam, which aims to be the *lingua franca* of stream processing.

For example, for computing integer indexed sums of 30-minute windows, we could use the following:

```
PCollection<KV<String, Integer>> output = input
  .apply(Window
  .into(FixedWindows.of(Duration.standardMinutes(30)))
  .triggering(AfterWatermark.pastEndOfWindow()))
  .apply(Sum.integersPerKey());
```

Here, we are summing integers by key, with a fixed 30-minute window, and triggering the sum output when the watermark passes the end of a window, which reflects "when we estimate the window is complete."

One element of note is that contrary to Structured Streaming, triggers and outputs are not independent of the query itself. In Dataflow (and Beam), a window must also select an output mode and trigger, which conflates the semantics of the identifier with its runtime characteristics. In Structured Streaming, one can also have these for queries that don't logically use windows, making the separation of concepts simpler.

Apache Beam offers its API in a Java SDK, along with Python SDK and a smaller but still notable Go SDK and a few SQL primitive queries. It allows one single language supporting a series of concepts that are universally adaptable to stream processing and hopefully can run on almost every stream computing engine. Besides the classic aggregates that we have seen in previous chapters, like the window-based slicing, and event-time processing, the beam API allows triggers in processing time including count triggers, allowed lateness, and event-time triggers.

But where Beam shines is offering portability between different streaming systems, centralizing one single API (sadly with no Scala SDK) for streaming programs that can run almost anywhere. This is exciting, but note that when executed under a particular computation engine, it has only the capacities that this computation engine and its "runner" plug-in have in implementing the totality of the API of Apache Beam.

In particular, the computational engine of Apache Spark is exposing the capabilities of Spark Streaming, not those of Structured Streaming. As of this writing, it does not implement stateful streams fully, or any event-time processing, because those capabilities are either limited in Spark Streaming alone or because the "runner" plug-in has not caught up to the changes in Spark Streaming itself. As a consequence, expressing your program with Apache Beam is often a game of being slightly behind the expressivity of Structured Streaming while the developers of the Spark runner for Apache Beam catch up.

Naturally, the Spark ecosystem is made greater only through collaboration with other related streaming projects, so we would, of course, encourage you to do so, to help contribute to the Spark runner for Apache Beam (*https://github.com/apache/beam*), so that projects using the Beam API can benefit from the gains in efficiency of Spark's streaming engines.

In summary, Apache Beam is an open source project that aims at offering a single SDK and API for a very expressive stream-processing model. It is an API that is efficiently implemented in Google's Cloud Dataflow which allows you to run such a program on Google Cloud as well as a flurry of related streaming systems, under the caveat that they do not all have the same capabilities. You would be well advised to refer to the Apache Beam capability matrix (*https://beam.apache.org/documentation/runners/capability-matrix/*), which presents an overview of the differences.

However, note that the Google Cloud also allows running native Apache Spark, either on nodes or on Kubernetes, and, in practice, it might therefore not be necessary to switch to the Beam API if you know that you are going to run your program on systems that support deploying Apache Spark easily. If you need to support both the Google Cloud and other streaming systems as deployment systems, Apache Beam might make a lot of sense.

## CHAPTER 30

Looking Ahead

Apache Spark is a fast moving project.

We have seen that Spark Streaming is an older, relatively low-level API built on top of Resilient Distributed Datasets (RDDs) and the usual Java, Scala, or Python objects that every programmer is used to. Spark Streaming is battle tested and deployed at many production-level applications. We can consider it a stable API where the efforts go mostly to maintenance.

Structured Streaming, being built upon the Dataset and Dataframe APIs of Spark, takes full advantage of this the impressive optimization work Apache Spark introduced through Spark SQL, such as the Catalyst engine and the code generation and memory management from project Tungsten. In this sense, Structured Streaming is the future of streaming in Apache Spark, and where the main development efforts will lie for the foreseeable future. As such, Structured Streaming is delivering exciting new developments such as continuous processing.

We need to mention that Structured Streaming is a newer framework for stream processing and, as such, is less mature, something we have outlined in particular in the machine learning chapters of this book. It is important to keep this in mind, especially when embarking on a project heavy on machine learning. Given the current interest in machine learning, we should expect that future versions of Spark will bring improvements in this area and more algorithms supported in streaming mode. We hope to have equipped you with all the elements to make an accurate evaluation of the offerings of both APIs.

There is one remaining question that we would like to address: how to keep learning and improving in this space.

Stay Plugged In

One of the strongest aspects of Apache Spark has always been its community.

Apache Spark, as an open source project, has been very successful at harnessing contributions from individuals and companies into a comprehensive and consistent code base, as is demonstrated in Figure 30-1.

Figure 30-1. Spark contribution timeline

The GitHub page of Apache Spark is evidence of its steady development pace, where more than 200 developers contribute to each release and the total number of contributors is into the thousands.

There are several established channels to get in touch with the community.

Seek Help on Stack Overflow

Stack Overflow (*http://www.stackoverflow.com*), the well-known Q&A community, is a very active place to discuss Spark-related questions. It's advisable to first search for existing answers in this website before asking new questions, because the chances are that people before you already had the same or similar query.

Start Discussions on the Mailing Lists

The Apache Spark community has always relied heavily on two mailing lists, where the core developers and creators of Apache Spark are committed to helping users and fellow contributors on a regular basis. The user mailing list, at *user@spark.apache.org* is for readers who are trying to find the best ways to use Spark, while the developer mailing list, at *dev@spark.apache.org*, caters to those who are improving the Spark framework itself.

You'll find up-to-date details on how to subscribe to those mailing lists for free online (*https://spark.apache.org/community.html*).

Attend Conferences

The Spark Summit is the bi-annual conference cycle promoted by Databricks, the startup that is the direct shepherd of the Apache Spark project. On top of events with a conference program dedicated to Spark, this conference has offered a watering hole for Spark developers to meet with the community and one another. You can find more information online (*https://databricks.com/sparkaisummit*).

Attend Meetups

If you live near a city with a big technology footprint, consider attending user groups or meetups (*http://bit.ly/2wBBXyd*). They are often free and a great opportunity to see early previews of conference talks or more intimate demonstrations and use cases of Apache Spark applications.

Read Books

We have previously mentioned the 2015 book *Learning Spark* by Matei Zaharia and the other founders of the Spark project as a good entry point to build a foundation on the functioning of Apache Spark. Numerous publications on Spark, in general by O'Reilly, are volumes we would definitely recommend, as well. Let us mention just the 2017 volume *Spark: The Definitive Guide* by Matei Zaharia and Bill Chambers as an essential refresher on more recent evolutions in the Spark platform.

On the more theoretical side, you might find yourself looking for more in-depth knowledge about streaming algorithms and machine learning in the abstract, before implementing more of those notions using Apache Spark. There is too much material in this domain for us to recommend exhaustively, but let us just mention that Alex Smola's 2012 course on data streams at Berkeley (*http://bit.ly/2WiE0Xc*) is a good entry point, with a rich bibliography.

Contributing to the Apache Spark Project

When you do want to contribute back what your algorithmic adventures have created to the open source community, you'll find that the Apache Spark development is organized as follows:

- On Github (*https://github.com/apache/spark*)
- On a JIRA bug tracker (*http://bit.ly/2wwt8Wq*)

The developer workflow for Spark includes design documents for the larger developments, which you'll find listed in the resources mentioned previously, and that offer a wonderful window into the development process. Another way to get this entry into the developer work on Apache Spark is to watch the videos of Holden Karau, Apache

Spark developer and PMC member, who live streams her pull request reviews and even coding sessions. You'll find this unique "day in the life of a Spark developer" experience on:

- YouTube (*http://bit.ly/2KlkMZK*)
- Twitch (*http://bit.ly/2EQ9WYj*)

All of these resources should give you the tools to not only master stream processing with Apache Spark, but also provide you with the means to contribute to the collective endeavor that makes this system better every day.

We hope you have enjoyed this book!

References for Part V

- [Akidau2013] Akidau, Tyler, Alex Balikov, Kaya Bekiroglu, Slava Chernyak, Josh Haberman, Reuven Lax, Sam McVeety, et al. "MillWheel: Fault-Tolerant Stream Processing at Internet Scale." *Proceedings of the VLDB Conference*, Vol. 6, No. 11 (August, 2013). *http://bit.ly/2KpYXYT.*

- [Akidau2014] Akidau, Tyler, Robert Bradshaw, Craig Chambers, Slava Chernyak, Rafael J. Fernandez-Moctezum, Reuven Lax, Sam McVeety, et al. "The Dataflow Model: A Practical Approach to Balancing Correctness, Latency, and Cost in Massive-Scale, Unbounded, Out-of-Order Data Processing." *Proceedings of the VLDB Endowment*, Vol. 8, No. 12 (September, 2014). *http://bit.ly/316UGQj.*

- [Akidau2016] Akidau, Tyler. "Why Apache Beam? A Google Perspective," Google Cloud Big Data and Machine Learning blog, May 3, 2016. *http://bit.ly/2Kmwmny.*

- [Akidau2017] Akidau, Tyler, Slava Chernyak, and Reuven Lax. *Streaming Systems.* O'Reilly, 2017.

- [Alexandrov2014] Alexandrov, A., R. Bergmann, S. Ewen, et al. "The Stratosphere Platform for Big Data Analytics." *The VLDB Journal*, 23 (2014): 939. *http://bit.ly/2JSQu15.*

- [Amazon2017] Amazon Web Services. "Streaming Data Solutions on AWS with Amazon Kinesis," Whitepaper, July 2017. *http://bit.ly/2MpQSpZ.*

- [Carbone2017] Carbone, P., S. Ewen, G. Fóra, S. Haridi, S. Richter, and K. Tzoumas. "State Management in Apache Flink." *Proceedings of the VLDB Endowment*, 10: 12 (2017): 1718-1729. *http://bit.ly/2wAW7s6.*

- [Chen2016] Chen, Zhong. "Spark Streaming and Azure Stream Analytics," Azure Stream Analytics Team blog, June 16, 2015. *http://bit.ly/2QPBwtz.*

- [Chintapalli2016] Chintapalli, S., D. Dagit, B. Evans, R. Farivar, T. Graves, M. Holderbaugh, Z. Liu, et al. "Benchmarking Streaming Computation Engines at Yahoo!", Yahoo! Engineering blog, December 2015. *http://bit.ly/2HSkpnG.*

- [Chiu2014] Chiu, Oliver. "Announcing Azure Stream Analytics for real-time event processing," Microsoft Azure blog, October 29, 2014. *http://bit.ly/2Kp8FuL.*

- [Ewen2015] Ewen, S.; "Off-heap Memory in Apache Flink and the Curious JIT Compiler," Flink blog, September 2015. *http://bit.ly/2Xo83sO.*

- [Georgiadis2018] Georgiadis, Georgios, Vikram Agrawal, et al. "Kinesis Connector for Structured Streaming," Github, March 2018. *http://bit.ly/2wxS3Jf.*

- [Hueske2015] Hüske, F. "Juggling with Bits and Bytes," Flink blog, May 2015. *http://bit.ly/318oThA.*

- [Kreps2016] Kreps, Jay. "Introducing Kafka Streams: Stream Processing Made Simple," Confluent blog, March 10, 2016. *http://bit.ly/2WlkjOh.*

- [Marz2014] Marz, Nathan. "History of Apache Storm and Lessons Learned," Thoughts from the Red Planet blog, October 6, 2014. *http://bit.ly/2JVEMme.*

- [Noll2018] Noll, Michael. "Of Streams and Tables in Kafka and Stream Processing," personal blog, April 5, 2018. *http://bit.ly/2wvOR0A.*

- [Tejada2018] Tejada, Zoiner, Mike Wasson, Mary McCready, Christopher Bennage, and Romit Girdhar. "Choosing A Stream Processing Technology in Azure," Azure Architecture Center, October 24, 2018. *http://bit.ly/2HStQnt.*

Index

About the Authors

Gerard Maas is a Principal Engineer at Lightbend, where he works on the seamless integration of Structured Streaming and other scalable stream processing technologies into the Lightbend Platform. Previously, he worked at a cloud-native IoT startup, where he led the data processing team on building the streaming pipelines that pushed Spark Streaming to its limits in terms of throughput. Back then, he published the first comprehensive guide to tune Spark Streaming performance.

Gerard has held leading roles at several startups and large enterprises, building data science governance, cloud-native IoT platforms, telecom platforms, and scalable APIs. He is a regular speaker at technology conferences and contributes to small and large open source projects. Gerard has a degree in Computer Engineering from the Simón Bolívar University, Venezuela. You can find him on twitter as @maasg.

François Garillot is based in Seattle, where he works on distributed computing at Facebook. He received a PhD from École Polytechnique in 2011, and worked on Spark Streaming's back-pressure while working at Lightbend in 2015. His interests include type systems, leveraging programming languages to make analytics simpler to express, and a passion for Scala, Spark, and roasted arabica. When not at work, he can be found enjoying the mountains of the Pacific Northwest.

Colophon

The animal on the cover of *Stream Processing with Apache Spark* is the Eurasian magpie (*Pica pica*). It is found throughout northern Europe and Asia, ranging from Spain and Ireland all the way to the Kamchatka Peninsula in northeast Russia. In English, "magpie" refers to the Eurasian magpie, although there are variations on this member of the crow family all over Europe, Asia, the Middle East and North Africa, and North America.

Both male and female European magpies have striking plumage. The belly and shoulders are bright white in contrast to the glossy black head, breast, and wings. These black areas shimmer with a gloss of blue or green depending on the light. The male magpie is 17 to 18 inches in length (about half of which is the tail) and has a wingspan of 20 to 24 inches; the female is slightly smaller. Magpies generally avoid humans, but you may be able to hear their loud, chattering call.

The Eurasian magpie is omnivorous. It will feed on insects, carrion, small mammals, and even the chicks and eggs of other birds as well as acorns, grains, and seeds. It is among the most intelligent of all animals, with cognitive abilities like those found in great apes: tool use, memory, reasoning, and social interaction. These traits led to a number of superstitions regarding magpies. European and Scandinavian cultures associate these birds with thievery and even witchcraft. By contrast, in Asia, they are associated with good fortune and the arrival of guests.

Although the Eurasian magpie population is widespread and thriving, many of the animals on O'Reilly covers are endangered. All of them are important to the world. To learn more about how you can help, go to *animals.oreilly.com*.

The cover image is a color illustration is by Karen Montgomery, based on a black and white engraving from *Meyers Kleines Lexicon*. The cover fonts are Gilroy Semibold and Guardian Sans. The text font is Adobe Minion Pro; the heading font is Adobe Myriad Condensed; and the code font is Dalton Maag's Ubuntu Mono.

O'REILLY®

There's much more where this came from.

Experience books, videos, live online training courses, and more from O'Reilly and our 200+ partners—all in one place.

Learn more at oreilly.com/online-learning